THE SOCIAL FABRIC

AMERICAN LIFE
FROM 1607 TO 1877

THOMAS L. HARTSHORNE
Cleveland State University

ROBERT A. WHEELER
Cleveland State University

JOHN H. CARY
Late, Cleveland State University

JULIUS WEINBERG
Late, Cleveland State University

Longman

New York   San Francisco   Boston
London   Toronto   Sydney   Tokyo   Singapore   Madrid
Mexico City   Munich   Paris   Cape Town   Hong Kong   Montreal

FOR MARTHA AND MELISSA

R. W.

Vice President and Publisher: Priscilla McGeehon
Acquisitions Editor: Ashley Dodge
Executive Marketing Manager: Sue Westmoreland
Supplements Editor: Kelly Villella
Production Manager: Mark Naccarelli
Project Coordination, Text Design, and Electronic Page Makeup: Nesbitt Graphics, Inc.
Cover Designer/Manager: John Callahan
Cover Photo: Memories Past (1992); Jane Wooster Scott (20th C./American); Collection of
    Mr. & Mrs. Kazanjian/Jane Wooster Scott/SuperStock
Photo Researcher: Photosearch, Inc.
Manufacturing Buyer: Roy Pickering
Printer and Binder: The Maple-Vail Book Manufacturing Group
Cover Printer: Coral Graphics, Inc.

Library of Congress Cataloging-in-Publication Data

The social fabric.—9th ed. / [edited by] Thomas L. Hartshorne . . . [et al.].
        p. cm.
    Rev. ed. of: The social fabric / [edited by] John H. Cary . . . [et al.]. 8th ed. © 1999.
    Includes bibliographical references.
    Contents: v. 1. American life from 1607 to 1877—v. 2. American life from the Civil War to the
present.
    ISBN 0-321-10139-1 (v. 1)—ISBN 0-321-10140-5 (v. 2)
    1. United States—Social conditions. I. Hartshorne, Thomas L. II. Cary,
John H. (John Henry), 1926–

HN57 .S623 2003
306'.0973—dc21   2002020670

Please visit our website at http://www.ablongman.com

ISBN 0-321-10139-1

1 2 3 4 5 6 7 8 9 10—MA—05 04 03 02

CONTENTS

I know histhry isn't thrue Hinnessy, because it ain't like what I see ivry day in Halsted Sthreet. If any wan comes along with a histhry iv Greece or Rome that'll show me th' people fightin', gettin' dhrunk, makin' love, gettin' married, owin' the grocery man an' bein' without hard-coal, I'll believe they was a Greece or Rome, but not befure.

Mr. Dooley, Finley Peter Dunne's comic Irish philosopher, expressed those sentiments in the early twentieth century, and at the time he spoke it certainly was true that "history"—that is, what the people who called themselves "historians" wrote—dealt only with politics, diplomacy, government, and famous leaders and that it ignored the daily lives of ordinary men and women. In the last few decades, however, the historical profession has staged a conscious and determined reaction against this tendency. Increasing numbers of historians have been mining a wide variety of materials to learn about the mass of men and women who tilled our fields, built our cities, and fought our wars. While it may be true, as one historian has said, that "the past is another country," reading this new sort of history can help to remind us that we have a great deal in common with the people who lived there. Furthermore, understanding what they did and why they did it can help us gain an understanding of our own lives.

This anthology of readings for college history courses was created out of the belief that adding the kind of history described by Mr. Dooley to conventional political, diplomatic, and constitutional history would make the mixture more meaningful to college students. This and the companion volume of *The Social Fabric*, which covers the period from 1865 to the present, touch on marrying and making love, fighting and getting drunk, owing the grocer, and going without heat. Covering the time from the earliest settlement of America to Reconstruction, this volume contains descriptions of what it was like to cross the ocean in an immigrant ship and the Great Plains in a covered wagon; what marriage and family were like in the seventeenth century and what farm life was like in the nineteenth century; what life was like for workers in New England factories and for slaves on southern plantations; and how people fought on the frontier and tried to conquer demon alcohol.

In addition to offering pictures of the lives and attitudes of ordinary Americans, we have made a conscious effort to portray the diversity of American life. Thus, there are essays dealing with women as well as men, Native Americans and African Americans as well as whites, immigrants as well as the native-born, and the poor and oppressed as well as the rich and powerful. We also focus on the way in which sectional, class, racial, ethnic, and religious differences have often divided the nation and even, on occasion, threatened to tear it apart. In the end however, for all their diversity, the American people have also shown an abiding respect for values and traditions they hold in common and that bind them together.

We have prefaced each of the readings with an introductory note which explains the relation of the particular subject to broader developments in the history of the period. Each selection is also accompanied by an illustration which provides a visual commentary on the topic. At the end of each selection there are a series of questions which students may use to review what they have just read and which also suggest subjects for further reflection or class discussion. Finally, we add some suggestions for further reading for those who want to go into particular subjects more deeply.

THE NINTH EDITION

Six new essays appear in this new edition of Volume I of *The Social Fabric*. Most of the additions were suggested by those who use the book regularly in their classes. In the first section we have added two new essays. The first, by Colin Calloway, shows how European and Native cultures borrowed a great deal from each other by the end of the colonial period. A second new essay focuses on slavery and the creation of tobacco plantations in the Chesapeake Bay region. We have also added a new essay on temperance reform to highlight this important movement. The previous edition included an essay on Hispanics: we have updated the selection with a new essay which shows the contributions Tejanos, the native Texans, made to early Texas. The fifth selection by Stephen Ash shows a different side of the Civil War—what it was like to live in the occupied areas of the South. The final reading focuses on Louisiana and how the violence of the war continued through Reconstruction and beyond. We hope these additions enhance the usefulness of *The Social Fabric*.

We are extremely gratified by the response of both teachers and students to this anthology. Their comments and suggestions for improvement have been important and valuable aids to us in our continuing effort to make these volumes as useful and interesting as possible. We are grateful for their help.

It is also our hope that these volumes will live up to the high standards established and maintained for so long by our late colleagues John H. Cary and Julius Weinberg. The original idea for these volumes was theirs, and we hope that we have succeeded in being true to their intention and that our efforts would meet with their approval.

T. L. H.

R. W.

THE SOCIAL FABRIC

COLONIAL AMERICANS

*A*ll Americans are descended from ancestors who came to the western hemi-sphere from other parts of the world in what was to be the largest migration of people in recorded history. For some 15,000 years, the land we know as the United States was inhabited by Indian peoples who had crossed from northern Asia to Alaska and made their way across both American continents. When Jamestown, Virginia, was founded in 1607, the native population of North America numbered between 500,000 and 4,000,000 people and was gathered in tribes from the warlike Iroquois hunters of the Northeast to the pueblo dwellers of the Southwest.

During the next 150 years, one tribe after another encountered invaders from England and other European countries who brought with them very different social values, agricultural traditions, governmental institutions, technology, and diseases. The Europeans also brought hundreds of thousands of African slaves to the New World, and the encounter of these three peoples makes up much of the sometimes tragic and occasionally positive history of early North America. People of English descent com-prised half the population of newcomers in the colonies under English government by the middle of the eighteenth century. Thus, English influences were naturally predomi-nant in shaping colonial institutions and social life. However, Africans, continental Europeans, and Native Americans comprised the other half of the population, and their languages, religions, and social attitudes modified English institutions and contributed significantly to the rich variety of North American society.

The first article in this section shows how the lives of Native Americans and Europeans were influenced by their growing contact with each other. The way people dressed, what they ate, and where they lived all changed, in some cases dramatically. The second essay shows how slavery changed in the Chesapeake Bay region before the Revolutionary War. The third reading suggests how New England males attempted to control their social environment by justifying their superiority and the divine laws of women's submissiveness. The final essay examines one way in which women were in command as the drama of the witch trials at Salem unfolded.

CHAPTER 1

Collection of The New-York Historical Society, (Neg. No. 7723)

Hendrick, or Theyanoguin, a Mohawk sachem, shows both his Native roots in the wampum string he holds and his facial tattoos and his adoption of European ways in his clothing.

NEW WAYS: INDIAN AND EUROPEAN

COLIN CALLOWAY

*N*ative American groups comprised a wide variety of traditions, languages, and political structures long before Columbus ventured into the Carribean. As these numerous cultures evolved, they constantly changed but not so much as when natives met Spanish, French, and English explorers and colonists. In fact, historians think that if North America had truly been uninhabited, colonial America and American history would have been very different. But there were native residents, and recently we have learned how much both groups borrowed and adapted from each other. The change was so dramatic that by the end of the eighteenth century they lived in a new blended society—very different from their own separate traditions.

This essay concentrates on some of the many things which the cultures adapted and adopted from each other. We learn that the Irish would have had no potato famine without Native Americans and how modes of transportation, crops, ways of farming, and dressing changed in both cultures. Lives changed in fundamental ways because of the cultural contact between natives and Europeans.

In 1719, William Tapp or Taptico, the last werowance (district chief) of the Wicomoco Indians of Chesapeake Bay, died. Three Englishmen compiled and appraised the inventory of his estate. Tapp owned goods and livestock valued at £100. His wardrobe consisted of English-style clothing—hats, vests, breeches, garters, and shoes. His house was furnished with chests, tables and chairs, and four feather beds, and there was an assortment of spoons, pewter plates, table linen, old books, and paper. The chief had lived in a manner comparable to that of neighboring English planters. But he also left fishhooks and line, a canoe, guns, and axes, indicating that he had continued to practice the traditional activities of an Algonkian male—fishing, hunting, and clearing the land. The presence of sheep, cattle, chickens, and a spinning wheel indicated that his wife, Elizabeth, had added spinning, knitting, and dairying to the traditional tasks of an Algonkian woman—preparing food, making pottery, and rearing children.

The clash of Indians and Europeans was a conflict between two ways of life; but even as the protagonists fought to preserve or impose their way of life, each way of life was undergoing substantial changes as a result of contact with the other. Nowhere in North America did Europeans and Indians fight each other all the time. They had to achieve ways of coexisting, however cautiously, and their daily interactions produced changes in their daily lives. As Indians and Europeans learned and borrowed from each other, they developed or adopted new diets and new ways of procuring food, new styles of architecture, new styles of clothing, and new ways of speaking, and they added new items to the things they used in their everyday lives.

The diffusion of different items and different ways of living was nothing new in North America. Throughout history and throughout the world, nomadic hunting peoples and sedentary farming peoples have developed reciprocal trade relations, and such networks functioned in North America at the edges of different ecosystems, with Plains hunters, for example, trading with settled farming peoples on the banks of the Rio Grande or the Missouri River. Trade networks crisscrossed Indian America before Europeans arrived. Turquoise from New Mexico, copper from Lake Superior, pipestone from Minnesota, marine shells from the coasts, flint, feathers, tobacco, hides, and different strains of corn made their way across vast distances. Ideas and influences followed the same trade routes, so that, for instance, pottery made by Mahicans, Munsees, and New England Algonkians came to reflect the ceramic styles of the Iroquois in New York, or vice versa. Some Indian peoples—the Ottawas of the Great Lakes and the Jumanos in the Southwest, for example—gained an early reputation as far-ranging traders, moving other peoples' goods to other people.

Indians' reasons for trade differed somewhat from Europeans'. Trade was a way of cementing alliances, preventing conflict, making and renewing friendships; it was an activity hedged around by social and ceremonial considerations. Existing trade networks and trading experiences provided a ready-made avenue for the incorporation of European traders and their items. . . .

Early French traders recognized the ceremonial aspects of trade and accommodated themselves to the customs of the country. When Samuel de Champlain opened trade with the Hurons early in the seventeenth century, he did so by following Huron rules of trade, giving generous gifts, which obligated Huron people to be more generous and encouraged them to return for more trade the next year. The French, says Denys Delâge, "had decoded the Amerindian system of ex-change" and recognized that, over time, gifts given were sure to bring a good re-turn. Rather than engage in hard bargaining for immediate profits, early French traders learned "the language of gifts" and gave them in ceremonies "that joined the parties in a pact of generosity." The more lavish the French were with their gifts of metal and manufactured goods, the more lavish the Hurons were with their gifts of furs. Traders in other regions and in later years also adopted the Native custom of ceremonial gift-giving as a way of initiating trade, although they were rarely as sensitive or as skilled as the French in employing Native trading practices to their advantage. Nevertheless, the flow of European manufactured goods into Indian country continued unabated.

Once an item passed from European to Indian hands, it did not necessarily stop there. It had entered a world of extensive contacts and intertribal communi-cation that might carry it across half a continent and more. . . . An incised copper plate, unearthed in Georgia in 1984, illustrates the possibilities. An Aztec evi-dently made the plate as an adornment for a Bible or a box some time in the mid-sixteenth century. It made its way to northwestern Georgia, where it was traded to a Coosa Indian. . . . "The Coosawattee Plate provides a tangible and remarkable example of the crosscurrents of change sweeping through the Western Hemisphere in the sixteenth century. The history of the artifact parallels the his-tory of the era: manufactured by a native of Mexico, influenced by the Christian religion of Europe, carried hundreds of miles to an unsettled frontier, traded for food or given as a gift, adapted for use by another culture, and finally buried with a child in a village soon thereafter abandoned." In such "small things forgotten" lie stories of people's lives and changing lifestyles.

Early explorers and chroniclers insisted that Indians regarded Europeans with awe and even attributed to them godlike qualities because of the impressive new technologies they possessed. But if Indians were awestruck at first, they soon got over it and started adapting the new items into their lives. When Giovanni da Verrazzano, a Florentine sailing for the king of France, put in to Narragansett Bay in 1524, the Indians there evidently had not met Europeans before. They were not interested in trading for cloth or metal goods; they wanted blue beads, bells, and copper trinkets, objects similar to what they might have obtained in inter-tribal trade and that occupied a familiar place in their lives. As Verrazzano fol-lowed the coast northeast to Maine, however, he encountered Abenaki Indians, who clearly had had previous experiences with European sailors. They hid their women, "mooned" Verrazzano's crew, and refused to trade for anything but knives, fishhooks, and metal goods. By the 1620s, Montagnais Indians near the mouth of the St. Lawrence were using large quantities of metal tools and weapons and woolen clothing; they recognized the utility of the new items, but they hardly held European traders in awe. "The English have no sense," said one Montagnais. "They give us twenty knives like this for one Beaver skin." . . . When Nicholas Denys arrived in Acadia in 1638, the Indians there were already using portable iron kettles, metal axes, knives, and arrowheads.

European merchants funneled into Indian country an inventory of manufac-tured goods that included steel axes and knives, iron and copper kettles, spoons, metal hoes, ice chisels, fishhooks, gorgets, combs, scissors, awls, mirrors, needles, thread, thimbles, woolen clothing and blankets, linen shirts, jackets, hats, guns, and alcohol. In time, some Indian peoples' tastes extended to books and paper, spinning wheels, pewter and glassware, china, lace and silk, buckles, shoes, and feathered hats. Metal drills made possible the mass production of wampum. Glass beads from Italy, and even from Czechoslovakia, became a standard trade item. They flooded into Indian country by the thousands, supplanting or supplement-ing traditional sources of shells and porcupine quills in the manufacture of wampum belts and the decoration of clothing. Beadwork came to be regarded as a traditional craft in American Indian life. Woolens from Yorkshire, linen from Ireland, strouds (a cheaper cloth made from woolen rags) from the Midlands, guns from Birmingham, all became commonplace in Indian America. So perva-sive was the influx of manufactured goods that, by the time of the American Revolution, Mohawks at Fort Hunter reportedly were living much better than most of their colonial neighbors. Some of their Oneida relatives lived in frame houses with chimneys and painted windows, ate with spoons from pewter plates, drank from teacups and punch bowls, combed their hair with ivory combs, used silk handkerchiefs, and wore white breeches. . . .

Indian peoples accepted European goods because they made life easier, more comfortable, warmer, and more pleasurable. Scissors and metal knives allowed Indian women to fashion traditional clothing from hides and skins with greater ease and precision. Metal pots were more durable and transportable than stone or bark ones, and they could be heated directly over a fire rather than having to drop heated stones into the contents. Steel hatchets surpassed stone axes. Guns possessed some advantages over bows and arrows. Indians also valued certain goods for aesthetic and spiritual reasons.

Archaeologists excavating eighteenth-century sites in the eastern United States often find it difficult to determine whether a settlement was Indian or European on the basis of the materials unearthed. Indian peoples quickly became tied into European trade networks, and by the eighteenth century they, like their colonial neighbors, were becoming part of an Atlantic economy and a growing consumer revolution that shaped their tastes, their lives, and the world they inhabited.

The new goods came with hidden costs—increasing violence, declining craft skills, and dependency on outsiders. As they became dependent on trade goods, some Indian communities found it difficult to preserve their lands and their inde-pendence. . . . The first European products reached the Senecas of western New York in the second half of the sixteenth century; by the end of that century, most Senecas had discarded stone axes and flint knives in favor of metal tools. . . . A Creek Indian named Handsome Fellow said in 1777: "We have been used so long to wrap up our Children as soon as they are born in Goods procured of the white People that we cannot do without it." Anthropologist Oscar Lewis maintained that the Blackfeet could not remember how to make pottery a mere ten years after they first acquired iron pots from British traders.

Where Native pottery survived, it underwent changes. Spanish missionaries among the Hopis discouraged the use of pottery as burial offerings and encouraged potters to replace Native designs—which might involve association with animal spirits and other sources of power—with Christian designs such as flowers, Maltese crosses, and eight-point stars. . . . As Indian women married Spanish men, Native pottery, whether of traditional or Spanish design, or incorporating elements of both, became part of daily life in their households. . . .

. . . However, it was not a simple substitution of Indian artifacts for European goods. Indians often took new items and refashioned them into traditional designs, or sought them for their symbolic and spiritual rather than their utilitarian value. European tools and implements became part of their everyday world in ways Europeans neither expected nor understood. East Coast Algonkians used the woolen stockings they got from Dutch traders in the seventeenth century as tobacco pouches, and they wore steel hatchet blades around their necks in place of stone ornaments. Europeans often thought Indians were gullible traders who would exchange beaver pelts for "beads and baubles," but in the world of eastern Algonkian people, colored glass beads and metal objects often possessed powerful symbolic and spiritual significance and were incorporated into ceremonial objects along with native crystal, shells, and copper. Invested with Indian meanings and put to Indian uses, trade items became, to a large extent, Indian goods of European manufacture.

Indians also made their own versions of European things. Spaniards appear to have introduced playing cards into the Southwest in 1598. Apache Indians later made their own decks of cards out of rawhide, copying and modifying the Spanish ones. Since the king, knight, and other figures on the Spanish cards meant nothing to the Apaches, they substituted their own designs, painting figures in Apache costume. Appreciating the value of hard cash, Indians were not above making their own: two Apalachees living near St. Augustine were arrested in 1695 for counterfeiting Spanish coins out of tin.

European traders sometimes included in their inventory of trade goods for one tribe items manufactured by Indians of other tribes, with the result that some artifacts and customs of indigenous but particular tribal origin spread throughout Indian America. Indians were discriminating customers, and European manufacturers responded to their demands and accommodated their preferences to make goods specifically for the Indian trade: pipe tomahawks, muskets with large trigger guards for northern Indians wearing mittens, cloth of preferred colors as in the famous Hudson's Bay blankets, which became almost ubiquitous in northern regions of America.

Some Indian crafts, such as basket making, wood carving, and beadworking, were actually stimulated by European influences and demands. . . . In the second half of the eighteenth century, goods from factories half a world away poured into Indian communities on the Northwest Coast, producing increased wealth, more elaborate ceremonies, and an artistic florescence. When those tribes obtained steel chisels and other metal tools from maritime traders, they used the new tools to work wood on a scale never before possible and to develop new levels of artistry and intricacy. Huge totem poles—a symbol of "Indianness" in the popular imagination, but exclusive to the Northwest Coast, where they bore family and clan crests—proliferated. Unprecedented supplies of copper allowed more elaborate decorations and crests on dance masks. In the Northeast, Indians sometimes resorted to making baskets for sale to colonists as a way of earning a meager living after their traditional economies were disrupted. Working for a market and catering to the tastes of customers who might want baskets for decoration rather than use, they took basket-making skills to new heights and produced objects of great beauty.

Europeans also adapted items of Indian manufacture into their material culture. In addition to baskets and bowls peddled by Indian women in the settlements, frontiersmen employed Indian-style hatchets. Colonists traveled by Indian snowshoes, Indian toboggans, and Indian canoes. Birchbark canoes, manufactured from the bark of the paper birch, with ribs of white cedar and pitch from the balsam fir, were unmatched for travel in the rivers and lakes of northeastern forests. . . .

Contemporary observers agreed that bark canoes were impressive craft. An anonymous Frenchman said the Indian canoes he saw on the Great Lakes in 1672 were "so light that one or two men at most carry them, and yet so made that some will hold six to eight persons with their belongings." Birchbark canoes enabled the French and the British to penetrate the north country. The fur trade, which introduced so many items of European manufacture into Indian country, depended itself on transportation by Indian canoe, often with Indian paddlers. Farther south, Indians used more cumbersome dugout canoes, but they were a vital means of travel. John Lawson noted how settlers in the Carolinas had adopted them from their Indian neighbors: "Many of the Women are very handy in Canoes, and will manage them with great Dexterity and Skill, which they become accustomed to in this watery Country."

The European invasion of America produced a dietary revolution in the Old World. Potatoes, corn, tomatoes, squash, beans, pumpkins, and a host of other foods, hitherto unknown in Europe, enriched people's diets, improving their health and allowing them to live longer. Balances of power shifted north, away from the Mediterranean, as Prussia, Russia, and Britain fed their populations with potatoes, a plant that thrived despite short growing seasons. European population expanded dramatically, increasing the human pressure on an already overtaxed land base. Thousands, and eventually millions, of people left their overcrowded continent in search of more plentiful land in America. So dependent did the population of Ireland become on potatoes that when the crops failed year after year in the late 1840s and early 1850s, as many as 1 million people died, and another 1.8 million were propelled into emigration to America.

Diets also underwent substantial change within America where European crops and livestock altered Indian lifestyles, and European pioneers took to growing Indian corn and hunting in Indian fashion.

By the time Europeans came to America, Indian peoples were growing corn, usually supplemented with beans and squash, from the Rio Grande to the St. Lawrence. Introduced from Mexico, corn had spread north, and Indian peoples in New Mexico were growing a kind of corn by 3000 B.C. Elsewhere, Indian farmers developed new strains, like northern flint, suited to the soils and climate of their homelands. This maize or "Indian corn," which one scholar called "a marvel of Indian ingenuity," was said to be "the most remarkable plant breeding accomplishment of all time." It played a major role in Americanizing the diets of European settlers. . . .

Corn was higher in nutrition than most other grain crops, and it gave higher yields. John Lawson, who traveled in South Carolina and into the interior Indian country in 1701, was one of many colonists who sang the praises of corn. "The *Indian* Corn, or *Maiz,* proves the most useful Grain in the World," he wrote, "and had it not been for the Fruitfulness of this Species, it would have proved very difficult to have settled some of the Plantations in *America.*" It grew virtually anywhere. "It refuses no Grounds, unless the barren Sands, and when planted in good Ground, will repay the Planter seven or eight hundred fold. . . ."

In New England, the Pilgrims at Plymouth benefited from Indian knowledge and food surpluses to survive their first hard years. The Pilgrims stole caches of corn before the Patuxet Indian Squanto came along and "directed them how to set their corne." Indians in southern New England traded agricultural surpluses to hunting peoples farther north; it was easy for them to share surplus food with English settlers in the initial years of contact, providing the basis for the "first Thanksgiving" so ingrained in the popular mythology about early America. Colonists also adapted Indian corn agriculture into their new way of life. "Many ways hath their advice and endeavor been advantageous to us," said one man, "they being our first instructors for the planting of their Indian corn, by teaching us to cull out the finest seed, to observe the fittest season, to keep distance for holes and fit measure for ills, to worm it, and weed it, and dress it as occasion requires."

After Indian men cleared the fields for planting, Indian women hoed the soil and planted the kernels in small hillocks formed by hand. They also planted beans and pumpkin seeds, which added nitrogen to the soil. The growing cornstalks served as beanpoles and also afforded shade to the pumpkin vines. Indian people taught the settlers how to harvest corn, how to grind it into meal, and how to preserve it through the year. . . . The Indians also showed them how to cook corn and beans together to make succotash, how to tap maple trees for sugar, and how to cook beans in earthen pots, to produce a dish that has since become known as Boston baked beans.

Corn fed colonists, and it provisioned colonial armies. From the Spanish invasions of the Southeast by Pánfilo de Narváez in 1528 and Hernando de Soto in 1539–43, to John Sullivan's invasion of Iroquois country in 1779, colonial expeditions relied on the corn they found in Indian fields and villages to feed the troops and keep the campaign alive. Colonists fed corn to their chickens, turkeys, and pigs, adding more meat to their diets than was common in Europe. They exported it to the Caribbean, where it fed slaves working on sugar plantations. Corn from America also stimulated population growth in Africa, the labor pool for America's plantations. Slaves and poor whites in the southern United States became so dependent on corn as a staple food that they succumbed to a new disease, a nutritional ailment called pellagra (something that Indians had avoided because their cooking methods, which included adding wood ashes to the food, enhanced the niacin in corn). Settlers planted European grains whenever they could, but corn agriculture became a way of life in much of pioneer America. Henry Adams, in his history of the United States during Thomas Jefferson's first administration, said simply that "Indian corn was the national crop. . . ."

. . . Despite its American origins, the potato was not widely used in English colonies until north country Britons arrived in the eighteenth century and made the crop they had adopted at home an important part of the diet of backcountry settlers. The pattern by which newcomers adopted new foods was not straightforward. . . . Settlers used what was available to create new varieties of old foods and drinks: cornmeal replaced oatmeal to produce "grits"; scotch whisky (distilled from barley) gave way to bourbon (made mainly from corn and rye).

Indian crops, combined with Euro-Indian farming techniques, produced prolific yields and an American backwoods farming culture that blended ethnic traditions. Finnish settlers in the Delaware Valley brought their own methods of cutting, clearing, settling, and fencing the land, but they adopted Indian practices of crop selection, hoeing, and mound cultivation. Colonial settlers also followed their Indian neighbors in gathering wild plants and berries, drawing on knowledge that Indian people had accumulated during centuries of living in the forests of eastern America. Berries, walnuts, pecans, hickory nuts, wild grapes, nettles, papaws, crab apples, and maple sugar supplemented the diets of European colonists, too.

Indians provided English colonists with another major crop, one cultivated for inhaling rather than eating. After experimenting with several cash crops, colonists in Virginia finally settled on Indian tobacco as the most lucrative. The English found they preferred Caribbean to Virginian tobacco, and John Rolfe, who married Pocahontas, the daughter of Powhatan, imported seeds from the Caribbean and began turning tobacco into a large-scale commercial crop. The English experimented with a variety of procedures until they hit upon the right one for mass production. In [one historian's] view, "The final tobacco culture combined traditional aspects of both native American and European knowledge with some innovations developed in Virginia and neighboring tobacco colonies." With tobacco smoking a common and addictive social vice in seventeenth-century Europe, tobacco cultivation and export became the basis for the prosperity of colonial Virginia and many of its "first families." Tobacco smoking was also popular among European colonists in North America. Writing in the mid-eighteenth century, Swedish traveler Peter Kalm observed, "The Frenchmen's whole smoking etiquette here in Canada, namely the preparation of the tobacco, the tobacco pouch, the pipe, the pipe-stem, etc. was derived from the natives, with the exception of the fire-steel and flint." Many Indians found that European curing processes made the new tobacco more desirable than their own varieties, and some stopped growing tobacco except for use in religious rituals.

Indians taught Europeans how to hunt and fish. As John Smith acknowledged, English settlers at first were out of their depth in America, unable to harvest the natural resources they found there: "Though there be fish in the sea, fowls in the air, and beasts in the woods, their bounds are so large, they so wild, and we so weak and ignorant, we cannot much trouble them." William Wood, who lived in the Massachusetts Bay area in the 1630s, said that the local Indians were "experienced in the knowledge of all baits, and diverse seasons; being not ignorant likewise of the removal of fishes, knowing when to fish in rivers, and when at rocks, when in bays, and when at seas. . . ."

. . . Most Europeans came from societies where hunting was a gentlemen's sport, and those who hunted for food often did so as poachers. Europeans had to adopt the Indians' hunting culture in order to survive in their new world. European hunters learned from Indians the use of animal skins as camouflage, decoys, various whistles and calls to attract the prey, and methods (such as deer runs) of taking animals. They borrowed from Indian woods lore to become familiar with animals and their habits and habitats, and they adopted Indian hunting gear. . . .

European missionaries and other groups intent on "civilizing" Indians urged them to give up hunting and concentrate on farming, and many Indians incorporated new crops, poultry, and livestock into their economies. Meanwhile, many European settlers who lived in the backcountry were becoming more dependent on hunting and less tied to agriculture. As hunters, they chose to live in less populated areas, moved over greater distances, and lived more like their Indian neighbors. Seventeenth-century Puritans had feared the wilderness; by the mid-eighteenth century, backcountry settlers were living and hunting in it, much as the Indians did. Eastern elites and European travelers who ventured into the American backcountry commonly remarked with repulsion the extent to which frontiersmen and their families resembled Indians in their way of life. Missionary David McClure said that backcountry Virginians were "generally white Savages, and subsist by hunting, and live like the Indians." What they were witnessing was the emergence of a new way of life, a new frontier culture that drew on Indian and European traditions and centered on hunting as a means of subsistence. In this way . . . "the Indians Americanized the settlers." Many conflicts between Indians and backcountry settlers, notes Daniel Boone's biographer John Faragher, occurred "not because they were so alien to each other but because they were so much alike" and competed for the same forest resources.

But the transformation was not complete. Backcountry hunters did not usually adopt the Indian hunting ethic that required respectful treatment of the prey and restraint in the kill. Wasteful and disrespectful hunting practices on the part of Euro-American hunters remained a constant source of friction between Natives and newcomers, even as market pressures began to undermine the Indians' own hunting ethics.

Indian diets also changed considerably with the introduction of European crops and domestic animals. De Soto's conquistadors brought hundreds of pigs to the Southeast. Indian villages soon had their share of chickens, pigs, and cattle. The Cherokees were eating pork by the middle of the eighteenth century. When English explorers reached the interior of Georgia and the Carolinas, they found peaches growing wild in the woods and assumed they were an indigenous fruit. In fact, peaches had been introduced in Florida by Spanish or French colonists. The Indians developed a taste for them and traded and transplanted them farther north. When William Bartram visited Indian villages in northern Florida and Georgia on the eve of the American Revolution, he noted that the surrounding fields "were plentifully stored with Corn, Citruels, Pumkins, Squashes, Beans, Peas, Potatoes, Peaches, Figs, Oranges, &c." The Spaniards also introduced watermelons to Mesoamerica. Indian people quickly adopted them and traded them from one group to another ahead of the Spanish advance northward. Oñate found Pueblo people growing watermelons by the time he got to the Rio Grande in the 1590s; the French explorer René Robert Cavelier de La Salle saw them among the Caddoes in eastern Texas in 1682. La Salle also saw peach trees in Quapaw villages in Arkansas. Spaniards brought fruit trees and grain cereals from Europe, and they brought tomatoes and chilies from Mexico to the Pueblos on the Rio Grande, adding permanent ingredients to New Mexican cuisine.

Pueblo Indians in New Mexico and the Hopi Indians in Arizona kept corn as the center of their subsistence base, but took on domesticated plants and livestock introduced by the Spaniards. By the eighteenth century, sheep were replacing deer and antelope as food items, wool replaced cotton as the most popular textile, cowhide and sheepskin replaced deerskin for moccasins and other leather goods. Hopi people also learned knitting and blacksmithing from the Spaniards. Spanish missionaries in the 1770s remarked on the large herds of cattle, horses, and sheep grazing around Hopi villages. Apaches and Navajos raided Spanish and Pueblo livestock, but in time the Navajos became shepherds themselves, and they had large flocks of sheep by the end of the eighteenth century.

Dietary changes proved a mixed blessing. Spanish missionaries enforced agriculture as a key component of "civilization," and mission agriculture eventually produced food surpluses that were less vulnerable to seasonal and annual fluctuations than were traditional Native resources. However, the wide variety of foods enjoyed by Indian peoples before contact tended to be replaced by a steady diet of wheat, corn, and beans, supplemented occasionally with fruit and vegetables in season. Mission Indians could expect three meals a day, but it was a diet very high in carbohydrates. The monotonous diet was also deficient in high-quality proteins, vitamins A and C, and riboflavin. These deficiencies made Indian neophytes, especially women and children, more susceptible to disease. . . .

European contact changed how Indian people procured their food, just as contact with Indians changed how Europeans procured theirs. Spaniards introduced horses into the Southwest, and Indian peoples quickly recognized the new animals as a tremendous asset. Horses spread north on to the Great Plains in the late seventeenth and eighteenth centuries, opening a new world of mobility for the Indian inhabitants and changing the way they harvested the enormous herds of buffalo. Instead of hunting on foot and by dangerous buffalo drives, Plains Indians became efficient mounted hunters. A sophisticated horse-buffalo complex evolved that brought Plains peoples unprecedented prosperity and became ingrained as the core of their way of life. New groups of people moved on to the plains to take advantage of new opportunities, embrace the new way of life there, and acquire new identities as Plains Indians. Their increasing efficiency and their numbers subjected the buffalo herds to new pressures even before white hide-hunters entered the area. . . .

Contrary to popular opinion, all Indian peoples did not inhabit tepees or wigwams. They had many different styles of architecture, suited to their particular needs and appropriate to their specific environments. Constructed from the available raw materials and following time-honored techniques, Indian lodgings—whether the longhouses and wigwams of the Northeast, the earth lodges and tepees of the Great Plains, the plank houses of the Northwest Coast, or the pueblos of the Southeast—served to shelter the people, keeping them warm in winter and cool in summer. Indian architecture made arrangements of space that catered to peoples' social, ceremonial, and subsistence needs. Algonkian wigwams were typically versatile and movable: Giovanni da Verrazzano said that the Indians he met on Long Island in 1524 "change their habitations from place to place as circumstances of situation and season may require." When people moved they often carried elm or bark coverings, portable roofing that they laid over the sapling frames they had left standing at familiar campsites. Iroquoian longhouses of 100 feet and more in length, constructed from sheets of bark laid over such frames, were multifamily dwellings where people related by clan through their mother's line lived year-round. Southeastern Indian towns often contained council houses, ball fields, and ceremonial plazas.

European observers varied in their opinions of Indian housing, but some recognized its utility. Daniel Gookin, an astute observer of the Indians in Massachusetts in the seventeenth century, said, "I have often lodged in their wigwams, and found them as warm as the best English houses." Jesuit missionary Joseph François Lafitau said the Iroquois were "the most comfortably lodged of all America. . . ."

Indians were not always impressed by the Europeans' houses. A Micmac chief in the seventeenth century asked French visitors why men who were five or six feet tall needed houses sixty to eighty feet high: "Do we not have in our dwellings all the conveniences and advantages that you have in yours, such as reposing, drinking and sleeping, eating and amusing ourselves with our friends . . . ?"

Colonists borrowed from Indian housing techniques, if only temporarily, as they adjusted to their new environment. At Salem, in Massachusetts Bay Colony early in the seventeenth century, a settler adapted a local Indian wigwam, adding a door at one end and a fireplace at the other. However, when European colonists resorted to Indian-style housing, it usually was a makeshift measure until they could build a more substantial and permanent home. More often, Europeans employed American materials and American labor in constructing European-style buildings. Hispanic women learned from Pueblo women how to plaster adobe houses. Indian converts built many of the Spanish missions, and Spaniards set up *encomienda* and *repartimiento* systems, requiring Indian towns to provide teams of laborers. Pueblo Indian workers built Santa Fe, New Mexico. . . .

More often, it was Indian architecture that changed in response to European influences. Indians modified and adapted their dwellings for centuries before Europeans arrived, and Pueblo Indians in the Southwest continued to live in their settled, multistoried towns long after, but by the eighteenth century in the eastern woodlands, changes in Indian housing were widespread and permanent. Europeans brought new building materials and tools—iron nails and hinges, hammers and saws. They also generated dramatic changes in Indian societies and demographic changes in Indian country, which often resulted in fewer people living in communities farther apart. Iroquois peoples in New York began to live in single-family log cabins rather than in the communal longhouses that traditionally sheltered many families of the same clan. Iroquois villages that formerly were surrounded by palisades now tended to be scattered. Cherokee towns in Tennessee and the Carolinas followed a similar pattern of dispersal as people began to farm family plots, European-style, rather than tend communal fields shared by the whole village. Peter Kalm, who visited the Hurons at Lorette on the St. Lawrence River in the mid-eighteenth century, said that the Indians no longer lived in huts but had "built all their houses after the French fashion." The log cabin, built with notched-log construction and first introduced by Finnish and Swedish settlers into the Delaware Valley in the mid-seventeenth century, became almost the standard lodging of American backwoods pioneers and was also extensively adopted by Indian communities.

Single-family homes proliferated and communal lodgings like longhouses decreased, which altered social uses of space. Relations between people changed, and the bonds within and between clans, families, and communities sometimes weakened. In times of severe social stress, changing living arrangements surely had far-reaching repercussions. Many Indians grew up in what, in the context of their societies, constituted "broken homes."

When Don Juan de Oñate and a wagon train of colonists set out to establish the first Spanish settlement in the Southwest, they brought with them the clothes they had been accustomed to wearing in Mexico. The men had velvet suits with high collars and lace cuffs, sateen caps, and richly embossed and stitched leather shoes from Cordova in Spain. The women had full silk dresses decorated with gold piping and lace trim, wore dainty and brightly colored slippers, and covered their heads with fringed and embroidered shawls imported from Manila. Such clothing had no place on the Rio Grande frontier. "Before long," notes historian Marc Simmons, "the colonists packed away their finery and took to dressing like the Indians." Velvet suits and silk dresses gave place to clothes made of gamuza (chamois) or buckskin, the softly tanned hide of deer and antelope. Buckskin remained the standard clothing of New Mexicans, whether Indian or Hispanic, until the Santa Fe Trail opened in 1821, which meant large quantities of cheap American cloth appeared in the New Mexican market, and it did not disappear until the second half of the nineteenth century when railroads brought cheap cloth from New England mills.

The Spanish experience in New Mexico was mirrored by other Europeans in other parts of the country. Europeans of status sometimes insisted on wearing their European clothing, however impractical, as a mark of their "civilization" in a land of "savagery" and "wilderness." In Europe, clothes symbolized one's position in society. In Indian country, however, practicality usually outweighed social status, and most colonists who ventured there found it made sense to wear Indian clothing or a version thereof. High-ranking Spaniards might try to preserve a style of dress appropriate to their status, but common Hispanics replaced worn-out shoes and boots with Indian moccasins or moccasinlike shoes. Peter Kalm said that French colonists who traveled in Canada "generally dressed like the natives." Backcountry settlers in eighteenth-century America wore moccasins, leggings, and hunting shirts. Men from the British borderlands were long accustomed to wearing such shirts and leggings, but in America they added moccasins and breechcloths. Young men in backcountry Virginia reportedly were proud of their "Indian-like dress" and wore it to church, where the sight of leggings, breechcloths, and bare thighs caused quite a stir among young women in the congregation. . . .

Wearing Indian clothing was more than a matter of comfort and practicality for Europeans in Indian country: dressing in "the Indian fashion" made a statement and increased their cultural mobility. In the same way, Indians who donned ruffled shirts and three-cornered hats often were announcing their role as cultural mediators and their ability to deal with Europeans. As European colonists living in or near Indian country pulled on Indian moccasins, leggings, and hunting shirts, Indian people living near colonial settlements acquired shirts and jackets, trousers and shoes. Cloth shirts and pants were more comfortable than garments fashioned from hide. Indians attributed their own meanings and values to the articles of clothing they adopted, and they sometimes wore European clothes in very non-European ways—shirts hanging loose, hats on backwards or sideways, jackets unbuttoned, trousers cut off at the thighs and worn as leggings—attracting the ridicule of European visitors. Like Europeans in Indian country, Indians who had contact with Europeans often mingled European and Indian clothing. . . . An early French observer noted how Indians in that region readily utilized European clothing: "In Summer, they often wear our capes, and in Winter our bed-blankets, which they improve with trimming and wear double. They are also quite willing to make use of our hats, shoes, caps, woolens and shirts, and of our linen to clean their infants, for we trade them all these commodities for their furs."

Alexander Hamilton, a Scottish physician traveling in New England in the 1740s, met two "French Mohawks," presumably from Caughnawaga, on the road outside Boston. The Indians were on horseback, "dressed *à la mode Français* with laced hats, full trimmed coats, and ruffled shirts," but behind one of them sat "a pritty woman all bedaubed with wampum. . . ."

In other times and places, Indian people adopted European clothing almost completely. An observer said that the members of one of John Eliot's Indian congregations wore English clothing—"You should scarce know them from English people." Other Indians in Massachusetts dressed so like their neighbors that they were "very often mistaken for English." By the first decade of the eighteenth century, Indians on Martha's Vineyard were "generally clothed as the English are." In Rhode Island, Alexander Hamilton visited the Niantic leader Ninigret or "King George," who had built himself a huge mansion and whose wife "dressed like an English woman" in silks, hoops, and stays. In 1759, traveler Andrew Burnaby said Indians in Virginia "commonly dress like the Virginians" and were sometimes mistaken for lower-class whites. . . .

Europeans, and later white Americans, often assumed that if Indian people adopted the outward trappings of "civilization" they would become like white people; wearing European-style clothing and using manufactured goods would ease their spiritual transformation into Christians. However, Indians, like Europeans, took what they wanted from their new neighbors to make their lives easier, more comfortable, more productive. European clothes and metal goods did not transform Indians into Europeans any more than Indian leggings and moccasins made colonists into Indians. The battle for spirits and souls went deeper than such surface adjustments.

FOR FURTHER STUDY

1. How does the Coosawattee plate show the changes happening to natives and Europeans?

2. As the trade for European goods increased, how did some become "Indian goods of European manufacture."

3. How did Indian baskets and even totem poles change because of the influx of European materials and new markets?

4. Explain how and why canoes and corn were two of the most important items adopted by Europeans.

5. How did two European animals change native lifestyles?

6. Ben Franklin often wore a coonskin cap in Paris. How was he typical of the cross-cultural clothing worn by both natives and colonists?

FOR FURTHER READING

Recent works have added to our knowledge of the exchanges between Europeans and natives. For food see Jack Weatherford, *Indian Givers* (1988) and Nelson Foster and Linda S. Cordell, editors, *Chiles to Chocolate: Food the Americas Gave the World* (1992). For corn in particular see Nicholas Hardeman, *Shucks, Shocks, and Hominy Blocks* (1981). An interesting work on the canoe is John McPhee, *The Survival of the Bark Canoe* (1976). For hunting ways see John Mack Faragher, *Daniel Boone: The Life and Legend of an American Pioneer* (1992) and for architecture: Peter Nabokov and Robert Easton, *Native American Architecture* (1989). For changes in the Southwest see Marc Simmons, *Coronado's Land: Essays on the Daily Life in Colonial New Mexico* (1991) and for all Spanish North America see David J. Weber, *The Spanish Frontier in North America* (1992).

For a comprehensive look see James Axtell, editor, *The Indian Peoples of Eastern America: A Documentary History of the Sexes* (1981) that uses contemporary examples to trace native cultural traditions from birth through vision quests to marriage and death. Much work has been done on southern Indians. Some good examples are James H. Merrell's *The Indians' New World: Catawbas and Their Neighbors from European Contact through the Era of Removal* (1989), Karen O. Kupperman, *Settling with the Indians: The Meeting of English and Indian Cultures in America, 1580–1640* (1980), and Philip L. Barbour's *Pocahontas and Her World* (1970). Historians also looked at cultural exchange between Indians, European colonists, and African Americans. Several works, especially Gary B. Nash's *Red, White, and Black: The Peoples of Early North America*, 3rd ed. (1992), show how all these groups changed because of their contact with each other. Apparently, some Europeans even preferred living with Indians as J. Norman Heard shows in *White into Red: A Study of the Assimilation of White Persons Captured by Indians* (1973).

CHAPTER 2

Abby Aldrich Rockefeller Folk Art Museum, Williamsburg, VA

Slaves perform a West African dance in the detail of this eighteenth-century painting.

THE CREATION OF A SLAVE SOCIETY IN THE CHESAPEAKE

IRA BERLIN

$\mathscr{S}$lavery became the labor system of choice in the colonial South near the end of the seventeenth century. Along the shores of the Chesapeake Bay in Virginia and Maryland the intense cultivation required of the region's main crop, tobacco, and the limited supply of white indentured servants produced a transition from white to black labor. The change, completed by 1750, transformed the essence of the society from one with a few slaves to a society which at its heart was a slave society.

In this essay Ira Berlin contrasts early Chesapeake society—which he calls the charter generations when society was fluid and most workers were European—with later developments in the 1700s, which created the planter class, the slave economy, and the beginnings of African American society. The dynamic changes which happened before 1750 altered Chesapeake society in several ways. The slave population, itself, changed from one brought to the region from the Carribean to a heavily African population, and then back to a new mix where colonial-born, African Americans predominated. As these dynamics took place the Chesapeake emerged as the primary colonial slave region before the Revolutionary War.

Be aware that when Berlin uses the term *charter generations* he means those Africans first brought to the Carribean and then sold to the Chesapeake before direct importations from Africa became the rule. They were creoles because they combined two cultures, African and Carribean, and they often spoke English. The author also uses two geographical terms you need to know: *tidewater* means those areas close to the Chesapeake and the rivers which feed it; *Piedmont* means the area above the tidewater region closer to the foothills of the Appalachian mountains. As you read look for these four elements: enslavement, Africanization, the new plantation system, and the destruction of the charter generation.

The plantation revolution came to the Chesapeake with the thunder of cannons and the rattle of sabres. Victory over the small holders, servants, and slaves who composed Nathaniel Bacon's motley army in 1676 enabled planters to consolidate their control over Chesapeake society. In quick order, they elaborated a slave code that singled out people of African descent as slaves and made their status hereditary. In the years that followed, as the number of European servants declined and white farmers migrated west, the great planters turned to Africa for their workforce. During the last decades of the seventeenth century, the new order began to take shape. The Chesapeake's economy stumbled into the eighteenth century, but the grandees prospered, as the profits of slave labor filled their pockets. A society with slaves gave way to a slave society around the great estuary.

Although black people grew tobacco as before, the lives of plantation slaves in no way resembled those of the charter generations. White indentured servants might graduate to tenantry or gain small holdings of their own, but black slaves could not. Planters restricted the slaves' access to freedom and stripped slaves of their prerogatives and free blacks of their rights. Rather than participate in a variety of enterprises, slaves labored single-mindedly under the direction of white overseers whose close supervision left little room for initiative or ambition. The slaves' economy withered and with it the robust network of exchanges that had rested upon the slaves' independent production. But even as the great planters installed the new harsh regime, African slaves and their descendants, sometimes in league with remnants of the charter generations, began to reshape black life. In the process, they created a new African-American society.

The triumph of the planter class began the transformation of black life in the Chesapeake. Following the legalization of chattel bondage in the 1660s, slaves slowly but steadily replaced white indentured servants as the main source of plantation labor. Planters enslaved Indians where they could under new legislation that declared "all Indians taken in warr be held and accounted slaves dureing life." But the Native-American population was dwindling fast at the end of the seventeenth century, so Africans became the object of the planters' desire. Between 1675 and 1695 some 3,000 black slaves entered the region. During the last five years of the century, Chesapeake tobacco planters—most of them located along the York River—purchased more slaves than they had in the previous twenty years. In 1668

From *Many Thousands Gone: The First Two Centuries of Slavery in North America* by Ira Berlin, pp. 116–127, Cambridge Mass.: The Belknap Press of Harvard University Press. Copyright © 1998 by the President and Fellows of Harvard College. Reprinted by permission of the publisher.

white servants had outnumbered black slaves more than five to one in Virginia's Middlesex County and much of the Chesapeake region. By 1700 the balance of bound labor had been reversed, and the county of Middlesex—like many other jurisdictions in the Chesapeake—counted more black slaves than white servants. In all, slaves constituted one-third of the laborers growing tobacco in Maryland and Virginia, and, since the great planters could best afford to purchase slaves, slaves composed an even greater share of the workers on the largest estates. Still, black people remained a minority of the population. In 1720 no more than one-quarter of the region's population was black. Twenty years later, black people made up 40 percent of the population in parts of the Chesapeake. Although black people never challenged white numerical dominance, they achieved majorities in a few localities. For many whites it seemed like the Chesapeake would "some time or other be confirmed by the name of New Guinea."

As demand for slaves surged upward, planters turned from the West Indies and other parts of the Atlantic littoral to the African interior as their primary source of slaves. During the 1680s some 2,000 Africans were carried into Virginia. This number more than doubled in the 1690s, and it doubled again in the first decade of the eighteenth century. Nearly 8,000 African slaves arrived in the colony between 1700 and 1710, and the Chesapeake briefly replaced Jamaica as the most profitable slave market in British America. The proportion of the Chesapeake's black population born in Africa grew steadily. By the turn of the century—eighty years after the first black people arrived at Jamestown and some forty years after the legalization of slavery—newly arrived Africans composed nearly 90 percent of the slave population, and their dramatic influx into the Chesapeake profoundly transformed black life.

The transformation sped forward with increasing velocity in the 1730s. During that decade, the number of forced immigrants averaged over 2,000 per year and sometimes rose to twice that number, as slaves replaced indentured servants not only on large plantations but on smaller units as well. Men and women with filed teeth, plaited hair, and ritual scarification (which slaveowners called "country markings" or "negro markings") were everywhere to be seen. Their music—particularly their drums—filled the air with sounds that frightened European and European-American settlers, and their pots, pipes, and other material effects left a distinctive mark on the landscape. An Anglican missionary stationed in Delaware found "difficulty of conversing with the Majority of Negroes themselves," because they have "a language peculiar to themselves, a wild confused medley of Negro and corrupt English, which makes them very unintelligible except to those who have conversed with them for many years." The language of black America turned from the creole lingua franca of the Atlantic world to the languages of the African interior—most probably various dialects of Igbo. Whereas Atlantic creoles had beaten on the door of the established churches to gain a modicum of recognition, the new arrivals showed neither interest in nor knowledge of Christianity. Their religious practices—probably polytheistic although sometimes Islamic—were dismissed as idolatry and devil worship by the established clergy, who placed them outside the pale of civilization as most white men and women understood it.

Europeans and European-Americans found the manner in which the new arrivals spoke, prayed, married, and buried their dead to be foreign in ways the charter generations were not. Africa had come to the Chesapeake.

The Africanization of slavery marked a sharp deterioration in the conditions of slave life. With an eye for a quick profit, Chesapeake planters imported males and females disproportionately, at a ratio of more than two to one, and by the end of the seventeenth century this sharply skewed sex ratio manifested itself in the plantation population. Such a sexual imbalance made it difficult for the newly arrived to establish families, let alone maintain the deep lineages that had framed so much of their African life. Since planters employed slave women much as they used slave men—dividing the labor force by age and physical ability but rarely by sex—the special needs of women during pregnancy went unaddressed, and this neglect undermined the ability of the slave population to reproduce itself. Moreover, just as direct importation drove birth rates down, it pushed mortality rates up, for the transatlantic journey left transplanted Africans vulnerable to New World diseases. As long as the main source of slaves was the African trade, fertility remained low and mortality high in the Chesapeake. Whereas Anthony and Mary Johnson, like other members of the charter generations, had lived to see their grandchildren, few of the newly arrived Africans would reproduce themselves. Indeed, within a year of their arrival, one-quarter of all "new Negroes," as they were called, would be dead. . . .

The loss of their names was only the first of the numerous indignities newly arrived Africans suffered at the hands of Chesapeake planters. Generally, planters placed little trust in Africans, with their strange tongues and alien customs. They condemned the new arrivals for the "gross bestiality and rudeness of their manners, the variety and strangeness of their languages, and the weakness and shallowness of their minds." Whenever possible, planters put the newly arrived African slaves to work at the most repetitive and backbreaking tasks in some upland quarter, denying them access to positions of skill that Atlantic creoles frequently enjoyed. Planters made but scant attempt to see that the new arrivals had adequate food, clothing, or shelter, because the open slave trade made "new Negroes" cheap, and the disease environment in which they were set to work inflated their mortality rate no matter how well they were tended. Residing in sex-segregated barracks, African slaves lived a lonely existence, without families or ties of kin, and often separated by language from supervisors and co-workers alike. Rude frontier conditions made these largely male compounds desolate, unhealthy places that narrowed the vision of their residents. The physical separation denied the new arrivals the opportunity to integrate themselves into the mainstream of Chesapeake society, and prevented them from finding a well-placed patron and enjoying the company of men and women of equal rank, as their predecessors had done. The planters' strategy of stripping away all ties upon which the enslaved persona rested—name, village, clan, household, and family—and leaving slaves totally dependent upon their owners was nearly successful. . . .

But restrictions on movement were only one small indicator of the narrowing of slaves' lives. Whereas members of the charter generations had slept and eaten under the same roof and had worked in the same fields as their owners, the new arrivals lived in a world apart. Even the ties between black slaves and white servants atrophied, as blacks sank deeper into slavery while whites rose in aspiration if not in fact. The strivings of white servants necessitated their distinguishing themselves from African slaves, who were the recipients of harsh treatment that whites laborers would no longer accept. No matter how low the status of white servants, their pale skin distinguished them from society's designated mudsill, and this small difference became the foundation upon which the entire social order rested. Nothing could be further from the "drinkinge and carrousinge" that had brought black slaves and white servants together for long bouts of interracial conviviality than the physical and verbal isolation that confronted newly arrived Africans. Whiteness and blackness took on new meanings. . . .

Slavers peddled their human cargo in small lots at the numerous tobacco landings that lined the Bay's extensive perimeter. Planters rarely bought more than a few slaves at a time, and larger purchasers like Carter frequently acted as jobbers, reselling their slaves to upstart planters. Once purchased, African slaves were further separated according to the various and changing circumstances of individual planters. Only occasionally did members of one nation congregate on a single plantation. Thus the slave trade in the Chesapeake operated to scatter men and women of various nations and diminish the importance of African nationality. And whatever fragile communities slaves had managed to create in their cramped, terrifying journey to the New World were also often disbanded as soon as the slave ships entered the Chesapeake Bay. . . .

Such a social order required raw power to sustain it; and during the early years of the eighteenth century, planters mobilized the apparatus of coercion in the service of their new regime. In the previous century, maimings, brandings, and beatings had occurred commonly, but the level of violence increased dramatically as planters transformed the society with slaves into a slave society. Chesapeake slaves faced the pillory, whipping post, and gallows far more frequently and in far larger numbers than ever before. Even as planters employed the rod, the lash, the branding iron, and the fist with increased regularity, they invented new punishments that would humiliate and demoralize as well as correct. What else can one make of William Byrd's forcing a slave bedwetter to drink "a pint of piss" or Joseph Ball's placement of a metal bit in the mouth of persistent runaways. . . .

The state ratified the planters' actions, affirming the masters' right to take a slave's life without fear of retribution. After 1669 the demise of a slave "who chance to die" while being corrected by his or her owner or upon orders of their owner no longer constituted a felony in Virginia. Such legislation soon became general throughout the region. In the years to follow, Chesapeake lawmakers expanded the power of the slaveholder and diminished the rights of the slaves in many other ways. The Virginia slave code, enacted in 1705, recapitulated, systematized, and expanded these sometimes contradictory statutes, affirming the slaveholders' ascent.

Confined to the plantation, African slaves faced a new harsh work regimen as planters escalated the demands they placed on those who worked the tobacco fields. With the decline of white servitude, slaves could no longer take refuge in the standards established for English servants. During the eighteenth century, slaves worked more days and longer hours, under closer supervision and with greater regimentation, than servants ever had in the seventeenth. Although the processes of production changed but little during the first third of the eighteenth century, slaveholders reduced the number of holidays to three: Christmas, Easter, and Whitsuntide. Saturday became a full workday, and many slaves worked Sunday as well. Planters shortened or eliminated the slaves' mid-day break. In many places, planters extended the workday into the evening, requiring that slaves grind corn and chop wood for their masters on their own time. Winter, previously a slack season, became filled with an array of tasks, including grubbing stumps, cleaning pastures, and repairing buildings. Shorter winter days did not save slaves from the new regimen, as some planters required that they work at night, often by firelight.

Although they worked harder and longer than had English servants, African slaves rarely received equivalent food, shelter, and medical attention. The customary rights accorded English workers lost their meaning as the field force became increasingly African. Slaves might protest, but their appeals stopped at the plantation's borders. Whereas slaveholders in the seventeenth century had petitioned the courts to discipline unruly slaves, in the eighteenth century they assumed near sovereignty over their plantations. The masters' authority was rarely questioned, and, unlike white servants, African slaves had no court of last resort. . . .

Meanwhile, the grandees steadily expanded their holdings and tightened their grip on colonial legislatures and county courts. Their plantations became the seats of small empires, as much factories as farms, which extended to mills, foundries, weaving houses, and numerous satellite plantations. Planters took on the airs of English gentlemen, making much of their sociability and cultivating a sense of stewardship. The seat of their domain—a large mansion house with accompanying "Kitchins, Dayry houses, Barns, Stables, Store hourses, and some . . . 2 or 3 Negro Quarters"—towered over the community with near perfect symmetry. It became the hub of the planter's universe. The home plantation, declared the tutor on one such estate, was "like a Town; but most of the Inhabitants are black." Writing after the Revolution, George Mason, himself a substantial planter, remembered that his father "had among his slaves carpenters, coopers, sawyers, blacksmiths, tanners, curriers, shoemakers, spinners, weavers and knitters, and even a distiller." The great plantation towns of the Chesapeake—Carter's Grove, Corotoman, Sabine Hall, Shirley, Stafford Hall, and eventually Doorhoregan, Monticello, and Mount Vernon—dominated the countryside and symbolized the rule of the planter class. . . .

The growth of the paternalist ideology meant many things for slaves, but its first meaning was work. Regimented labor was all-encompassing. During the seventeenth century, few planters had owned more than one or two laborers, and most had worked in the field alongside their slaves and servants in a manner that necessarily promoted close interactions. African importation and the general increase in the size of holdings permitted planters—along with their wives and children—to withdraw from the fields. They hired overseers to supervise their slaves and sometimes employed stewards to supervise their overseers, dividing their workforce by age, sex, and ability. There were few economies of scale in to-bacco culture, and planters—believing close supervision increased production—kept work units small by dividing their holdings into "quarters." But the small units rarely meant slaves worked alongside their owners. To squeeze more labor from their workers, planters also reorganized their workforce into squads or gangs, often placing agile young workers at the head of each gang. Rather than work at their own pace, slaves found their toil subject to minute inspection, as planters or their minions monitored the numerous tasks that tobacco cultivation necessitated. The demands placed on slaves to work longer and harder grew steadily throughout the eighteenth century as planters—particularly in the older, settled areas—encountered diminishing yields and rising production costs. Slaves suffered as planters prospered from the increased productivity, and the size of slave-grown crops far exceeded those previously brought to market. . . .

Violence, isolation, exhaustion, and alienation often led African slaves to pro-found depression and occasionally to self-destruction. But slaves contested the new regime at every turn—protesting the organization, pace, and intensity of la-bor and challenging the planters' definition of property rights. Over time, they perfected numerous techniques to foil their owners' demands and expand con-trol over their own labor and lives. . . .

Resistance required guile as well as muscle. If the imposition of the new regime began with the usurpation of the Africans' names, slaves soon took back this signa-ture of their identity. While slaves answered to the names their owners imposed on them, many clandestinely maintained their African names. If secrecy provided one shield, seeming ignorance offered another. In the very stereotype of the dumb, brutish African that planters voiced so loudly, newly arrived slaves found protec-tion, as they used their apparent ignorance of the language, landscape, and work routines of the Chesapeake to their own benefit. Observing the new Negroes on one Maryland estate, a visitor was "surprised at their Perseverance." "Let an hun-dred Men shew him how to hoe, or drive a Wheelbarrow, he'll still take the one by the bottom, and the Other by the Wheel." Triumphant planters had won the initial battle by gaining control over Chesapeake society and placing their imprint on the processes of production, but slaves answered that the war would be a long one.

Rather than embrace Chesapeake society in the manner of the charter genera-tions, transplanted Africans joined together to distance themselves from the source of their oppression—sometimes literally. Runaways fled toward the moun-tainous backcountry and lowland swamps. They generally traveled in large bands that included women and children, despite the hazards such groups entailed for a successful escape. As with African fugitives in lowland South Carolina and Louisiana, their purpose was to recreate the only society they knew free from white domination. During the 1720s, reports that fugitive slaves had established a settlement in the "Great Mountains" circulated widely in Virginia, and fear of maroonage grew among colonial officials. In 1729 a dozen slaves had left a new plantation near the falls of the James River, taking provisions, clothing, tools, and arms to a settlement of their own creation near Lexington. Two years later, Harry, a recently arrived African slave who had escaped from Prince George's County, Maryland, joined a small company of maroons beyond the line of European settlement. About the same time, a planter, surveying the Great Dismal Swamp on the south side of Virginia, stumbled upon a black family who "call'd themselvs free, tho' by the Shyness of the Master of the House, who took care to keep least in Sight, their Freedom seem'd a little Doubtful." . . .

But the risk might well be worth the chance, especially for slaves caught up in the westward expansion of the plantation regime. Tobacco was hard on Chesapeake soils; and during the middle years of the eighteenth century, productivity had begun to slip, especially in the places of initial settlement. Unable to maintain the yields of earlier times, planters searched for ways to increase their return by finding fresh tobacco lands. Beginning in the 1720s, they pushed beyond the fall line, where the Atlantic coastal plain meets the piedmont, liquidating maroon villages and removing Indians to the west. The younger sons of great planters and ambitious small planters staked out new quarters and prepared to plant tobacco. Many took their slaves with them, and others purchased slaves from tidewater estates—dismembering nascent slave communities at their very point of formation. But upcountry planters also relied heavily on African imports. The hub of the slave trade moved from the York River to the upper James during the middle years of the eighteenth century. Between 1720 and the Revolution, slave traders and planters carried more than 15,000 Africans beyond the fall line, transferring the center of African life from the tidewater to the piedmont and making the upcountry the most thoroughly African portion of the Chesapeake region. Africans made up the majority of the black population in many places, and in some parts of the piedmont they composed the majority of the entire population.

Africanization again marked the debasement of black life. As the piedmont's slave population grew, the familiar demographic characteristics of an open slave trade appeared: imbalanced sex ratios, low fertility, high mortality, and of course an African majority. In 1730, when the black population had begun to achieve a rough sexual parity in the tidewater, it stood at 120 males for every 100 female slaves in the piedmont. Reflecting the limited resources of upland planters and the desire of tidewater grandees to keep their most productive workers at home, the piedmont also had a disproportionately large number of children and young adults. Planters in general purchased "men boys" and "women girls," the words one slave trader used to characterize teenaged slaves. . . .

Isolated from the mainstream of Chesapeake life, newly arrived Africans had no sense of the standards by which Chesapeake slaves had earlier worked. Old hands sometimes supplied guidance as to the established routine, but the forced migration to the upcountry was extremely disruptive, dividing established families and sundering communities. Even experienced hands faced new tasks, as the heavily forested piedmont had to be cleared, fresh land broken, cabins built, and crops planted—all in rapid succession. In such circumstances, slaveholders found numerous ways to ratchet up the level of labor expected from slaves. While pressing slaves too hard might send them to the woods, slaveholders and their subordinates, eager to extend the tobacco kingdom, were quick to wield the lash. . . .

During the half century following legal enslavement, lawmakers in the Chesapeake region filled their statute books with legislation distinguishing between the rights accorded black and white persons, barring free persons of African descent from the most elemental liberties, and denying slaves access to freedom. Free black people lost the right to employ white indentured servants, hold office, bear arms, muster in the militia, and vote. They were required to pay special taxes, were punished more severely for certain crimes, and were subjected to fines or imprisonment for striking a white person, no matter what the cause.

The opportunities for black people to escape slavery or enjoy liberty all but disappeared. In the same motion that slaveowning legislators degraded the free people's legal standing, they narrowed the avenues to freedom. In 1691 the Virginia lawmakers transformed manumission into a legislative prerogative and required slaveholders to transport former slaves out of the colony, discouraging the freeing of slaves. Legislators also tried to seal another route to freedom by confining the children of white women and black men to thirty-one years of servitude and, as if to make sure such men and women would never gain freedom, stipulating that children born during this period—the grandchildren of the original offenders—would also be enslaved for thirty-one years. . . .

The exodus altered the size and character of the remaining free black population. While the number of slaves in the Chesapeake grew ever larger, the number of free people of African descent declined, if not in absolute numbers, certainly as a proportion of the black population. By midcentury, free people of African descent constituted a small and shrinking share of the black population, probably not more than 5 percent. Nowhere did free people of color comprise more than 20 percent of the black population, as they once had on Virginia's eastern shore.

Along with their diminishing numbers, free people of African descent acquired another distinguishing characteristic. In 1755 about 80 percent of this group in Maryland were of mixed racial origins. Like white Marylanders, about half of the free colored population was under sixteen years of age, and of these, almost nine out of ten were of mixed ancestry. In other words, Chesapeake free blacks were becoming progressively light-skinned. In the "bleaching" of the free black population, planters found additional evidence of the identification of whiteness with freedom. . . .

The close connection between free and slave blacks, their illegitimacy, and their inability to protect themselves at law made it easy for white planters to treat them as one. Unscrupulous planters and traders sold numerous free black apprentices and servants into slavery simply by removing them beyond the reach of evidence that they had a legal title to freedom, thereby demonstrating the disdain in which they held the liberty of people of African descent. A complaint brought by Moll, a black servant in the Virginia piedmont against her former owner, for "claiming her as a slave and Threatning to carry her out of the colony," captures the dangers free blacks regularly faced at midcentury. Those black men and women who maintained their freedom could scarcely hope for the opportunities an earlier generation of free people of color had enjoyed. The transformation of the free black population in the century between 1660 and 1760 measured the changes that accompanied the plantation revolution in the Chesapeake. The growth of a slave society and the degradation of free people of African descent were part of the same process of making slavery and making race.

Enslavement, Africanization, the imposition of the new plantation regimen, and the destruction of the charter generations—the various elements of the plantation revolution—altered black life in the Chesapeake region, almost always for the worse. But during the fourth decade of the eighteenth century, black society was again transformed as a new generation of African Americans eclipsed the African majority, ending the era of African domination. Native-born black people were healthier and lived longer than the African newcomers. Like members of the charter generations, they too were familiar with the landscapes and economies of the region. Perhaps most importantly, the new creoles had control of the word, as English was their native tongue. They could converse easily with one another, as well as with their owners and other whites. Indeed, many native-born slaves had developed particular variants of English and spoke in a "Scotch-Irish Dialect" or "Virginia accent."

Language allowed them to adjust their inherited cosmology, sacred and secular, to the requirements of tobacco cultivation and the demands of their status. Traveling through the countryside as messengers, watermen, and jobbing tradesmen, native-born slaves exuded confidence as they mastered the terrain, perfected their English, and incorporated the icons and institutions of their owners' culture into their African inheritance. The culture that emerged enabled African Americans to challenge their owners from a position of knowledge.

The passage from an African to an African-American majority began slowly. The transition had its demographic origins in the slaves' development of immunities to New World diseases and the steady growth in the size of slaveholding units. At midcentury, Chesapeake slaves not only lived longer but they also resided in units whose large size made it possible to find partners and form resident families. During the 1720s the slave population began to edge upward through natural increase. Planters, encouraged by the proven ability of Africans to survive and reproduce, strove to correct the sexual imbalance within the black population, importing a larger share of women and perhaps reducing the burdens on slave women during pregnancy. Although planters continued to purchase Africans at a brisk pace and the sex ratio remained imbalanced, by 1730 almost 40 percent of the black people in the Chesapeake colonies were native to the region. At midcentury, African Americans formed four-fifths of the slave population. On the eve of the American Revolution, the vast majority of Chesapeake slaves were native Americans, most several times over.

Chesapeake planters delighted in the growth of an indigenous slave population, as it allowed them to transfer much of the cost of reproducing the workforce to the workers themselves. Thomas Jefferson declared that "a woman who brings a child every two years [is] more profitable than the best man on the farm [for] what she produces is an addition to the capital, while his labor disappears in mere consumption." Jefferson was not the only slaveholder who appreciated the value of a self-reproducing labor force. "Nothing is more to the advantage of my son,"

NATIVE BORN

declared one ambitious planter in 1719 as he purchased two fifteen-year-old girls, "than young breeding negroes." Although mortality rates remained high, African importation declined steadily as the indigenous slave population increased. By the 1770s, only 500 of the 5,000 slaves added annually to the black population of Virginia derived directly from Africa.

As the native population grew, the Chesapeake once again became a creole society, although its point of reference was not the Atlantic but the North American interior. The charter generations and their descendants had been all but obliterated by the plantation revolution, so that only small remnants survived. Its members' occasional presence—especially in the likes of Azaricum Drighouse—reminded both white and black that people of African descent had once played a different role in Chesapeake society. But the charter generations no longer shaped the course of black life.

Africans—or so-called saltwater slaves—also remained important, at least as long as an open slave trade continued to renew knowledge of the Old World. But even in those areas where Africans composed a majority—parts of the piedmont during the 1740s and 1750s, for example—their numerical dominance dwindled, as rapid settlement quickened the pace of creolization. The majority of black people in the piedmont had also become African American, living in families and working in a manner familiar to slaves of native birth. Rather than shaping the lives of the creole majority, Africans were incorporated into the ongoing evolution of black society.

At midcentury, the African moment in Chesapeake history was passing, as the African population aged and the rising generation of African Americans came into its own. During the next two decades the linguistic and material evidence of an African presence, so visible in the early decades of the eighteenth century, would all but vanish. Slaves with teeth filed, hair plaited, or skin scarred in the ritual manner disappeared from the countryside. Some African words, gestures, and forms continued to shape speech, but no distinctive language emerged, and parents rarely gave African names to their children. The pottery they made, the pipes they smoked, and perhaps most importantly the way they celebrated rites of passage—particularly birth and death—incorporated ancestral Africa into everyday African-American life so thoroughly as to become almost invisible. African-American culture in the Chesapeake evolved parallel with Anglo-American culture and with a considerable measure of congruence.

The emergence of the new culture marked the transformation of the relationship between master and slave and with it the very definition of race. As Chesapeake slaves gained control of the word, the landscape, the productive processes, and much else, notions of blacks as a dull, brutish people fell away. In their place reappeared the stereotype of the artful, sensible charlatan, men and women who gain their way not through force but through guile and manipulation: forged passes, mimicked dialectics, and artfully constructed stories. The belief that such men and women could transform themselves—as erroneous as the older depiction of the brutish slave—was a product of the changing realities of slave life. . . .

To create families to their liking, African-American slaves pressed their owners with demands for a modicum of domestic security. Husbands and wives petitioned for permission to reside together on the same quarter or to allow husbands to visit "broad wives" and other kin, often flattering masters and mistresses with their supplications. Such off-plantation relationships disrupted the smooth operation of plantation life, making slaveowners reluctant to acquiesce. However, if the appeals to planter benevolence failed, slaves—particularly slave men—raised the cost of disapproval by withdrawing their labor. When Sam, a thirty-three-year-old carpenter, fled his plantation in central Maryland, his owner knew he could be found "lurking in Charles County . . . where a Mulatto woman lives whom he has for some time called his wife." According to her owner, a young fourteen-year-old fugitive with an iron collar was "harbour'd in some Negro Quarter, as her Father and Mother Encourages her Elopements, under a Pretence that she is ill used at Home." The separation of family members was probably the single largest source of flight and the root cause of other dissension within the plantation. . . .

Slaves established other conventions to provide them with a modicum of domestic stability. While slave women demanded time to feed their children at the breast, slave men saw to it that their families were fed beyond their masters' rations. Slaves also began to wrench control of the naming process from their owners, and parents increasingly named their children after a respected ancestor or other notable. A number of naming patterns appeared, but among the names that were missing from the quarter were those of the master and mistress. Few slaves named their children after the plantation's putative father and mother, a tacit recognition that the "family, black and white," were no kinsmen. Before long, a system of inheritance emerged within the slave community. By the middle years of the eighteenth century, it became common for slave artisans and domestics to pass their skills and special positions within the plantation hierarchy to their children.

Slaves also won a measure of privacy for their domestic lives. Unlike the barracks that housed newly arrived Africans, native-born slave families generally resided in individual cabins, often of their own construction. Most were small, rude buildings, little different from the outbuildings where slaveholders housed their animals and stored their tools, although they generally took a neater, more permanent form in the great plantation towns. But even when ramshackle and dilapidated, the separate slave quarter marked the acceptance of the slaves' demands for an independent family life and a grudging concession to the slaves' right to privacy—a notion that was antithetical to the very idea of chattel bondage. With the maturation of the plantation generations, the family once again became the center of black life in the Chesapeake and the locus of opposition to the planter's rule. . . .

Nevertheless, the slave family remained a fragile institution, as slaves had few resources to sustain ties and fewer still to protect—let alone advance—their interests. Slaveholders continually intervened in the slaves' family affairs, undercutting parents and other figures of authority, affirming their power as they rationed visitation rights and forced slaves to solicit their approval for the most routine engagements. Even under the best of circumstances, the long-distance relationships between husbands and wives were difficult to maintain and the authority of parents difficult to sustain, when they had no power to protect, few resources to reward, and little authority to punish. The frailty of family ties grew with the distance, as from afar kin relations did not even have the force of propinquity. Nonetheless, slaves recognized the centrality of their own domestic institution, and put it in the center of their own world.

With the reestablishment of the black family came responsibilities not only as husbands and wives, parents, and even grandparents but also as community leaders: men and women who set the standards and defined the norms of the slaves' society and then established strategies and created the tactics by which they might be achieved. Leadership placed some slave men and women squarely in opposition to the planters' belief that they were metaphorical fathers and mothers of the slave community. The development of black family life, and the restructuring of the black community which the new kinship patterns affirmed set in motion a new series of conflicts over the fruits of the slaves' labor, as slaves tried to roll back the stringent labor requirements that accompanied the growth of the plantation and to reinvigorate their own economy. The issues were many: customary workload and pace of labor, division of labor within slave families, the nature of supervision, character of discipline, all of which slaveowners claimed as their exclusive prerogative and all of which slaves determined to alter in their own favor.

The African-American family did not end at the household's edge. Sometimes extended families occupied a single plantation or quarter; sometimes slave families spilled across plantation boundaries. In Folly's Quarter of Charles Carroll's great Doorhoregan estate on the western shore of Maryland, Fanny lived surrounded by her children, grandchildren, and nephews and nieces, forty in number. Likewise, all but thirty of the 128 slaves residing on Riggs, Carroll's home quarter, belonged to two extended families. Sometimes the quarter took the name of the family matriarch or patriarch. But the small size of most Chesapeake estates forced slave men and women to look beyond plantation borders for a spouse. As slaves intermarried across plantation lines, the extended network of kin spread through the countryside, joined together by consanguinity and shared obligations. Scattered among the dozen quarters, mills, and forges that comprised Charles Carroll's vast holdings, some twenty slaves bore the names of their grandparents and others that of aunts and uncles and of course parents.

The quarter, whether the home of a single extended family or a group of unrelated individuals who had been transmuted into kin, became the institutional embodiment of the slave community in the Chesapeake. On the home plantation, the quarter was generally neatly tended, often along a street that led to the planter's Great House. Outside the orbit of the great plantation towns, the quarter was little more than a ramshackle collection of huts and outbuildings. Surrounded by equally disorderly gardens, animal pens, and scrawny barnyard fowl, this farrago of small dwellings—each rarely more than a single spartan room with an earthen floor—was much like the west African villages or compounds from which slaves or their ancestors derived. Within its bounds, slaves plotted their own ascent, socializing among themselves, educating their children to the harsh realities of enslavement, and honing the weapons which they would employ to reclaim what their owners usurped. . . .

During the middle years of the eighteenth century, slaves recovered some of the prerogatives that members of the charter generations had taken for granted. The free Sunday had become an entitlement rather than a privilege, so almost all Chesapeake slaves had Sundays to themselves. According to a historian of eighteenth-century Chesapeake agriculture, "slaves had converted that practice into a right that could not be violated arbitrarily." Occasionally, slaves enjoyed part of Saturday as well. When owners impinged upon the slaves' free days, they generally compensated them in time or money.

Still, planters resisted, refusing to surrender the very essence of slavery's value. To prevent slaves from elevating customary practices into entitlements and from manufacturing yet additional rights, slaveholders sought to confine the slaves' economy. They were especially adamant about the independent trading, as they understood how the slaves' entry into the marketplace enlarged their understanding of the value of their own labor and sharpened their appreciation of the planter's usurpation. Moreover, planters were not above countering with new demands of their own—for example, requiring slaves to process as well as grow tobacco and to manufacture candles and other necessities for the Great House. The maturation of tobacco culture did not end the contest between master and slave; it only moved the struggle to new ground. . . .

FOR FURTHER STUDY

1. What does the Africanization of slavery mean? What was its impact?

2. In what ways did planters increase coercion and work load on slaves in the early eighteenth century?

3. What measures did slaves use to resist their masters' increasing demands?

4. How did the plantation owners keep the proportion of free blacks from growing? Why did it become harder to be free and black in the Chesapeake?

5. When did the transition from African to African American begin and why it is important?

6. How was the slave family reestablished?

FOR FURTHER READING

Berlin's study is part of a vast literature on slavery. For another synthesis see Philip D. Morgan, *Slave Counterpoint* (1998). See also Donald R. Wright's *African American in the Colonial Era: From African Origins through the American Revolution* (1990). For an even broader perspective see Peter Kolchin *American Slavery, 1619–1877* (1993). If you want to learn about the relationships between the three races of colonial America the best work is Gary B. Nash, *Red, White, and Black: The Peoples of Early North America,* 3rd ed. (1992). Of course, one place to start is with the origin of the trade itself and the African context. One excellent study is John Thompson's *Africa and Africans in the Making of the Atlantic World, 1400–1680* (1992). The extent of the slave trade and the horrors and realities of the Atlantic or "middle" passage are discussed in Philip D. Curtin's *The Atlantic Slave Trade: A Census* (1969) and in Daniel P. Mannix with Malcolm Cowley, *Black Cargoes: A History of the Atlantic Slave Trade, 1518–1865* (1962). For an overview see John Thornton, *Africa and Africans in the Making of the Atlantic World, 1400–1864* (1992).

Racism and slavery are intimately connected and historians have long-debated the relationship between the two. The seminal work is Winthrop D. Jordan's *White Over Black: American Attitudes Toward the Negro, 1550–1812* (1968). Edmund Morgan sees the commitment to large-scale slavery in colonial Virginia as a combination of racism and economics in *American Slavery American Freedom: The Ordeal of Colonial Virginia* (1975).

For a study of early relations in Virginia where some slaves were not only able to buy their own freedom but accumulate considerable estates see T. H. Breen and Stephen Innes, *"Myne Own Ground": Race and Freedom on Virginia's Eastern Shore, 1640–1720* (1980) and Douglas Deal, *Race and Class in Colonial Virginia: Indians, Englishmen, and Africans on the Eastern Shore during the Seventeenth Century* (1993). Alan Kulikoff's *Tobacco and Slaves: The Development of Southern Cultures in the Chesapeake, 1680–1800* (1986) traces the region's slaves and the development of a distinct African American culture in the eighteenth century. See also Lorena S. Walsh, *From Calabar to Carter's Grove: A History of a Virginia Slave Community* (1997). Georgia slaves are studied in Betty Wood *Slavery in Colonial Georgia, 1730–1775* (1985) and Julia Floyd Smith, *Slavery and Rice Culture in Low Country Georgia, 1750–1860* (1985). For a unique cultural adaptation see Gwendolyn Midlo Hall, *Africans in Colonial Louisiana: The Development of Afro-Creole Culture in the Eighteenth Century* (1992). Slaves also developed their own culture "in the chill Yankee air" of New England according to William D. Piersen in *Black Yankees: The Development of an Afro-American Subculture in Eighteenth-Century New England* (1988).

Slaves did resist slavery and many of the works above discuss slave actions including several later chapters of Peter Wood's, *Black Majority.* For more detailed attention to slave efforts Gerald W. Mullin *Flight and Rebellion: Slave Resistance in Eighteenth-Century Virginia* (1972) and Thomas J. Davis, *A Rumor of Revolt: The "Great Negro Plot" in Colonial New York* (1985) are especially useful. During the American Revolution slaves could and did make choices based on their quest for freedom as Sylvia R. Frey notes in *Water from the Rock: Black Resistance in a Revolutionary America* (1991).

CHAPTER 3

Courtesy of the Massachusetts Historical Society, (MHS No. 1495)

An artist known as the Pollard Limner manages to portray the indomitable spirit of the elderly Puritan woman Ann Pollard in this painting.

HUSBANDS AND WIVES

LYLE KOEHLER

*A*s children, most of us take marriage and family very much for granted, as part of the natural order of things. Eventually, we may come to wonder just how natural matrimony is, whether it exists because of love or social necessity, and what the role of parents and children in the family is and should be. Several factors account for the heightened skepticism about marriage and the family in recent years. One, of course, is the rising divorce rate, and another may be the lessened economic dependence of women and children upon the father of the family.

In recent years, historians have turned their attention to the makeup of the family and household in earlier times and have examined how our views have changed with respect to the relationships between men and women. Some historians believe women were more highly valued members of the family and had greater equality in earlier centuries, when they were vital to the household economy, than in the period since industrialization. Men, most of whom were farmers or home craftsmen, spent their day in the household, rather than away in factories and offices.

Most of the colonists' views, including those of marital relationships and child rearing, were heavily influenced by English and continental European traditions. But these customs—like their language, government, and class attitudes—slowly and subtly changed in the New World. The following selection by Lyle Koehler emphasizes the continuity of English traditions in Puritan New England and the pervasive influence of Calvinism on family life. Koehler argues forcefully that the colonial period was far from being a golden age for women. He views men as striving for male dominance and women as being forced into abject submission.

Other historians might well question these conclusions. Some scholars have suggested that one cannot get a reliable view of the day-to-day life of average people by studying the sermons and laws written by a small elite. Others have suggested that we cannot really speak of a monolithic, New England, Calvinist society. Some students believe that men and women were closer to having an equal status in the colonial period than in the nineteenth century. In any case, Koehler's article cannot be assumed to give a clear portrait of the family in the middle or southern colonies.

Calvinists in England and in America expected each person to keep his or her proper place in God's social design. They placed virtually everyone on a grid of inferiority and superiority—servant before master, non-church member before church-member, idler before working man, wife before husband, child before adult. Such a system facilitated supervision, because each master was legally accountable for overseeing the behavior of designated subordinates.

Crucial to the maintenance of religious and social order was the Puritans' attention to proper child rearing. Godly parents were to make sure that their "unstaid and young" charges did not become addicted to the "greasy sensuality" of play—to "rattles, baubles, and such toyish stuff." Pilgrim pastor John Robinson described the difficulty of such a task:

> . . . surely there is in all children . . . a stubborness, and stoutness of mind arising from natural pride, which must, in the first place, be broken and beaten down; that so the foundation of their education being laid in humility and tractableness, other virtues may, in their time, be built thereon . . . . For the beating and keeping down of this stubborness parents must provide carefully. . . . Children should not know, if it could be kept from them, that they have a will in their own, but in their parents' keeping; neither should these words be heard from them, save by way of consent, "I will" or "I will not."

As Robinson indicated, the parent was to crush the child's drive or desire for self-assertion or independence, for such feelings might advance the child's "natural pride." Instead, adults were to inculcate in youngsters a sense of virtual helplessness before parental whim and God's authoritarian will. . . .

. . . If children cursed or struck their parents—except "to preserve themselves from Death or Maiming"—Puritan law specified the death penalty. New Hampshire and Connecticut also prescribed hanging for any son who refused to heed his mother's or father's voice after chastisement. The authorities neglected to prosecute youngsters under such capital laws, but they did use the laws to inspire fear. In 1647 the authorities also expended some time and effort attempting to revive "the ancient practice in England of children asking their parents' blessing upon their knees," which would presumably symbolize the child's "Obedience unto the commands" of his or her parents. Ipswich minister Thomas Cobbett went still further, explaining that children "should rise up and stand bare [headed] before their Parents when they come to them, or speak to them. . . . It stands not with

---

Parents' Honour for children to sit and speak, but rather they should stand up when they speak to Parents." . . .

The archetypal Puritan patriarch kept his children in a state of repressive bondage. He was a classic example of what clinical psychologist Diana Baumrind calls the authoritarian parent, who

> values obedience as a virtue and favors punitive, forceful measures to curb self-will at points where the child's actions or beliefs conflict with what he or she thinks is right conduct. He or she believes in keeping the child in his place, in restricting his autonomy, and in assigning household responsibilities in order to inculcate respect for work. This parent regards the preservation of order and traditional structure as a highly valued end in itself. He or she does not encourage verbal give and take, believing that the child should accept the parents' word for what is right.

Such a parent believed that "too much doting affection" distracted children from thoughts of God, or led them to consider themselves their parents' equals. Minister Thomas Cobbett warned that "fondness and Familiarity breeds . . . contempt and irreverence in children." Robert Cleaver believed "cockering" children with affection could only ruin them: "For as the Ape doth with too much embracings, well neer kill her young whelpes: so likewise some indiscrete parents, through immoderate love and over-much pampering and cherishing do utterly despoil and mar their children. Therefore, if parents would have their children live, they must take heed that they love them not too much."

Puritans stressed discipline more than affection. In English Puritan households, according to one scholar, "the rod was most favored" as a punitive device. In America, the Massachusetts *Body of Liberties* (1641) prohibited "unnaturall severitie" toward the young, but did not specify when punishment became "severe" or "unnatural." The adult faced prosecution when he broke a child's bones, endangered the child's life, or delivered a cudgeling with "a walnut tree plant, big enough to have killed a horse"—but only three of nearly three dozen such offenders received more than an admonition or a very small fine. Still, New England Puritans did not oppose the use of the "Rod of Correction"; in fact, they considered it "an ordinance of God," suitable to inspire "love and fear." Cotton Mather stated it simply: "Better whipt, than Damn'd." . . .

Growing up in a Puritan home was certainly painful. Strict control through the family and all other social institutions often created a feeling of profound helplessness in children. This phenomenon had wide-ranging impact, for, as psychologist Martin Seligman has shown, repeated and sustained perceptions of an inability to control one's outcomes can lead to a state of chronic despair. Many boys and girls, in true Puritan fashion, lamented their own despicability and great sinfulness. Elizabeth Butcher, aged two and one-half, purportedly asked herself often from the cradle "the question, What is my corrupt Nature? and would make answer to herself, It is empty of Grace, bent into Sin, and only to Sin, and that continually." Jerusha Oliver, "While her infancy was hardly yet expired," professed many sins. Depressed by her backsliding, at age twelve she began sequestering herself for entire days, so that she could repent. Sarah Derby "set up almost all night, crying to the Lord, that He would please apply unto her, by His own Holy

Spirit, a Promise, which might Releive the Disconsolations of her Soul." Recurrent melancholia assailed Samuel Sewall's daughter Elizabeth between the ages of seven and fifteen. One minister's son, Nathaniel Shrove, hoped for death, that he might avoid sin—and then decided he was too despicable to deserve even that.

These were anxiety-ridden, insecure, unhappy children—the products of a culture which devalued independent thought, self-satisfaction, exuberance, and real closeness. A consideration of their anguish and preoccupations can help us understand the Puritan psyche, particularly as it affected attitudes toward the female sex. . . .

Like so many of their European contemporaries, New England's male Puritan leaders assumed that the obvious physical differences between the sexes had important social consequences. Throughout the seventeenth century these authorities argued and acted as if they believed anatomy alone determined destiny. In virtually all avenues of behavior Puritans affirmed the differences and deemphasized the similarities between the sexes—a practice which usually worked to the disadvantage of women. Because Puritan men had a high need to prove that they wielded some sort of power, in the face of the impotence inculcated in childhood and a theology of man's ultimate powerlessness before God, they tended to exaggerate prevailing notions of male superiority. While such men referred to themselves as the "Magnanimous, Masculine, and Heroicke sexe," every woman became a "poor fraile" creature—the "weaker sex." As Elnathan Chauncy scrawled in his commonplace book, "Y^e soule consists of two portions inferior and superior[;] the superior is masculine and aeternal. Y^e inferior foeminine and mortal." Custom meshed with psychological need for Puritans and non-Puritans alike with sometimes bizarre results.

Beginning with conception and birth, profound developmental differences were assumed between male and female infants. Some physicians hypothesized that the male child was conceived earlier than the female because the male, as a higher, more sophisticated form of life, needed more time to develop in the womb. On the other hand, some religious leaders asserted that the male embryo, in recognition of its ultimate superiority, received his soul on the fortieth day, while the female embryo had to wait until the eightieth day before she acquired hers. When a woman had conceived twins of each sex, those twins supposedly occupied segregated uterine chambers to breathe into them the "laws of chastity." When the twins or a single child was ready to enter the outside world, the birth of a male was easier, according to the English obstetrical expert Thomas Raynalde. The reason for this was simple: babies were presumed to find their way into the outer world under their own power, and boys, being more vigorous than girls, got out faster. After delivery, the attending midwives cut a girl's navel string shorter than a boy's, "because they believe it makes . . . [females] modest, and their [genital] Parts narrower, which makes them more acceptable to their husbands."

Daughters were "less long'd for" than sons, perhaps in part because English obstetrical guides asserted that mothers who were carrying boys enjoyed fair complexions, red nipples, and white milk, while girls gave them "a pale, heavy, and swarth[y] countenance, a melancolique eye," black nipples, and watery bluish milk. At birth Puritan daughters, in particular, often received names which providentially reminded them of the limitations of their feminine destiny: Silence, Fear, Patience, Prudence, Mindwell, Comfort, Hopestill, and Be Fruitful. No Calvinist girl would ever bear an impressive name such as Freeborne, Fearnot, or Wrestling.

Puritan males, like so many of their English contemporaries, valued those characteristics in women which would insure submissiveness. The ideal woman blushed readily and chose "to be seen rather than Heard whenever she comes." She held her tongue until asked by her father or husband to speak; then only good, comforting words flowed from her mouth. "The greatest Nuisance in Nature," Joseph Beacon unequivocatingly wrote, "is an immodest impudent Woman." The ideal female displayed "an Eminence in Modesty, reserve, purity, temperance, humility, truth, meekness, patience, courtesie, affability, charity, goodness, mercy, [and] compassion," taking special care to avoid the "monstrous" decorative habit of painting the face with "varnish." Tender, consoling, and in need of careful direction, she was viewed as a defenseless creature, "that naked Sex that hath no arms but for imbraces."

In Puritan terms, women needed men, not only for physical protection and financial support but also to prevent themselves from going intellectually astray. Since the woman was presumed less able to ground her spiritual development in the cold logic of reason, Puritan divines told her to consult her father, her husband, or a minister whenever she wished to comprehend a theological issue. In fact, too much intellectual activity, on a theological or any other plane, might overtax her frail mind and thereby debilitate her equally weak body. In 1645 Emmanuel Downing claimed his wife, Lucy, made herself sick "by trying new Conclusions"; he suggested riding as a cure. In the same year Downing's brother-in-law, Massachusetts Governor John Winthrop, asserted that Ann Hopkins, the wife of the Connecticut governor, had lost her understanding and reason by giving herself solely to reading and writing. This statesman commented that if she "had attended her household affairs, and such things as belong to women, and had not gone out of her way and calling to meddle in such things as are proper for men, whose minds are stronger etc., she had kept her wits, and might have improved them usefully and honorably in the place God had set her.". . . Thomas Parker, the Newbury pastor, reacted to his own sister's writing with particular sharpness. "Your printing of a Book," he wrote, "beyond the custom of your sex, doth rankly smell.". . .

Many English and American Puritans believed the virtuous woman should walk in the shadow of her male masters from the cradle to the grave. A daughter owed almost complete allegiance to her father's wishes. He was to supervise whom she might choose as friends, direct her to the service of others, and remind her to keep constant watch over the state of her soul. He was expected to reprimand her for tending to become a "Busie-Body" or "Pragmatical." Whatever he commanded (with exception of something sinful), she was to obey. His pleasure was her goal, and "her heart would melt/When she her Fathers looks not pleasant felt." The ideal daughter was like "a nun unprofest," a girl who never read lust-inducing plays and romances, who avoided the comb and the looking glass, and who relished serving her parents with a demeanor of "Virgin Modesty." When she reached a marriageable age, a daughter should "do nothing" without her father's approval; in marriage matters, she should be "very well contented . . . to submit to such condition[s]" as her parents "should see providence directing." In every familial relation the father, that "soul of the family," served as "governor of the governed." Apparently to emphasize the potency of such paternal overlordship, John Cotton in 1641 actually suggested hanging any maiden who allowed a lover to have sexual intercourse with her in her father's house.

In marriage the woman traded her father's surname for her husband's, in a symbolic transferral of the male right to "govern, direct, protect, and cherish" her. Her lack of an independent name accented the fact that she could not exist independent of men: as daughter she was to give "Reverence, subjection & Obedience" to her father, and as wife she was to give the same to her marital "master." Since he possessed more "quickness of witte . . . greater insight and forecast," that "Prince and chiefe Ruler" deserved her assistance, "reverand awe," and silent submission—if not outright fear. . . .

Theologians directed the "true wife" to be constantly concerned for her husband's welfare, even at the expense of her own. In Cotton Mather's words:

> When she Reads, That Prince Edward in his Wars against the Turks, being stabbed with a poisoned Knife, his Princess did suck the Poison out of his Wounds, with her own Royal Mouth, she finds in her own Heart a principle disposing her to shew her own Husband as great a Love. When she Reads of a woman called Herpine, who having her Husband Apoplex'd in all his Limbs, bore him on her Back a thousand and three Hundred English Miles to a Bath, for his Recovery, she minds herself not altogether unwilling to have done the Like.

Mather urged the wife to address her husband by the appropriate title of "My Lord." If she felt any "passion" against her mate, she left it unexpressed; but when he was in passion, she quickly strove to mollify it. The virtuous wife was to "carry her self so to her husband as not to disturb his love by her contention, nor to destroy his love by her alienation." She was to be at his beck and call, acting "as if there were but One Mind [His] in Two Bodies.". . .

A wife's major purpose in life, besides working on religious salvation, was to minister to her husband's needs. Her personal identity and social rank were derived through him. She was his appendage, as Cotton Mather explained in a letter to his sister-in-law, Hannah Mather. To be the "best of women in the American World," he urged Mistress Mather, "Go on to love him [her husband], and serve him, and felicitate him, and become accessary to all the Good which *he* may do in the world.". . .

. . . [It] was the Puritan contention that female activities ought to be largely limited to the home's safe environment, even though many non-Puritan women worked in various English agricultural pursuits. William Perkins wrote, "The woman is not to take libertie of wandring, and staying abroad from her owne house, without the man's knowledge and consent." Considering her an ineffective manager of "outward business and affairs," Puritan leaders urged the wife to busy herself with cooking, cleaning, spinning, child care, and other household tasks. Indeed, worldly concerns constituted a potential threat to her health in a way that monotonous household activities did not. A woman achieved respect largely by the extent to which "She looks well to the Wayes of her Household.". . .

In the final analysis, the spokesmen for the several Biblical Commonwealths posited an ideology of female weakness, deference, patience, and nurturance. Sex roles were sharply separated, with the male viewed as the stronger, ruling sex, one more protective than nurturant. As much as and perhaps more than their English contemporaries, the Puritan spokesmen of New England viewed male characteristics as expressions of their own "obvious" superiority. Michael Wigglesworth held that women's weakness made them "generally more ignorant, and Worthless." Nathaniel Ward found it hard to view women as anything other than "featherheaded" spendthrifts and "Squirrel-brained" friskers after the latest fashions, ladies "fitter to be kickt . . . then either honour'd or humour'd." He called "these nauseous shaped gentlewomen" no more than "gant-bar-geese, ill-shapen-shotten-shell-fish, Egyptian Hyeroglyphics, or at the best . . . French flurts of the pastery." This acerbic minister maintained that "The world is full of care, much like unto a bubble/Woman and care, and care and Women, and Women and care and trouble." Another minister, William Hubbard, believed women to be little better than property; concerning a case wherein two men claimed the same woman as wife, he wrote that it took much time "to find who was the right *owner* of the *thing* in controversy."

Misogyny in New England had its limits, however. Although they affirmed the need for women to seek male theological advice, Puritans did allow women to work out their individual reckonings with God in the isolation of their closets. Some ministers attacked their male associates for refusing to recognize female worth. Cotton Mather wrote:

> Monopolizing HEE's, pretend no more
> Of Wit and Worth, to hoard up all the store.
> The Females too grow Wise & Good & Great.

This divine informed his readers, "It is a Common, but Causeless report that women's tongues [wag ceaselessly] and are frequently not governed by the fear of God." Similarly, John Cotton asserted that those men who viewed women as "a necessary Evil" were "Blasphemers." Yet another man, John Saffin, in a poem entitled "Cankers touch fairest fruites" directed his male readers away from the belief that women were "Woe to men.". . .

The reader may object that I have been painting too bleak a picture of the Puritans' ideas about the "weaker sex." After all, many scholars have pointed out that these religious reformers emphasized the importance of love—an attitude which theoretically facilitated the liberation of women from the shackles of male dominion. On the surface this argument seems plausible, as some Puritans indicated their approval of affection and the emotional closeness which sometimes develops with physical closeness. John Winthrop addressed his wife Margaret as

"My Chiefe Ioye in this World" and, when away from her on business, wrote letters containing the following affectionate remarks:

> [April 28, 1629] I kisse and loue thee with the kindest affection and rest
>   Thy faithful husbande,
> [May 8, 1629] the verye thought of thee affordes me many a kynde re-
>   freshinge, what will then the enjoyinge of thy sweet societye, which I
>   prize aboue all worldly comforts,
> [February 5, 1629/30] My sweet wife, Thy loue is such to me, and so
>   great is the bonde between vs, that I should neglect all others to hold
>   correspondencye of lettres with thee.

Edward Taylor viewed his relationship with his wife as "the True-Love Knot, more sweet than spice/ And set with all the flowre of Graces dress." To this divine, the wedding knot was the place "Where beautious leaves are laid with Honey Dew./ And Chanting Birds Cherp out sweet Musick true." Thomas Hooker described the ideal husband very romantically, as "The man whose heart is endeared to the woman he loves, he dreams of her in the night, hath her in his eye and apprehension when he awakes, museth on her as he sets at table, walks with her when he travels and parlies with her in each place where he comes." Such a husband cradled his wife's head on his bosom and "his heart trusts in her . . . the stream of his affection, like a mighty current, runs with ful Tide and strength." Thomas Thatcher wrote poetically to Margaret Sheafe, his betrothed, in the 1660s:

> Thy Joy I seek, thy comfort's my desire
>   Whilst to enjoy thy bosom I aspire;. . .

Puritans like Thatcher, Hooker, Taylor, and Winthrop certainly expressed loving sentiments, quite in accord with those English Puritan divines who described "set-led affection," "companionship," and "tender loue" as the "glue" between marital "yoke-fellows." Many a divine directed the husband to support his wife, praise her virtues, honor her, and "bee not bitter, fearce, and cruell vnto her." Yet, when ministers celebrated the mutual delight and concord existing in "louing" union, they considered love "not so much the cause as . . . the product of marriage." A "duty" owed one's spouse and God, it became "nothing but Christian charity, and marriage supplied the chief form for the exercise of that charity." As one minister explained, love was "the Sugar to sweeten every addition to married life *but not an essential part of it.* Love was Condition in the married Relation." Since a couple need not love to marry, either sex could wed for less romantic considerations. A young man could legitimately search for a "goodly lass with aboundation of money" or a "very convenient" estate, as long as he had a desire to respect his wife-to-be and did not keep his motives from her. And a maiden could accept the hand of a suitor for equally mercenary motives, as long as she was honest about it. Such marriages had little to do with love; it magically appeared at some later date, if at all.

Nor did Puritans view love in egalitarian terms. Although a couple "are combined together as it were in one," Calvinists agreed that, even in the closest human relationship, "one is alwaies higher, and beareth rule, the other is lower, and yeeldeth subjection.". . . . William Gouge pointed out that a couple "are yoak-fellows in mutuall familiaritie, not in equall authoritie. . . . If therefore he will one thing, and she another, she may not thinke to haue an equall right and power. She must giue place and yeeld," even if he be "a drunkard, a glutton, a profane swaggerer, an impious swearer, and blasphemer." Gouge and his contemporaries urged the wife, as a specific manifestation of her love, "to guid the house &c. not guid the Husband." The male-centered nature of such love becomes particularly clear in admonitions for her "wholly to depend on him, both in judgment and will." When the husband brought home unexpected dinner guests or failed to take her moods seriously enough, the enduring wife was to grin and bear it, for discontentment over such matters "argueth not a louing affection, nor a wiuelike subjection." Love meant that she empathized with his moods, in a nurturant man-ner, but that he did not need to reciprocate. In fact, even if she were "wiser, more discreete, and prouident then the Husband," those traits could not "overthrowe the superioritie of the man." The wise wife could advise him, but only with "hu-militie and reuerence; shewing her selfe more willing to heare, then to speake."

 . . . [T]he disobedient or contentious wife became one of the world's most de-spicable creatures—not only "an heart-sore to him that hath her," but no better than a wolf, a wart, a cancer, a gangrene, or even excrement. (By comparison, the harsh or churlish husband became only "a wild beast.") Quite revealingly, Puritan Alexander Niccoles explained the prevailing notion of male-centered love: a man "not only unitest unto thy selfe a friend," a "comfort for society" and "a compan-ion for pleasure," but "in some sort a servant for profite too." Thomas Gataker went a step further, referring to the wife as a form of the husband's property. She "must resolue to giue herselfe wholly to him," Gataker wrote, "as her Owner, on whom God hath bestowed her." Still, in their effort to maintain security within the familial unit, as a counterpart to the insecurity occurring in the world outside, many Puritans disliked calling the wifely role "servitude" or "slavery." However, their overt endorsement of female subjection, coupled with affirmations of the husband's "superiority" and "authoritie" in "all things" at home, revealed that Puritans perceived marriage as servitude, although in a slightly different cast.

The Puritan notion of love served, then, not to liberate women; instead, it insti-tutionalized sex-role oppression for both men and women. Whatever the realities of any particular interaction, as an idea it reinforced female submission and made it difficult for males to be anything other than controlling.

Such a concept of love fed male egocentricity. The Puritan male tended to em-phasize what his wife could do for him, rather than what he could do for her. He loved her not for her uniqueness but for the extent to which she fulfilled the role expectations of the ideal female, including a self-sacrificing concern for his needs. Joseph Thompson cared for his wife because she studied how "to make my life Comfortable to me, as far as she could." Similarly, Richard Mather's wife was ac-counted "a Woman of singular Prudence" when she managed his secular affairs so well that he could devote himself totally to his own studying and "Sacred Imployments." Thomas Shepard applauded his mate for her "incomparable meekness of spirit, toward myselfe especially." Edward Taylor's wife, Elizabeth

Fitch, was, in his opinion, "a Tender, Loving, Meet,/ Meecke, Patient, Humble, Modest, Faithful, Sweet/ Endearing Help," a woman "Whose Chiefest Treasure/ of Earthly things she held her Husbands pleasure." . . .

. . . Puritans could not agree with the Antinomian and Quaker belief that an intense feeling between husband and wife served as a reflection of, instead of a danger to, love for God. When Antinomian William Hutchinson said he thought more of his wife than of their church, the Puritans could only call him a man of "weak parts," one incapable of constraining his own affection or of regulating his wife's behavior.

Despite the Puritan desire to limit the genuine, earthly love that could develop between two people by subordinating it to the love of God and to demand arising out of sex role dominance and submission, some couples did marry for love and enter into very close relationships. That closeness developed not because of, but in spite of Puritanism. Ideologically, the egalitarian impulse of pure affection was undercut by the Puritan need to regard love first and foremost as duty—not as deep feeling brought to a marriage by the couple, but as a network of obligations imposed upon the couple by God. Such a notion of love, coupled with a belief system which accentuated male superiority, constituted an effort not only to be true to biblical prescriptions and to the sometimes conservative ethos of English culture, but also to countermand the Puritan male's peculiar feelings of impotence. . . .

An important issue arises at this point: Was Puritan sex-role ideology consistent with Puritan practice, or simply an unenforceable vision? Was it a purely intellectual identification with a glorified biblical past, or the genuinely descriptive adjunct of socially institutionalized sex roles? Such questions necessitate an examination of the extent to which the prevailing sex-role ideology was implemented.

Puritan society was organized in a way that explicitly affirmed the belief in sex segregation as a reminder of men's and women's different destinies. In church the men, women, maidens, and youths all sat separately, with the most prominent men sitting in the foremost, highest-status pews. Each sex also entered the meetinghouse by a separate door. . . .When the little girl attended a dame school to learn the rudiments of education, she studied at a curriculum somewhat different from that of the boys; while the latter grappled with Latin, penmanship, spelling, reading, and religion, the former learned cooking, weaving, and spinning, as well as reading, writing and religion.

. . . [I]n other realms Puritans used institutional prohibitions to distinguish between the respective roles of men and women. Both spinsters and widows could own property, but neither could vote for public officials. Puritans considered the franchise an important means for protecting civil liberties, but for men only—as Nathaniel Ward wrote, without such protection, "men are *but* women." Nor could women vote in church affairs, prophesy, or even ask questions in church, for in all such cases "speaking argues power." A woman could speak only when singing hymns or, in a few churches, when she made a public request for the privilege of membership. Male members not only reserved full participation in church affairs for themselves, but also were reluctant to admit to membership women who were "full of sweet affection" but "a little too confident."

Puritan society provided virtually no avenues for women to seek fulfillment outside marriage. The school curriculum emphasized the importance of the woman staying in the home, and the apprenticeship system trained girls for no trade other than housewifery. There is no record of any New England mercantile establishment hiring a maiden to work outside the home until after King Philip's War, although in England a daughter could receive apprenticeship training as a shopkeeper. Maidens, wives, and widows could not hawk or peddle goods throughout the countryside, as was true in their Puritan homeland. An unwed woman could attempt to build some savings by working as a domestic servant, a doctor, or a schoolmistress; however, such occupations were very poorly paid. Without marriage, a woman could hardly expect to have any financial security.

Even if a woman did manage to accumulate a sizeable estate or income (through an inheritance, for example), she faced great social pressure to marry. If a lass remained single until age twenty-three, neighbors called her a "spinster." If she was still unwed at twenty-six, she received the more odious appellation of "thornback." Bookseller John Dunton remarked in 1686 that "an old (or Superannuated) Maid, in Boston, is thought such a curse as nothing can exceed it, and [look'd] on as a Dismal Spectacle." Some of Dunton's Puritan contemporaries believed that deceased old maids could do no better than to lead apes in Hell.

Men were expected to marry also, but community gossip did not focus on the bachelor as it did on the spinster. There was, in fact, no term of opprobrium comparable to "spinster," "thornback," or "old maid." The church members of at least one town, Salem, chose a thirty-six-year-old bachelor, Nicholas Noyes, as their minister (1683). Puritans did, however, establish vehicles for the regulation of bachelors' behavior, since Satan reportedly loved to provide erotic fantasies to tempt the minds of unwed males. Medfield, Massachusetts, set aside segregated housing, a special Bachelors' Row, to facilitate their supervision. The Middlesex County magistrates prosecuted many "singlemen" who failed to place themselves under family government between 1665 and 1679, while Plymouth, New Haven, and Connecticut colonies required bachelors to live with "licensed families." The Connecticut enactment actually specified that bachelors living alone pay a £1 fine each week—which undoubtedly helps to explain why Madame Knight wrote in 1704 that half of Connecticut's males were married by the time they reached twenty years of age.

Despite such pressures to marry, the prospective suitor could not simply court any girl he wished. He first had to secure the permission of the maiden's father, or face prosecution on a charge of "inveigling" the girl. All Puritan-controlled locales except Maine punished by a £5 fine or a whipping any man who "stole away" the affections of a maiden by "speech, writing, message, company-keeping, unnecessary familiarity, disorderly night-meetings, sinful dalliance, gifts, or in any other way." The severity of the punishment for inveigling suggests that Puritans took very seriously the father's right to convey his overlordship to another male, thereby depriving the daughter of any initial decision about whom she wished to woo her. A father could not "wilfullie and unreasonably deny any childe timely or convenient" marriage, but he could largely determine whom she married. The daughter could, of course, reject any suitor allowed to court her, but she then had to deal with the consequences of her decision. For example, when Lucy Downing refused to wed a candidate of whom her parents approved, her mother informed her that such behavior was unwise and disreputable. When a depressed Betty Sewall withdrew from Grove Hirst's suit, her father reminded her that such action would "tend to discourage persons of worth from making their Court" to her. A young woman capable of such independence could hardly be expected to transform herself into a submissive, obedient wife, a fact which further restricted her marital possibilities.

Young men had fewer limitations. Even though a father might attempt to "control" his sons by refusing to give them any of his property, they could hire themselves out to artisans, become fishermen, or enter a number of other occupations. Once a young man decided he wanted to marry, he could secure the appropriate paternal permission to court one or more lasses. His father did not need to approve of his choices, although certainly that was the preferred route.

Once a couple had wed, no law specified that the wife had to obey her husband's every wish. However, the law did give him great supervisory control over her property and behavior. At marriage, a wife had to relinquish control over whatever real estate she possessed or income she received. She could, through a prenuptial contract, attempt to retain some control over her own property, but the English Court of Chancery and the Massachusetts Assistants did not recognize the validity of such an agreement. Not until 1762 did the Bay Colony accept prenuptial contracts as binding, although Connecticut had done so as early as 1673. The authorities of New Haven, New Hampshire, and Plymouth never heard a case concerning the legitimacy of such a contract. Whatever their position on prenuptial agreements, all of the colonies respected the husband's "right" to regulate his wife's realty. Only some of her personal estate—her dresses, quilts, needles, and so on—remained in her hands after marriage.

Puritan legal practice reinforced the notion that a husband was his wife's overseer, and therefore held him accountable if she stepped out of line. When a woman committed a minor crime, the courts usually ordered her husband to pay for it, in a fit punishment for his indiscretion in allowing her to break the law. If a wife did not attend Sabbath services, for instance, her husband was held responsible for failing to bring her to the meetinghouse. If she sold alcoholic beverages without a license, he paid £5 to £10 for tolerating her behavior. With the husband lay the decision of whether to pay a fine assessed against his wife, or to subject her to a whipping instead. In one case the Plymouth General Court actually allowed the husband to punish his wife "att home" after she had beaten and reviled him (1655). The wife had almost no opportunity to discharge a fine by enlisting the aid of her family or a charitable neighbor. Of course, no woman received a trial by a jury of her female peers.

Although, as in English local and customary law, a wife could sue in court for wrongs done her (provided she had her husband's permission), usually her husband brought suit in her behalf. Whenever a wife hurled scurrilous remarks at a neighbor, both she and her husband automatically became parties to the suit. If the husband neglected to take civil action when his spouse was the injured party, her parents might bring suit on her behalf (in a slander suit, for example). Without husbandly or parental allowance, a wife could not seek damages for any injury, irrespective of its severity. Her honor belonged to her father or her husband, who protected it at his discretion. Under no circumstances could a woman sue her own husband for tortious acts (e.g., slander, assault) against her, although she could give evidence against him in a criminal case.

A wife's activity in "outward matters" was always contingent upon her husband's approval. She could contract for rents and wages, sell goods, and collect debts, but only if her husband had authorized her activity. Since Puritans believed the "weaker sex" had little ability in such dangerous matters, they wished to keep women within the home's protective confines. To prevent weak Puritan wives from unwarily responding to some sinner's solicitations, the Massachusetts General Court in 1674 barred any wife, in the absence of her husband, from entertaining any traveler without the allowance of the town selectmen, under the penalty of a £5 fine or ten lashes. She also had to busy herself with household tasks, in order to avoid prosecution on a charge of idleness. . . .

In Puritan ideology and practice, a wife could have few outright belongings. Neither her premarital possessions (with the exception of some personality) nor her subsequent acquisitions, nor the use of her free time, nor even her criminal sentences were hers alone. Her status seemed quite like that of a servant, even though the latter's period of servitude was limited by contract.

. . . Still, despite such disadvantages, women were not completely under male control in Puritan New England. Single, widowed, or divorced women of means could open mercantile shops, own land, and maintain inns. These women could sue on their own behalf in court. Three extant petitions indicate that women attempted to have some political impact by petitioning the Massachusetts General Court or a Connecticut magistrate. In half of all cases where a deceased husband left a widow, she received the right to act as the executor of his estate—a position of some administrative importance.

Even though the husband could restrict his wife's activity in many ways, she retained certain legitimate claims on him (based not on her "rights" but on her supposed weakness, or need for protection). In Plymouth and New Haven, a wife's permission was necessary before a husband could sell their house or any of their land. In contrast, however, Connecticut and much of Massachusetts conceded that property transferral was the husband's prerogative. In his will the Connecticut husband usually referred to the couple's acquisitions as "my" lot or "my" dwelling house. When a husband made his will, he could not leave his wife penniless. In Massachusetts before 1649, Connecticut before 1696, Plymouth, and New Haven, the law reserved to the widow a dower right of one-third of the lands, houses, tenements, rents, and hereditaments her husband possessed. This widow's third was free from all debts, rents, judgments, and executions against her deceased mate's estate. Plymouth and New Hampshire also allowed the widow either all or part of her husband's personal estate, while in Massachusetts after 1649 the magistrates determined what portion she would receive. . . .

A husband could not beat his wife in order to reduce her to abject submission. As early as 1599 the English Puritan Henry Smith asserted, "If hee cannot reform his wife without beating, he is worthy to be beaten for choosing no better." Almost a century later Cotton Mather agreed that for "a man to Beat his Wife was as bad as any Sacriledge. And such a Rascal were better buried alive, than show his Head among his Neighbours any more." The Bay Colony's initial law code, the "Body of Liberties," in 1641 freed the wife from "bodily correction or stripes by her husband, unlesse it be [given] in his owne defence upon her assalt." Nine years later the Massachusetts General Court specified a fine of up to £10 or a whipping as punishment for any man who struck his wife, or for any woman who hit her husband. None of the other four Puritan colonies enacted such a law, although they did lightly penalize husbands who abused their wives too readily. . . .

We cannot know the extent to which wives possessed real "private power" or derived satisfaction from the marital power arrangement. . . . As a general rule, the specter of male overlordship is so apparent in institutional, intellectual, economic, and family life throughout the seventeenth century that it leaves little room to doubt women's difficulty in achieving, much less exerting, a sense of their own assertive independence. All of woman's protections and the few privileges she enjoyed as a widow did not, in the final analysis, facilitate her development beyond the limitations imposed by her sex-role conditioning.

 ## FOR FURTHER STUDY

1. Summarize the seventeenth-century Calvinist view of the nature of children and proper child rearing. How do these views differ from the predominant attitudes of American society today, especially with regard to parental concerns about child development?

2. Describe the particular characteristics of the ideal wife in the seventeenth century as set forth in the sermons and laws. Develop an argument as to why such historical sources are or are not reliable guides to the actual relations of men and women in day-to-day family life.

3. What were the limitations on women's equality in economic life, church, government, and social activities?

4. The changing status of women in our time has occurred as a result of a complex variety of factors. Which of the following do you believe to be most important: the decline of traditional religious views, industrialization, creation of new social agencies to handle needs that formerly rested on the family, modern household technology, or women's suffrage?

FOR FURTHER READING

The two classic studies of family in New England are Edmund S. Morgan, *The Puritan Family*, rev. ed. (1966), and John Demos, *A Little Commonwealth: Family Life in Plymouth Colony* (1970). Philip Greven placed the family in its social context in *Four Generations: Population, Land, and Family in Colonial Andover, Massachusetts* (1970). Greven's later work, *The Protestant Temperament: Patterns of Child-rearing, Religious Experience, and the Self in Early America* (1977), shows how parents treated their children depending on their religious views. One important aspect of early New England society is discussed in Roger Thompson's *Sex in Middlesex: Popular Mores in a Massachusetts County, 1649–1699* (1986).

In the past three decades the study of women in colonial America has expanded dramatically. Laurel T. Ulrich, *Good Wives: Image and Reality in the Lives of Women in Northern New England, 1650–1750* (1980), is an interesting study of three ideal types of women. Ulrich continued her work with a fascinating study of one midwife in *A Midwife's Tale: The Life of Martha Ballard, Based on Her Diary, 1785–1812* (1990). The importance of midwives is discussed in Jane Donegan, *Women and Men Midwives: Medicine, Morality, and Misogyny in Early America* (1978).

Roger Thompson's *Women in Stuart England and America: A Comparative Study* (1974) shows that colonial patterns differed from English conditions, and Marylynn Salmon discusses the advantages of colonial women in *Women and the Law of Property in Early America* (1986).

We know less about the southern family in the colonial period. For a general history of the elite see Daniel Blake Smith, *Inside the Great House: Planter Life in Eighteenth Century Chesapeake Society* (1980). For a study of a southern community see Darrett Rutman and Anita Rutman, *A Place in Time: Middlesex County, Virginia, 1650–1750* (1984).

Not surprisingly, the Revolutionary period has received a good deal of attention. Two excellent studies of the period are Mary B. Norton, *Liberty's Daughters: The Revolutionary Experience of American Women, 1750–1800* (1980), and Linda Kerber, *Women of the Republic: Intellect and Ideology in Revolutionary America* (1980). For a collection of essays on various aspects of women at the time see Ronald Hoffman and Peter Albert, eds., *Women in the Age of the American Revolution* (1989). For an interesting look at one family see Richard Buel and Joy Buel, *The Way of Duty: A Woman and Her Family in Revolutionary America* (1984).

CHAPTER 4

By permission of the Folger Shakespeare Library

This engraving is from Matthew Hopkins's The Discoveries of Witches. *Hopkins was a professional witch-hunter who sent more than 300 people to the gallows in England.*

THE WITCHCRAFT SCARE

JOHN C. MILLER

*O*ne of the striking phenomena of recent years has been widespread interest in witchcraft, the occult, and occurrences beyond normal, sensory perception. Hollywood producers have beaten paths to the bank with the box office receipts from dozens of films on vampires, ghosts, and satanic possession. Thousands of readers have believed quite as firmly in the reality of supernatural forces haunting the house in Amityville as in the astrological forces in their own lives. One major university has a center for the study of extrasensory perception, and many others offer courses on magic, the devil, and the mystery of evil. If, after all, one believes in God and the forces of good, is it illogical to believe in Satan and the forces of evil?

One might, however, ask why the belief or at least the interest in magic and witchcraft seems to be especially strong in certain periods and to be the subject of skepticism or ridicule at other times. Some scholars have suggested that a society is more likely to turn to supernatural explanations in an especially troubled time and to charge unpopular or deviant members of the society with witchcraft when it needs scapegoats. For many years, this was the fundamental historical explanation of the Salem witchcraft episode that staggered Massachusetts in 1692. In recent years, historians have reexamined Salem witchcraft and have developed a number of other explanations. One writer has suggested that witchcraft was actually practiced in Salem, and that the victims who felt tormented by witches were suffering from hysteria, rather than deliberately misleading the community by false accusations. Another writer has suggested that a peculiar fungus in the rye grain, which some of the citizens in one part of the town used in baking, caused them to experience hallucinations similar to an LSD trip. Others have argued that the witchcraft affair was a religious and socioeconomic conflict between two different parts of the town.

The Salem episode has fascinated novelists and dramatists from Nathaniel Hawthorne to Arthur Miller. Like historians, they have seen very different things in the outbreak of witchcraft. Miller, writing his play *The Crucible* in the 1950s when Senator Joseph McCarthy was conducting a Communist witch hunt, saw parallels between the events of his own day and those of 1692. In the conclusion of a French film about the affair, a crowd storms the gallows areas in a scene reminiscent of events at the Bastille in 1789. Other writers have viewed Salem witchcraft as little more than the logical outcome of a narrow-minded religious outlook, whether in Catholic Europe where thousands perished or in Puritan Massachusetts where twenty men and women died.

The following selection by John C. Miller represents an eclectic, and perhaps a somewhat old-fashioned, point of view in the sea of new interpretations. Miller suggests that socioeconomic conflict, the troubles the colony had recently experienced, and a lack of enlightenment all contributed to the hysteria. He is a bit harsher on the Mathers than some recent writers, but on the whole his essay gives a concise and balanced summary of the whole episode. His comments on witchcraft in Europe suggest that some restraint is in order before we label seventeenth-century Salem as an especially dark and bloody chapter of our past.

During the period 1670–1690, among the evidences of backsliding noted by the New England clergy was a growing disposition on the part of the people to take witchcraft lightly. The Reverend Increase Mather observed with alarm that even some church members were beginning to say that people possessed by demons mentioned in the Bible were simply epileptics or lunatics. Taking what he regarded as an extraordinarily tolerant attitude toward these skeptics, Mather said that he would not "suspect all those as guilty of witchcraft, nor yet of heresie, who call the received opinion about witches into question." But neither did he admit that they had a right to advance such heretical opinions.

To alert these skeptical citizens to their danger, Mather included in his *Essay for the Recording of Illustrious Providences* (1684) a long discourse upon witchcraft. The elder Mather prided himself upon taking a dispassionate, scientific view of witchcraft and of other natural phenomena. He admitted, for example, that many accounts of possession by demons were mere fables, and he denied that it was possible for spirits to generate bodies or beget children or that witches could transform themselves or others into another species of creature such as a horse, wolf, cat and mouse. "It is beyond the power of all the devils in hell to cause such a transformation," he asserted. "They can no more do it than they can be the authors of a true miracle." Moreover, he disapproved of many of the "superstitious and magical ways" of detecting witches—"whereby," he said, "much innocent blood hath been shed." Only by exhaustive cross-examination and scientific appraisal of the evidence, said Mather, could the guilt of witches be proved beyond all doubt.

The "Invisible World" was also very real to Cotton Mather—more real, it sometimes seemed, than the little world of churchgoers over which he presided. He invested commonplace events with supernatural, portentous meaning. For example, when he suffered from toothaches "he considered whether or not he had sinned with his teeth. How? By sinful and excessive eating; and by evil speeches." Thus even a simple case of caries was endowed with theological significance.

In sounding the alarm against witchcraft, Cotton Mather acted under what he supposed was a special mandate from Heaven. In 1686, God appeared to him in a vision and told him that his mission was to fight witchcraft. Accordingly, after protracted fasting and prayer, Mather took up his pen—specially consecrated, he believed, by the Almighty to expose "the whole Plot of the Devil against New England in every branch of it"—to write against witches. The result of his revelation was the publication in 1689 of *Memorable Providences Relating to Witchcraft and Other Possessions.*

Both Increase and Cotton Mather were impressed by the inability of science to explain the phenomena they studied. To them, science left the ultimate mysteries untouched. Lacking a scientific explanation for many baffling events in human affairs, they were driven to the conviction that demons were constantly at work among men and that the Devil, for God's own purposes, had been permitted to act through the medium of witches—always, however, within definite restrictions laid down by the Almighty.

The Mathers tried to buttress the case for witchcraft with pseudoscientific "evidence" derived from their observation of people under seizure. What they recorded were cases of abnormal psychology, but they presented them as irrefutable "proof" of the existence of demons. By their books and sermons they succeeded in inculcating the idea that witchcraft was increasing by leaps and bounds in New England and that God's own plantation might fall before the wiles of stratagems of Satan. "'Tis *our* Worldliness, *our* Formality, *our* Sensuality, and *our* Iniquity," said Cotton Mather, that had provided Satan with an entering wedge into God's own plantation.

In the jeremiads, the clergy portrayed the crusade against sin and worldliness within their favorite frame of reference—the struggle between God and the Devil. All history, as they saw it, consisted of variations on this cosmic theme. Although the last thing the clergy wanted to see was a plague of witches descend upon New England—by their reckoning no greater disaster could befall a country—yet by their books and sermons they inadvertently prepared the way for Salem witchcraft. People who fear witches and who talk about them constantly are likely to be assailed by them sooner or later.

Salem witchcraft was merely an episode—hardly more than a footnote—in the history of an ancient superstition, for evidences of belief in the malefic power of certain individuals has been found in the most primitive societies. But it was not until the late Middle Ages, when witchcraft was identified with heresy and therefore came within the purview of the Holy Inquisition, that a witchcraft mania really began. The Reformation intensified the zeal of the witch-hunters. While Roman Catholics and Protestants disagreed upon many points, they agreed in holding witches in abhorrence and in putting an end to their existence as summarily as possible. In the sixteenth and seventeenth centuries—the age of the Renaissance and the New Science—over 100,000 people charged with having leagued themselves with the Devil were put to death.

Witchcraft was believed to originate in a bargain between a man or woman and the Devil by which he or she agreed to sell his or her soul to Satan. This transaction, of course, was a great victory for Satan: he had turned against God one of God's own creatures and ensured the damnation of a human being. It was supposed that the Devil insisted that his victims sign a book agreeing to renounce the Christian religion, pay homage to the Prince of Darkness, and join in celebrating the Black Mass. Not until it was all down in writing did Satan feel that the bargain was truly consummated. Everything was neat, orderly and legal, the Devil having served his apprenticeship in Heaven where making contractual obligations—or so the Puritans believed—was the approved procedure. After the signatories signed the "contract," they were permitted to have carnal intercourse with devils, join in the witches' sabbat, revel with the Devil himself, and enjoy the power to subvert God's order on earth. Women who put their signatures to this horrid affidavit became witches; men who joined the Devil's legion were known as wizards.

Witchcraft was therefore treated as a legal crime—an offense against God— which merited the death penalty. Every country in Christendom enacted laws against witchcraft and hauled suspects into civil or ecclesiastical courts to stand trial. . . . The act need not be malefic or destructive: if it were proved to have been performed through "conference with the Devil," it became a capital offense.

Witches were held responsible for storms, droughts, the death of cattle, sexual impotence, epidemics—and all the evils, in short, that the Devil chose to inflict upon mankind. But, clearly, malice, spite, and unreasoning fear played an important part in determining who were the Devil's agents. Unpopular eccentrics and "far-out" people were always candidates for suspicion. Old women were particularly vulnerable: being accused of practicing witchcraft was one of the hazards of being old, ugly, and unwanted.

The Devil was no respecter of persons. James I, who regarded himself as God's own anointed, also believed that he was the victim of a witches' conspiracy. He was firmly persuaded that they had almost succeeded in drowning him by brewing up a storm while he was at sea. As was his custom when he was particularly exercised by anything from tobacco to theology, James wrote a book against it. *Demonologie,* a dialogue upon witchcraft, appeared in 1597.

As a rule, outbreaks of witch-hunting occurred especially in countries distinguished by clerical power, popular ignorance, the breakdown of government, and the use of torture. Germany, where all these conditions existed, was the site of the most sanguinary efforts to suppress witchcraft. At the height of the mania, no one was safe from the suspicion of being in league with the Devil. The estates of wealthy people made them particularly vulnerable, and a lenient judge was liable to incur the charge of being an accomplice of the accused. Even the expression of disbelief in witchcraft was apt to be construed as circumstantial evidence of guilt. As James I said in *Demonologie*, the author of a book casting doubt on the existence of witches betrayed himself to be "one of that profession."

In whipping the people into a frenzy of fear of witches, intellectuals played a vital role. The belief in witches and the determination to stamp them out was in part a by-product of the scholarship of the age: the more learned and religious the individual, the more zealous and remorseless was his attitude toward witches likely to be. In the great witch-hunts of the sixteenth and seventeenth centuries, the prime instigators were men of learning who instilled their fear of the prevalence of witchcraft into the minds of the common people.

Vast ingenuity was expended by scholars upon the problem of determining how a witch could be detected. While such signs as moles or warts, an insensitive spot which did not bleed when pricked, a capacity to float in water, and an inability to recite the Lord's Prayer constituted only circumstantial evidence, they gave witch-hunters a clear lead in tracking down the Devil's agents.

On the European continent, torture was used to extract confessions from those accused of witchcraft. The rack, red-hot pincers, thumbscrews, scourges, leg-crushing machines—the familiar appurtenances of torture—together with a novel instrument, the witches' chair (a seat under which a fire was kindled), were the ultimate resorts of judges and inquisitors confronted with people who obstinately protested their innocence. By express orders of the Pope, issued in 1468, there were no limits upon the amount or degree of torture that could be applied. But the inquisitors were not content with a confession procured under torture: the accused had to be tortured until he or she confessed voluntarily.

In England, although those accused of witchcraft were not tortured, they were subjected to intensive interrogation, sometimes lasting for weeks or even months without benefit of habeas corpus. Those convicted in England were hung rather than burned at the stake—a distinction which, however finely drawn, was important to those who suffered the penalty. Moreover, James I and other authorities on witchcraft enjoined judges and juries strictly to observe the rules of evidence. Even so, about 30,000 people were convicted of witchcraft in the British Isles.

During the centuries when witchcraft was in flower, the professional witch-hunter and informer flourished in Europe. Judges welcomed the services of these itinerants who ferreted witches out of their deepest lairs. One of the most successful witch-hunters on record was Matthew Hopkins, who, during the 1640s, was personally responsible for the death of over 200 English witches. But Hopkins enjoyed an unfair advantage over his rival witchhunters: he was said to have secured the Devil's own list of witches commissioned to operate in England.

As a result of the bloodletting of the period 1600–1660, when the mania reached its height, a reaction against witch-hunting set in. On the Continent, torture had been carried to such lengths that the confessions which had brought thousands of men and women to their deaths seemed worthless. During this period, thousands of people saw one or more of their relatives suffer death under one of the most terrible charges that could be made against a human being—selling his or her soul to the Devil and contracting to aid the Devil against God.

Being the most militant of English Protestants in the struggle against the Roman Catholic Counter-Reformation, the Puritans were peculiarly prone to believe in witchcraft and the ubiquitous power of Satan. Literal believers in the Bible, they took the injunction "Thou shalt not suffer a witch to live" to mean that they were under a religious duty to exterminate witches. As Calvin said, "The Bible teaches that there are witches and that they must be slain. . . . God expressly commands that all witches and enchantresses shall be put to death; and this law of God is an universal law." In Geneva, Calvin suited the action to the word. Before he came to that city, little had been heard of witchcraft, but in the 60 years that followed, over 150 witches were burned. It is not therefore merely coincidental that the most destructive witch craze in English history occurred during the period of Puritan ascendancy.

By the last quarter of the seventeenth century, the maniacal phase of witchcraft was clearly on the wane. Fewer and fewer of the "Accursed tribe" were sent to the stake or the gallows. As Montaigne said, "After all, it is rating one's conjectures at a very high price to roast a man alive on the strength of them." In the late seventeenth century, Holland abolished witchcraft trials altogether. In Geneva, the final witch burning occurred in 1652, and the last mass holocaust took place in Germany in 1679 when the Archbishop of Salzburg consigned 97 witches to the flames. In 1672, Louis XIV of France ordered that all prisoners recently condemned to death for witchcraft by the Parlement of Rouen should have their sentences commuted to banishment.

But the belief in witchcraft could not yet be dismissed as a mere peasant superstition. What had really changed was not the belief in witchcraft but confidence in the effectiveness of the methods used to detect it. While few doubted that many of those who perished at the stake were genuine witches who richly deserved their fate, it began to dawn upon the sober-minded, particularly after the mania had spent itself, that many had fallen victim to biased evidence, rumor, hearsay, envy, and malice.

What is truly remarkable about Salem witchcraft is that it occurred so late in the history of an ancient superstition. Far from playing a leading part in the mania, the Puritans did not enter upon the stage until the final act. That, in part, is why they became so conspicuous: most of the other actors, having already played out their terrible parts, had left the scene.

In Puritan New England, the outbreak of witchcraft occurred in a social context characterized by instability, clerical power, tension, and fear. The decade 1680–1690 had seen the loss of the Massachusetts charter, the establishment of the despotic Dominion of New England, the revolution of 1688–1689, and an abortive expedition against Quebec. The "great fear" abroad in the land was the fear of crypto-Roman Catholics in high places who were believed to be plotting the overthrow of the Protestant religion. It is significant that the witch-hunt was preceded by a hunt for Roman Catholics. To a marked degree, Salem witchcraft was a continuation of the anti-Roman Catholic agitation. Puritans would have been hard pressed to tell which of the two—Roman Catholics or witches—was more malefic. In any event, at the very time that the threat of Roman Catholicism was approaching its climax, the country was infested with swarms of witches.

In Salem Village—now Danvers, Massachusetts—the anxiety and apprehension felt by all the people of the colony were aggravated by dissension between the pastor and his congregation (just before the outbreak of witchcraft, two ministers had successively taken their parishioners to court to collect their salaries, and both had won judgments); by educational backwardness; by petty squabbles among the villagers over land, animals, and crops; and by the presence of Tituba, a slave woman of mixed black and Indian ancestry whose mind was filled with the primitive lore of her people. Tituba was a slave in the household of the Reverend Samuel Parris, who had come to Salem Village in 1689 and who, like his predecessors, had quarreled with his parishioners over his salary. The Reverend Mr. Parris's family consisted of his wife, his daughter, and his niece. Tituba regaled these highly impressionable adolescents with tales of the occult: Salem witchcraft was the product of the conjunction of the pagan superstition of Africa with the Christian superstition of Western Europe.

The Reverend Mr. Parris was a firm believer in witchcraft, and his young daughter and niece had probably learned at his knee all about black magic and the Invisible World. It certainly seemed very real to them; at the age of twelve they were experts on demonology. Growing up in the narrow world of a country parsonage in an intellectual atmosphere that came straight from the Middle Ages, with overtones of voodooism, and living in a backward, tension-ridden, credulous, quarrelsome community, these girls were in a strategic position to start a witch-hunt. Not surprisingly, they were seized with fits and convulsions, pinched and choked by unseen hands, pricked with invisible pins and needles, and visited by specters who tried to entice them into selling their souls to the Devil.

In 1691, few people doubted that the long-heralded assault on New England by the Invisible World had begun. . . . The most dismal predictions of the jeremiads seemed mild in comparison with the horrible reality. Cotton Mather declared that "prodigious Witch-Meetings" were being held all over the country at which "a fearful knot of proud, ignorant, envious and malicious creatures" volunteered for the Devil's service. But Mather was not surprised by this untoward event: "Where," he asked rhetorically, "will the Devil show most Malice, but where he is hated, and hateth most?" Mather rejoiced at the prospect of a decisive encounter with his old enemy who, he was persuaded, had sent the witches "as a particular Defiance unto *my* poor *Endeavours* to bring the Souls of men unto Heaven." . . . But at least the enemy was identifiable. From reports he had heard, Mather pieced together a picture of the Devil; "a short and a Black Man . . . no taller than an ordinary Walking-Staff," wearing "a High-Crowned Hat, with strait Hair, and had one Cloven-Foot."

In May 1692, at the advice of the clergy, Governor Phips appointed a special court of oyer and terminer in which those accused of witchcraft could be tried.

This court was composed of merchants, public officials, and doctors. Most of the members were college graduates. There was not a lawyer among them, but this circumstance was not accounted important: college graduates were deemed sufficiently learned in the law to qualify as judges, and in any event, the problem of ridding the country of witches was thought to transcend the skill and erudition of any mere lawyer. Only the most pious, God-fearing men could cope with this assault.

In Salem witch trials, despite the strong sense of urgency and crisis, no precipitate action was taken. There was a three-month delay between the first accusations and the first trial. During this interval, the bodies of the accused were carefully examined for such telltale evidence of guilt as insensitive spots, supernumerary teats, warts, or moles. The physical checkup over, the accused were asked to recite the Lord's Prayer. If they stammered, stuttered, or missed a word, it was all up with them, for it was a well-known fact that the Devil could not get through the Lord's Prayer without stumbling. Inability to shed tears was likewise accounted an incriminating sign, since the Devil was incapable of feeling remorse for any of his misdeeds. Those who failed to clear themselves of suspicion were indicted and bound over for trial. Without legal counsel, they conducted their own defense— no easy task in view of the fact that the judges and jurors, who were all church members, were strongly inclined to regard them as guilty until proved innocent.

Among the accused was a backwoods preacher, the Reverend George Burroughs. Burroughs was alleged to be the "black man" who sounded the trumpet that summoned the witches to their rendezvous, and he was also accused of having successively murdered his two wives by incantation. The first witness against Burroughs was his own granddaughter! During his examination and trial, spectators cried out that he was biting them—and, wonderful to relate, marks made by his teeth were found on their arms even though he had not stirred from the dock. Evidence was presented that Burroughs had performed feats of running and weightlifting clearly beyond the powers of mortal man unless aided by the Devil.

For Cotton Mather, the clinching evidence against Burroughs was supplied by five witches from Andover who testified that he was their ringleader and that in that capacity he had presided over their infernal get-togethers. Thenceforth, Mather took a personal interest in seeing Burroughs brought to the gallows, unusual as it was for one clergyman to display such zeal for putting a halter around the neck of another wearer of the cloth.

Burroughs was duly convicted and sentenced to death. But as he was being prepared for the noose, he made a moving plea of innocence and recited the Lord's Prayer without making a single mistake, and the spectators were almost persuaded that Burroughs was not a wizard after all. At this point, Cotton Mather, mounted on a horse, proved that he was as effective an orator in the saddle as in the pulpit. He turned the crowd against Burroughs by pointing out that the condemned man was not really an ordained minister and that all the persons hitherto executed had died by a righteous sentence. Burroughs was strung up, and Cotton Mather rode home satisfied with having done a good day's work for the Lord.

A convicted witch could save herself by confessing; indeed, the object of the prosecution was not to kill witches but to extract confessions from them. Some of the accused took this easy way out, implicating others in their accounts of their dealings with the Devil. These confessions brought an everwidening circle of people under suspicion. As in England, torture was not used to procure confessions, but wizard or witch could go to the gallows protesting his or her innocence or stubbornly refusing to speak.

Confession, while it usually saved a person's life, led to forfeiture of property. Giles Cory, who would have been found guilty in an ordinary court of law of nothing more serious than eccentricity, refused to answer his accusers when charged with entering into a compact with the Devil—in the hope thereby of preserving his estate for his heirs. By English law (not repealed until 1772), *peine forte et dure* —pressing by weights until a confession, or death, was forthcoming—was prescribed for those who stood mute. The weights were placed upon Cory, and after several days of torture, he died without opening his lips. At that incredible cost, he made it possible for his heirs to inherit his property.

Salem witchcraft was not merely the result of a welling up of ignorance, superstition, and fear from the depths of society. The clergy, the magistrates (including Governor Phips himself), and educated people in general shared the conviction of the most ignorant and deluded people that they were witnessing an outbreak of "horrible Enchantments and Possessions" instigated by Satan.

As long as the accusations were made against friendless old women and people of low degree, the clergy hallooed on the witch-hunters and sanctified the good work by quoting the injunction of the Book of Exodus: "Thou shalt not suffer a witch to live." In the trials, every kind of "evidence"—hearsay, gossip, old wives' tales—was admitted provided that it indicated the guilt of the accused. Some of this so-called evidence went back many years and obviously originated in personal spite. None of the defendants had counsel to raise objections to the admission of this kind of evidence or, indeed, to question the legality of the procedure or the jurisdiction of the court. As a result, there was no one to contest the legality of "spectral evidence."

In their confessions, or in giving evidence on the witness stand, many people alleged that they had been approached by people who passed as respectable members of society yet who now appeared in the guise of the Devil's agents urging their victims to sign the Devil's book and to commit other enormities. This was "spectral evidence," and if it were indiscriminately admitted to be valid, there was obviously no limit to the number of people who might be accused of witchcraft. The weighty question raised by spectral evidence was whether or not the Devil could assume the shape of an innocent person or whether or not every person who appeared to the afflicted actually served the Devil's purposes.

When their opinion was asked, the Mathers recommended that the judges observe "a very critical and exquisite caution" lest they be taken in by the Devil's legerdemain. Caution was especially important, they warned, in cases of "persons formerly of an unblemished reputation." "It was better for a guilty witch to live," said

Increase Mather, "than for an innocent person to die." Cotton Mather admitted that the Devil might, by God's permission, appear in the shape of an innocent person, but he thought that this permission was rarely given.

In essence, Cotton Mather took the position that spectral evidence merely offered grounds for suspicion and, at most, a presumption of guilt but that corroborative evidence was required before a verdict could be rendered. The immediate danger, as he saw it, was that evil spirits would confuse the judges by appearing in the guise of innocent people, thereby permitting bona fide witches to escape scot-free. Chief Justice Stoughton, much as he revered the Mathers, did not accept their views on the admissibility of spectral evidence. In his opinion, the fact that the Devil assumed the form of a respectable individual, even though he was a pillar of the community, must mean that that individual had sold his soul, for, he declared, the Devil could not impersonate an innocent man or woman. He therefore instructed the jury that "as the Devil had appeared in the form of many of the accused, according to the eyewitnesses there, the defendants must be guilty." This instruction resulted in the conviction of several of the accused.

Nor did the people follow the Mathers in drawing these fine distinctions regarding the admissibility of spectral evidence. To them, any person who took the form of a specter must be an agent of Satan. In consequence, Massachusetts was gripped by a reign of terror. Ties of friendship and of blood ceased to matter. It was a case of every man for himself and the Devil take the hindmost. Wives testified against their husbands; children charged their parents with practicing witchcraft; a wife and daughter gave evidence against their husband and father in order to save themselves; and a seven-year-old girl helped send her mother to the gallows. When two young men would not confess, they were tied together by the neck until they accused their own mother. The roll of specters began to read like a *Who's Who* of New England. Captain John Alden, the eldest son of John and Priscilla Alden, was accused of being a wizard on the strength of spectral evidence, but the resourceful captain escaped from jail. Dudley Bradstreet, the son of a former governor, fled the colony before he could be brought to trial. The wife of the Reverend John Hale, secretary of the colony of Connecticut, was denounced as a witch, and one woman who was hung at Salem was a church member. Cotton Mather himself was not safe: in October 1693, a young woman swore that Mather's image threatened and molested her. "I cried unto the Lord," Mather wrote in his Diary, "for the Deliverance of my *Name*, from the Malice of Hell." Thus the work of casting out devils seemed likely to lead to the depopulation of Massachusetts. Who would be alive to hang the last witch?

Clearly, events were escaping from the control of the clergy and magistrates. Witch-hunting had reached the height of mass hysteria: the people clamored for more victims, and no one was safe from their zeal and fear.

To add to the danger, although Salem Village continued to be "the Chief Seat of these Diabolical Vexations," witches began to expand their operations until all Massachusetts reeled under "the horrible Assaults made by the Invisible World." The citizens of Gloucester, expecting to be attacked by an army of witches, took refuge in a stockade. In Andover, where an epidemic was blamed on witches, more than 50 people were accused of having had dealings with the Devil. One of the magistrates who dared to defy public opinion by refusing to institute proceedings against the suspects was himself accused of sorcery. But the mania was short-lived: one of the accused instituted action for defamation of character against his accusers. "This wonderfully quenched zeal," it was observed, "the accusers saw *his* spectre no more."

By September 22, 1692, the Salem judges had tried 27 suspects, one-third of them church members; all had denied being witches. All 27 had been sentenced to death, and of this number 19 had been hanged and 1 pressed to death. A man accused of bewitching a dog barely escaped with his life, but the dog, presumably possessed by devils, was killed. None of the 50 who confessed that they were witches had been executed; 100 persons accused of being witches were in jail awaiting trial; and an additional 200 had been accused but had not yet been imprisoned. Two judges had resigned from the court of oyer and terminer to protest the course the proceedings had taken. Among the suspects were Lady Phips, the wife of the Governor of the province, and the Reverend Samuel Willard of Boston, the president of Harvard College. Willard was under suspicion because he had questioned some of the evidence presented at the trials.

On September 22, 1692, at the advice of the clergy, now thoroughly alarmed by the use to which spectral evidence was being put, Governor Phips suspended the proceedings of the court of oyer and terminer. In December the accused were brought before the Superior Court for trial. Spectral evidence was sparingly admitted, with the result that of the 52 persons brought to trial, 49 were acquitted. Only three were found guilty and condemned, but Phips first reprieved them and then granted a general pardon to all under suspicion. In 1957, the Massachusetts Legislature adopted a resolution absolving all the Salem witches of wrongdoing.

Chief Justice Stoughton bitterly lamented the decision to call a halt to the trials: "We were in a way to have cleared the land of them," he said. "Who it is that obstructs the cause of justice I know not; the Lord be merciful to this country!"

It is ironical that Cotton Mather, who wished to be known above all as a man of God and a do-gooder, should be remembered chiefly for his part in the Salem witch trials and therefore held to be typical of all that was most narrow, bigoted, and repellent in Puritanism—the very epitome of the blackfrocked, bluenosed zealot. He was by no means the most remorseless and bloodthirsty of the witch-hunters; indeed, his position on spectral evidence marks him as a moderate and a stickler for the observance of legal formalities. The people, and some of the clergy, demanded more witch trials and more executions, but Mather tried to calm the storm he had helped create. In his poem dealing with Salem witchcraft, Longfellow makes Mather say:

> Be careful. Carry the knife with such exactness, That on one side no innocent blood be shed By too excessive zeal, and, on the other, No shelter given to any work of darkness.

Yet Cotton Mather did not question the justice of the verdicts handed down at Salem, nor did he doubt that all who had been executed were guilty. Those who asked God to attest to their innocence were guilty, in his opinion, of "monstrous impudence." Lest it be supposed that innocent people had been condemned on the basis of inadequate evidence, Mather wrote a book entitled *Wonders of the Invisible World* (1692). Yet Mather was not as sure as he professed to be that justice had been done: in 1696, he recorded in his diary his fear that God was angry with him for "not appearing with Vigor enough to stop the proceedings of the Judges, when the Inextricable Storm from the Invisible World assaulted the Country."

The period of the Salem witchcraft marked the last occasion on which witches and wizards were executed in the colonies, but the belief in witchcraft did not end, nor did the indictment and trial of suspects stop. In Virginia in 1705, a woman was accused of practicing witchcraft. The court ordered that her body be examined for witch marks and that she be subjected to the trial by water. The incriminating marks were found, and she floated while bound—strong evidence of guilt. Nevertheless, she was not tried as a witch, nor, for that matter, was she given an opportunity to clear her reputation.

Nevertheless, even during the trials at Salem, doubts had been expressed by one of the judges and by some clergymen regarding the guilt of some of the condemned. Not, however, that they doubted the existence of the Devil and of witchcraft: their reservations extended only to the kinds of evidence held admissible by the court. Yet the feeling gained ground that New England lay under the heavy indictment of having shed innocent blood. For this reason, some of the jurors and witnesses publicly repented their part in the proceedings at Salem. In 1697, Judge Samuel Sewall stood before his congregation and acknowledged his "blame and shame . . . asking pardon of men, and especially desiring prayers that God, who has unlimited authority, would pardon that sin and all others his sins." On the other hand, Chief Justice Stoughton went to his death insisting that he had been in the right.

It was the educated laity rather than the clergy who took the lead in discrediting witchcraft. In 1700, Robert Calef, a Boston merchant, published *More Wonders of the Invisible World,* an attack upon Cotton Mather and witchcraft. Calef believed that a great deal of innocent blood had been shed at Salem, and he held Cotton Mather primarily responsible for it. The girls who had started the frenzy he called "a parcel of possessed, distracted, or lying Wenches, accusing their Innocent Neighbours." Cotton Mather denounced Calef's book as "a firebrand thrown by a madman," and Increase Mather, as president of Harvard College, ordered the book publicly burned in the College Yard.

The eighteenth-century Enlightenment completed the rout of witchcraft. Science shifted the attention of educated men from the supernatural to the natural world, thereby resuming a process which, having begun with the Renaissance, had been interrupted by the Reformation. Satan suffered the second of the two great disasters that befell him in his long and checkered career: having been cast out of Heaven, his power to control human events now began to be questioned. In short, Satan lost the thing upon which his power over men had always depended—his credibility. Witchcraft, after a long and bloody history, was relegated to the igno-minious status of a mere superstition, and the thousands of men and women who had perished in the flames or on the scaffold were seen to have been the victims of a great delusion.

 ## FOR FURTHER STUDY

1. In the opening section of this essay, Miller suggests certain broad social condi-tions that are likely to exist in a country in which witch hunting arises. What are these conditions, and to what extent did they exist in Massachusetts in the 1690s?

2. Miller says witch hunting died out not because people no longer believed in witchcraft, but because they doubted the tests used to discover witches. What were these tests? Which were used in the Salem trials and which were not?

3. The special court appointed in Salem had no lawyers on it, though witchcraft was a crime. On the other hand, clergymen played a prominent role in advising the court and in other respects. Can you think of ways in which the participation of trained attorneys might have affected the evidence, the examination of wit-nesses, or the outcome? Or would the lawyers in that society have acted much the way laymen did?

4. Some modern cults embody elements of satanic worship and witchcraft; others do not, but some of the psychological motivation of the cultists may be similar to that exhibited at Salem. Considering such phenomena as the Branch Davidians, how do you explain the psychology of the modern cult member?

FOR FURTHER READING

The Salem witch trials have interested scholars and students alike for many years. Students interested in learning more about the Salem witch trials can read a number of excellent studies. Chadwick Hansen argues in *Witchcraft at Salem* (1969) that the girls suf-fered from hysterical fits that were interpreted at the time as proving witches were in Salem. Paul Boyer and Stephen Nissenbaum found community conflict at the root of the witchcraft scare in *Salem Possessed: The Social Origins of Witchcraft* (1974). John Demos placed the presence of witches at Salem in its New England context in *Entertaining Satan: Witchcraft and the Culture of Early New England* (1982). Carol Karlsen takes a very different approach when she examines why women were the brunt of the attacks because of their position in society, in *The Devil in the Shape of a Woman: Witchcraft in Early New England* (1987).

For a broader context Richard Godbeer's *The Devil's Dominion: Magic and Religion in Early New England* (1992) and David D. Hall's, *Worlds of Wonder, Days of Judgement: Popular Religious Belief in Early New England* (1989) are welcome additions.

PART II

*R*EVOLUTIONARY *P*EOPLES

*T*he seventy-five years that followed 1750 were a remarkable period in American history. The transformation from a loose conglomeration of English colonies to an independent nation was possible because many residents had a growing feeling that the societies of these colonies had become a separate people—no longer just immigrants but Americans. Finally having broken from the mother country, Americans thought of themselves at the beginning of a new era—one where they could not only design a new republic but form a new, more open society. Together, the American people established a truly national government and enunciated ideas that became deeply embedded in the national consciousness as they struggled to find a place in their new social context.

Besides the enduring monuments of American political and constitutional practice that were created, these years also witnessed remarkable achievements in other areas. The break from England did much to accelerate the development of American democratic thought and egalitarian social attitudes. It also encouraged a spirit of nationalism in literature, architecture, and other aspects of American cultural life. Basic directions in foreign policy were enunciated, and there were significant developments in American economic life. Social life also changed considerably as some groups, including Native Americans, were treated with less respect. At the same time, social and economic opportunity for many others expanded as the country moved west to the Mississippi and beyond.

Of course, our ancestors could not foresee the extraordinary economic and political success of the United States. The first essay in this section treats the views that colonists had of Native women in the Southeast. Their relative power and importance in their own culture was in stark contrast to the relative powerlessness of many colonial women. The second reading exposes an important segment of the life cycle of most ordinary Americans of the Revolutionary period, the servant. These poor immigrants faced innumerable challenges as they journeyed to America in the years just before independence. The third reading gives us a graphic picture of the deprivation and suffering experienced by Washington's army. The next selection focuses on the Loyalists, Americans who questioned the wisdom of declaring independence from Britain and suffered the consequences. The final essay examines an important ritual that emerged in the frontier culture of the southern United States. It suggests simple contests may tell a great deal about the fabric of a segment of American society.

CHAPTER 5

The Trapper's Bride, Alfred Jacob Miller, Joslyn Art Museum, Omaha, NE

This later painting depicts traders and their Indian wives.

NATIVE AMERICAN WOMEN—FROM PRINCESSES TO WENCHES

EIRLYS M. BARKER

*A*s we discovered in Reading 3, most colonial women were subordinate to their husbands legally and socially throughout the colonial period. Their independent action took place within the context of other women, exchanging goods, such as clothing and fabric and services such as caring for the sick and helping with births. But not all women in North America were treated as part of their husband's household once they were married. Some European women experienced a brief time early in the colonial period when they were more powerful than their European counterparts. This was especially true of women who lived in colonies when the number of women was small. Moreover, in many colonies some women who outlived their mates experienced brief control of a considerable estate and a few refused to remarry to prolong their control. In fact, one historian has argued that these independent women threatened male-dominated society and that, at least at Salem, some accused of being witches were targets partly because they were independent.

Native American women led much more independent lives. Although tribal differences prevent sweeping generalization, many Native women held positions of power and responsibility unknown in European society. For instance, many performed most of the agricultural work in their societies unlike European women. Moreover, in some tribes goods were inherited through the female rather than the male line. In almost every way these Native American women challenged the common practices of Europeans. In one particular region, the southeastern area, ancient tribal traditions placed women in important positions. Native women had more freedom over their choice of a mate and often in the education of children than virtually any European colonist or their progeny. One wonders if some colonial wives envied the independence of Native women or if they were too focused on the differences between the two worlds to notice.

This essay concentrates on how colonists' views of Native women in the Southeast changed over the colonial period. As you read, look for when and why they went from valued trade partners to wenches in European eyes and how Native societies changed to marginalize their former importance.

By the eighteenth century white males in North America and Europe knew exactly what the status of women was, both in the home and in the world at large. Women of European origin were born into a patriarchal society. They were reared from birth to be obedient to their fathers and submissive helpmeets for their future husbands. This was not so in Native American society. Many of the earliest colonists commented on what seemed to them a woman's high degree of freedom over personal matters, including choosing a husband and even, in some instances, making the decision to end a marital relationship. In the southeastern tribes women exercised control over their personal lives and bodies to a greater extent than did contemporary women of European descent. The structure of native society led to the high degree of respect and freedom that Native American women experienced.

The area of the American Southeast is vast, extending from the Atlantic coast west to the Mississippi River and from the Ohio River to the Gulf of Mexico. It is an area containing many Indian tribes—more properly referred to as nations—descended from peoples of varied traditions and language groups. These included the Creeks, the Cherokees, the Catawbas, the Yamasees, the Choctaws, the Chickasaws, and the Natchez. By the beginning of the seventeenth century these nations had experienced times of great upheaval and change. Throughout the Americas the native inhabitants suffered a dramatic decline in population as a result of European contact. The consequences of this disaster forced remnants of nations that were once numerous to seek an existence as part of new units or federations that European invaders called, for example, Creek and Catawba, by the eighteenth century. Yet, the old clan and family structures remained in place. Most of the southeastern tribes maintained a traditional matrilinear system of inheritance. They were not matriarchies, and the division of labor was gender-based; however, outsiders often believed Indian women had more personal free-

From Eirlys M. Barker, "Princesses, Wives, and Wenches: White Perceptions of Southeastern Indian Women to 1770" in Larry D. Eldridge (ed). *Women and Freedom in Early America.* Copyright © 1997. Reprinted by permission of Greenwood Publishing Group, Inc., Westport, CT.

dom and wielded more influence over the lives of their families and villages than their European peers did.

Among the cultural baggage that the first European settlers brought with them to North America was the concept of patriarchy, one at odds with Indian ideas of an orderly society. The trend toward a nuclear family composed of husband, wife, young children, and perhaps some servants was accelerating, along with an increase in the wish for privacy. This removed influential female role models, such as grandmothers or mothers-in-law, from the household. In contrast, Native American society in the Southeast at the time of contact was based on extended families living together in dwellings headed by an older female member.

The southeastern Indians lived in settled villages where a woman's clan built huts closely clustered together. The women were in charge of providing food for their extended households, from planting seeds of corn, squash, and beans, to gathering berries and nuts. They also dried meat into jerky and turned deerskins and furs into clothing. Older women taught the children to fish and to trap small animals such as rabbits and directed all such daily operations for their extended family network. The men were often absent for long periods of time pursuing their primary economic function, hunting to provide their kin with meat. With the presence of Europeans came a new market demand for furs and skins—deerskins became the major commodity and currency of the area. It became necessary to go farther afield to acquire enough skins to exchange for essential trade goods. This also led to an increase in warfare when Indians roamed into and poached on their neighboring tribes' traditional hunting grounds. The longer men are absent, the more women exercise effective control in any situation.

Outsiders sometimes depicted Indian women as embodying the savagery of the "New World," as being too free, too close to nature, and too apt to follow their own whims and desires. The earliest European accounts often commented on the minimal clothing worn by the natives, and this was reflected in the popular engravings made of Caribbean and Florida Indians and those based on John White's 1580s watercolors of the Carolina tribes closest to the Roanoke colony. They especially dwelt on the scant nature of women's dress—a contrast to the European woman, who, humble or noble, hid most of her body under layers of heavy fabrics. Indian women had to be licentious if they did not follow the basic Christian rules of dress and decorum. According to Amerigo Vespucci at the turn of the sixteenth century, the "women go about naked and are very libidinous. . . . Urged by excessive lust, they defiled and prostituted themselves." The perceived "lusty" and libertine nature of Indian women was often used as an excuse for rape by the "Christian" soldiers.

Some of the early English writers, such as Robert Beverley in Virginia, tried to dispel the idea that the women were "Incontinent" in their affections. They were merely "inspir'd with Mirth and good Humor," he said. Beverley was also unusual in promoting the idea of intermarriage with the Indians as a means of gaining and keeping their friendship. By the mid-eighteenth century most writers stressed the "mild, amiable, soft disposition" of the women and the modesty of their clothing.

During the seventeenth century an increasing number of Europeans moved into the interior of the continent. Some were soldiers, others prospective planters. Among the first wave who both observed and cohabited with Indian women for lengthy periods of time were those men who risked much in the lucrative but dangerous Indian trade. The Europeans active in the southeastern deerskin trade—confusingly called Indian traders—realized that to be accepted, the best tactic was to marry Indian women and thus have a fixed place in native society. Many of these traders and the agents and soldiers who policed Indian-White relations and trade have given us the most accurate glimpses of the status and expectations of Indian women in their own societies, although the observers imposed their Eurocentric interpretations on much of what they saw and did not dwell on the minute details of everyday life.

The master traders always boasted that their consorts were important leaders in their tribes who had freely entered into lucrative relations with the newcomers. James Adair declared that he wrote his *History of the American Indians* while enjoying the company of a "Chikkasah female, as great a princess as ever lived among the ancient Peruvians, or Mexicans." In the early years of the trade, even humble traders wielded great power in their native villages. They came with desirable goods that enhanced the quality of life, so that tribal leaders encouraged marriage with their relatives. The marriage of the Powhatan "princess" Pocahontas to the Virginia planter John Rolfe was merely one of the first and most famous of such alliances. One of the most prominent Native Americans in the early eighteenth century was the Creek leader Coosaponakeesa, the much-married Mary Musgrove Mathews Bosomworth. She was Georgia's counterpart to Pocahontas in the "Indian Princess" mystique. Despite her prominence, her lineage is obscure and much debated. She was probably closely related through her mother to the Lower Creek "Emperor" Brims and thus exerted influence over his successor, Chigelly. Mary's father was a British trader named Griffin, but it was her Creek connections that gave her authority among the Indians. By her later years she acquired the status of "Beloved Woman," which enabled her to be an effective interpreter of culture and language to the early Georgia colonists.

The Indian women who were leaders in their tribes insisted on receiving privileges such as their share of the presents the colonial governments issued. When influential Indians visited Charles Town, the center of government in South Carolina, for formal conferences with the governors, their wives and other female relatives expected to receive gifts and often took part in the ceremonies. Senawki, wife of Tomochichi, the Yamacraw chief, who welcomed the first Georgia colonists, not only visited London and attended the royal court with her husband in 1734, but two years later took the initiative in talks with John Wesley, one-time Indian agent for Georgia.

Most Indian women had a freer choice of marriage partners than most European women of this time, for "a marriage is settled by the agreement of both people," meaning those directly involved, not their parents. It was the woman's freely-given acceptance that sealed an alliance. There were no essential religious ceremonies or vows, merely an acknowledgment by the couple and their town that an acceptable union was taking place. Surveyor Bernard Romans in the 1760s was struck with the simplicity of Creek marriage. It was "without much ceremony, seldom any more than to make some presents to the parents, and to have a feast. A 1683 description of Lousiana's Indians mentioned that "very frequently they marry without any noise," although there would often be "feasts with pomp and rejoicing." Sexual relationships with unattached Indian women were acceptable to most of the southern tribes as long as the women consented, for young girls "are the mistresses of their own bodies," as related to a young Frenchman in the 1720s.

Because these clans were exogamous—it was necessary to marry outside the clans—Indian women were free to marry any foreigners. Although a new husband moved to live with his wife's clan, he did not become a member of that clan. Even so, the union gave him a whole new group of relatives. Initially, it was probably not much more exotic for a Creek woman to cohabit with a white Carolinian than for her to marry a Chickasaw or a Cherokee. According to South Carolina's first Indian agent, Thomas Nairne, the southeastern Indians believed that marriage within one's own clan or one's father's clan was "an unclean thing . . . the greatest crime in the world," comparable to the "worst sort of Incest" in European society. This, combined with the catastrophic decline in population, underscored the need for new sources of strangers to serve as marriage partners. As early as 1708 Nairne had commented on the "break up of their Townships . . . since the use of firearms the fatell small pox and other European distempers. There were possibly ten times as many women as men among the tribes by the mid-eighteenth century, indicating another practical reason for accepting European husbands, whatever qualities particular individuals might bring with them.

The wives of Indian traders chose a lavish and exotic way of life, compared with most of their peers. The traders came with goods that made lives easier for all, but especially for the women. Many Europeans had commented that the women were "the Chief, if not the only manufacturers." Some, such as William Byrd II of Virginia, thought they did "the little Work" that was done in native society, regarding them as mere beasts of burden. As the women's primary economic function was to be in charge of the food, the trader wives gained status by being the first to acquire metal hoes, axes, and knives, sturdy but lightweight copper kettles to cook the food instead of having to fashion earthenware pots that were brittle and heavy, and metal fishhooks and needles. Such items freed them from much of the drudgery of their lives, as did manufactured cloth. Byrd seemed particularly incensed that the men were "at most employ'd only in the Gentlemanly Diversions of Hunting and Fishing." He neither understood the men's role in helping to clear the land for farming nor realized their role in providing meat for their communities. John Brickell, who in the 1730s updated Lawson's work on North Carolina, noted that the "Industry of Wives" produced crops without the use of plows, with the "Men's minds being wholly taken up in Hunting." Adair, however, that long-term resident in Indian country, knew that Creek men would not go to war until they had "helped the women to plant a sufficient plenty of provisions." Still, the women's crucial economic role gave them influence over clan or village decisions. If they were against a war sortie, they could refuse to parch corn, dry jerky, or make the moccasins that were needed for such a venture.

The social ties that came through marrying Indian women were crucially important to the newcomers. All the nations were subdivided into totemic clans, which were the most meaningful social element for the southeastern Indians. Within Cherokee society, "to be without a clan . . . was to be without any rights, even the right to live." It was fellow clansmen who avenged a murder. Nairne described the Chickasaws' clan system and its usefulness to Europeans: "It is the easyest thing in the world, for an English Traveller to procure kindred among the Indians, It's but taking a mistress of such a name, and he has at once relations in each Village, from Charles Town to the Missisipi." This was illustrated many times; for example, in 1758 some Indians refused to surrender to South Carolina authorities Samuel Jarron, who had "escaped the Watch" at Keowee, a Cherokee town. The Indians' leader explained, "We look upon him . . . as one of our Brothers. He has lived among us several Years; he has had some of our Women, and has got Children by them. He is our Relation, and shan't be taken up." Adair also recounted some instances of wives saving their husbands' lives with the help of their families. One trader was told by his wife to run away when foreign Indians raided his storehouse, and he had a few qualms about leaving her because "her family was her protection."

One of the most confusing differences observed by Europeans was the Indian system of matrilineal inheritance. Inheritance in societies derived from Germanic antecedents came through the male line; primogeniture had become the norm in Western Europe, with the oldest son claiming his father's property, or, if there were no direct male heirs, the closest legitimate male relative. For Native Americans, because inheritance was matrilineal, a foreign father did not disrupt their society. Nairne understood that "the Chiefs sisters son alwaies succeeds and never his own." A Frenchman in Louisiana in 1703 had asked why this was so and was told that "nobility can come only from the woman, because the woman is more certain than the man about whom the children belong to." Alien blood would not therefore confuse issues of clan, town, or tribal status, so it was not essential to police the personal aspect of women's lives.

The Indian conception of property was also very different, again benefitting females. Under English law a married woman owned nothing "without the license of her husband. For all her personal chattels are absolutely his own." Indians in North America owned what they used every day or what they fashioned themselves. Males, therefore, traditionally owned the weapons they used, as well as their clothes and what Europeans regarded as personal possessions. Dwellings and agricultural tools, used mostly by women, were owned by the women. Thus, the gender-based division of labor gave women ownership over the products from, and the implements used in, those tasks. Because husbands lived in their wives' dwellings, it was easy for a man to remove his possessions from his wife's home if the relationship ended, for everything he owned was portable.

Divorce for most of the southeastern tribes was "at the choice of either of the parties," another shock to Europeans, whose women enjoyed no such inherent right. Among the Creeks the man could remarry immediately, but the wife had to wait until the end of the annual harvest festival, the Busk, with its purification ceremonies and significance. Divorce for the Native Americans, as compared with Europeans, was a matter with more religious than civic significance. Widows, as in Europe, were free to marry after a set period of mourning and purification. This varied from "the tedious space of four years" among the Creeks, to three years among the Chickasaws.

Europeans were startled by the disposition of children from dissolved Indian unions, for the children stayed with the mother. John Lawson, raised in the English patriarchal system at the turn of the eighteenth century, commented with surprise on both the ease of divorce and how "all the Children go along with the Mother." William Bartram, the Quaker naturalist, mentioned that Indians seldom separated once they had children, but if they did, "the mother takes the children under her own protection." This was in stark contrast to English law; before 1837 mothers in Britain had no guardianship rights at all.

As many European fathers would find to their astonishment, they had little control over the education of any *metis* (half-Indian) children—even teaching sons the arts of war and hunting was a role for the mother's brother or another close male relative within the mother's clan. Indian wives and their clan kin expected to remain in charge of the children's education and upbringing. It came as a shock to traders even toward the end of the eighteenth century when their wives refused to let them send their sons to be educated in Charleston or Savannah. A Creek trader, James Germany, had married a Creek women [sic] "of a very amiable and worthy character and disposition industrious, prudent, and affectionate." But even this paragon to British eyes refused to be parted from her children. It was her and her clan's responsibility to educate them. Access to European ideas and customs was not regarded as necessary for the children—in fact, devoted mothers who had experienced Eurocentric attitudes within their households might believe that the children would lose, not gain, freedom if exposed to Charleston or Savannah and racial prejudice. A woman's traditional role gave her the freedom to dictate how her offspring should be educated.

Although divorce was a common occurrence, and marriages often resembled serial monogamy, adultery was a heinous crime in all the southeastern nations except, perhaps, the Cherokees. In some nations it was punished merely by cutting off a woman's hair. In others the penalty could be death. The Chickasaws were "very jealous of their wives," and adultery was punished by "the loss of the tip of the [male adulterer's] nose, which they sometimes cut, but more generally bite off." The Creeks tended to punish both parties equally by "severe Flagellations"; a trader named Cockran lost his ears in the 1730s for this crime. The Cherokees did not punish either, believing that adultery was a meaningless concept, given either marriage partner's freedom to separate at any time.

Polygyny was allowable, but most Indian marriages were probably monogamous. A few chiefs might have more than one wife, but this became less prevalent with time among the nations closest to the Europeans. An observer of the Yuchis of Georgia in the 1730s, a tribe close to the settlers, remarked that "among them no one knows of polygamy. Sororal polygyny, however, remained common: a man might take a wife's unmarried or widowed sister as a second wife, but only with the first wife's consent. William Bartram believed that the Creeks continued to allow polygyny, but even if "every man" could take as many wives as he pleased, "the first is queen, and the others her handmaids and associates." . . .

Indian women . . . had the freedom to decide the fate of captives taken in war. Women who had lost family members and partners could opt to save captives from death, to take the place of the deceased family members through adoption. Adoption was never automatic, although it became more common with the de-population of the eighteenth century and especially after the devastating 1738 smallpox epidemic. If the captive's fate was death, women made it a long, drawnout affair, inflicting pains and mutilations as the fiery torture was prolonged over several days. It was they who scalped and dismembered the victim, all the while singing "with religious joy." In 1750 South Carolina's governor James Glen referred to the Indians as "Cruel & Barbarous. . . . Even their Women, those who in all other Nations are called the Soft & tender Sex, with them are Nursed up in Blood, & taught to delight in Murders & Torturing."

While it is tempting to view trader wives as persons used by the foreign partici-pants in the trade, this is a gross oversimplification. In the Southeast no Indian woman could be forced into a marriage against her will, and divorce, or at least an informal end to a relationship, was possible on either side without stigma or pun-ishment. The Indian wives of the European traders freely chose that role. It gave them an enviable position, providing the latest technical innovations and luxuries and allowing them an easier and more comfortable existence than that enjoyed by many of their peers. This element of choice sometimes led wives to act against their own village, as during the outbreak of the Cherokee War in 1760, when some women tried to sneak provisions to the soldiers in Fort Loudoun during the Cherokee siege of that fort. To the chroniclers, their actions stemmed from their appreciation of the ribbons and other baubles the soldiers had given them; a bet-ter explanation, however, is their loyalty to men considered their lawful partners in their society. Interestingly, the Cherokees did not regard these actions as trea-sonable but understood that the women were acting on behalf of family members.

Whatever the official colonial policy on interracial unions, such liaisons were inevitable, given the lack of European women on the frontier. As early as 1737 an agent for Georgia commented on the huge number of mixed offspring: "All the Indian Traders had wives among the Indians . . . and he believed there were 400 children So begotten." Unfortunately, we know few of these wives or offspring by name except for those who were extraordinary in one way or another, perhaps through their talents as interpreters or for being victimized in some way.

Indian women had the liberty of choosing a nontraditional career without be-ing ridiculed. A feature of native society that struck nearly all European visitors was their hospitality toward strangers. One common custom in the South was to offer a stranger an unmarried woman as a "She-Bed Fellow" for the length of his stay. John Lawson and William Byrd II early in the eighteenth century had noted this custom among the North Carolina nations. There, the trading girls sported a haircut that set them apart from the other, unavailable women. These women were not outcasts in their villages. They could retire from their profession to marry a man of their choice without loss of status and with a dowry. Nor was this a localized custom. Emperor Brims unsuccessfully offered "Bedfellows" to a royal official and his clerical cotraveler on their official 1729–31 visit to Creek country. In Louisiana Father Hennepin remarked that a trading girl's parents found nothing to "censure in this; very far from that, they are glad to have their daughters earn some clothes or some furs."

Other women volunteered to take part in the hunting expeditions that became an integral part of village life with the increasing demand for deerskins and other furs. This was an extension of their food-preparation function; women ground the corn for making bread. In March 1740 the Indians attacking St. Augustine with General George Oglethorpe of Georgia had to be given "rice . . . having no women with them to parch or pound their Corn." Women also began the work of preparing the skins for market, including scraping away excess meat and fur, soaking them in a solution of brains, and finally smoking the prepared skins. If this process was not begun in a timely fashion, these valuable trading items would rot. On those occasions when a hunting band was attacked by enemy Indians, the women would "sing their enlivening war song," which spurred their men to "become as fierce as lions."

Among the Chickasaws, women on expeditions did more than such household-type chores—they had the choice to go into combat if they wished. Nairne had himself seen Chickasaw women in battle, and Bernard Romans mentioned that he had "several times seen armed women . . . going in pursuit of the invading enemy." Accounts of women warriors typically mix admiration for their bravery with condemnation of the "savagery," or primitiveness, of their actions. When summoned to fight against Hernando de Soto's men in a life-and-death situation, the women of Mauvila "attacked with utter rage and determination, thus showing well that the desperation and courage of women in whatever they are determined to do is greater and more unbridled than that of men." Women were usually treated more leniently when captured by native enemies, but some were killed and scalped.

By the 1760s Indians were regarded increasingly as a barrier to expansion, rather than as allies against the French and Spanish or as partners in a lucrative trade. Paralleling this, Indian women in the official records are increasingly disparaged as "wenches," a word reserved in the British Empire for women of the lowest ranks, including prostitutes, servants, and slaves. The women described in early accounts were usually called "wives." By 1751 even women who warned their trader husbands that their lives were in danger from a roving band of enemy Indians are officially dismissed as the "Wenches kept by the white Men." There were no more accounts of Indian "princesses" and their virtues. Mary Bosomworth's Indian ancestry was used increasingly to explain her deficiencies—her frequent temper tantrums, her obesity, and her occasional drunkenness were examples of an excess of freedom and her failure to control herself—even by her last, very proper English husband.

Freedom clearly meant very different things to Native American women and to European males. To most native women it meant a continuation of their traditional way of life, one that had struck so many early European observers as a free, if not libertine, existence. Whatever the actual status of the women within their own societies, most colonial venturers initially responded to the women in two ways. One response came from the men who for trade or diplomatic reasons were destined to live in the interior of the colony for at least part of the year. They might rationalize that an Indian consort's status in her society would help him, but, as many noted, such aid was forthcoming only if the woman saw advantages to her and her possible offspring from such an alliance. Initially, such unions were of great benefit to both parties, and the Europeans wrote in terms of Indian princesses and leaders of their nations helping them in their common economic venture. The other response was the one that, with time, became the norm. As the European peddlers of trade goods within the nations became increasingly smaller cogs in the great machine of the British Empire, they minimized the part played by their Native American wives. By the 1770s women were regarded merely as personal sexual perks and sources of comfort in an increasingly hostile environment.

By the 1770s the decline in status of the Indian trade and Indian diplomacy was reflected in a return to the original perception of Indian women as wantons. Trade and a desire for peace were no longer the prime motivations for Indian policy. As settlers advanced into "Indian country," the old way of life changed for those at the edges. Over time, changes affected all Indian women, even in remote villages, as their society was modified by the goods, diseases, and doctrines imported by traders and missionaries. The new doctrines of Christianity and patriarchy stripped women of their age-old control over their homes and the means of production, as well as their freedom to enter into and leave marital arrangements.

 ## FOR FURTHER STUDY

1. How did the first Europeans view Native women? How did this view of their dress and "disposition" change by the mid-eighteenth century? Why did it change?

2. What did the marriage between Pocahontas and John Rolfe symbolize?

3. How did Native marriage customs and attitudes toward sexual relations give Native women power and flexibility? How did clan practice of exogamy play an important role? What was the role of disease in expanding women's importance?

4. Define the matrilineal inheritance system and conception of property. How were they different from European beliefs?

5. Who controlled the children in a divorce, and what culture was responsible for the education of children of Native mothers? Why?

6. Identify some of the occupations Indian women chose, and compare their options to those of colonial women.

7. Why were Native women viewed as wenches by 1760?

FOR FURTHER READING

For a unique look at the original sources see James Axtell (Ed.), *The Indian Peoples of Eastern America: A Documentary History of the Sexes* (1981). For the South see J. Leitch Wright, *The Only Land They Knew: The Tragic Story of the American Indians in the Old South* (1981). For one newly-created tribe see James H. Merrell, *The Indians' New World: Catawbas and Their Neighbors from European Contact through the Era of Removal* (1989). For a discussion of slavery and one prominent nation in the region see Theda Perdue, *Slavery and the Evolution of Cherokee Society, 1540–1866* (1979). On the fur trade see Calvin Martin, *Keepers of the Game: Indian-Animal Relationships and the Fur Trade* (1978). For Indians in another area see Daniel Usner, Jr., *Indians, Settlers, and Slaves in a Frontier Exchange Economy: The Lower Mississippi Valley Before 1783* (1992). On the role of southern women in one area see Kathleen M. Brown, *Good Wives, Nasty Wenches, and Anxious Patriarchs: Gender, Race, and Power in Colonial Virginia* (1996). For Native women in the North see Carol Devens, *Countering Colonization: Native American Women and Great Lakes Missions, 1630–1900* (1992). For an overview of Native peoples see James Axtell, *The European and the Indian* (1981), and for all colonial people see Gary B. Nash, *Red, White, and Black: The Peoples of Early North America,* 3rd ed. (1992).

CHAPTER 6

ELIZABETH CANNING,

Drawn from the Life, as she stood at the Bar to receive her Sentence, in the Session's-House, in the *Old-Bailey*.

THIS unfortunate young Girl was indicted for wilful and corrupt Perjury, for swearing against *Mary Squires*, commonly called the OLD GYPSEY, and her Evidence strongly corroborated by VIRTUE HALL, a Woman that liv'd with Mrs. *Susannah Wells*, that kept a House of Ill Fame at *Enfield Wash*, where *Canning* swore she was rob'd by the GYPSEY, and confin'd twenty-eight Days. Upon the Evidence of these two Parties, the GYPSEY was capitally convicted, and receiv'd Sentence of Death accordingly, and Mrs. *Wells* burned in the Hand, with six Months Imprisonment, for concealing the Felon after the Felony was committed. Soon after that abandon'd Wretch *Virtue Hall* recanted, and said that what she had sworn against the GYPSEY, was intirely false, and that she never saw ELIZABETH CANNING till the Time she was brought down by some Gentlemen to survey Mrs. *Wells*'s House. This Recantation occasion'd a strict Enquiry into this mysterious Affair.

Upon that Enquiry a Bill was preferr'd, and found to be a true Bill by the Grand Jury on that Head. Some of her Friends entered into a Recognizance of a large Sum, that she should appear, and take her Tryal at the Sessions following: Accordingly on the first Day of *May* 1754 she surrender'd, and appear'd at the Bar, and was arraign'd; and immediately the Court proceeded to Tryal, which lasted that Day, and the six successive Days following. When the Tryal was over, the Recorder of *London* repeated the Evidence on both Sides, and gave his Charge to the Jury in a very impartial Manner. The Jury then withdrew, and was out of Court about two Hours; and on their Return, the Jury was about two o'Clock, on the 8th, in the Morning, gave in their Verdict that she was GUILTY, but not of wilful and corrupt Perjury. Upon that Verdict the Court was pleas'd to inform them, that they must consider what they were about, that they must either acquit her, or bring her in guilty of the Indictment; they went out a second Time, and soon return'd, that she was guilty.

Immediately she was by the Court committed to *Newgate*, where she continu'd till the 30th, then she was brought to the Bar again, to receive Sentence in Pursuance of an Adjournment from the 13th. When the Court proceeded to pass Sentence, which was one Month's Imprisonment, and Transportation for seven Years, to one of his Majesty's Colonies in *America*; after hearing every Thing that could be urged in behalf of the Prisoner, to obtain an Arrest of Judgment, or a new Tryal, by several learned Council. There were present in Court at that Time the Right Hon. *Thomas Rawlinson*, Esq; Lord-Mayor of the City of *London*, who always presides in this Court during the Mayoralty; the Right Hon. Lord Chief Justice *Willes*, Mr. Justice *Dennison*, Mr. Justice *Gloss*, the Baron *Legg* and *Smyth*, and the Recorder, with ten worthy Aldermen, two of which joined with the Judges, *viz.* Mr. Alderman *Janssen*, and Mr. Alderman *Dickinson*, who all concurred in the above Sentence. The Court was mov'd by Sir *John Barnard*, senior Alderman, and Member in Parliament for the City of *London*, that the Sentence might be mitigated to six Months Imprisonment, which met the Approbation of seven more of the *Aldermen* then present, *viz.* Mr. Alderman *Bean*, Sir *Robert Ladbroke*, Mr. Alderman *Alsop*, Mr. Alderman *Cockayne*, Mr. Alderman *Bethell*, Mr. Alderman *Alexander*, and Sir *Richard Glynn*; but was over-rul'd.

In pursuance to her Sentence, she was remanded back to *Newgate*. During her Confinement, the great Resort of Persons occasion'd an Order from the Sheriffs, that Nobody be admitted without their special Licence; after which she had the Misfortune to fall dangerously ill, as was suppos'd, by a Gaol Distemper; whereupon both Physicians and Surgeons were by special Order sent to visit her, and by such proper Attendance she was recovered of her Indisposition; and on *July* 17th, at the Opening of the Sessions, a Motion was made, that the Court should contract with another Person, instead of Mr. *Stewart* (who is the present Contracter) for the Transportation of Felons, to carry her to *America*; and Mr. *Stewart* in Court consented to wave his Contract; the Motion was granted, on a Division, (as we are inform'd) the present Contracter being to transport her to some of his Majesty's Colonies in *America*, according to her Sentence, under the usual Penalty. There were present in Favour of this Application, the five following worthy Aldermen, Sir *Robert Ladbroke*, Sir *Joseph Hankey*, Mr. Alderman *Alsop*, Mr. Alderman *Alexander*, and Mr. Alderman *Scott*; Lord Chief Baron *Parker* and the Recorder against it. And *July* 20th, about Four in the Afternoon, she was by a Warrant directed to the Keeper of *Newgate*, ordering him immediately to deliver her to her Friends, to transport herself according to the Contract, made and provided in that Case; and on *Wednesday*, *August* the 7th, she embark'd on board the *Myrtilla*, Capt. *Budden*, bound for *Philadelphia*.

Elizabeth Canning, convicted of perjury in England, was sentenced to indentured servitude in the American colonies and left for Pennsylvania in 1754.

Indentured Servants—Voyage, Sale, Service

Sharon V. Salinger

*M*any poor European teenagers had to go to work early in their lives
to reduce the burden on their families. Most found jobs as indentured servants in the households of more prosperous residents. They agreed to work
for three to seven years in exchange for food, clothing, a place to sleep, and,
maybe, a chance to learn a skill. Some adults who had few resources also
worked as servants. Often, in difficult economic times, few servant positions
were available and many looking for work were easily convinced to come to
America.

They agreed to leave behind a network of family and friends and become
servants. They promised four or more years of work to pay for their transatlantic passage because after their terms were over and their debt repaid,
they hoped to become independent, perhaps even buy their own land—two
prospects which were nearly impossible in Europe.

Their future looked better in North America than in Europe but they did
not know how perilous the passage and servitude might be. Conditions on
ships were difficult and in some cases life-threatening. If they survived, servants were often exploited by con-artists and sold in slave market conditions.
Once they were indentured to a particular master they were at the mercy of
their owner who could treat them as family members (although that might
not be good) or could mistreat them in many ways. Ironically, the very fact
that labor was more valuable in the colonies than in Europe meant that masters used devious means to force the most work out of their servants and
keep them as long as possible. Also, during their terms servants were their
master's property and could be rented out or sold for the remainder of their
terms at any point.

Some colonial parents, especially those from New England, indentured their children to others in the community so they would be raised with proper discipline and not be indulged by their parents.

The passage below, taken from Salinger's *"To serve well and faithfully,"* describes servants who came to Pennsylvania from Europe, especially Germany, in the eighteenth century. Their experiences, even accounting for the language difficulties they encountered, were shared by many migrants to the colonies. As you read this passage, remember that many who left Europe were looking for any job and would have taken one under similar or less promising conditions in Europe if they had not decided to travel to America.

In 1773 John Harrower chronicled his personal trail from freedom to servitude. Harrower had been a businessman in Scotland but was forced to leave his home and family on December 6, 1773, to find relief from his economic woes. With only eight and a half pennies and stockings to sell, Harrower hoped to find work in eastern England. He certainly would go no farther from home than Holland. But at each stop along the way, no work was available and no ships had space to take him to Holland. He survived by selling his small inventory of stockings, borrowing a bit of money, and living very frugally.

Harrower's travels took him first from Scotland to Newcastle. There he contemplated "engaging the M[aste]r of the *Elizabeth* Brigatine bound for North Carolina" but, he wrote, "the thoughts of being so far from my family prevented me." After a futile search for work in Newcastle and no better luck at the next stop, Portsmouth, Harrower trudged eighty miles to London. Six weeks after leaving home, Harrower lamented that he "was like a blind man without a guide, not knowing where to go, being friendless and having no more money but fifteen shillings and eight pence farthing a small sum to enter London with."

Harrower survived in London on almost no money. One day, while waiting for a possible business contact, he drank three pennies worth of punch and "was obliged to make it serve me Dinner." The only advertisement for employment Harrower felt qualified to answer was one for "bookkeepers and Clerks to go to a Gentlemen [in] Philadelphia." He arrived at the stated address but was too late; the position had been filled. With each further effort Harrower faced the same dilemma: "more than a dozen Letters before me, so that I hade little expectation."

On January 24, Harrower wrote "a petition in generall to any Merch[an]t or Tradesman setting forth my present situation . . . offering to serve any for the bare support of life fore some time." But, he recorded, it was "all to no effect, for all places here at present are entirely carried by friends and Interest." Harrower dis-

From *"To Serve Well and Faithfully": Labor and Indentured Servants in Pennsylvania, 1682–1800,* by Sharon V. Salinger. Copyright © 1987 by Sharon V. Salinger. Reprinted by permission of the author.

covered that the city of London was full of "many Hundreds . . . starving for want of employment, and many good people are begging." By this time, he was reduced to his last shilling and was "obliged to engage to go to Virginia [as an indentured servant], for four years as a schoolmaster for Bedd, Board, washing and five pounds during the whole time."

Although indentured servants rarely kept journals, we know that Harrower's tale was not unique. Hundreds of others shared similar economic circumstances. Their quest for work forced them to leave their families and homes and trek to the nearest seaports. After a futile search for employment and with resources depleted, these individuals often solved their most immediate problem, their economic condition, by signing on as indentured servants. Perhaps by the end of their servitude, the future would look more promising. It is unlikely that prospective servants had any realistic notion of what awaited them in the New World. But thousands came. And most signed their contracts voluntarily, spurred by economic difficulties, concerns of conscience, and "the ever present factor of encouragement from America."

Emigrating servants did leave a record of what pushed them to leave their homelands and drew them to Pennsylvania. Servants embarking from London, Stomaway, and Leith longed to "procur[e] better livelihoods"; for "want of employ," to better "pursue ones calling"; or to "better [their] fortune." Servants on board the ship *Clementine* bound for Philadelphia echoed the hope of "procuring a better livelihood." Passengers and servants on board the *Friendship* thought that Philadelphia would provide a better opportunity to "better their fortunes and pursue their callings than remaining in England." Emigrants from Scotland expressed similar sentiments:

> The chief cause which gave rise to and propagated the prevailing spirit of Emigration among the Highlanders is that for some years the Land holders and Chieftans of the North have rais'd their rents so high and screwed their Tenants to such a degree that they have been greatly oppressed and reduced to Indigent and necessitous Circumstances . . . It is easily conceived that a people oppressed in this manner would grasp at any opportunity to be relieved from a condition but one degree removed from slavery.

Customs officers in Wigtown summarized the cases of David Ireland, a smith, and George McCandlish, a farmer. Ireland and McCandlish opted to go to Pennsylvania because "they were informed and understood they could live much better and with more ease in the country to which they are going than they could in their country."

German servants held similar hope for life in the New World. Jacob and Hannah Duncan agreed to indenture themselves because in exchange for four years of labor they would receive a "stake in the future." For these individuals, emigration meant removing the shackles that burdened them in the Old World and replacing them with opportunity in the New.

Tantalizing reports in letters from Pennsylvania drew them to the Quaker colony. . . .

Because letters from the New to the Old World were not always favorable, a group of forgers and shady ship captains emerged to censor the correspondence. Some shipmasters involved in the Irish trade felt little aversion "to censoring the letters they carried and making sure that unfavorable reports of America never reached their destinations." German immigration agents also altered unfavorable accounts. These letters were either discarded or "falsely copied." A few individuals in Germany earned their living forging these letters. Advertisers wanted the view of America to be synonymous with the "promised land."

Less commonly, potential servants were encouraged to emigrate by colonial recruiting agents. Merchant Thomas Clifford sent a former servant back to his native Bristol to "acquaint poor laboring people with the genuine State of this Country, and the Opportunities industrious honest poor men have of supporting themselves by their labor here." Visitors in Europe or departing emigrants occasionally advertised for servants. John Harrower may have answered an advertisement like the one Charles Taylor placed in a London newspaper in 1773—Wanted "blacksmiths, taylors, coopers, shoemakers and a genteel lad that understands waiting on a single person" to accompany him to Pennsylvania.

Shipping advertisements bolstered the image of the colonies as a source of relief for those in the throes of economic misery. Potential servants from Ireland were tempted by the pictures of a pleasant passage and the promise of a successful future. A 1766 advertisement for the departure of the *Hopewell* declared,

> It would swell the advertisement to too great a length to enumerate all the blessings those people enjoy who have already removed from this country . . . suffice to say, that from tenants they . . . become landlords, from working for others they now work for themselves, and enjoy the fruits of their own industry.

How could anyone have resisted a 1767 advertisement in the *Belfast News Letter* that equated the departure of the *Britannia* to a religious experience? "The ship, by the blessing of God, will then proceed on her intended voyage for the Land of Promise." Writing from the colonies in the 1770s, emigrant William Eddis claimed that the streets of London were filled with advertisements

> offering the most seducing encouragements to adventurers under every possible description; to those who are disgusted with frowns of fortune in their native land and to those of an enterprising disposition, who are tempted to court her smiles in a distant region.

From Scotland, people were tempted by many "enticing accounts of America published everywhere by the shipmasters and agents, [which] have a great affect."

Women who traveled the distance alone confronted special difficulties, and we can only imagine how they must have felt as they contemplated the journey to America. They too left their homes and families to escape a desperate poverty, to seek some alternative to the increasingly difficult lives of their mothers and sisters before them. Perhaps, like many of their contemporaries, they had already moved from the countryside to seek work in the cities, to labor as domestic servants in the homes of wealthy families. Most likely, they cherished dreams of a better life than they had known, a modest prosperity, stalwart husbands, homes, and perhaps servants of their own. They could not have known that merchants were warning their agents abroad to "send no more women."

Once they had made the decision to go to America, prospective servants arranged for the indenture, boarded ships advertised as "well suited for passengers," and soon found themselves in the midst of a nightmare. The journey to the "promised land" became a "middle passage" with horrors that sometimes rivaled those of the slave trade. Illness and death from overcrowding, crude sanitary conditions, and meager diets plagued the passengers, who found themselves thrust into the role of human cargo in an eighteenth-century profit business. The onboard provisions were generally calculated to last for twelve weeks, fourteen if the captain was "liberally inclined." The daily diet at sea consisted of bread, ship's biscuits, meat, peas, cheese, and, if the passengers were fortunate, fish. But when the ship's progress was delayed, usually owing to inclement weather or unfavorable winds, provisions dipped dangerously low, especially since quantities were calculated to accommodate "freights" rather than the number of people. A "freight" was a passenger over the age of fourteen. Children between the ages of four and fourteen counted as half-freights. On voyages where there were a high proportion of children, as on the redemptioner ships, provisions were less adequate and delays at sea often disastrous.

The most vivid account of the transatlantic journey comes from the journal of Gottlieb Mittelberger. His graphic descriptions make the sounds and smells almost palpable. Mittelberger was witness to a tragic journey even though he had paid for his ticket. He made the trip from Germany to the New World with a commission to deliver an organ to a Lutheran congregation in Pennsylvania. In May 1750 he left his birthplace in the district of Vailhinger for Heilbronn, picked up the organ, and then followed the typical route down the Neckar and the Rhine rivers to Rotterdam. The Rhine boats had to stop at thirty-six customshouses between Heilbronn and Holland, where officials examined the ship and required passengers to pay a toll. After four to six weeks, the ships finally arrived in Holland, where once again they were detained. "In Rotterdam and to some extent also in Amsterdam, the people are packed into the big boats as closely as herring." The sleeping area for each person measured only two by six feet. Between four hundred and six hundred passengers were crammed into these ships, forced to share quarters with "the immense amount of equipment, tools, provisions, barrels of fresh water, and other things."

With favorable winds, the passage from Holland to Cowes, off the southern coast of England, might take eight days or less; with contrary winds, it could take as long as four weeks. In Cowes, everything was reexamined and additional customs charges were levied. Mittelberger writes, "It can happen that ships have to ride at anchor there from eight to fourteen days, or until they have taken on full cargoes." By the time the ship sailed, most of the passengers had spent their last remaining money, had consumed their meager stock of provisions, and had nothing left. Families that had planned to arrive in Pennsylvania free were now forced to travel as redemptioners.

When the ship weighed anchor for the last time, "both the long sea voyage and misery begin in earnest." Almost five hundred passengers crowded onto the *Osgood* for this journey to Pennsylvania. Signs of distress filled the ship:

> smells, fumes, horrors, vomiting, various kinds of sea sickness, fever, dysentery, headaches, heat, constipation, boils, scurvy, cancer, mouth-rot, and similar afflictions, all of them caused by the age and the highly-salted state of the food . . . as well as by the very bad and filthy water.

Mittelberger also witnessed food shortages, frost, heat, thirst, and "so many lice, especially on the sick people, that they have to be scraped off the bodies." The climax of the journey was reached, Mittelberger claimed, when a storm hit, and for two or three days, "everyone was convinced that the ship with all on board" would sink. Six months of steady traveling finally brought Mittelberger to Pennsylvania; the journey from Rotterdam to Philadelphia had taken fifteen weeks.

If the shipboard accommodations were miserable for paying passengers like Mittelberger, the conditions below deck were even worse for indentured servants. The tragic nature of the trade in servants was not merely a function of the enormous number of immigrants who poured into the Quaker colony after the second decade of the eighteenth century. Thousands of immigrants had arrived in Pennsylvania during the seventeenth century as well. The difference resides in the nature of the transportation system. In the early period, servants were not segregated from paying passengers, nor was the transportation of servants a special business. Indeed, servants often accompanied their masters. In the eighteenth century, however, the transportation of servants became a profitable enterprise. Traders delivered thousands of bound laborers to Pennsylvania and exhibited a callous disregard for their servant cargoes. As a result, passengers on these voyages suffered from a high rate of disease. . . .

Death was also common on the transatlantic voyages. Encouraged to seek their fortunes in the flourishing Quaker society and promised suitable provisions for the voyage, prospective servants suffered a staggering loss of life on board eighteenth-century vessels. Although it is difficult to derive precise mortality figures, a crude rate approximation at various points throughout the eighteenth century can be calculated using scattered data. In 1710 fully 25 percent of the German immigrants to Pennsylvania perished. Of the sixteen ships that arrived in Philadelphia in 1738, only two could land passengers without a quarantine period. On one of the ships, 70 percent of the passengers died. Overall, a total of 1,600 individuals perished, a crude mortality estimate of more than 50 percent. In 1749, the year of heaviest German immigration into the colony, approximately one of five passengers died on route. Although only spotty data exist for the mortality on vessels carrying servants from Ireland, Irish servants may have fared even worse. In 1729 statistics from two vessels indicate a mortality of more than 50 percent. A 43 percent mortality occurred on the *Seaflower* voyage in 1741 and a 26 percent death rate on the voyage of the *General Wolfe* in 1772.

Scattered data reveal that the mortality for servants at certain times equaled that for slaves in the "middle passage," and during other periods actually exceeded the death rate for slaves. Analyses of mortality in the eighteenth-century French slave trade from Nantes yield a mean rate of 16.2 percent for the period from 1715 to 1775. These data also show a general decline in mortality between 1748 and 1792. A recent study of the middle passage reports a death rate of 9.3 percent over the entire eighteenth century as well as a decline in the rate as the century progressed. Thus slave mortality throughout the eighteenth century fell within the 10 to 20 percent range, compared with almost 25 percent for servants traveling to Pennsylvania.

A number of factors contributed to excessive servant death. Although profit motivated both trades, slaves were more valuable than servants. Each slave represented a substantial investment well before reaching the slave market. In contrast, transporters of servants paid at most a small sum to an agent to procure the servant and were out of pocket only for the provisions on the transatlantic voyage. In addition, slave traders operated ships designed and used exclusively for the transportion of their human cargo and the business of slaving was the sole venture. Servant traders did not make quite the same commitment nor reap comparable profits. They were content to make operating costs or have additional cash, but servant cargoes usually accounted for only a portion of a venture.

The high mortality in the servant trade was avoidable. As horrible as the middle passage was, death rates actually improved through the eighteenth century. Servant transporters were aware of the requirements for a healthy voyage. Merchants Abel James and Henry Drinker cautioned their Captain Enoch Story to pick out healthy servants and warned him that the journey's success depended upon the "Provisions laid in and furnished for the Voyage." Merchant Thomas Clifford prescribed that his vessels have frequent washings with vinegar "every ten days if weather permits, fore and aft between decks." When the ships were not crowded, Clifford ordered them scrubbed with water. Servant traders were also aware of the advantages of citrus and proper ventilation. It had been known for some time that citrus prevented scurvy. In addition, proper air circulation had been identified with healthy voyages and well before the midcentury a ventilation system for ships had been developed. When the English Board of Trade planned to send a group of settlers to Halifax in 1749, they commissioned the inventor of the "Sutton Air Pipes" to estimate the costs of installation of the system for the transport vessels. Sutton agreed to outfit the ships at a cost of thirty pounds per ship, "or thirty-five if with furnace." The board ordered the work and was pleased to discover that the English arrived in Halifax in excellent health, "while John Dick's Germans, who came on a ship without ventilation, were all sickly." Whether ventilation systems did in fact provide a more healthy atmosphere on ship is not our concern, since contemporary wisdom thought that proper ventilation would protect the health of passengers. By not incorporating ventilation technology, shippers revealed that the health of their servant passengers was not a priority.

Transporters took great pains to reassure paying passengers that their transportation was separate from that of servants. In an advertisement announcing the departure of the *Elizabeth and Mary* for Philadelphia in 1769, paying passengers were urged to travel on this ship because they would experience a superior voyage. The advertisement promised that "as she will take no servants, will have good accommodations for passengers." Thus if servant traders had wanted to, they could have protected the health of their servants. Clearly, few incentives motivated them to do so, and as long as they did not jeopardize the health of paying passengers and separated free from bound travelers, both businesses could operate.

In order to make the maximum pecuniary gain in the servant trade, shippers crammed as many souls as possible into their vessels, confident that even with the most callous disregard for human life, the monetary return would still make it worth the effort. A number of immigrants testified that the treatment during the voyage caused much of the suffering. On the vessel carrying John Harrower to Virginia, the servants came close to mutiny on two different occasions. They were incensed because the captain had put them on strict rations. Harrower also reported that two servants were placed in irons "for wanting other than what was served." Testimony from a 1729 trip suggests that the danger to the passengers came from a combination of too many passengers and too much time spent in travel. A hard trip was made nightmarish when "meanly provided, many starve for want and may die of Sickness being crowded in such numbers on board one Vessel." The ship *Love and Unity* left Rotterdam bound for Philadelphia in 1731. Hardly living up to its name, the passengers endured a dreadful voyage, many lives were lost, and the vessel was unable to reach Philadelphia. It landed instead off the coast of Massachusetts. In testimony written by five survivors, the captain was accused of being "a wicked murderer of souls, thought to starve us, not have provided provisions enough, according to agreement." An English emigrant who traveled to Baltimore in 1774 reported that as soon as the vessel left Land's End the master "used the passengers in a most cruel manner." He reduced the food to "one and one half biscuits, three small potatoes, and two ounces of salt beef, six spoonfuls of pea soup being substituted for potatoes and beef on Tuesdays and Fridays." The traveler alleged that complainers met severe punishment. Captains involved in the redemptioner trade also gained an infamous reputation. Transportation rules specified that if the passenger survived the voyage beyond the halfway point in the journey, the family would be responsible for the cost of passage, whether or not the individual survived. Many masters were notorious for providing adequate provisions for only the first half of the trip and then virtually starving their captives to the journey's end. . . .

If prospective servants survived the passage, the next ordeal began as the ship neared the port. Servants did their best to wash, groom, and gather their belongings. Often, chests were missing or possessions had been pilfered. At other times, passengers discovered that their trunks had never made it on board. In 1749 the *Pennsylvanische Berichte* reported the arrival of a ship that carried the personal belongings of Germans who had arrived some weeks before. The article lamented that many found their chests had been broken open "but the Germans pay and must pay when their chests are robbed or when famished with hunger even though their contracts are expressly to the contrary."

Servants and their belongings were so mistreated at the hands of the Pennsylvania traders that the 1765 law not only clarified matters of health, but addressed a whole range of abuses. To prevent ships' crews from gouging the passengers, the maximum profit from the sale of items to passengers could not exceed 50 percent. To ensure that German passengers were not ignorant of the law, an interpreter was to board the ship before landing and explain their rights. To increase the chances that servants' baggage made the journey, shippers were required to issue bills of lading and were liable for losses and damage. This law also forbade masters from charging family members for the cost of passage of any who died in transit.

After the ship docked, announcements appeared in the local papers noting the ship's arrival and advertised all of the goods on board, including the indentured servants. In the seventeenth century, most servants had arranged their indentures on the eastern shores of the Atlantic. For eighteenth-century servants, the docking signaled the opening of the servant market in which they were the commodities. A typical advertisement read that newly arrived servants were available for all "sorts of business, inquire at Willing and Shippen." Philadelphia residents could purchase a general assortment of imported spring goods, as well as a few barrels of Irish beef and Scotch herring, and, in addition, examine the 250 servants included in the ship's cargo.

Those interested in purchasing a servant boarded the ships to inspect them. Reminiscent of the slave market, servants were displayed like cattle. Prospective buyers felt their muscles, checked their teeth and health, verified occupations, inquired about their behavior, and then, if satisfied, paid the master the costs and took the servant home. As the ship neared its return departure date, the remaining servants were removed from the vessel and housed in the merchant's buildings. Newspaper advertisements directed buyers to the places of business.

Female servants were particularly "troublesome" and difficult to place. To a great extent, the problems were caused by the limited demand for domestic laborers. In 1754 Thomas Willing wrote to his agents requesting a cargo "with 20 to 30 man and boy servants. . . . The servants should not be above 30 or less than 16 years old and no women." In their instructions to a ship's captain, Abel James and Henry Drinker requested that "if servants are dealt in avoid women altogether or as much as possible." In 1764 Benjamin Marshall warned Thomas Murphy that "the less Women the better as they are very troublesome." In the same year, Marshall wrote to Barnaby Eagen that "Stout able Labouring men and Tradesmen out of the Country with Young Boys and Lads answer best, Women are so troublesome it would be best to send few or none as there is often so many Drawbacks on them." Because domestic servants were in such close contact with their masters' families, prospective owners were particularly selective and required more detailed information than most servants could provide. In 1769 Thomas Clifford warned his captain to "avoid so much as possible bringing women servants, [for] 'tis not easy to get good places for them . . . without Character reference."

For redemptioners, the landing was followed by a frantic search to procure the funds to repay the captain or to contract for the most favorable indenture. The process often proved frustrating. Announcements appeared in newspapers warning redemptioners to pay or "they will be proceeded against according to Law." If the servant market was poor, redemptioners were thrust into society. "For none would take a man with the encumbrances of a Wife or small Children . . . and by that means many of them . . . are hardly able to maintain themselves."

For eighteenth-century German servants, the jarring experience of being a piece of cargo in the labor market was complicated by language problems. For every servant like Johannes Fierly or Hans Surnan who was purchased by a German family, there was a Christopher Stoffel or Johannes Fretzel acquired by an English-speaking master. Comments like "broken English" or "little or no English" testify to the difficulties.

Henry Muhlenberg, a minister of the Lutheran Church, arrived in Pennsylvania in 1742 and experienced the language problems firsthand. On his way home from missionary business, Muhlenberg stopped in Providence and was asked to preach a sermon in German. "An English justice of the peace," Muhlenberg writes, "said there was [*sic*] a great many poor German servants, men and women, indentured to the English people in this neighborhood." Muhlenberg commented that these German servants spoke no English and longed for a sermon they could understand. Apparently redemptioners received the service eagerly, for Muhlenberg wrote, "There was weeping among the Germans, as is usually the case when they have been deprived of the Word of God for a long time."

Once servants had been purchased, their lives were filled primarily by rigorous work and inflexible schedules. Male servants labored at a great variety of jobs. Those who toiled in the homes of the city's elite included among their responsibilities driving carriages, running errands, and caring for the horses. The bound laborers in the city's inns and taverns were expected to perform household chores, wait on tables, do the marketing, and tend horses. In a city board yard, the servant was counted on to take care of the accounts and to be familiar with the varieties of lumber. In merchants' businesses, servants performed as clerks and were expected to "write a tolerable hand and understand figures."

The majority of Philadelphia's eighteenth-century servants worked for artisans in a tremendous array of craft establishments. Petty commodity production was organized around the household, and servants and masters lived and worked together. Servants were part of a household labor force, supplementing rather than replacing family members. James Gardener, a tanner, skinner and leather dresser, was indentured in 1745 to tanner John Howell. They probably worked side by side, performed many of the same tasks, and shared the stench of the tan yard. Paul Mahoney arrived in Philadelphia one year later and was indentured for four years to shipwrights John Lawton and Simon Sherlock. For Mahoney, each day seemed like another because he spent his time sawing, an indispensable skill in the shipyard. John McCan was indentured to Philadelphia cabinetmaker Matthew Hand. McCan was "most accustomed to chair making." Servant John Hopkins, who was owned by a shoemaker, made children's shoes and pumps, "of which he was uncommonly ready."

Work was hard in early America and not without its dangers, especially for servants. An article in the *Pennsylvania Gazette* reported that "a man ordered his servant to take some Fowls in from Roost every night for fear of the Fox." Thinking he was a fox, the master shot the servant in the arm. John Martin was a brewer's servant. While loading beer casks on board Captain Annis's ship, he "missed his footing and fell into the River"; the cask tumbled after him, striking him in the head, and he drowned.

Much of urban production in the eighteenth-century port city was controlled by the weather. More hours of daylight meant longer periods at the workbench. When it rained or snowed, housewrights, shipwrights, and others who labored out-of-doors were forced to call a halt to their labors. When the weather turned severe, the river froze and supplies were stuck on board ships until the thaw. Winter sleet prevented the cooper from molding the barrel staves outside or the ropemaker from walking the rope. No doubt, during these downtimes, servants and masters performed other necessary jobs. While huddled around the fire, they could sharpen or fix tools. Perhaps they sought new jobs or discussed new styles. At times masters may have given up getting anything accomplished and trudged off to the neighborhood tavern to hear the latest news and to drink to the health of the king and the end of winter. If all else failed and winter stayed around too long, masters might be forced to sell their servants. In January 1775 a cooper fell victim to the vagaries of the weather and placed this advertisement: "To Be Sold, a servant man with three years and ten months to serve, a cooper by trade, and is a good hand at making flaxseed casks and pork barrels. Sold for no faults but their master's declining business."

The work pace for female laborers was similarly difficult and varied. Domestic servants were accountable for a wide range of chores, from cooking and housework to carding and spinning, washing and "doing up the linen." Domestic tasks were endless, often disagreeable, and occasionally dangerous. Servants were required to be available twenty-four hours per day. Child care took up much of the time, and servants acted as wet nurses, as well as baby nurses, and tended the children. Household chores often fit into a set pattern, so that a day of clothes washing was invariably followed by a day at the ironing table. It was not unusual in the Drinker household for servants to be required to prepare a meal for twelve to fifteen people—the family, visitors, and boarders.

Domestic servants were called upon by their masters for the slightest excuses—a barking dog or a scary noise. They were also to be on hand for more serious matters in case of illness or when the fire alarm sounded. The chambermaid slept at the foot of Elizabeth Drinker's bed. She was expected to rise before the family and stoke the fires to spare the Drinkers the inconvenience of dressing in a cold house or to make sure that family members did not wait for their hot morning beverage. One particularly rainy winter, Elizabeth Drinker reported that the privy filled and flowed into the house. The cleanup was a most objectionable job and fell to the servants. . . .

Domestic servants shouldered a special group of burdens. As servants in a household, they found themselves thrust into an ambiguous position. They were simultaneously workers to be controlled and extended members of the family to be disciplined. Conflict is inevitable in all economic relationships defined by inequality, no matter how well intentioned the employer. In such an exploitative relationship as that between domestic servant and master, when the servant resided and labored within the household, where living and working spaces were close, and when the relationship was to last for four years or even longer, latent conflict could easily become overt.

Urban life affected the tone and character of the servants' experience. Servants belonged to a distinct subculture that embraced both the free and unfree laboring classes. Not only did these social relations separate the working classes from those above them, but their "betters" were aware of the association and felt threatened by it. Throughout the eighteenth century, petitions to colonial officials from the inhabitants of Philadelphia complained about the social gatherings of the unfree classes. In 1741 the Philadelphia Grand Jury reported "the great disorders" committed on Sundays by "servants, apprentice boys and numbers of Negroes." During the weekday evenings, "many disorderly persons" gathered at the courthouse, the Grand Jury claimed, "and great numbers of Negroes and others sit [until late] and many disorders were committed." The semiannual fairs in Philadelphia, held in May and November, were important occasions of lower-class life. In 1731 city residents complained that "diverse inhabitants . . . by custom think they have a right to liberty of going out." Not only did these individuals partake of spiritous drink, but they "conspired to run away more than at any other time." Even worse was the corruption of the city's youth, "who are at times induced to drinking and gaming in mix'd companies of vicious servants and negroes." By 1775, at the urging of the mayor and Common Council, the Assembly abolished the fairs. Fairs, according to the Assembly, were "useless" and tended to "debauch the morals of the people." The people "debauched" were not just the servants but the journeymen and slaves who participated in the gaming and drinking.

All classes frequented the many taverns and dram shops in the city, even though the law prohibited tavern keepers from serving spirits to servants or slaves. Lawrence Herne, who was indentured to a tavern keeper, managed nicely. And Thomas Minor, a servant owner, petitioned the court for "considerable damage and trouble by his servants getting liquor and giving a pledge for it at the house of Robert McKee tavernkeeper and by . . . running away from his master's service when intoxicated with liquor."

Urban life not only provided servants with access to strong drink, the drinking establishments frequented by the "lower sort" were virtually segregated from the middling and upper classes. In 1744 the Philadelphia Grand Jury referred to Hell Town, a neighborhood where the proportion of houses that served strong drink was extremely high. The great number of tippling houses presumably caused a great "temptation to entertain Apprentices, Servants and even Negroes." The activities in these places, "nurseries of Vice and Debauchery," changed little through the course of the century. "Spiritous liquors" were an important part of the lives of the laboring classes and stealing away from one's master to share a pint must have eased the pain of servitude.

Paternalism still governed the associations between servants and masters because productive relations in prerevolutionary Philadelphia remained unchanged. Masters and servants continued to live under the same roof, paused together over the midday pint, perhaps shared the supper table, and worked toward the same productive goals. Unlike the paternalism characteristic of a slave society, the class structure did not prevent the servant classes from developing a social network. Although the same productive relations dominated labor, the institution of indentured servitude had changed, mainly because of the ordeal servants suffered in reaching America, the shifting ethnic balance of the population, and the erosion of skill. The behavior of servants leaves little question that a heightened level of social conflict induced servants to seek ways of escape. This is evident from the steady rise in the number of runaways in the eighteenth century. Only three seventeenth-century servants are known to have escaped from service. In contrast, at least 10 percent of the servants indentured in 1745 were advertised as runaways over the next five years. Throughout the late colonial period approximately 6 percent of the city's servants protested by running away. . . .

. . . Although servants from all ethnic groups ran away, including a few French and Spanish servants, the majority of Pennsylvania's runaways were from Ireland. Only a small number were from Germany, with a few more from England. The reasons for this are not clear. Part of the explanation may be that many German redemptioners emigrated as family units, and running away may have been logistically more difficult or less desirable. Occasionally, when German servants did abscond, husbands and wives traveled together. Another explanation for the low incidence of German runaways is that they may have been inhibited by language difficulties. Most likely, the Irish ran away at a high rate in response to the profound anti-Irish sentiment in Pennsylvania. The English had a long history of anti-Irish feeling, and the large proportion of Irish servants must have inspired the colonists' hatred. The Irish were more abused than any other ethnic group in Pennsylvania, and much of the abuse was overt. German servants were described as industrious; the Irish "have such an ill-name, they won't sell for any tolerable price." Irish runaways were portrayed like Dennis Hurly, who was "remarkably subject to swearing and drinking," or Patrick Tumony, who although he writes a good hand "pretends to be a miller."

The variation in runaway patterns among the servile classes exposes the basic distinction between the two forms of bondage for the individuals involved. Servitude and slavery did have much in common. Both were highly exploitative labor systems. White and black unfree laborers performed the same tasks, had little to say about their lives, were at the whim of their masters, and were subject to a very similar legal code. And during the eighteenth century, the nature of the servant market dispelled any doubts that this was a humane and benign institution. Although the distinctions between the systems of servitude and slavery were blurred, the psychological realities for the bound workers were vastly different. For all of the horrors in both systems, the one fundamental difference was that the servant's bondage was for a finite period of time. The slave's burden of perpetual bondage was hardly comparable to a three- to four-year indenture. The level of frustration for skilled slaves might very well push them beyond the threshold. The master reaped the benefit not only of his own labor but of his slaves' as well.

 ## FOR FURTHER STUDY

1. How does John Harrower's decision to come to the colonies typify decisions made by other unemployed Europeans? What factors encouraged others but were left out of Harrower's story?

2. What was the journey to America like? Compare the trip for servants and slaves.

3. How did the servants find masters? What was their work schedule like after they began to repay those who bought them?

4. How did servants develop a network and culture in colonial Philadelphia? Why did Irish servants run away most often?

5. What was similar and different about the lives and prospects of servants compared to slaves?

FOR FURTHER READING

The conditions indentured servants faced were difficult throughout the American colonies. Several older studies by Richard B. Morris, *Government and Labor in Early America* (1946), and Abbot Emerson Smith, *Colonists in Bondage: White Servitude and Convict Labor in America, 1607–1776* (1947), cover most colonies and are particularly interested in the convicts who were freed if they agreed to become servants in the New World. A more recent study of convicts is A. Roger Ekirch, *Bound for America: The Transportation of British Convicts to the Colonies, 1718–1775* (1987). Two other works discuss specific aspects of servitude: David W. Galenson, *White Servitude in Colonial America: An Economic Analysis* (1981), and John Van der Zee, *Bound Over: Indentured Servitude and American Conscience* (1985).

Servants were part of other important aspects of colonial life. They came in the wave of immigrants captured in a compelling work by Bernard Bailyn, *Voyagers to the West: A Passage in the Peopling of America on the Eve of the Revolution* (1986).

- Of course, many colonial families indentured their children to other residents, especially in New England. These native servants shared some of the same problems with new immigrants because they lived away from their parents. Two works treat these relationships in rich detail: John Demos, *A Little Commonwealth: Family Life in Plymouth Colony* (1970), and Edmund S. Morgan, *The Puritan Family: Religion and Domestic Relations in Seventeenth Century New England* (1966).

CHAPTER 7

This engraving of Washington's soldiers at Valley Forge depicts suffering and poor conditions.

BUILDING AN ARMY

JOHN E. FERLING

$\mathscr{D}$uring much of their history, Americans have considered themselves to be a special people, destined by God to serve as an example for the rest of humanity. The religious sects that settled here, including the Puritans, saw their colony as "a City upon a Hill, the eyes of all people uppon us." In the eighteenth century, many revolutionary leaders believed that there was a conspiracy in England aimed at suppressing colonial liberties and that they had a sacred duty to defend America as the last bastion of freedom. Americans, they felt, were a virtuous people who were destined by God to lead the world in establishing a free and noble republic that would abolish the kings, armies, and corrupt ministries that enslaved Europe. The defense of liberty would be made by untrained citizen-soldiers, moved to courageous deeds by their love of freedom and their faith in God. Their fear of regular, standing armies gave rise to a long tradition of antimilitarism, a commitment to civilian control of the military, and a belief that American wars could be fought by voluntary enlistment of average citizens. It also perpetuated a myth that the Revolutionary War was won by patriotic farmers who turned out in large numbers to promote the glorious cause.

During the first year of the war, a considerable amount of such enthusiasm was displayed in the patriotic songs and poetry, in the parades and celebrations, and even in the number of men who joined the ranks. By 1776, however, the enthusiasm had waned, and men deserted, went home on leave and never returned, or refused to enlist unless a bounty was paid for their doing so. Washington's army seldom exceeded 25,000 troops and was frequently much smaller. Increasingly, Washington saw the need for a regular army of long-term enlistees, and increasingly the war was fought not by middle-class patriots but by others who were hired to fight—the slave and servant who thus bought their freedom, or the young and the poor who saw so few opportunities in civilian life that even the meager pay in the Continental army looked good. If the enthusiasm of the volunteer soldier soon flagged, so too did that of the civilian population, which complained about taxes and

97

sometimes sold food and supplies to the British army rather than donating them to Washington's forces.

The book by John E. Ferling, from which the following selection is taken, is a study of colonial warfare from the early Indian conflicts through the Revolution. Its graphic portrayal of the suffering of revolutionary troops helps us understand why Washington had such difficulty in recruitment.

America's rebel soldiers sustained incredible deprivation during the War for Independence. The suffering of the luckless troops quartered at Valley Forge in the winter of 1777–1778, in fact, has become part of the national mythology. One soldier complained of "Poor food—hard lodging—Cold Weather—fatigue—Nasty Clothes—nasty Cookery. I can't Endure it—Why are we sent here to starve and Freeze." Another soldier complained of having received just half a day's allowance of food in eight days. As often as not, alleged one soldier, when the troops were provided with "beef" it was actually horse meat. The bread frequently "had nearly as much flesh as bread being . . . full of worms." It "required a deal of circumspection in eating it," he added. One soldier claimed that for four days he had tasted only "a little black birch bark which I had gnaw'd off a stick of wood." Other men, in their desperation, boiled their shoes for food. Some troops purchased foodstuffs wherever they could locate a seller. Others lived by stealing provisions. "I would have taken victuals or drink from the best friend I had on earth by force," one trooper ruefully acknowledged.

The deprivation experienced at Valley Forge almost paled beside the forlorn experiences of the men in Benedict Arnold's 1775 invasion of Canada. Few American soldiers have endured the miseries to which these men were subjected. Although the expedition was undertaken in the autumn and winter months in the northeastern corner of the mainland colonies, and, of course, into Canada, the troops were dispatched with an inadequate number of tents. The general shortage of provisions was exacerbated by the destruction of many of the serviceable goods the men did possess; since few of the men were familiar with the bateaux provided to transport the items through the swampy terrain, it was not uncommon for a diarist among the troops to record that the soldiers "lost all the Baggage, Arms, & Provisions of 4 men" when several craft capsized. On the eve of entering Canada, General Arnold noted that his "detachments are as ready, as naked men can be. . . ." Food supplies for the expedition quickly dwindled, and much that remained was palatable only to someone facing starvation. The men first substituted salt pork and flour for the accustomed regimen. Soon their diet consisted of water and flour, a drab concoction which the men christened

From *A Wilderness of Miseries: War and Warriors in Early America*, by John E. Ferling, (Westport, CT: Greenwood Press, 1980), pp. 93–126. Copyright © 1980 John E. Ferling. Excerpted and reprinted with permission of the author and Greenwood Press, an Imprint of Greenwood Publishing Group, Inc.

"Lillipu." Ultimately, the men ate soap, candles boiled in water, gruel, wood, boiled rawhide and leather, carcasses of animals discovered in the forests, and even the pet dogs that had accompanied some of the soldiers. The latter fare, which was made into a green stew, was eaten with gusto, particularly by those who did not realize the contents of this culinary delight. . . .

Many times troops suffered for prolonged periods with inadequate supplies of clothing and blankets. Early in the war, Congress legislated to outfit each enlistee in the Continental army with two hunting shirts, two pairs of overalls, a leather or woolen coat, a hat or cap, one pair of trousers, two shirts, two pairs of hose, and two pairs of shoes. Nevertheless, during an entire winter campaign in the South, General Greene had coats for only 10 percent of his troops. A visitor to a Virginia regiment discovered some troops "with one coat, some hoseless, with their feet peeping out of their shoes; others with breeches that put decency to blush." A British officer thought "no nation ever saw such a set of tatter-demalians. There are few coats among them but what are out at elbows and in a whole regiment there is scarce a pair of breeches." Even the troops in Philadelphia celebrating the first anniversary of the Declaration of Independence "paraded thro' the streets with great pomp, tho' many were barefoot & looked very unhealthy." Numerous soldiers complained of endless cold nights, of sleeping under leaves, or of huddling together in a vain attempt to stay warm. One contingent, without blankets or shelter, discovered that the "only way to avoid freezing was to be constantly walking, running, or jumping." Another, according to a bitter new recruit, just kept "marching and countermarching, starving and freezing." Even so, these troops were lucky. Soldiers who got lost while on night patrol were known to die of exposure. In one horrid instance, a crew of eighty on a privateer perished from the cold during a storm.

Those who died quickly and relatively painlessly in the cold may have been fortunate. The chronic inadequacy of food and other provisions produced incredible suffering among thousands of soldiers. The common cold, respiratory diseases, and a wide variety of apparent viral ailments were endemic to the camps of the Revolutionary armies. At best, these ills could immobilize and entire army; at worst, soldiers so weakened by deprivation and these minor ills could become susceptible to more serious ailments. Malaria and dysentery, usually referred to as "the flux," repeatedly struck at the soldiery. But smallpox probably frightened the soldiers more than any enemy. Colonel Jeduthon Baldwin of Massachusetts left a graphic account of his successful three-month battle with the disease. He was one of 29,000 soldiers who fell ill with smallpox in May 1776. At the outset, Baldwin's appetite waned and he grew listless. He also developed severe headaches "over my eyes" that left him "very full of pain & distress"; on the second day, chills tore through his body, and he was scarcely able to lift his head. After five days the fever abated, but a sore throat developed and the "hard head ache" persisted. He was without energy and quickly grew faint if moved. The fever returned a few days later, accompanied now by the pox, which provoked "an extream fire and itching [and] made me Very uncomfortable." Sixteen days after his ills commenced, Baldwin at least seemed well. Three months later, he suffered a relapse and endured a similar period of headaches, "fever and ague."

Conditions in Baldwin's environment must have resembled those witnessed by General John Lacey of Pennsylvania. He toured a camp of New England soldiers where he saw "some men in and some out of Tents sick on the bare ground—infected with Fluxes, Fevers, Small Pox and over run with legions of Lice. . . . The Lice and Maggots which seemed to vie with each other, were creeping in Millions over the Victims." Lacey departed hastily to acquire some "good old Spirits" and become "handsomely Drunk" in order to forget the horrors he had seen. But the sight of troops so inflicted with "rhumatism" from exposure that they were unable to care for themselves "any more than a new born infant," of men with "every joint . . . inflexible and swelled to an enormous size," of soldiers who could not see, speak, or walk tightly packed into a barn for shelter, of men infested with "large maggots, an inch long, Crawl[ing] out of their ears" were not sights easily forgotten. . . .

Under these conditions, the death rate from illnesses could be astronomical. For thirty months after July 1776, never less than 16 percent of the troops were incapacitated by illness; at times more than one-third of the army was on sick call. When an epidemic swept a camp, soldiers by the score might die daily. A chaplain who visited Ticonderoga in August 1776 reported that about thirty men perished each day. These disasters left little opportunity for customary burial procedures. Corpses were hurriedly buried without a coffin. Sometimes large pits were dug to accommodate scores of victims. A visitor to a camp saw

> several Corps brought, carried by four Soldiers in a blanket, one holt of each corner. On their arriving at the pit or Grave, those next to it let go of the blanket, the other two giving a Hoist rolled the dead body into the pit where lay several bodies already deposited in the same way, with no other covering but the Rags in which they dyed, heads and points as they happened to come to the place. In this manner the burial continued all day.

Those soldiers who escaped illness, and many who did not, endured a steady regimen of grinding physical toil. While in camp, a work day of twelve hours or more was common for those on fatigue duty, which involved principally cooking, cutting wood, and building entrenchments and barracks. Work commenced at about six in the morning and continued, with one hour for breakfast, until noon; work resumed at about two o'clock and continued without abatement until sunset. The length of the work day was comparable to that of farmers and artisans, but the nature of the work was more onerous. The "fall business in Flaxseed time is nothing to be compared to the Fatigues I undergo Daily," one farmer-soldier assured his wife. Some details were less arduous than others, but far less pleasant. To the "Camp Colour men" fell the unhappy duty of cleaning the area of all "nausances," defined in written orders as "filth, bones, &c.," and of "throwing the Same into the pits and Covering the filth therein with fresh dirt every morning"; these men additionally faced the even less enviable task of covering "the excrements in the holes of their Respective Regiments every morning."

Still, most troops probably preferred the loathsome tasks and the boredom of camp life to the endless, and what often must have appeared pointless, marches. Washington's forces were extraordinarily mobile. One soldier mentioned marching forty-five miles in twenty-four hours. Another calculated that his outfit had marched 160 miles during the last three weeks of November 1781, followed by 281 miles in December and 60 additional miles in January; his diary typically notes marches on successive days of sixteen miles, sixteen miles, twenty-three miles, ten miles, and eleven miles. One company marched nearly eight hundred miles in six months in 1777, followed by marches totaling over seventeen hundred miles between April and December of 1780, over two thousand miles in 1781, and in excess of twelve hundred miles in the first four months of 1782. . . .

Occasionally the troops marched until they encountered an adversary. Then the pain of camp duty and training gave way to the terror of battle, an ordeal of agony and spasmodic fear unlike anything ever experienced by these men. The thought of battle was sufficient to knot a man's stomach, to leave his mouth dry with nervous anticipation. Few displayed their anxiety to the comrades, but instead masked their feeling with a false display of joviality "as if they were Wholly at peace." On the eve of combat they spent their time "either sleeping, swimming, fishing, or Cursing and Swearing, most generally the Latter." One observer was fooled by their jocosity and bravado. They "laugh at death," he thought, "mock at Hell and Damnation, & even call the Deity to remove them out of this World."

But these men did confide in their families. They often thought of death, and they prepared their wills and put their business in order "in case that my maker should . . . ordain that I should not live to Come off the Hill." Some men were fatalistic in the face of battle. "Heaven is the Prize for which we all contend," one soldier believed. Some were idealistic, claiming to fear not "Tory *George,* & his "War-worn Army!" All wondered what combat would be like. "When two such powers impinge there must be a dreadful Impulse," Philip Fithian speculated. Typically, Fithian immediately tried to shake off his fear: "I prefer my Situation here . . . to any Situation whatever of *Eligence, Safety,* or *Ease.*"

Eventually the confusion and noise of combat descended on the men. Fear, paralyzing to some, numbing to others, was the predominant sensation. Private Fithian, the young man brimming with Whig principle and pretended dauntlessness, summarized the shock of his first battle in the briefest of diary entries: "O doleful! doleful! doleful!—Blood! Carnage! Fire!" Another, less poetically, registered his feelings: "Good God, how the balls flew,—I freely acknowledge I never had such a tremor.". . .

Although not unanticipated, no one could fathom the incredible carnage wrought by battle until it had been experienced. Physicians sometimes broke after a prolonged period of "beholding mutilated bodies, mangled limbs and bleeding, incurable wounds." A soldier might be expected to waffle when he saw his comrades take "a musket-ball through his cheeks, cutting its way through the teeth on each side, and the substance of his tongue." Others saw men with half their faces "torn off by a cannon-ball, laying mouth and throat open to view." Men were decapitated or rendered paraplegics within a moment of the commencement of a battle. Many unravelled when they saw soldiers "split like fish to be broiled." Those who had not previously experienced the scores of wounded men "weltering in their blood . . . in the most horrid tortures" could never be adequately prepared for such a sight. Many men broke into tears when confronted with a view of their buddies lying "in heaps on all sides," or when they heard the "groans of the wounded" pierce the otherwise silent night. Equally surprising and disturbing was the bovine indifference to suffering which some callous men exhibited. With horror, one soldier related a scene he witnessed at the Battle of Monmouth, where a "wounded captain . . . lying on the ground and begging his sergeant, who pretended to have the care of him, to help him off the field or he should bleed to death. The sergeant and a man or two he had with him were [too] taken up in hunting after plunder" to provide assistance. . . .

As in all wars, untested men wondered how they would perform in combat, and they particularly speculated at whether they could kill another man. Those men who left accounts of their battle activities during the War for Independence were not inclined to mention inaction because of paralyzing fear, but they did discuss their feelings about killing. In one breath they told of taking "as deliberate aim at him as ever I did at any game in my life," and candidly confessing in the next breath that "I hope I did not kill him, although I intended to. . . ." And they acknowledged their reluctance to kill. "When we got so near we could fairly see them they looked too handsome to be fired at; but we had to do it," a soldier at Bunker Hill remembered. In all likelihood, that was not the full story.

Unlike many modern wars wherein technology has depersonalized killing, the American Revolution was the kind of war in which soldiers frequently saw their adversaries. Men formed ranks and marched toward one another; a volley might be fired at point-blank range into a massed regiment, or the battle might conclude with hand-to-hand combat following a bayonet charge. Of course, psychological studies were not made following the War for Independence, but an abundance of evidence . . . indicates that men perceived their situation much the same as the combat soldiers in World War II, who were subjected to elaborate studies and tests. The technology of war differed in these two eras. There were no aerial attacks in the Revolution, nor were there tanks or machine guns; perhaps most important, whereas men are thought to panic in modern wars because the enemy is often unseen, the adversary usually was quite visible during the Revolution. Yet, at bottom, battles always involved noise, confusion, the terrible sights of tangled destruction, and, above all else, the churning presence of inextinguishable fear.

Recent studies indicate that fear reaches its zenith just before the battle commences. The soldier experiences a pounding heart, rapid pulse, tense muscles, a sinking feeling in his stomach, dryness of mouth and throat, constant perspiration, and an involuntary desire for elimination. Psychologists have concluded that every "soldier engaged in any form of combat is apprehensive before, and fearful during, the action. The situations of war, for the civilized man, are completely abnormal and foreign to his background." Men enter combat wondering why they were so unfortunate to be in this ghastly predicament; they question the purpose of the war, and they speculate whether they will survive and how they will perform. The soldier does not seriously consider being wounded until he has seen his comrades maimed. He is more fearful of artillery shells and bayonets than of bullets. He worries most about wounds to the face and genitals; then he fears wounds in the abdomen, chest, and extremities. He has little hatred for the enemy; indeed, he even tends to empathize with his adversary. During combat, well over half the American soldiers in World War II acknowledged that they "lost their heads for a moment, couldn't control themselves and were useless as soldiers for a little while." Many experienced tremors, grew weak or dizzy, alternately sobbed or laughed uncontrollably, were disoriented. . . .

Men, of course, did take note of the suffering about them, and they protested against their miseries in a variety of ways. The easiest, least dangerous means of recrimination was to refuse to reenlist when one's term of service expired. Not that it was always pleasant or even safe to depart from the army under these perfectly legal means. Those packing to leave were the target of jeers and depredations by their officers. General Charles Lee even smashed the butt of a musket over the skull of one soldier who tried to persuade a comrade to come with him. Yet, so many soldiers refused to reenlist at the end of the first year of hostilities that some historians, such as Don Higginbotham, believe it "was the much berated militia that pulled Washington through the . . . crisis." Late in 1775 Washington reported that less than 150 men in a regiment of 650 men agreed to reenlist. The problem persisted through the next year, prompting Thomas Paine, in his now famous words, to characterize some men as "summer soldiers and sunshine patriots." Frequently, Washington spoke of his fears that the rebellion might collapse for lack of troops, and, in despair, he was driven to complain of the "egregious want of Public Spirit" that prevailed. Nor was it just the common soldier who went home. Officers resigned, too. At the end of 1775, Washington told Congress that up to 50 percent of all officers beneath the rank of captain were quitting the army. By 1778 so many officers were departing that Washington, alarmed and caustic, wondered aloud if he would be left alone with his privates and corporals to wage the war. Arrears in pay induced many officers to quit, but many others departed when "fatigued through wet and cold" they returned to their tent to find a letter from home "filled with the most heart-aching tender complaints a woman is capable of writing," and begging him "to consider that charity begins at home."

Other soldiers sought escape from the horrors of military life by deserting. Nearly a full year before the woes of Valley Forge, Adjutant Alexander Hamilton reported that "hardly a day passes without some deserter" bolting from the ranks. During periods of great suffering, the desertion rate dramatically increased. Joseph Galloway, the Loyalist intelligence official from Pennsylvania, reported nearly 1,500 defections—a figure that included civilian as well as military activity—during the winter of 1777–1778. A recent study indicates that about ten soldiers deserted each day from Washington's camp at Valley Forge. During the long course of the war, roughly two of every ten soldiers deserted. Even more might have departed, but, when challenged, officers sometimes made concessions—as General Montgomery was compelled to do to keep his Canadian invasion force intact—of more abundant food and clothing, or even cash bounties.

Men deserted for numerous reasons. Many deserting soldiers reflected the poor state of recruiting. Some of these "hungry lean fac'd Villians" took their enlistment money, then took leave of the army at the first opportunity. Some deserters were of foreign birth, and the ideological and nationalistic sentiments that motivated others were alien to them; one contemporary, for instance, estimated that early in 1778 three out of four deserters had been born abroad.

But most deserters simply skipped out because of the difficulties and dangers that confronted them daily. Not all men fled with the intention of never returning. Some absented themselves from duty, as an officer reported, "to produce a draught of milk from the cows in a farmer's yard." Many intended to escape temporarily from the hazards of battle or from the fatigue of camp duty, like the private who was discovered "stowed . . . away snugly in an old papermill." A few soldiers deliberately overstayed legitimate furloughs, figuring that "my country should give me a day to return to camp." One private was prepared to return when his lieutenant arrived home on leave and encouraged his subordinate to linger for another week; the young private no doubt joyfully "remained another week and then went with the officer to camp and had no fault found." Many, however, deserted with the hope of never returning, and many struck out because they believed the soldiers were forgotten by the civilians back home. "[W]e doubt the Willingness of our Countrymen, to Assist us," wrote one soldier, who probably spoke for many. "You cannot blame us," he added. "I despise My Countrymen. I wish I could say I was not born in America. . . . I am in Rags, have lain the Rain on the Ground for 40 hours past, & only a Jerk of fresh Beef & that without Salt to dine on this day. . . ." Amid such distress the bounties afforded by home grew more alluring. "How impatient of Home am I at this Distance, in so inclement a Season, when a little unwell—Home, Home, Home, O Dear Home," a private lamented to his diary. . . .

From the outset the officers of the Continental army adopted the view of European officers. They saw themselves as a special caste, within both the army and society generally. Although they were hardly the only men who gave up economic enterprises at home to risk life and limb, they manifested an air of selflessness. A spirit of élan emerged quickly among officers. They depicted the army as a "place for sociability, friendship, and happiness" for those within this elite cadre. Certain badges of honor—codes of conduct—sprang up among army leaders. To an officer, one explained, "honor is so feelingly alive that it must smart and agonize at the least show of aspersion." A "range of duelling," commonplace in the officer corps of many European armies, grew fashionable in the Continental army among men who believed their honor had been besmirched. Failure to attain promotion was regarded as such a blow to one's personal honor that it drove some officers to quit the army; at least one officer, Abiel Leonard, a chaplain, committed suicide when he was not elevated to a more important command. More than anything, the officers longed for fame and flattery, a craving that led some to act recklessly, exposing their men to unnecessary risks.

These attitudes aroused suspicions in a society pledged to increased egalitarianism. John Adams grew weary "with the wrangles between military officers, high and low. They quarrel like cats and dogs. They worry one another like mastiffs, scrambling for rank and pay like apes for nuts." In addition, he concluded early in the war that it was unwise to "trust your generals, with too much power, for too long," and he argued that it "becomes us to attend early to the restraining" of officers. . . .

The leadership felt no moral constraints in ordering a variety of physical punishments, although most leaders, with an eye toward morale, attempted to mingle the velvet glove with the mailed fist. Still, most officers believed that brutality was sometimes required, and many leaders were impatient with what they regarded as leniency. Joseph Reed, Washington's secretary, believed that the time-honored military punishment of thirty-nine lashes was ineffective. He urged even harsher codes, believing that the men were so "contemptible" of this form of excoriation—"it is very frequent for them," he claimed, "to offer to take as many more [stripes] for a pint of rum"—that disorder was rampant. Alexander Hamilton likewise exhorted his chiefs to order more drastic punishments. "An execution or two, by way of example, would strike terror, and powerfully discourage the wicked practices going on" among the troops. Hamilton believed corporal punishment merely tended to "excite compassion" for the victim and to "breed disgust" toward the officers.

Initially, Washington modestly punished even serious offenders. In 1775, for instance, he ordered a deserter to forfeit nine days' pay, to perform latrine duty for six days, and to wear at all times during the ensuing week a sign bearing the word "Deserter." This attempt to mobilize peer pressure as a deterrent against a multiplicity of practices was made in an endless variety of ways. Some officers attempted to embarrass soldiers who refused to reenlist by cursing them in the presence of their comrades and denouncing them as the "worst of all creatures." At times the soldiers themselves took the initiative. Captain Simon Thayer, who served under Arnold during the invasion of Canada, noted the time several soldiers seized four men who refused to do their share in a work detail and "led them from place to place with Halters round their necks, exposing them to the ridicule of the soldiers, as a punishment Due to their effeminate courage."

However, whatever constraints Washington might have displayed initially were quickly abandoned. In fact, the civilian authorities at times were compelled to restrain the commander. At one point Washington requested that the maximum number of lashes that the army was permitted to apply to an offending culprit should be increased from thirty-nine to five hundred. Congress refused, and set the maximum in the Articles of War at one hundred lashes. Many Congressmen believed discipline was essential for "preserving the health and spirits of the men," but they also felt that soldierly attributes could be acquired without resorting to "cruelty, severity, tyranny." Still, during the Battle of Long Island, when the fate of the rebellion seemed to hang on its outcome, Washington ordered that any soldier attempting "to skulk, lay down, or retreat, without orders . . . be instantly shot as an example." When the fighting commenced, the General rode among the troops and "laid his Cane over many of the Officers who showed their men the Example of running."

Flogging was the preferred form of punishment. An established ceremony normally accompanied the practice. The troops were assembled and the convicted soldier was marched—quite literally marched, for he stepped to a drummed cadence—to the punishment area, where, after his shirt was removed, he was tied to a tree or post. The sentence was read and the "drummer" began to administer the flogging. A "whip formed of several small knotted cords" was the usual tool. Often the lash "cut through the skin at every stroke," providing a ghastly sight, as was intended, for the soldiers who were compelled to watch the spectacle. While the lash ordinarily was laid on the back, there is evidence that some were whipped on the "naked Buttocks." Additional humiliations were often conjured up. Some men, for instance, were "dress'd in Petticoats & Caps" for their flogging. Often, following the final stripe, salt was rubbed liberally into the lacerated flesh to heighten the torment. . . .

Other forms of punishment often were inflicted. Some men were compelled to "ride the wooden horse" or to stand in the pillary. Others were dry-shaved, and still others had their hair curled or plaited in the prevailing feminine fashion. Also, soldiers were made to run the gauntlet. This practice called for the bare-backed victim to walk, not run, between two rows of men furnished with sticks or switches. A drummer held a bayonet-equipped rifle to the chest of the victim and backed very slowly down the line, insuring that each soldier was permitted to strike the condemned man. Sometimes men died from the floggings received, whether at the whipping post or from the ordeal of the gauntlet. . . .

One of the most noticeable aspects of army life to men subjected to such a brutal regimen was the extraordinary difference between their lot and the life enjoyed by the officer caste. The army, of course, was modeled on the prevailing caste attitudes of civilian society in the 1770s. Many leaders of America's rebellion did not find it hypocritical to embrace the new republican principles while openly fretting over the growing power of the people. As can be seen from Elbridge Gerry lamenting that "the people . . . feel rather too much their own importance" and the South Carolina clergyman trembling at the prospect that "every silly clown, and illiterate mechanic" might govern, the old class values of the ruling elite died slowly. In addition, the American army was still patterned on the European model, and in this age, according to Professor Corvisier, the Continental "military hierarchy conformed fairly closely to the social hierarchy" of the ancien regime. In Washington's army of the rebellion, therefore, as in American society in general, a wide gap existed between the living conditions and perquisites of the rulers and the ruled. It should not be surprising, therefore, that men might be punished for intemperance while they daily witnessed officers appearing openly in an inebriated state. Moreover, the very leader who might have a man flogged for excessive drinking was powerless to do more than complain about "Effeminate officers, who [would] rather pass their time in tippling than turn it to the profit and advantage of their country." Soldiers might be punished brutally for accidentally discharging a weapon, but the duel, in which one officer might deliberately kill or maim another officer, was regarded as a mark of honor within the officer caste. The common soldier additionally could readily perceive that substantially different supplies were allotted to officers. On General Sullivan's expedition against the Indians in Pennsylvania and New York in 1779, officers were furnished with a quart of whiskey for every pint issued to the men; moreover, officers were ordered to see "that water be immediately mixed with the soldiers' whiskey." At the same time in 1779 that soldiers were complaining of monotonous sustenance and inadequate food supplies, and Washington was urging Congress to increase the quantity of victuals, the commander, in one week, dined on ham, bacon, roast beef, greens, beefsteak pies, crab, and apple pie. . . .

Resentment toward the officers often threatened to blow up, and sometimes individuals or small groups, did erupt. Once a death sentence was commuted at the last moment following "secret and open threats" by the soldiers against the officers who had sanctioned the execution. "I believe it was well" that the commutation was ordered, a private stated, for the condemned man's "blood would not have been the only blood that would have been spilt: the troops were greatly exasperated." A Pennsylvanian witnessed the execution of a Virginian who had shot an officer, then he calmly recorded that the murderer was "certainly justified" in his deed. Another soldier longed for the courage to drill an officer who needled him. "I heartily wish," he wrote, that "some person would make an experiment on him to make the sun shine thro' his head with an ounce ball.". . . Full-fledged mutinies occasionally erupted, and during these riots some soldiers hunted down and murdered officers who angered them.

Securing nonmilitia soldiers had never been an easy task in the colonial years. Many colonists had fled Europe because of their strong antipathy to warfare and, having made their escape, they were not about to join a military force in the New World. Nor did these predominately rural peoples wish to abandon their farms during the planting season or at the harvest. . . .

Some enlistments were solicited by a combination of fast talk and alcohol. Many men signed up under the influence, but few were as lucky as the drunken Maryland carpenter whose release was granted when his enraged wife accosted the authorities with "every vile name she could think of." Recruiters also used barbecues and even dances to fill their quotas. The general patriotic fervor that swept the colonies netted some recruits, particularly in the early days of the conflict. Many men joined in those days in the belief that the war would be short and relatively bloodless. These men, one such idealist noted, "had a fixed expectation and a strong desire of meeting the british in real combat. Those feelings absorbed the more *tender* ones." Another recruit of this ilk was "unconscious of danger, and animated by a hope of applause from [his] country." It was, in the words of a popular poem of the day. "Fame and dear freedom" that induced many to volunteer.

Some enlisted for psychological reasons they could not hope to fathom. One recruit spoke of his father's pride upon "seeing me dressed in military uniform, with epaulets on my shoulders, and a sword by my side." Another enlistee mentioned that when he agreed to serve he was the center of attention in his village for a few shining hours. The wholehearted support of the endeavor by women helped provoke men to join. "It was not necessary to urge anyone to enlist," one soldier wrote. "I presume," he added, "that female influence . . . was never more evident than at this time: they appeared to vie with their brethren in sustaining the idea of a fixed and determined resistance."

Many men were forcefully persuaded to join. One soldier claimed a recruiter told him he would see that his grain and fields would be destroyed if he refused to serve. Another soldier acknowledged that he enlisted to escape jail for some offense at home. Those already in the army were urged to reenlist, and some were threatened with suicidal missions or the prospect of inadequate food supplies during the remaining weeks of their tour if they refused to continue to serve. . . .

Who did serve in the Revolutionary forces? Probably about 100,000 men, of a total population in excess of 3 million persons, actually bore arms at one time or another between 1775 and 1783. Washington hoped to have 75,000 soldiers in the field for the campaign of 1777, but his peak strength was 18,472, and that was attained on October 1, 1778. The armies included British deserters, slaves, free blacks, indentured servants, even children twelve to thirteen years of age. The bulk of these forces, however, consisted of young adult and teenage white freemen. A recent study of Maryland recruits in 1782 indicated that about 40 percent were foreign-born. The average age of the native-born soldier was twenty-one years, but the median age of the foreign-born was twenty-nine years. Many had only recently completed a period of indentured servitude. Economically, the average soldier among these Marylanders was in the bottom third of his state. Some troops in the Continental army were conscripted, but most enlisted. "As a group," John Shy has written, "they were poorer, more marginal, less well anchored in the society. Perhaps we should not be surprised; it is easy to imagine men like this actually being attracted by the relative affluence, comfort, security, prestige, and even the chance of satisfying human relationships offered by the Continental Army."

The soldiers are "so sick of this way of life, and so home sick," General Greene wrote at the end of the first year of the war, that most were unlikely to reenlist. He was correct. Perhaps as many as 80 percent of those who bore arms in 1775 were home again by early 1776. Thomas Paine railed at the "summer soldier" in 1776, and in 1781, a few months before Cornwallis's defeat at Yorktown, another patriot lamented that if "the Salvation of the Country had depended on their staying Ten or Fifteen days, I don't believe [the soldiers] would have done it." Most soldiers, this writer anguished, believed that "he was a good Soldier that served his time out," and nothing beyond. Daniel Morgan, the Virginia laborer who rose to the rank of general, wondered "what is the reason we cant Have more men in the field—so many men in the country Nearby idle for want of employment." John Adams knew precisely the answer to Morgan's query. It hardly was "credible," he thought, "that men who could get at home better living, more comfortable lodgings, more than double the wages, in safety, not exposed to the sickness of the camp, would bind themselves during the war. . . ."

The experience of war, then, was a blend of monotony and anticipated danger, of brutal discipline and an exacting regimen that circumscribed one's personal liberties, of exhilaration mingled with churning terror, of physical toil, needless tasks assigned by callous taskmasters, deprivation, disease, indecency, guilt, hatred, loneliness, homesickness, inequities, and, above all else for most men, the ardent, ever-present longing for the end of one's tour of duty.

But this was the experience of those in the army. Some—the political leaders who shared responsibility for the war—had the luxury of facing the war well out of harm's way.

FOR FURTHER STUDY

1. The conduct of war—like governmental institutions and class attitudes—may reflect the national characteristics of different societies. Some people, for example, believe there is a distinctive Prussian, English, or American way of making war. Do you see any peculiarly "American" traits in the attitudes of revolutionary soldiers?

2. The kinds of extraordinary disciplinary, recruiting, and desertion problems described by Ferling are not usually associated with our army in World Wars I and II. Tell how the following factors might help to explain the apparent contrast: differences in governmental authority and organization, the backgrounds of the soldiers in the two periods, and developments in propaganda.

3. The Revolutionary War might also be compared to the Vietnam War. Some people today see the former as the embodiment of selfless sacrifice and patriotism, while viewing the widespread draft dodging and dissent during the Vietnam War as a national disgrace. How does Ferling's article modify your view of these and other American wars?

4. What evidence do you see in modern America that our society has seriously modified its distrust of a standing army and militarism?

FOR FURTHER READING

For an interesting look at the emergence of a separate American identity in the military see Fred Anderson, *A People's Army: Massachusetts Soldiers and Society in the Seven Years' War* (1984). An excellent broad study of the establishment of a revolutionary army and the ideals of the new republic is Charles Royster's *"A Revolutionary People at War": The Continental Army and American Character, 1775–1783* (1979). James K. Martin and Mark E. Lender, *A Respectable Army: The Military Origins of the Republic, 1763–1789* (1982), argues that most of the fighting was done by the poor and unfortunate, rather than by the middle and upper classes. Several other studies include Lawrence Cress's *Citizens in Arms: The Army and the Militia in American Society to the War of 1812* (1982), John Shy's *A People Numerous and Armed: Reflections on the Military Struggle for American Independence* (1976), and E. Wayne Carp's *To Starve an Army at Pleasure: Continental Army Administration and American Political Culture, 1775–1783* (1984).

Many students are interested in military leaders. One excellent study is Don Higginbotham, *George Washington and the American Military Tradition* (1985). For more general military history of the war see Piers Mackesy, *The War for America, 1775–1783* (1964), and for an overall guide to this important period use either Edward Countryman, *The American Revolution* (1985), or Robert Middlekauf, *The Glorious Cause: The American Revolution, 1763–1789* (1982).

The social context of the revolution in the South is discussed in Rhys Isaac's *The Transformation of Virginia, 1740–1790* (1982); for the North see Robert A. Gross, *The Minutemen and Their World* (1976). Gary B. Nash concentrates on cities in *The Urban Crucible: Social Change, Political Consciousness, and the Origins of the American Revolution* (1979). If you are interested in just how radical the revolution was, read Gordon S. Wood, *The Radicalism of the American Revolution* (1992).

CHAPTER 8

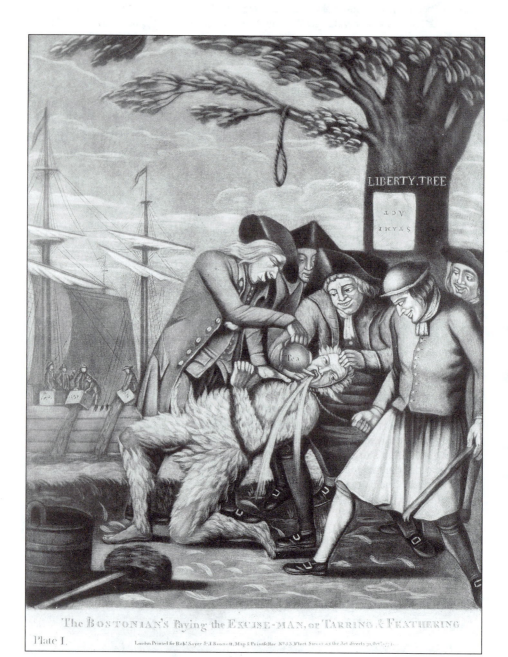

Metropolitan Museum of Art, Bequest of Charles Allen Munn, 1924 (24.90.32)

"The Bostonians Paying the Excise-Man," (detail) by Philip Dawe, 1774, shows the punishment of John Malcolm, discussed in this reading.

SOCIAL WAR

WALLACE BROWN

One of the most elusive goals of the historian, and of the human mind in general, is objectivity. In our time, most historians recognize that, try as they may to avoid it, some prejudice and personal values are bound to creep into their thought and into the history they write. One illustration of this is in the difference in treatment that history accords to the winners and losers in any revolution. Rebels who fail don't get a very good press from historians, since their society is likely to denounce the revolutionary leaders as traitors or madmen. If the revolution succeeds, the same men may be celebrated as patriots and statesmen, while the ruling group that is overthrown is castigated as oppressive or corrupt.

Between 1765 and 1775, British colonial society developed some serious internal divisions and antagonisms. Upon the outbreak of war, provinces, towns, and families were split, and brother fought brother with all the hatred that civil war can engender. By 1783, as many as 80,000 people had been driven out of the colonies; farms and businesses of Loyalists were confiscated, and thousands of these British adherents were intimidated and mistreated. Many of them had been distinguished contributors to colonial society—governors, judges, ministers, farmers, craftsmen, and laborers. Had the British won the war, Thomas Hutchinson, Joseph Galloway, William Franklin, and Jonathan Boucher would today be as celebrated as are John Adams, Thomas Jefferson, Patrick Henry, and John Hancock.

One question worth pondering is what American society may have lost by the exile of the Loyalists and the victory of the Patriot cause. A substantial reservoir of political talent and experience certainly evaporated, but among the many who cast their lot for independence were an extraordinary number of men of talent to take the Loyalists' places. More difficult to judge is the loss to American thought and culture. A number of Loyalists were able or distinguished scientists, artists, writers, and religious leaders who made their contributions in Canada or Europe rather than here. More important than such

individuals was the effect of the break on American political and constitutional thought, which—it has been argued—suffered the loss of a valid conservative tradition with the exile of the Loyalists.

Another question that has interested historians since the Revolution began is just what a Tory or Loyalist was. The simplest definition is that he was
one who remained loyal to England. This raises the question of why they
were loyal, whereas immediate neighbors of similar background and position
became revolutionary leaders. Many answers to this question have been offered—that it was one's religion that made the difference, or one's wealth, age,
occupation, national origins, or temperament. Yet for all the Loyalists who
were influenced by such factors, there were at least as many men of the same
class who chose the Patriot side.

Wallace Brown, a contemporary student of these questions, has made
use of statistical techniques to try to determine the percentage of Loyalists of
different occupations, religions, and so forth. Since the statistical parts of his
studies are based on fragmentary records, they have been criticized by some
historians. However, his book *The Good Americans,* from which the following
selection is taken, is a general study of Loyalism that is less dependent on statistics than his earlier work. Chapter 5 of *The Good Americans* presents a vivid
account of the suffering that Loyalists endured during the American War for
Independence. If few groups have since been subjected to such direct violence, the persecution of the Loyalists nonetheless reminds one of the fate of
many another unpopular minority in later American history. And it should
make us cautious about accepting only a "winner's" view of historical losers.

In November, 1777, the Continental Congress recommended the confiscation of
Loyalist estates, a suggestion already made by Thomas Paine, and in some places
already acted upon. All states finally amerced, taxed, or confiscated much Loyalist
property, and in addition New York and South Carolina taxed Loyalist property in
order to compensate robbery victims. Some towns simply raffled off Tory property. Patriot officers requisitioned horses and supplies from Loyalists rather than
Whigs, and, of course, there was much old-fashioned looting, particularly of the
property of exiles. . . .

Although the majority of active Loyalists suffered much loss of property, some
attempted by various subterfuges to preserve their estates quite apart from having
a wife or third party act as purchaser. One scheme was to make over one's property, or make a sham sale, to a sympathetic, moderate friend who had escaped
suspicion.

Abridgement of pages 127–146 from *The Good Americans: Loyalists in the American Revolution,* by Wallace Brown.
Copyright © 1969 by Wallace Brown. Reprinted by permission of the author.

Much commoner was the device used by exiles of leaving their wives or relatives behind in order to keep a foot in both camps. For example, Benjamin Pickman fled from Salem, Massachusetts, in 1775, but left his wife behind to look after their property, to which he returned ten years later. Some brothers may even have chosen opposite sides for such a reason. As the British claims commissioners commented on one split family, "it is possible that this may be a shabby family Compact . . . to preserve the property whether Great Britain or America prevailed."

The overall severity of the various laws against the Loyalists has been estimated as follows:

"Harshest"—New York, South Carolina.
"Harsh"—Massachusetts, New Jersey, Pennsylvania.
"Light"—Rhode Island, Connecticut, Virginia, North Carolina.
"Lightest"—New Hampshire, Delaware, Maryland, Georgia.

With some exceptions, notably Georgia, laws were harshest in states where Loyalists were most powerful, and as the war progressed, the purpose of the laws changed from conversion to "revenge and hate." Similarly, enforcement varied and was usually severest where danger was greatest and civil war bitterest.

A prominent Southern Tory reported that in Virginia, where the Loyalists were weak and little problem, the property of those who joined the British army went to their wives and children "on the Spot . . . as if the Father was dead," and he noted that his own wife "had never been molested but on the contrary treated with the utmost Kindness and Respect." Other Loyalists described being turned off their property with only the clothes on their backs.

But perhaps more typical was the fate of the Chandler family of Worcester, Massachusetts. Colonel John Chandler, a very prominent citizen of distinguished Massachusetts pedigree, dubbed "Tory John" and later in England the "Honest Refugee," fled from Boston with the British army to become a permanent, proscribed exile. For over two years his wife and family continued to enjoy their property undisturbed, until the Worcester Committee of Correspondence began a process that resulted in the confiscation of all but a third of their real and personal property, which third was reserved for Mrs. Chandler's use as long as she remained in the United States. Her husband did not return (he was forbidden to by an act of October, 1778), and on her death special legislation was needed to secure her property for her children.

A myriad of particularities could play a part in determining the extent of persecution. A well-liked or respected Tory (and there were a few such) might well escape, as might someone whose skills were especially valued, for example, a doctor. Influential but quiet Loyalists were more apt to avoid penalties than those of lower social standing or those more vociferous in their beliefs.

The zeal of the patriots could be extremely capricious and, as always with witchhunts, frequently ridiculous and heavy-handed. One citizen was accosted for naming his dog "Tory," the implication being that a Tory was forced to lead a dog's life. In 1776 at Stratford, Connecticut, an Episcopal minister was brought before the local committee because he had officiated at a baptism where the child was named Thomas Gage. The committee viewed the action as a "designed insult" and censured the cleric. In the same state Zephaniah Beardslee reported that he was "very much abused" for naming his daughter Charlotte, after the queen. It may be noted that Beardslee, apparently a very serious Loyalist, had also been found drinking the king's health. The frequent persecution of Tories for this activity, however, is not as picayune as it seems, because toasts presuppose groups in taverns and the chance of Loyalist plots and associations. Thus, Abraham Cuyler held a gathering in Albany, New York, In June, 1776, that featured drinking and the singing of "God Save the King." At last the enraged Whig citizens crashed the party and carried the royal merrymakers off to jail. . . .

The results of Loyalism might simply be social ostracism—being sent to Coventry—as, for instance, happened to James Allen, who noted in his diary for February 17, 1777: "I never knew how painful it is to be secluded from the free conversation of one's friends"; and to George Watson, a mandamus councillor, when he entered a church at Plymouth, Massachusetts, and "a great number of the principal inhabitants left." Or it might mean serious loss of services, as when the blacksmiths of Worcester County, Massachusetts, refused to work for any Loyalists, their employees, or their dependents; or an economic boycott, as in Connecticut, where the local committee forbade "all Persons whatever viz. Merchants Mechanicks Millers and Butchers and Co. from supplying . . . John Sayre or Family with any manner of Thing whatever." Lawyers, teachers, doctors, apothecaries, and others often lost their customers and hence their livelihoods. Mathew Robinson, a Newport trader, from the first branded as "a Rank Torey," suffered several indignities, including the pulling down of his fences by a "multitude . . . under colour of laying out a Highway" and climaxing in 1781 when, after *"a New England Saint"* charged that Robinson "drank the King's Health, and damn'd the Congress and call'd them damn'd Rebels and Presbyterians," he was imprisoned by the rebels without examination, this being even "against their own Bill of Rights."

In many areas—for example, New York—the Loyalists were allowed to sell their property before departing, but such hurried, desperate sales were unlikely to net a fair price, and the result amounted to confiscation.

All wars and revolutions cause great mental strain and suffering, most of which goes unmeasured. The history of the Revolutionary era is liberally punctuated with stories of Loyalists who succumbed to melancholia, became mad, died, or committed suicide.

Alexander Harvey, a Charleston lawyer, wound up in a private English madhouse, having been "driven to Distraction" by his experiences as a Loyalist; George Miller, a North Carolina merchant whose fright had conquered his Loyalist principles, was thrown "into Convulsions" by the strain of serving in the American militia; Peter Harrison's death came after the shock of Lexington, and with it America lost its greatest colonial architect; several Loyalists, including the wife of William Franklin, simply died of "a Broken Heart"; the widow of Dr. Robert Gibbs of South Carolina recounted that the prospect of the loss of his property "so preyed upon his Spirits" that he died. Andrew Miller, of Halifax, North

Carolina, was estranged from all his friends by his Loyalism, which literally killed him; others chose suicide—Millington Lockwood of Connecticut was wounded in the head, lost his reason, and drowned himself, while some years later, in London, after years of fruitless waiting for compensation, an unnamed, ruined Loyalist shot himself in despair, blaming an ungrateful country.

Although Americans at the time of the Revolution would clearly have found it odd, today one of the sharpest historical debates is over the question of how far the American Revolution was a *real* revolution. Even those historians who, noting the social dislocation, argue that the American Revolution was rather like the French Revolution stress the absence of the Terror. Mass executions there were not, a guillotine there was not, yet atrocities and terror there most certainly were. It is fitting that in the beginning the rebels "hoisted the Red Flag or Flag of Defence."

Leaving aside civil-war aspects such as the execution and maltreatment of prisoners and the burning of towns (by both sides; for example, the Americans fired Norfolk and Portsmouth; the British, Falmouth and Fairfield), we can cite a great range of fates that awaited the Loyalists; they were catalogued by "Papinian" as tarring and feathering, rail riding,

> . . . chaining men together by the dozens, and driving them, like herds of cattle, into distant provinces, flinging them into loathsome jails, confiscating their estates, shooting them in swamps and woods as suspected Tories, hanging them after a mock trial; and all this because they would not abjure their rightful Sovereign, and bear arms against him.

Tarring and feathering (pine tar and goose feathers) became the classic Whig treatment of the Tories, and the British Government believed there was "no better proof of Loyalty" than suffering this punishment. A famous instance of it occurred in Boston on January 25, 1774, and is worth recounting in some detail.

At about eight o'clock in the evening a club-wielding mob milled along Cross Street. Their objective was John Malcolm, a distinguished but hot-tempered veteran of the French and Indian War, a native Bostonian, an ex-overseas merchant turned royal customs official, and a highly unpopular man for many reasons connected with both his personality (he was inordinately quarrelsome) and his job.

His recent arrival in Boston had been preceded by the unpopular news that in 1771 he had helped the governor of North Carolina against those reputedly Whiggish rebels known as the Regulators and that in October, 1773, he had officiously seized a brigantine at Falmouth (now Portland), Maine. Malcolm waited, ready and armed, behind barred doors. Undeterred, the mob raised ladders, broke an upstairs window, captured their prey, dragged him onto a sled, and pulled him along King Street to the Customs House, or Butcher's House, as it was popularly known, where the spectators gave three mighty cheers.

Although it was "one of the severest cold nights" of the winter, so cold that both Boston Harbor and even the very ink as it touched paper had frozen hard, the wretched man was put in a cart, stripped "to buff and breeches," and dealt the punishment of tarring and feathering, which American patriots were soon to convert into a major spectator sport. Malcolm, self-styled "Single Knight of the Tarr," as opposed to English Knights of the Garter, had already suffered the same indignity the year before for his conduct at Falmouth. He later claimed to be the first in America tarred for loyalty.

A contemporary description gives a good idea of how Malcolm and many others were treated:

> The following is the Recipe for an effectual Operation. "First strip a Person naked, then heat the Tar until it is thin, and pour it upon the naked Flesh, or rub it over with a Tar Brush, *quantum sufficit.* After which, sprinkle decently upon the Tar, whilst it is yet warm, as many Feathers as will stick to it. Then hold a lighted Candle to the Feathers, and try to set it all on Fire; if it will burn so much the better. But as the Experiment is often made in cold Weather; it will not then succeed—take also an Halter and put it round the Person's Neck, and then cart him the Rounds."

Malcolm, flogged and otherwise molested at intervals, was paraded around various crowded streets with his neck in a halter and was finally taken to the Liberty Tree, where he refused to resign his royal office or to curse Thomas Hutchinson, the hated governor of Massachusetts.

The crowd then set off for the gallows on Boston Neck. On the way Malcolm gasped an affirmative when one of his tormentors asked if he was thirsty and was given a bowl of strong tea and ordered to drink the king's health. Malcolm was next told to drink the queen's health; then two more quarts of tea were produced with the command to drink to the health of the Prince of Wales.

"Make haste, you have nine more healths to drink," shouted one of the mob.

"For God's sake, Gentlemen, be merciful, I'm ready to burst; if I drink a drop more, I shall die," Malcolm implored.

"Suppose you do, you die in a good cause, and it is as well to be drowned as hanged," was the reply.

The nine healths, beginning with the "Bishop of Osnabrug," were forced down the victim's throat. Malcolm "turned pale, shook his Head, and instantly filled the Bowl which he had just emptied."

"What, are you sick of the royal family?"

"No, my stomach nauseates the tea; it rises at it like poison."

"And yet you rascal, your whole fraternity at the Custom House would drench us with this poison, and we are to have our throats cut if it will not stay upon our stomachs."

At the gallows the noose was placed in position around Malcolm's neck and he was threatened with hanging, but he still refused to submit, whereupon he was "basted" with a rope for a while, and finally, on pain of losing his ears, he gave in and cursed the governor. The stubborn, brave man was further carted around the town, made to repeat various humiliating oaths, and finally deposited back at his home just before midnight, half frozen, an arm dislocated, and, as he said, "in a most mizerable setuation Deprived of his senses." Five days later, bedridden and "terribly bruised," he dictated a complaint to Governor Hutchinson, which his injuries obliged him to sign with an X.

The frost and tar caused an infection that made his skin peel extensively. However, he was careful to preserve a piece of skin with the tar and feathers still adhering (the stuff was the very devil to get off), which he carried to England as proof of his sufferings when, somewhat recovered, he set sail on May 2, 1774, to try to gain compensation for his loyalty.

Another Tory punishment that became traditional was the gruesome riding on a rail that sometimes followed tarring and feathering, but was severe enough in itself. It consisted of jogging the victim roughly along on "a sharp rail" between his legs. The painful effect of these "grand Toory Rides," as a contemporary called them, can readily be imagined. Seth Seely, a Connecticut farmer, was brought before the local committee in 1776 and for signing a declaration to support the king's laws was "put on a Rail carried on mens Shoulders thro the Streets, then put into the Stocks and besmeared with Eggs and was robbed of money for the Entertainment of the Company."

Persecution of the Loyalists came in many forms. In 1778 prisoners in Vermont were made to tread a road through the snow in the Green Mountains. The wife of Edward Brinley was pregnant and waiting out her confinement at Roxbury, Massachusetts, accompanied by "a guard of Rebels always in her room, who treated her with great rudeness and indecency, exposing her to the view of their banditti, as a sight 'See a tory woman' and striped her and her Children of all their Linens and Cloths." Peter Guire, of Connecticut, was branded on the forehead with the letters *G. R.* (George Rex). Samuel Jarvis, also of Connecticut, related that the following treatment made his whole family very ill:

> That your Memorialist for his Attachment to constitutional Government was taken with his Wife and Famely, consisting of three Daughters and one little Son by a Mob of daring and unfeeling Rebels from his Dwelling House in the dead of Night Striped of everything, put on board Whale Boats and Landed on Long Island in the Month of August last about 2 oClock in the Morning Oblieging them to wade almost to their Middles in the Water.

Probably the best-known mobbing in Philadelphia was that of Dr. John Kearsley, whose widow finally submitted a claim to the commissioners. Kearsley, a leading physician, pill manufacturer, and horse dealer, was a pugnacious American with strong Loyalist views. He was seized by a mob in September, 1775, and had his hand bayoneted; then he was carried through the streets to the tune of "Rogue's March." Sabine reports that he took off his wig with his injured hand and, "swinging it around his head, huzzaed louder and longer than his persecutors." This display of spirit notwithstanding, he nearly died following this treatment, according to his widow. His house was later ransacked, he was arrested, and he finally died in jail.

Atrocious punishments of Loyalists were sometimes carried out by local authorities in semilegal fashion—it was noted that the tarring and feathering of a New York victim in 1775 "was conducted with that regularity and decorum that ought to be observed in all publick punishments." But just as often mobs, drumhead courts, and all the horrors of vigilante policing were found. Indeed it is possible that the term "lynch law" derives from Charles Lynch, a Bedford County, Virginia, justice of the peace who became renowned for his drastic, cruel action against neighboring Tories.

The number of Loyalists subjected to cruel, often extra-legal, punishments can only be estimated, and likewise the number of those murdered or executed "legally" will never be known, but no one familiar with the sources—Whig newspapers are full of accounts of executions—can doubt that it is substantial, although the statement by a New York Loyalist that the rebels "made a practice of hanging people up on a slight pretence" is no doubt an exaggeration. Probably only fear of reprisals kept numbers from being much larger than they were. The carrying out of the supreme penalty was usually reserved for some overt aid to the British such as spying, piloting ships, guiding troops to the attack, recruiting, counterfeiting.

One of the most notorious executions of a Loyalist was that of John Roberts, a native-born Pennsylvania Quaker, who had aided the British occupying forces in Philadelphia and rather foolhardily had not departed with them. His trial was in 1778, and even many Whigs petitioned the authorities for a pardon, but in vain. A contemporary described the situation thus:

> Roberts' wife, with ten children, went to Congress, threw themselves on their knees and supplicated mercy, but in vain. His behaviour at the gallows did honor to human nature. He told his audience that his conscience acquitted him of guilt; that he suffered for doing his duty to his Sovereign; that his blood would one day be demanded at their hands; and then turning to his children, charged and exhorted them to remember his principles, for which he died, and to adhere to them while they had breath. This is the substance of his speech; after which he suffered with the resolution of a Roman.

In 1792 the state of Pennsylvania restored Roberts' confiscated estate to his widow, Jane, a belated act of justice, for it seems Roberts had been a scapegoat, only one among so very many who had cooperated with the British. Roberts' behavior would doubtless have made him a remembered hero had he suffered for the other side. Similarly, in Connecticut, Moses Dunbar was tried and hanged for accepting a British commission and recruiting troops at about the same time that Nathan Hale suffered the same penalty. Connecticut honors Hale but forgets Dunbar. One of the more bizarre executions was reported by the *Boston Gazette* for November 3, 1777, under the date line Fishkill: "Last Thursday, one Taylor, a spy was hanged at Hurley, who was detected with a letter to Burgoyne, which he had swallowed in a silver ball, but by the assistance of a tartar emetic he discharged the same."

But perhaps more moving across the years than accounts of atrocities are the more pedestrian misfortunes of war. Women in particular are always the great sufferers, being separated from their husbands and sons, living in constant dread of bereavement. In 1780 Mary Donnelly petitioned the British authorities in New York for relief. Her husband had been serving on board a privateer when "about seven months ago as my youngest Child lay expireing in my Arms an account came of the Vessil being lost in a Storm." Mrs. Donnelly was now destitute, "frequently being affraid to open my Eyes on the Daylight least I should hear my infant cry for Bread and not have it in my power to relieve him. The first meal I had eat for three days at one time was a morsel of dry bread and a lump of ice."

On June 6, 1783, Phebe Ward, of East Chester, wrote to her husband Edmund, a native of the province of New York:

Kind Husband

I am sorry to acquant you that our farme is sold. . . .

thay said if I did not quitt posesion that thay had aright to take any thing on the farme or in the house to pay the Cost of a law sute and imprisen me I have sufered most Every thing but death it self in your long absens pray Grant me spedy Releaf or God only knows what will be com of me and my frendsles Children

thay say my posesion was nothing youre husband has forfeted his estate by Joining the British Enemy with a free and vollentary will and thereby was forfeted to the Stat and sold

All at present from your cind and Loveing Wife

phebe Ward
pray send me spedeay anser.

One of the most pathetic stories of all concerns Filer Dibblee, a native-born lawyer, and his family. In August, 1776, they fled from Stamford to Long Island, but a few months later the rebels turned Dibblee's wife and five children "naked into the Streets," having stolen the very clothes from their backs as well as having plundered the house. The family fled to New York city, where Dibblee obtained sufficient credit to settle at Oyster Bay, Long Island, but in 1778 the rebels plundered the family a second time and carried Dibblee as prisoner to Connecticut, where he remained imprisoned six months until exchanged. With further credit the family established themselves at Westhills, Long Island, where they were "plundered and stripped" a third time; then came a move to Hempstead, Long Island, and in 1780 a fourth ravaging. Dibblee now, for the first time, applied for relief from the commander in chief and received about one hundred dollars. In 1783 the whole family moved to St. John, New Brunswick, where they managed to survive a rough winter in a log cabin, but Dibblee's "fortitude gave way" at the prospect of imprisonment for his considerable indebtedness and the fate his family would suffer as a consequence. The result was that he "grew Melancholy, which soon deprived him of his Reason, and for months could not be left by himself," and finally in March, 1784, "whilst the Famely were at Tea, Mr. Dibblee walked back and forth in the Room, seemingly much composed: but unobserved he took a Razor from the Closet, threw himself on the bed, drew the Curtains, and cut his own throat."

Shortly afterward the Dibblee house was accidentally burned to the ground, was then rebuilt by the heroic widow, only to be accidentally razed again the same year by an Indian servant girl.

It is not surprising that imprisonment and escape loom large in Loyalist annals. The most celebrated prison was in Connecticut at the Simsbury (now East Granby) copper mines, where the ruins still afford a dramatic prospect. The isolated and strongly Whig back country of Connecticut was considered a good spot to incarcerate important Loyalists from all over the Northern colonies, and the mines, converted into a prison in 1773, were ideal. The "Catacomb of Loyalty," to quote Thomas Anburey, or the "woeful mansion," to quote an inmate, contained cells forty yards below the surface, into which "the prisoners are let down by a windlass into the dismal cavern, through a hole, which answers the purpose of conveying their food and air, as to light, it scarcely reaches them." The mere threat of the "Mines" could make a Loyalist conform. One prisoner regarded being sent there as a "Shocking Sentence (Worse than Death)." The mines received such celebrated Loyalists as Mayor Mathews of New York and William Franklin, who wrote of his "long and horrible confinement" and was described on his release as "considerably reduced in Flesh."

In May, 1781, there was a mass breakout. The leaders of the escape, Ebenezer Hathaway and Thomas Smith, arrived in New York some weeks later, and their alleged experiences were reported by Rivington's newspaper. Hathaway and Smith recalled that they had originally been captured on a privateer, sentenced, and marched the seventy-four miles from Hartford to Simsbury. The entrance to the dungeon was a heavily barred trap door that had to be raised

> by means of a tackle, whilst the hinges grated as they turned upon their hooks, and opened the jaws and mouths of what they call Hell, into which they descended by means of a ladder about six feet more, which led to a large iron grate or hatchway, locked down over a shaft about three feet diameter, sunk through the solid rock. . . . They bid adieu to this world,

and went down thirty-eight feet more by ladder "when they came to what is called the landing; then marching shelf by shelf, till descending about thirty or forty feet more they came to a platform of boards laid under foot, with a few more put over head to carry off the water, which keeps continually dropping." There they lived for twenty nights with the other prisoners, using "pots of charcoal to dispel the foul air" through a ventilation hole bored from the surface until the opportunity to escape came when they were allowed up into the kitchen to prepare food and rushed and captured the guards.

Some colorful Connecticut escapes in other places are also recorded. Nathan Barnum avoided appearing for trial in 1780 by inoculating himself with smallpox, whereupon he was "sent to the Hospital, where he was chained to the Floor to prevent his Escape, he found Means to bribe one of the Nurses, who not only brought him a File to cut off his Irons, but amused the Centinal, placed over him while he effected it. . . ."

Samuel Jarvis and his brother got out of prison "by the assistance of Friends who had privately procured some Women's apparel which they Dressed themselves in, and by that means made their escape through the Rebel Army." James Robertson asserted that while he was in jail at Albany, the British attacked and set the building on fire, whereupon, unable to walk, he managed to crawl into a bed of cabbages "and chewing them to prevent being suffocated" was found three days later badly burnt.

There was even a series of Tory hiding places between New York and Canada, rather in the fashion of the "Underground Railroad" of the pre-Civil War days.

The treatment of imprisoned Loyalists ranged over the widest possible spectrum. Simsbury was notoriously the worst prison, almost the Andersonville of the time. Many Loyalists suffered close confinement in much pleasanter conditions; others merely underwent house arrest; others were only prevented from traveling; some were on parole and, if banished to some remote part of America, were boarded with reluctant Whigs. Some worked in the normal way by day and simply spent the night in jail. In 1776 Thomas Vernon, a fanatically early riser, was removed, with three other prominent Rhode Island Loyalists, from Newport to Glocester, in the northern part of the state, because he had refused the test oath. The foursome's journey and their few months' stay in Glocester were pleasant and gentlemanly, almost Pickwickian. The friends walked and admired the countryside, ate, drank, and conversed well in the local inn where they lived; they planted beans, killed snakes, trapped squirrels, fished, played Quadrille (a card game); they were very well treated by the ladies of the house and by neighboring females. Their chief complaints were the lack of books, some local abhorrence of Tories, particularly by the men (their landlord said "the town was very uneasy" at their being there), a few fleas, tedium from the lack of friends and family, and some stealing of their food by their far from genial host. . . .

The Whigs suffered as the Tories did—legal persecution, mob action, imprisonment (the British prison ships were particularly horrible and gave rise to effective propagandist literature), and all the excesses of civil war. Adrian C. Leiby, the historian of the Hackensack Valley, for example, reports that there was barely a Whig family there that had not lost someone to a Tory raiding party. There is at least one recorded tarring and feathering of a Whig by British troops—of one Thomas Ditson, Jr., in Boston in March, 1775. In June, 1779, the *Virginia Gazette* reported the murder of a Whig captain by a party of Tories whom he had discovered robbing his house. A sentinel wounded him with a gunshot; then, after taking all the horses from the stables, the Tories pursued the captain into the house, where he was lying on a bed, and

> immediately thrust their bayonets into his body several times, continuing the barbarity while they heard a groan; and lest life might still be remaining in him, they cut both his arms with a knife in the most inhuman manner. The villain who shot him, had been his neighbour and companion from his youth.

The victim lived another two days.

 ## FOR FURTHER STUDY

1. Be prepared to discuss the following quotation from Sir John Harrington, who lived two centuries before the American Revolution:

   Treason doth never prosper; what's the reason?

   Why, if it prosper, none dare call it treason.

Evaluate Harrington's epigram with respect to Loyalists and Patriots in the War for Independence. Explain why the favorable historical reputation of the losing Civil War general Robert E. Lee is an exception to Harrington's view.

2. Summarize the various devices used to punish the Loyalists—both in their persons and in their property. What was the relation between official policy by state governments and actual treatment of Loyalists by neighbors and townsfolk?

3. Does the picture presented in this chapter modify your view of the American patriots? If so, how?

4. Is there any evidence here that would support the view that the Revolution was a civil war between different groups of colonials, as well as a war for independence from England?

FOR FURTHER READING

Only over the past three decades have historians devoted their attention to Loyalists. William H. Nelson's *The American Tory* (1961), Wallace Brown's *The King's Friends: The Composition and Motives of the American Loyalist Claimants* (1966), and Paul H. Smith's *Loyalists and Redcoats: A Study in British Revolutionary Policy* (1964) were part of the first wave of scholarship. More recently Mary B. Norton's *The British-Americans: The Loyalist Exiles in England, 1774–1789* (1972), Robert M. Calhoon's two works *The Loyalists in Revolutionary America, 1760–1781* (1973) and *The Loyalist Perception and Other Essays* (1989), and Janice Potter's *The Liberty We Seek: Loyalist Ideology in Colonial New York and Massachusetts* (1983) have added considerably to our knowledge.

CHAPTER 9

Crockett Almanac (1841) Prints and Photographs Division, Library of Congress

Rough-and-tumble fights like the one pictured here took place throughout the backcountry south.

FRONTIER FIGHTING: THE IMPORTANCE OF SAVING FACE

ELLIOTT J. GORN

We are often told we live in a violent society—the television news proves it nightly and movies and video games seem to celebrate violence for its own sake. Critics explain this by arguing that our lack of tightknit families and communities account for much of this increased violence. They think we have become too isolated and our society too impersonal. We all suspect our past was friendlier, more community-oriented, and less violent. If we think back a little, however, we remember we have another tradition in our past. Television shows of the 50s and 60s celebrated the wild west, a frontier where law and order was kept by individuals not by governments and where the threat of violence was ever-present.

Was violence typical in the new nation? Was it confined to the far west? Elliott Gorn thinks the nineteenth-century South, at least the frontier, was much more violent than we imagine. Like analysts who see cultural explanations for violence today, he argues that gouging and other forms of rough and tumble fighting explain a good deal about the region and its culture in the late eighteenth and early nineteenth centuries.

Keep in mind as you read that the South was different from the North in two important ways. First, the culture was largely oral, so your reputation depended on what people heard about you. If anyone suggested that you were inferior, you reacted quickly and decisively to let others know that what they heard was wrong and that you were willing to defend yourself to preserve your reputation and your honor. Second, many poor whites defended the privileges granted them because they were white with a vengeance, for these advantages proved they were not slaves.

The prevalence of physical mutilation in the southern backcountry is striking and is significant beyond the mere combat itself. See how it was embedded into the culture and why it was very important to those who participated, witnessed, and told about it.

"I would advise you when You do fight Not to act like Tygers and Bears as these Virginians do—Biting one anothers Lips and Noses off, and *gowging* one another—that is, thrusting out one anothers Eyes, and kicking one another on the Cods, to the Great damage of many a Poor Woman." Thus, Charles Woodmason, an itinerant Anglican minister born of English gentry stock, described the brutal form of combat he found in the Virginia backcountry shortly before the American Revolution. Although historians are more likely to study people thinking, governing, worshiping, or working, how men fight—who participates, who observes, which rules are followed, what is at stake, what tactics are allowed—reveals much about past cultures and societies.

The evolution of southern backwoods brawling from the late eighteenth century through the antebellum era can be reconstructed from oral traditions and travelers' accounts. . . .

As early as 1735, boxing was "much in fashion" in parts of Chesapeake Bay, and forty years later a visitor from the North declared that, along with dancing, fiddling, small swords, and card playing, it was an essential skill for all young Virginia gentlemen. The term "boxing," however, did not necessarily refer to the comparatively tame style of bare-knuckle fighting familiar to eighteenth-century Englishmen. In 1746, four deaths prompted the government of North Carolina to ask for legislation against "the barbarous and inhuman manner of boxing which so much prevails among the lower sort of people." The colonial assembly responded by making it a felony "to cut out the Tongue or pull out the eyes of the King's Liege People." Five years later the assembly added slitting, biting, and cutting off noses to the list of offenses. Virginia passed similar legislation in 1748 and revised these statutes in 1772 explicitly to discourage men from "gouging, plucking, or putting out an eye, biting or kicking or stomping upon" quiet peaceable citizens. By 1786 South Carolina had made premeditated mayhem a capital offense, defining the crime as severing another's bodily parts. . . .

Descriptions of . . . "fist battles," . . . indicate that they generally began like English prize fights. Two men, surrounded by onlookers, parried blows until

---

From: Elliott J. Gorn, "Gouge and Bite, Pull Hair and Scratch: The Social Significance of Fighting in the Southern Backcountry," *American Historical Review,* Vol. 90, February 1985, pp. 18–29, 31–38, 40–42. Copyright © 1985. Reprinted by permission of the author.

one was knocked or thrown down. But there the similarity ceased. Whereas "Broughton's Rules" of the English ring specified that a round ended when either antagonist fell, southern bruisers only began fighting at this point. Enclosed not inside a formal ring—the "magic circle" defining a special place with its own norms of conduct—but within whatever space the spectators left vacant, fighters battled each other until one called enough or was unable to continue. Combatants boasted, howled, and cursed. As words gave way to action, they tripped and threw, gouged and butted, scratched and choked each other. "But what is worse than all," Isaac Weld observed, "these wretches in their combat endeavor to their utmost to tear out each other's testicles."

Around the beginning of the nineteenth century, men sought original labels for their brutal style of fighting. "Rough-and-tumble" or simply "gouging" gradually replaced "boxing" as the name for these contests. Before two bruisers attacked each other, spectators might demand whether they proposed to fight fair—according to Broughton's Rules—or rough-and-tumble. Honor dictated that all techniques be permitted. Except for a ban on weapons, most men chose to fight "no holts barred," doing what they wished to each other without interference, until one gave up or was incapacitated.

The emphasis on maximum disfigurement, on severing bodily parts, made this fighting style unique. Amid the general mayhem, however, gouging out an opponent's eye became the sine qua non of rough-and-tumble fighting, much like the knockout punch in modern boxing. The best gougers, of course, were adept at other fighting skills. Some allegedly filed their teeth to bite off an enemy's appendages more efficiently. Still, liberating an eyeball quickly became a fighter's surest route to victory and his most prestigious accomplishment. To this end, celebrated heroes fired their fingernails hard, honed them sharp, and oiled them slick. "'You have come off badly this time, I doubt?'" declared an alarmed passerby on seeing the piteous condition of a renowned fighter. "'Have I,' says he triumphantly, shewing from his pocket at the same time an eye, which he had extracted during the combat, and preserved for a trophy."

As the new style of fighting evolved, its geographical distribution changed. Leadership quickly passed from the southern seaboard to upcountry counties and the western frontier. Although examples could be found throughout the South, rough-and-tumbling was best suited to the backwoods, where hunting, herding, and semisubsistence agriculture predominated over market-oriented, staple crop production. Thus, the settlers of western Carolina, Kentucky, and Tennessee, as well as upland Mississippi, Alabama, and Georgia, became especially known for their pugnacity.

The social base of rough-and-tumbling also shifted with the passage of time. Although brawling was always considered a vice of the "lower sort," eighteenth-century Tidewater gentlemen sometimes found themselves in brutal fights. These combats grew out of challenges to men's honor—to their status in patriarchal, kin-based, small-scale communities—and were woven into the very fabric of daily life. Rhys Isaac has observed that the Virginia gentry set the tone for a fiercely competitive style of living. Although they valued hierarchy, individual status was never permanently fixed, so men frantically sought to assert their prowess—by grand boasts over tavern gaming tables laden with money, by whipping and tripping each other's horses in violent quarter-races, by wagering one-half year's earnings on the flash of a fighting cock's gaff. Great planters and small shared an ethos that extolled courage bordering on foolhardiness and cherished magnificent, if irrational, displays of largess.

Piety, hard work, and steady habits had their adherents, but in this society aggressive self-assertion and manly pride were the real marks of status. Even the gentry's vaunted hospitality demonstrated a family's community standing, so conviviality itself became a vehicle for rivalry and emulation. Rich and poor might revel together during "public times," but gentry patronage of sports and festivities kept the focus of power clear. Above all, brutal recreations toughened men for a violent social life in which the exploitation of labor, the specter of poverty, and a fierce struggle for status were daily realities. . . .

Slowly, . . . rough-and-tumble fighting found specific locus in both human and geographical landscapes. We can watch men grapple with the transition. When an attempt at a formal duel aborted, Savannah politician Robert Watkins and United States Senator James Jackson resorted to gouging. Jackson bit Watson's finger to save his eye. Similarly, when a "a low fellow who pretends to gentility" insulted a distinguished doctor, the gentleman responded with a proper challenge. "He had scarcely uttered these words, before the other flew at him, and in an instant turned his eye out of the socket, and while it hung upon his cheek, the fellow was barbarous enough to endeavor to pluck it entirely out." By the new century, such ambiguity had lessened, as rough-and-tumble fighting was relegated to individuals in backwoods settlements. For the next several decades, eye-gouging matches were focal events in the culture of lower-class males who still relished the wild ways of old. . . .

Frontier braggarts enjoyed fulfilling visitors' expectations of backwoods depravity, pumping listeners full of gruesome legends. Their narratives projected a satisfying, if grotesque, image of the American rustic as a fearless, barbaric, larger-than-life democrat. But they also gave Englishmen the satisfaction of seeing their former countrymen run wild in the wilderness. . . . As they made their way from the northern port towns to the southern countryside, or down the Ohio to southwestern waterways, observers concluded that geographical and moral descent went hand in hand. Brutal fights dramatically confirmed their belief that evil lurked in the deep shadows of America's sunny democratic landscape. . . .

Thomas Anburey . . . believed that the Revolution's leveling of class distinctions left the "lower people" dangerously independent. Although Anburey found poor whites usually hospitable and generous, he was disturbed by their sudden outbursts of impudence, their aversion to labor and love of drink, their vengefulness and savagery. They shared with their betters a taste for gaming, horse racing, and cockfighting, but "boxing matches, in which they displayed such barbarity, as fully marks their innate ferocious disposition," were all their

own. Anburey concluded that an English prizefight was humanity itself compared to Virginia combat. . . .

. . . Thomas Ashe explored the territory around Wheeling, Virginia. . . . A
Wheeling Quaker assured Ashe that mores were changing, that the underworld
element was about to be driven out. Soon, the godly would gain control of the local government, enforce strict observance of the Sabbath, and outlaw vice. Ashe
was sympathetic but doubtful. . . .

To convey the rough texture of Wheeling life, Ashe described a gouging match.
Two men drinking at a public house argued over the merits of their respective
horses. Wagers made, they galloped off to the race course. "Two thirds of the population followed: —blacksmiths, shipwrights, all left work: the town appeared a
desert. The stores were shut. I asked a proprietor, why the warehouses did not remain open? He told me all good was done for the day: that the people would remain on the ground till night, and many stay till the following morning."
Determined to witness an event deemed so important that the entire town went
on holiday, Ashe headed for the track. He missed the initial heat but arrived in
time to watch the crowd raise the stakes to induce a rematch. Six horses competed, and spectators bet a small fortune, but the results were inconclusive.
Umpires' opinions were given and rejected. Heated words, then fists flew. Soon,
the melee narrowed to two individuals, a Virginian and a Kentuckian. Because
fights were common in such situations, everyone knew the proper procedures,
and the combatants quickly decided to "tear and rend" one another—to rough-
and-tumble—rather than "fight fair." Ashe elaborated: "You startle at the words
tear and rend, and again do not understand me. You have heard these terms, I allow, applied to beasts of prey and to carnivorous animals; and your humanity cannot conceive them applicable to man: It nevertheless is so, and the fact will not
permit me the use of any less expressive term."

The battle began—size and power on the Kentuckian's side, science and craft
on the Virginian's. They exchanged cautious throws and blows, when suddenly
the Virginian lunged at his opponent with a panther's ferocity. The crowd roared
its approval as the fight reached its violent denouement:

> The shock received by the Kentuckyan, and the want of breath, brought him in-
> stantly to the ground. The Virginian never lost his hold; like those bats of the South
> who never quit the subject on which they fasten till they taste blood, he kept his
> knees in his enemy's body; fixing his claws in his hair, and his thumbs on his eyes,
> gave them an instantaneous start from their sockets. The sufferer roared aloud, but
> uttered no complaint. The citizens again shouted with joy. Doubts were no longer
> entertained and bets of three to one were offered on the Virginian.

But the fight continued. The Kentuckian grabbed his smaller opponent and held
him in a tight bear hug, forcing the Virginian to relinquish his facial grip. Over
and over the two rolled, until, getting the Virginian under him, the big man
"snapt off his nose so close to his face that no manner of projection remained."
The Virginian quickly recovered, seized the Kentuckian's lower lip in his teeth,

and ripped it down over his enemy's chin. This was enough: "The Kentuckyan at length *gave out,* on which the people carried off the victor, and he preferring a triumph to a doctor, who came to cicatrize his face, suffered himself to be chaired round the ground as the champion of the times, and the first *rougher-and-tumbler.* The poor wretch, whose eyes were started from their spheres, and whose lip refused its office, returned to the town, to hide his impotence, and get his countenance repaired." The citizens refreshed themselves with whiskey and biscuits, then resumed their races.

Ashe's Quaker friend reported that such spontaneous races occurred two or three times a week and that the annual fall and spring meets lasted fourteen uninterrupted days, "aided by the licentious and profligate of all the neighboring states." As for rough-and-tumbles, the Quaker saw no hope of suppressing them. Few nights passed without such fights; few mornings failed to reveal a new citizen with mutilated features. It was a regional taste, unrestrained by law or authority, an inevitable part of life on the left bank of the Ohio.

By the early nineteenth century, rough-and-tumble fighting had generated its own folklore. . . .—the legends, tales, ritual boasts, and verbal duels, all of them in regional vernacular—made rough-and-tumble fighting unique.

It would be difficult to overemphasize the importance of the spoken word in southern life. . . . Southern society was based more on personalistic, face-to-face, kin-and-community relationships than on legalistic or bureaucratic ones. Interactions between southerners were guided by elaborate rituals of hospitality, demonstrative conviviality, and kinship ties-all of which emphasized personal dependencies and reliance on the spoken word. Through the antebellum period and beyond, the South had an oral as much as a written culture. . . .

The oral traditions of hunters, drifters, herdsmen, gamblers, roustabouts, and rural poor who rough-and-tumbled provided a strong social cement. Tall talk around a campfire, in a tavern, in front of a crossroads store, or at countless other meeting places on the southwestern frontier helped establish communal bonds between disparate persons. . . . But words could also divide. . . . Men were so touchy about their personal reputations that any slight required an apology. This failing, only retribution restored public stature and self-esteem. "Saving face" was not just a metaphor.

The lore of backwoods combat, however, both inflated and deflated egos. By the early nineteenth century, simple epithets evolved into verbal duels—rituals well known to folklorists. Backcountry men took turns bragging about their prowess, possessions, and accomplishments, spurring each other on to new heights of self-magnification. Such exchanges heightened tension and engendered a sense of theatricality and display. But boasting, unlike insults, did not always lead to combat, for, in a culture that valued oral skills, the verbal battle itself—the contest over who best controlled the power of words—was a real quest for domination. . . . Style and details changed, but the themes remained the same: comparing oneself to wild animals, boasting of possessions and accomplishments, asserting domination over others. Mike Fink, legendary keelboatman, champion gouger, and fearless hunter, put his own mark on the old form and elevated it to art:

> "I'm a salt River roarer! I'm a ring tailed squealer! I'm a regular screamer from the old Massassip! Whoop! I'm the very infant that refused his milk before its eyes were open and called out for a bottle of old Rye! I love the women and I'm chockful o'fight! I'm half wild horse and half cock-eyed alligator and the rest o' me is crooked snags an' red-hot snappin' turtle. . . . I can out-run, out-jump, out-shoot, out-brag, out-drink, an' out-fight, rough-an'-tumble, no holts barred, any man on both sides the river from Pittsburgh to New Orleans an' back ag'in to St. Louiee. Come on, you flatters, you bargers, you milk white mechanics, an' see how tough I am to chaw! I ain't had a fight for two days an' I'm spilein' for exercise. Cock-a-doodle-doo!" . . .

. . . Above all, fight legends portrayed backwoodsmen reveling in blood. Violence existed for its own sake, unencumbered by romantic conventions and claiming no redeeming social or psychic value. Gouging narratives may have masked grimness with black humor, but they offered little pretense that violence was a creative or civilizing force. Thus, one Kentuckian defeated a bear by chewing off its nose and scratching out its eyes. "They can't stand Kentucky play," the settler proclaimed, "biting and gouging are to hard for them." Humor quickly slipped toward horror, when Davy Crockett, for example, coolly boasted, "I kept my thumb in his eye, and was just going to give it a twist and bring the peeper out, like taking up a gooseberry in a spoon." To Crockett's eternal chagrin, someone interrupted the battle just at this crucial juncture. . . .

The danger and violence of daily life in the backwoods contributed mightily to sanguinary oral traditions that exalted the strong and deprecated the weak. Early in the nineteenth century, the Southwest contained more than its share of terrifying wild animals, powerful and well-organized Indian tribes, and marauding white outlaws. Equally important were high infant mortality rates and short life expectancies, agricultural blights, class inequities, and the centuries-old belief that betrayal and cruelty were man's fate. . . . Rather than be overwhelmed by violence, acquiesce in an oppressive environment, or submit to death as an escape from tragedy, why not make a virtue of necessity and flaunt one's unconcern? To revel in the lore of deformity, mutilation, and death was to beat the wilderness at its own game. The storyteller's art dramatized life and converted nameless anxieties into high adventure; bravado helped men face down a threatening world and transform terror into power. To claim that one was sired by wild animals, kin to natural disasters, and tougher than steam engines—which were displacing rivermen in the antebellum era—was to gain a momentary respite from fear, a cathartic, if temporary, sense of being in control. Symbolically, wild boasts overwhelmed the very forces that threatened the backwoodsmen.

But there is another level of meaning here. Sometimes fight legends invited an ambiguous response, mingling the celebration of beastly acts with the rejection of barbarism. . . .

Backwoodsmen mocked their animality by exaggerating it, thereby affirming their own humanity. A Kentuckian battled inconclusively from ten in the morning until sundown, when his wife showed up to cheer him on:

> "So I gathered all the little strength I had, and I socked my thumb in his eye, and with my fingers took a twist on his *snot box,* and with the other hand, I grabbed him by the back of the head; I then caught his ear in my mouth, gin his head a flirt, and *out come his ear by the roots!* I then flopped his head over, and caught his other ear in my mouth, and jerked that out in the same way, and it made a hole in his head that I could have rammed my fist through, and I was just goin' to when he hollered: 'Nuff!'"

More than realism or fantasy alone, fight legends stretched the imagination by blending both. . . . In this sense, gouging narratives were commentaries on backwoods life. The legends were texts that allowed plain folk to dramatize the tensions and ambiguities of their lives: they hauled society's goods yet lived on its fringe; they destroyed forests and game while clearing the land for settlement; they killed Indians to make way for the white man's culture; they struggled for self-sufficiency only to become ensnared in economic dependency. Fight narratives articulated the fundamental contradiction of frontier life—the abandonment of "civilized" ways that led to the ultimate expansion of civilized society.

Foreign travelers might exaggerate and backwoods storytellers embellish, but the most neglected fact about eye-gouging matches is their actuality. Circuit Court Judge Aedamus Burke barely contained his astonishment while presiding in South Carolina's upcountry: "Before God, gentlemen of the jury, I never saw such a thing before in the world. There is a plaintiff with an eye out! A juror with an eye out! And two witnesses with an eye out!" If the "ring-tailed roarers" did not actually breakfast on stewed Yankee, washed down with spike nails and epsom salts, court records from Sumner County, Arkansas, did describe assault victims with the words "nose was bit." The gamest "gamecock of the wilderness" never really moved steamboat engines by grinning at them, but Reuben Cheek did receive a three-year sentence to the Tennessee penitentiary for gouging out William Maxey's eye. Most backcountrymen went to the grave with their faces intact, just as most of the southern gentry never fought a duel. But as an extreme version of the common tendency toward brawling, street fighting, and seeking personal vengeance, rough-and-tumbling gives us insight into the deep values and assumptions—the *mentalité*—of backwoods life. . . .

What can we conclude about the culture and society that nourished rough-and-tumble fighting? The best place to begin is with the material base of life and the nature of daily work. Gamblers, hunters, herders, roustabouts, rivermen, and yeomen farmers were the sorts of persons usually associated with gouging. Such hallmarks of modernity as large-scale production, complex division of labor, and regular work rhythms were alien to their lives. . . . The southern uplands [are premodern] through most of the antebellum period. Even while cotton production boomed and trade expanded, a relatively small number of planters owned the best lands and most slaves, so huge parts of the South remained outside the flow of international markets or staple crop agriculture. Thus, backcountry whites commonly found themselves locked into a semisubsistent pattern of living. Growing crops for home consumption, supplementing food supplies with abundant game, allowing small herds to fatten in the woods, spending scarce money for essential staples, and bartering goods for the services of part-time or itinerant trades people, the upland folk lived in an intensely local, kin-based society. Rural hamlets, impassable roads, and provincial isolation . . . characterized the backcountry.

Even men whose livelihoods depended on expanding markets often continued their rough, premodern ways. Characteristic of life on a Mississippi barge, for example, were long periods of idleness shattered by intense anxiety, as deadly snags, shoals, and storms approached. Running aground on a sandbar meant backbreaking labor to maneuver a thirty-ton vessel out of trouble. Boredom weighed as heavily as danger, so tale telling, singing, drinking, and gambling filled the empty hours. Once goods were taken on in New Orleans, the men began the thousand-mile return journey against the current. Before steam power replaced muscle, bad food and whiskey fueled the gangs who day after day, exposed to wind and water, poled the river bottoms or strained at the cordelling ropes until their vessel reached the tributaries of the Missouri or the Ohio. Hunters, trappers, herdsmen, subsistence farmers, and other backwoodsmen faced different but equally taxing hardships, and those who endured prided themselves on their strength and daring, their stamina, cunning, and ferocity.

Such men played as lustily as they worked, counterpointing bouts of intense labor with strenuous leisure. What travelers mistook for laziness was a refusal to work and save with compulsive regularity. . . . Details might change, but penury, loose morality, and lack of steady habits endured.

Boatmen, hunters, and herdsmen were often separated from wives and children for long periods. More important, backcountry couples lacked the emotionally intense experience of the bourgeois family. They spent much of their time apart and found companionship with members of their own sex. . . .

Given the lives these men led, a world view that embraced fearlessness made sense. Hunters, trappers, Indian fighters, and herdsmen who knew the smell of warm blood on their hands refused to sentimentalize an environment filled with threatening forces. It was not that backwoodsmen lived in constant danger but that violence was unpredictable. Recreations like cockfighting deadened men to cruelty, and the gratuitous savagery of gouging matches reinforced the daily truth that life was brutal, guided only by the logic of superior nerve, power, and cunning. With families emotionally or physically distant and civil institutions weak, a man's role in the all-male society was defined less by his ability as a breadwinner than by his ferocity. The touchstone of masculinity was unflinching toughness, not chivalry, duty, or piety. Violent sports, heavy drinking, and impulsive pleasure seeking were appropriate for men whose lives were hard, whose futures were unpredictable, and whose opportunities were limited. Gouging champions were group leaders because they embodied the basic values of their peers. The successful rough-and-tumbler proved his manhood by asserting his dominance and rendering his opponent "impotent," as Thomas Ashe put it. And the loser, though literally or symbolically castrated, demonstrated his mettle and maintained his honor. . . .

Moreover, primitive markets and the semisubsistence basis of upcountry life limited men's dependence on goods produced by others and allowed them to maintain the irregular work rhythms of a precapitalist economy. The material base of backwoods life was ill suited to social transformation, and the cultural traditions of the past offered alternatives to rigid new ideals. Closing up shop in midweek for a fight or horse race had always been perfectly acceptable, because men labored so that they might indulge the joys of the flesh. Neither a compulsive need to save time and money nor an obsession with progress haunted people's imaginations. . . .

Whether judged positively as leisure or negatively as laziness, the southern sensibility valued free time and rejected work as the consuming goal of life. Slavery reinforced this tendency, for how could labor be an unmitigated virtue if so much of it was performed by despised black bondsmen? When southerners did esteem commerce and enterprise, it was less because piling up wealth contained religious or moral value than because productivity facilitated the leisure ethos. Southerners could therefore work hard without placing labor at the center of their ethical universe. In important ways, then, the upland folk culture reflected a larger regional style.

Thus, the values, ideas, and institutions that rapidly transformed the North into a modern capitalist society came late to the South. Indeed, conspicuous display, heavy drinking, moral casualness, and love of games and sports had deep roots in much of Western culture. . . . We must take care not to interpret the southern ethnic as unique or aberrant. The compulsions to subordinate leisure to productivity, to divide work and play into separate compartmentalized realms, and to improve each bright and shining hour were the novel ideas. The southern ethic anticipated human evil, tolerated ethical lapses, and accepted the finitude of man in contrast to the new style that demanded unprecedented moral rectitude and internalized self-restraint. . . .

The culture of honor thrived in hierarchical rural communities like the American South and grew out of a fatalistic world view, which assumed that pain and suffering were man's fate. It accounts for the pervasive violence that marked relationships between southerners and explains their insistence on vengeance and their rejection of legal redress in settling quarrels. Honor tied personal identity to public fulfillment of social roles. Neither bourgeois self-control nor internalized conscience determined status; judgment by one's fellows was the wellspring of community standing.

In this light, the seemingly trivial causes for brawls . . .—name calling, subtle ridicule, breaches of decorum, displays of poor manners—make sense. If a man's good name was his most important possession, then any slight cut him deeply. "Having words" precipitated fights because words brought shame and undermined a man's sense of self. Symbolic acts, such as buying a round of drinks, conferred honor on all, while refusing to share a bottle implied some inequality in social status. Honor inhered not only in individuals but also in kin and peers; when members of two cliques had words, their tested leaders or several men from each side fought to uphold group prestige. Inheritors of primal honor, the southern plain folk were quick to take offense, and any perceived affront forced a man either to devalue himself or to strike back violently and avenge the wrong.

The concept of male honor takes us a long way toward understanding the meaning of eye-gouging matches. . . . The southern upcountry fostered a particular style of honor, which grew out of the contradiction between equality and hierarchy. . . . Because black chattel slavery was the basis for the southern hierarchy, slave owners had the most wealth and honor, while other whites scrambled for a bit of each, and bondsmen were permanently impoverished and dishonored. Here was a source of tension for the plain folk. Men of honor shared freedom and equality; those denied honor were implicitly less than equal—perilously close to a slave-like condition. But in the eyes of the gentry, poor whites as well as blacks were outside the circle of honor, so both groups were subordinate. . . .

Southern plain folk, then, were caught in a social contradiction. Society taught all white men to consider themselves equals, encouraged them to compete for power and status, yet threatened them from below with the specter of servitude and from above with insistence on obedience to rank and authority. Cut off from upper-class tests of honor, backcountry people adopted their own. A rough-and-tumble was more than a poor man's duel, a botched version of genteel combat. Plain folk chose not to ape the dispassionate, antiseptic, gentry style but to invert it. While the gentleman's code of honor insisted on cool restraint, eye gougers gloried in unvarnished brutality. In contrast to duelists' aloof silence, backwoods fighters screamed defiance to the world. As their own unique rites of honor, rough-and-tumble matches allowed backcountry men to shout their equality at each other. And eye-gouging fights also dispelled any stigma of servility. Ritual boasts, soaring oaths, outrageous ferocity, unflinching bloodiness—all proved a man's freedom. Where the slave acted obsequiously, the backwoodsman resisted the slightest affront; where human chattels accepted blows and never raised a hand, plain folk celebrated violence; where blacks could not jeopardize their value as property, poor whites proved their autonomy by risking bodily parts. Symbolically reaffirming their claims to honor, gouging matches helped resolve painful uncertainties arising out of the ambiguous place of plain folk in the southern social structure. . . .

Eye gouging represented neither the "real" human animal emerging on the frontier, nor nature acting through man in a Darwinian struggle for survival, nor anarchic disorder and communal breakdown. Rather, rough-and-tumble fighting was ritualized behavior—a product of specific cultural assumptions. Men drink together, tongues loosen, a simmering old rivalry begins to boil; insult is given, offense taken, ritual boasts commence; the fight begins, mettle is tested, blood redeems honor, and equilibrium is restored. Eye gouging was the poor and middling whites' own version of a historical southern tendency to consider personal violence socially useful—indeed, ethically essential.

Rough-and-tumble fighting emerged from the confluence of economic conditions, social relationships, and culture in the southern backcountry. Primitive markets and the semisubsistence basis of life threw men back on close ties to kin and community. Violence and poverty were part of daily existence, so endurance, even callousness, became functional values. Loyal to their localities, their occupations, and each other, men came together and found release from life's hardships in strong drink, tall talk, rude practical jokes, and cruel sports. They craved one another's recognition but rejected genteel, pious, or bourgeois values, awarding esteem on the basis of their own traditional standards. The glue that held men together was an intensely competitive status system in which the most prodigious drinker or strongest arm wrestler, the best tale teller, fiddle player, or log roller, the most daring gambler, original liar, skilled hunter, outrageous swearer, or accurate marksman was accorded respect by the others. Reputation was everything, and scars were badges of honor. Rough-and-tumble fighting demonstrated unflinching willingness to inflict pain while risking mutilation—all to defend one's standing among peers—and became a central expression of the all-male subculture.

 ## FOR FURTHER STUDY

1. The author tells you in the first paragraph why he thinks fighting is important: who participates, who observes, which rules are followed, what is at stake, what tactics are allowed. If you can answer these questions as you read then you understand the article and Gorn's point.

2. Trace the evolution of fighting from the gentry and the eastern seaboard to the upcountry frontier and working class frontiersmen. What made rough-and-tumble fighting different?

3. An important part of the author's argument is that these fights toughened men for their real lives, which were violent and risky. How do these fights represent the lives of embattled poor frontiersmen who risked mutilation and death to beat the wilderness at its own game?

4. What functions did the exaggerated bragging of men like folk hero Mike Fink serve?

5. What aspects of this part of the South were premodern (as Gorn defines it) and why is it important?

6. What was the "southern ethic" and how did it differ from the ethic of the North?

7. Explain Gorn's view that rough-and-tumble was a poor man's duel with different rules and how the fighting reflected the social contradiction that ensnared the male culture of the frontier.

For Further Reading

On southern honor see Bertram Wyatt-Brown, *Southern Honor: Ethics and Behavior in the Old South* (1982). For the violence in the South see Edward L. Ayers, *Vengeance and Justice, Crime and Punishment in the Nineteenth-Century American South* (1983) and Dickson Bruce, *Violence and Culture in the Antebellum South* (1979). For a look at the colonial period see A. Roger Ekirch, *"Poor Carolina": Society and Politics in Colonial North Carolina, 1729–1776* (1981). A more general discussion can be found in Terry G. Jordan and Matti Kaups, *The American Backwoods Frontier: An Ethnic and Ecological Interpretation* (1989). For a history of the entire West see Malcolm J. Rohrbough, *The Trans-Appalachian Frontier* (1978). For a commentary on male roles see Peter N. Stearns, *Be A Man: Males in Modern Society* (1979).

THE TRIALS OF THE EARLY REPUBLIC

*O*ne of the questions frequently asked of historians is how closely their view of the past approximates the past as it truly was. We seldom think of ourselves as being part of an "age," and we are scarcely aware of the patterns of development that later historians may detect. Fifty years from now, historians may look back at our times as a revolutionary period, an age of reform, or a period of cultural decay. Of course, any such characterization is somewhat artificial because it ignores many contradictory developments of the time and applies simple labels to complex contexts.

The first quarter of the nineteenth century is generally regarded as a period of centralization and nationalism. Following the adoption of the Constitution of 1788, the Federalist period was characterized by the strengthening of the national government in both domestic and foreign affairs and the development of national interests quite distinct from those of European powers. This nationalistic thrust was continued under the Virginia presidents from Jefferson to Monroe, though support for domestic programs along these lines was stronger in Congress than in the executive mansion.

The second quarter of the nineteenth century has proved to be more difficult to characterize. Though some historians emphasize the democratic features of the "Age of Jackson," others have suggested that is was basically an age of business entrepreneurs and social inequality. There is little doubt that the years from 1830 to 1850 were a time of great social ferment when a startling variety of reforms were undertaken.

The first reading shows how industrial workers considered political action and union organization to help them reform their working lives. The second reading discusses an area where reform was badly needed but not attempted as it describes the callous and often brutal treatment of some Native Americans. The third essay emphasizes the changing position of middle-class women and the development of a new kind of family which changed the way many Americans were raised. The final selection describes one of the many groups that believed reform was necessary. In this case, converts to the cause of temperance believed that alcoholism was such an important problem that the country had to rid itself of demon alcohol to reach its full potential.

CHAPTER 10

TIME TABLE OF THE LOWELL MILLS,

Arranged to make the working time throughout the year average 11 hours per day.

TO TAKE EFFECT SEPTEMBER 21st., 1853,

The Standard time being that of the meridian of Lowell, as shown by the Regulator Clock of AMOS SANBORN, Post Office Corner, Central Street.

From March 20th to September 19th, inclusive.

COMMENCE WORK, at 6.30 A. M. LEAVE OFF WORK, at 6.30 P. M., except on Saturday Evenings. BREAKFAST at 6 A. M. DINNER, at 12 M. Commence Work, after dinner, 12.45 P. M.

From September 20th to March 19th, inclusive.

COMMENCE WORK at 7.00 A. M. LEAVE OFF WORK, at 7.00 P. M., except on Saturday Evenings. BREAKFAST at 6.30 A. M. DINNER, at 12.30 P.M. Commence Work, after dinner, 1.15 P. M.

BELLS.

From March 20th to September 19th, inclusive.

Morning Bells.	Dinner Bells.	Evening Bells.
First bell,...........4.30 A. M.	Ring out,.............12.00 M.	Ring out,............6.30 P. M.
Second, 5.30 A. M.; Third, 6.20.	Ring in,...........12.35 P. M.	Except on Saturday Evenings.

From September 20th to March 19th, inclusive.

Morning Bells.	Dinner Bells.	Evening Bells.
First bell,...........5.00 A. M.	Ring out,...........12.30 P. M.	Ring out at...........7.00 P. M.
Second, 6.00 A. M.; Third, 6.50.	Ring in,.............1.05 P. M.	Except on Saturday Evenings.

SATURDAY EVENING BELLS.

During APRIL, MAY, JUNE, JULY, and AUGUST, Ring Out, at 6.00 P. M.
The remaining Saturday Evenings in the year, ring out as follows :

SEPTEMBER.	NOVEMBER.	JANUARY.
First Saturday, ring out 6.00 P. M.	Third Saturday ring out 4.00 P. M.	Third Saturday, ring out 4.25 P. M.
Second " " 5.45 "	Fourth " " 3.55 "	Fourth " " 4.35 "
Third " " 5.30 "		
Fourth " " 5.20 "	DECEMBER.	FEBRUARY.
	First Saturday, ring out 3.50 P. M.	First Saturday, ring out 4.45 P. M.
OCTOBER.	Second " " 3.55 "	Second " " 4.55 "
First Saturday, ring out 5.05 P. M.	Third " " 3.55 "	Third " " 5.00 "
Second " " 4.55 "	Fourth " " 4.00 "	Fourth " " 5.10 "
Third " " 4.45 "	Fifth " " 4.00 "	
Fourth " " 4.35 "		MARCH.
Fifth " " 4.25 "	JANUARY.	First Saturday, ring out 5.25 P. M.
	First Saturday, ring out 4.10 P. M.	Second " " 5.30 "
NOVEMBER.	Second " " 4.15 "	Third " " 5.35 "
First Saturday, ring out 4.15 P. M.		Fourth " " 5.45 "
Second " · " 4.05 "		

YARD GATES will be opened at the first stroke of the bells for entering or leaving the Mills.

. *SPEED GATES commence hoisting three minutes before commencing work.*

Penhallow, Printer, Wyman's Exchange, 28 Merrimack St.

American Textile History Museum, Lowell, MA

The Lowell textile mills mandated a life of long hours. The constant ringing of bells ensured punctuality.

THE INDUSTRIAL WORKER

BARBARA M. TUCKER

$\mathcal{M}$any people equate the grand achievements of American business and industry with such remarkable men as Commodore Vanderbilt, Andrew Carnegie, and John D. Rockefeller. Important as leadership has been in American capitalism, one cannot understand the Industrial Revolution without an appreciation of the contribution of the millions of men, women, and children who made up the labor force in the new factory system. Besides its beneficial economic consequences, industrialization had some unfortunate social effects, and the history of labor was not necessarily characterized by steady improvement in either wages or conditions. Among the factors determining the condition of workers in a particular period were the available supply of labor, the skills necessary to a particular job, the type of industry in which one was employed, and the attitudes of courts and other governmental agencies toward labor and business. During much of our history, labor was considered a commodity whose value would fluctuate with supply and demand, just as the cost of raw materials or manufactured products might rise and fall.

The first half of the nineteenth century is an especially interesting period in American labor history. During these years, industrialization proceeded quite rapidly. Yet there was widespread ambivalence about the new machinery, the factory system, and the introduction of time clocks and factory whistles to regulate the cycle of one's life. There was also a well-established social philosophy as to the position of classes, the responsibilities of the employer, the relationship of work and leisure, and the roles of men and women in the labor force and in the home. Such deep social beliefs are not easily discarded; only grudgingly were they modified to meet the demands of the new industrialism. For a time, some of the new capitalists attempted to reconcile the old social philosophy of the paternalistic employer and his responsibility for the worker with the factory system of labor. Gradually management began breaking down older prerogatives of labor and insisting on punctuality, obedience, and a pattern of discipline that might enhance efficiency on the shop floor.

(1)

New Labor History

Early labor historians—the so-called Wisconsin School—concentrated their study on the organized labor movement and labor-management confrontations. A newer group of scholars has developed the "New Labor History," investigating a much broader range of subjects. Domestic servants, unorganized office workers, slaves, and others have been studied, with considerable attention devoted to workers' social and cultural values, rather than only their economic concerns. Barbara M. Tucker's book is a case study of the textile factories developed by Samuel Slater, but much of her attention is devoted to the relationship of family and religion to the development of the factory system.

Samuel Slater

To attract workers to his factories, Samuel Slater tried to construct a bridge to the past. The design of his factory colonies, the architecture of his company dwellings, and the institutions he established in the villages conformed in broad outline to those found throughout much of New England a century earlier. This link with tradition was not cosmetic, and it reached into the workplace. The occupations provided for men, women, and children, the conditions under which they labored, and the settlement of wages conformed to custom. Within the context of the new industrial order, familial values were preserved; alterations in the new economic orientation and structure of a society do not inevitably lead to major changes in its traditional units or beliefs.

In Slater's factory communities, a traditional division of labor based on age, gender, and the marital status of family members emerged. Married men performed customary tasks associated with a rural way of life, such as farming and casual labor, while their wives remained at home to care for the family. . . .

In the first decades of the nineteenth century, young children, adolescent boys and girls, and unmarried women comprised approximately three-fourths of the industrial labor force. From the outset few people opposed the employment of young people: quite the contrary, society condoned and encouraged it. H. Humphrey, noted author of child-training books, expressed the prevailing attitude toward the employment of children when he wrote:

> Our children must have employment—must be brought up in habits of industry. It is sinful, it is cruel to neglect this essential branch of their education. Make all the use you can of persuasion and example, and when these fail interpose your authority.

. . . If he will not study, put him on to a farm, or send him into the shop, or in some other way provide regular employment for him.

. . . The young labor force of Union Mills in Webster was typical. In 1840 thirty children and adolescents worked in the carding department under the direction of an overseer and several second hands. Approximately two-thirds of the workers there were female; 52 percent were children from nine to twelve years of age, 31 percent were from thirteen to fifteen years, and the remainder were sixteen or older. In the spinning department, the gender ratio approximated that of the carding room. Children as young as eight were introduced to the factory system through employment in this department. Of the twenty-five laborers employed there, 32 percent were from eight to twelve years of age, 44 percent were from thirteen to fifteen, and the remainder were sixteen or older. An overseer and a second hand monitored the labor of the spinning-department employees.

One of the largest rooms in the factory was the weaving department, and there young women, not children, dominated the labor force. At Union Mills in 1840 sixty-nine women wove either full or part time. With the exception of two young sisters. Mary and Sophia Strether, aged eleven and twelve, all of the women employed in the weaving department were between the ages of fourteen and twenty-four. Although some handloom weavers remained on the payroll, most of the cloth produced by Samuel Slater and Sons in 1840 was woven by machine.

Most of the people employed at Union Mills belonged to kinship groups. During the early years of industrialization family labor dominated the factory floors. Slater employed only a few people who had no kin working for a Slater enterprise or who did not live in the factory colonies; such employees were men who assumed skilled and supervisory positions and girls and unmarried women who tended power looms. . . .

Under the family system of labor, householders exercised considerable power within the factory, influencing the composition of the labor force, the allocation of jobs in the various departments, the supervision of hands, and the payment of wages. Bargaining between labor and management over the employment of children and labor conditions began before the youngsters entered the mills. On behalf of their children, householders negotiated a contract with Samuel Slater. Casual and verbal compacts at first, these agreements became more formal over time. Although written contracts certainly were initiated earlier, the first set of formal agreements found in the Slater company records are dated 1827; the last are dated 1840. Drawn up in February and March and effective from April 1, the annual contracts made between householders and Samuel Slater listed the names of kin employed, their rate of pay, and any special conditions pertaining to their employment. Typical of these agreements was one signed by John McCausland in 1828:

Agreed with John McCausland for himself & family to work one year from Apr. 1st next as follows viz:—
  Self at watching ⁵⁄₆ pr night = provided that any contract made with
  Saml. Slater for the year shall be binding in preference to this—

> Self to make sizing at 9/-pr. week
>   Daughter Jane—12 pr week—
>   Son Alex.   —7/ "   "
>   " James   —5/ "   "
> each of the children to have the privilege of 3 months Schooling and Alex to be let to the mule spinners if wished.

Education and training provisions were commonly included in the contracts. Parents sought release time from factory employment so that their children could attend school from two to four months annually, and permission was granted for both boys and girls to attend class. For their sons, householders sometimes sought further concessions. Like John McCausland, many parents wanted their sons to learn a skilled trade such as mule spinning, an occupation that commanded both prestige and high wages. . . .

While these contracts limited labor turnover and guaranteed Slater a steady supply of workers, they also ensured that parents would retain their position as head of the kinship unit and that children would not gain economic independence. Children looked to their parents to protect their interests. All children employed in the factory had to be sponsored by a householder; with few exceptions before 1830, Slater did not look beyond the kinship unit for labor.

Parents apparently also determined in which department their children would work and the conditions under which they would do so, although this is not stated specifically in the contracts. Family members often worked in the same department, attending machines side by side. Mule spinners hired and paid their sons, nephews, or close family friends to piece for them, and weavers hired kin to assist them at their machines. In 1840 Asa Day, a blacksmith employed by Union Mills, Webster, placed his daughters, Francis and Caroline, aged nine and thirteen, in the carding room. John Costis's six children, who ranged in age from nine to eighteen, also worked there, while the four Drake youngsters, aged ten to sixteen, worked together in the spinning department. In the weaving room, sisters often tended looms near one another. Mary Strether worked beside her older sister, Sophia; the Boster sisters, the three Faulkner girls, and the Foster and the Fitts sisters also worked there.

Parental concern did not end with the formal agreement. Although Samuel Slater established strict rules and regulations for the smooth, efficient operation of the factory, and although he demanded that workers be punctual, regular in attendance, industrious, and disciplined, he nevertheless bowed to parental pressures and allowed householders appreciable influence over the supervision of hands and the payment of wages.

The organization of the factory floor in the Slater mills was a reflection of the dominant position of the male householder. Within each department, the supervisory hierarchy came to reflect the hierarchy of the home. All positions of authority, from the second hand to the overseer, were filled by men. Although female labor was predominant in the industrial labor force, no woman filled a managerial position. Like children, women were the subordinates, not the supervisors. The prefactory family hierarchy, in which authority and power were vested in the husband, was transferred from the home to the new industrial order. The factory system did not challenge paternal authority; it perpetuated it. . . .

. . . In the organization and operation of his industrial communities, Slater respected the desires of householders and incorporated traditional values, practices, and customs within the new order. In return for his safeguarding of traditional prerogatives, householders provided Slater with a steady supply of tractable, industrious, reliable hands. The bargain that had been made between Samuel Slater and his workers in Pawtucket could be seen operating in Slatersville, Webster, Wilkinsonville, and the many other Slater-style communities throughout New England. As long as both labor and management adhered to its side of the agreement, harmonious relations between the two parties prevailed.

Industrial discipline posed some of the gravest problems faced by early factory masters, who had to devise various methods to teach people the so-called habits of industry: regularity, obedience, sobriety, steady intensity, and punctuality. Most manufacturers solved such problems in one of two ways: the stick-and-carrot approach as described by Sidney Pollard or the more subtle, internalized form of discipline as discussed by E. P. Thompson. Using the arguments of Max Weber and Erich Fromm, Thompson has maintained that rewards and punishments do not always succeed in creating a disciplined, tractable, steady, industrious laborer. Internal forces or "inner compulsion," he asserts, usually prove more effective in harnessing all energies to work than any other compulsion can ever be. For this method to be effective, each worker had to be made his or her own taskmaster, had to be made to feel guilty for "deviant" conduct, and had to develop an internal drive toward right and proper behavior. Among the British working class, Thompson ascribed that internal force to religion, especially Methodism. In Webster, Slatersville, and Wilkinsonville internal self-control also served to discipline the labor force. There the church and the family were the twin forces employed to exact compliance with factory rules and regulations. Discipline, however, did not begin and end at the factory door; beliefs taught in the church and the home circumscribed the behavior of the entire society. . . .

In Webster the Baptists, the Methodists, and the Congregationalists all received support from the Slater family, and although Samuel Slater and his sons belonged to the Congregational church, the Methodists in Webster received favored treatment. Samuel Slater encouraged the establishment of the Methodist church, and throughout the antebellum period his company continued to support it. Slater provided a plot of land for the church, laid its foundation, and bought sixteen of its forty pews for the exclusive use of his employees. Slater's company later built the parsonage and was responsible for the continued maintenance of church buildings. Whenever church officials required financial assistance, they turned first to the company and only later to the congregation. In effect the company became a church proprietor, exercising considerable influence over religious matters.

The Slater family encouraged its laborers to attend worship services and participate in other church activities. John Slater, Sr., expected all company employees to attend Sabbath services: "It has long been one of the established regulations of the mills, that the help are expected to attend public worship on the Sabbath. Also that no work will be done or repairs made by the company on that day." Manufacturers also allowed laborers leave to attend special church functions, often shutting down the mills and closing their shops so that all hands could attend revivals, camp meetings, and special quarterly sessions. During the summer revival of 1839, the mills were closed for several days to allow local Methodists to attend the meeting. "This being camp meeting with our Good Methodists," wrote factory agent Alexander Hodges, it "will be rather a broken one with the Mills." Clearly, Methodists formed such a large proportion of the labor force that their absence effectively curtailed operations.

By the late 1830s and early 1840s, Slater's labor force was predominantly Methodist. A comparison of employment ledgers and local church membership rolls reveals that prominent members of church boards, superintendents of Sunday schools, lay preachers, and stewards held important skilled and supervisory positions in local Slater factories. Charles Waite, resident manager of Slater's Phoenix Thread Mill, served variously as Sabbath school administrator, treasurer, and secretary-treasurer of the Methodist church. William Kimball, for ten years resident superintendent of the Slater and Kimball mill, served as the assistant secretary of the Methodist Sabbath school. At Union Mills, four of the six machinists, two of the four dressers, all of the bailers, and many of the mule spinners belonged to the church. Their sons and daughters filled the unskilled jobs in the carding, spinning, and weaving rooms. . . .

In part Samuel Slater and other manufacturers supported religion because they viewed it as a form of social control which facilitated the discipline of workers. The dictums and discipline advanced by the church became part of the foundation of a work ethic, and as such they served to train, discipline, and control workers. This was the case in Webster, where the Methodist church educated a whole generation in the dictates of their religion. The written tracts, hymns, sermons, and other literature used in the church all advanced the same messages: obedience, deference, industry, honesty, punctuality, and temperance. The lessons prepared the young operatives for ultimate salvation and also trained them to be good, obedient factory hands. In Webster the Methodist Sabbath school was the principal agency through which these values were taught.

The Webster Sabbath school flourished. In 1841 A. D. Merrill, minister of the local church, reported:

> The present state of the Sabbath School in the Webster Station of the M. E. Church must be viewed as in a state of more than ordinary prosperity. . . . It is the sentiment of the Superintendant that the school is more prosperous now than ever before at this season of the year since he resided in town. Such is the interest felt by the Superintendants and Teachers that they have during the last Quarter established a monthly Prayer meeting for the benefit and spiritual interest of the school.

This Sabbath school owed its origin to Samuel Slater. Like his mentor, Jedediah Strutt, Samuel Slater established Sabbath schools in each of his industrial villages.

Based on the British system he had observed, these schools were to "condition the children for their primary duty in life as hewers of wood and drawers of water."

Through these Sunday schools, Samuel Slater sought to foster attitudes toward right and proper conduct that would make children good citizens and good workers. A hymn from Dr. Isaac Watts's songbooks sung by the children in Slatersville and Webster began:

> Why should I deprive my neighbor
> Of his goods against his will?
> Hands were made for honest labour,
> Not to plunder or to steal.

When churches became firmly established in Webster and Slatersville, Slater disbanded his Sunday school and relinquished moral education and industrial training to the churches.

In transferring moral education to religious bodies, Slater could be confident that the church would continue to inculcate virtues and beliefs sympathetic to the new industrial order. In Webster, for example, the men who ran the Sunday school were the same men who supervised local factory operations. For twelve to fourteen hours each day, six days each week, children worked under Charles Waite and William Kimball, and on the seventh day they listened while the same men interpreted the scriptures. . . .

Values taught in the Sunday schools proved favorable to factory discipline. One of the first lessons taught to children concerned obedience. This was the first law of childhood, the first rule of the church, and the regulation deemed indispensable for the smooth, efficient operation of the factory. Sabbath school teachers stressed this dictum and condemned all children who disobeyed those in authority, whether at home, at school, or in the factory. One lesson used to instill this particular value might have been introduced to children in the following way: "As you sit here now, listening to me," the Sabbath school teacher might begin,

> can you remember any disobedient habits of yours, that make the father and the Mother unhappy, when they look at you and see how fast you are growing, without growing better? Is it true that you have had a bad temper, and do not love to be controlled? . . . Is it true that you have grown, but have not grown out of any of these habits: just as bad as ever, just as disobedient, just as wicked with the tongue as ever?

Punctuality, a cornerstone of any work ethic, also received considerable attention from the Methodists. They were concerned about time. In an era when people were accustomed to family time and to task-oriented labor, Methodist children were being taught: "Be punctual. Do everything exactly at the time." In his reports to the company, factory agent and Sabbath school administrator Charles Waite often stressed the need for punctuality: "Punctuality is the life of business whether in the counting house or the factory." The severe style of life demanded of the faithful allowed no place for carefree play, laughter, or harmless pranks. "No room for mirth or trifling here," began a child's hymn on amusement titled "And Am I Only Born to Die?" Children were constantly warned that "life so soon is gone," that although

> We are but young—yet we must die,
> Perhaps our latter end is nigh.

All hymns carried a similar warning: children should "sport no more with idle toys, and seek far purer, richer joys," devote themselves totally to Christ, and obey the teachings of the church.

Many values, including punctuality, attention to duty, and seriousness of purpose, were neatly summarized in the Webster Sabbath school constitution, which was drawn up by local church officials. The constitution was in fact a code of conduct similar to that maintained in the factory. In part the constitution required all children "to be regular in attendance, and punctually present at the hour appointed to open school. To pay a strict and respectful attention to whatever the teacher or Superintendent shall say or request. To avoid whispering, laughing and any other improper conduct." Altogether these values became the moral foundation for a strict work ethic. But one element essential to the successful operation of this ethic was missing: internal self-discipline.

As a work ethic these dictums and values would have been much less effective had not the church also taught self-discipline, self-restraint, and self-regulation of behavior. All efforts were made to internalize values in order to create an inner discipline that would control and limit the child's behavior. Children were taught to "do good" instinctively and to develop an internal drive toward right and proper conduct. In effect, they became their own taskmasters; conscience rather than rewards and punishments directed their actions.

To achieve this end, Sunday school teachers linked proper conduct to grace or, to put it conversely, disobedience to damnation. An exchange used to close an infants' class made the connection explicit:

TEACHER: Do you know who belong to Satan's army? Say after me—All who tell lies, all who swear and cheat; all who steal; all who are cruel.

In the child's mind, to cheat, to steal, to lie, or to misbehave in any way was to violate God's law, lose grace, and risk damnation. And such a risk was unthinkable. The songs published in *Hymns for Sunday Schools* describe hell in forceful and emotional terms:

> There is a dreadful hell,
>   And everlasting pains;
> There sinners must with devils dwell,
>   In darkness, fire, and chains.

Images of everlasting punishment and fears of eternal damnation worked to ensure a strict and steady compliance with the values advanced by the church.

The Sabbath school trained Webster's child workers well. In the factory, children quickly learned to obey all orders, for to disobey was to feel anxious and to risk censure or eternal damnation. Corporal punishment, fines, and the ultimate discipline—dismissal—were largely absent, and in fact were unnecessary when children readily and willingly, not to say cheerfully, obeyed the dictates of second hand and overseer. Operations almost always ran smoothly. Supervisors faced few disciplinary problems such as absence, theft, inattention to duties, or general mischievous behavior. The instructions children received in the Sabbath school were largely responsible for the exemplary behavior.

The tenets of the church were reinforced by lessons learned in the home. In the area of discipline the responsibility of parents was widely recognized. . . .

The values taught in the home were those required by industry: they served to make both dutiful, respectful children and submissive workers. Even the most liberal authorities on child-rearing practices, such as Lydia M. Child, cautioned parents that "implicit obedience is the first law of childhood," that "whatever a mother says always must be done." Other writers concurred. John Abbott, described by one historian as the Spock and Seuss to the people of the Civil War generation, went a step further and joined disobedience with wickedness. In *Child at Home* he wrote: "Think you, God can look upon the disobedience of a child as a trifling sin? . . . It is inexcusable ingratitude."

> The only path of safety and happiness is implicit obedience. If you, in the slightest particular, yield to temptation, and do that which you know to be wrong, you will not know when or where to stop. To hide one crime, you will be guilty of another; and thus you will draw upon yourself the frown of your maker, and expose yourself to sorrow for time and eternity.

All commands had to be immediately and cheerfully obeyed. Children were expected to respond to orders with glad and happy hearts. Again John Abbott: "Obedience requires of you, not only to do as you are bidden, but to do it with cheerfulness and alacrity"; and Theodore Dwight, Jr.: "Children should be obedient—must be obedient, habitually and cheerfully."

If obedience was the first law of childhood, then deference was the second. Children quickly realized their subordinate position within the patriarchal family. Mother taught that father was the head and ruler of the household, that he stood before them as God's representative on earth, and that, as supreme earthly legislator, he exercised complete control over their every action. According to Humphrey, "children must early be brought under absolute parental authority, and must submit to all the rules and regulations of the family during the whole period of their minority, and even longer, if they choose to remain at home." Once again religious injunctions were employed. Humphrey warned: "Now to disobey your parents, is to dishonor them. This you have done, and in doing it, you see you have broken God's holy law. We can forgive you, but that will not lessen your guilt, nor procure forgiveness from your heavenly Father. You must repent and do so no more."

Lessons taught in the home, reinforced by tenets learned from the scriptures, became the moral foundation for a disciplined labor force. Workers found little difference between disciplinary patterns in home and factory. Both home and factory were paternalistic, and both were controlled by men who expected unquestioning compliance with all commands. Children merely transferred their values and behavior patterns from the home and the church to the factory; old values were easily accommodated by the new institution.

Changes under way within the factory would have important consequences for the family system of labor. It was difficult for the Slater family to achieve a higher level of economic rationality while householders continued to influence factory operations. Disciplinary policies, placement procedures, and conditions of labor, customarily part of the domain of householders, were in conflict with the rational organization and operation of the factory floor. Authority could not remain divided between householder and factory master. By the 1830s management appeared to be ready to sacrifice the moral discipline associated with the family and the church in order to obtain more extensive control over the individual worker. Privileges once accorded the householder in the factory came under scrutiny and began to be dismantled as economic factors became the primary influence in the actions of management. . . .

Among the first issues addressed by the Slater family was the work schedule. The Slater family introduced Sunday and overtime work, and members of the same family began working different shifts. Some children worked extra hours on Tuesdays and Wednesdays, others on Thursdays and Saturdays; householders and older boys worked on Sundays. Mothers could not be certain when all members of the family or unit would be together. Sunday lost significance as the traditional day for family as well as for religious communion. Further inroads against tradition followed. Morning and afternoon breaks, which had long been periods for workers to meet and chat with kin, to exchange gossip with fellow workers, even to slip out of the mill and dash home or run errands, were abolished. Agents complained that workers took advantage of the breaks, that they stretched the allotted fifteen minutes into forty-five or sixty minutes. By eliminating rest periods, Slater forced more work from his laborers.

Parental supervisory prerogatives also came under attack. Samuel Slater and Sons assumed the power once vested in mule spinners to hire, pay, discipline, and dismiss piecers. A mule spinner no longer had the right to hire and supervise his sons or to teach them his trade. Parents were also forbidden to enter the mill and supervise their children while they were in the overseer's charge. Householders who objected to this regulation were fired. Peter Mayo's entire family, for example, was discharged because he attempted "to control his family whilst under charge of overseer and disorderly conduct generally." Economic incentives and penalties began to replace traditional forms of control within the factory. To encourage acceptable standards of work and behavior, the stick-and-carrot approach was introduced. Black marks were recorded against weavers for shoddy work and fines for tardiness, absence without leave, or disorderly conduct were deducted from their wages, while good work was rewarded by extra allowances.

A further assault against long-standing practices occurred when manufacturers abandoned the family wage system and began to pay wages directly to individual workers. Initiated in the mid-1830s, this method of payment was first introduced in the weaving department, but when parents complained, the former system was restored. In the early 1840s the firm tried once again, and this time it succeeded. By 1845 each worker received his or her wages. On settlement day in 1845 Daniel Wade, a watchman, and his two adolescent daughters, Laura and Elmira, both weavers, received separate pay slips. Children now could dispose of their own income. With the introduction of the new pay system, contracts were eliminated.

When the householder collected all wages, he controlled the available income and distributed it according to his priorities. With this new arrangement, however, economic power shifted in part to children and adolescent wage workers, and the householder's domination of the family was threatened. Parents had to negotiate with each child over the disposal of his or her wages. With economic independence, with jobs available to individuals in Webster and elsewhere, children, charges, and boarders could move out of the family home and take up residence in local boardinghouses or leave the community altogether. By this time the company operated two large factory boardinghouses, one that accommodated fifty-six men and women and another that housed twenty-eight people. Local residents also took in lodgers. . . .

While Slater checked the power of the householder, he also tried to introduce new policies that would increase the productivity of his labor force. The workday was stretched another fifteen, twenty, or thirty minutes, depending on the whim or the needs of the factory agent. It should be remembered that few workmen had clocks, and that a factory bell summoned hands to work, signaled breaks for lunch and dinner, and tolled again at quitting time. But factory time invariably fell behind true time, and agents exacted extra work from hands. This was the case not only in the Slater mills but throughout southern New England. At the Hope factory in Rhode Island, operatives started work approximately twenty-five minutes after daybreak and did not leave for home until the factory bell signaled the end of the day at 8:00 P.M. But as the *Free Inquirer* reported, 8:00 by factory time "is from twenty to twenty-five minutes behind the true time." Many manufacturers defended this practice, arguing that "the workmen and children being thus employed, have no time to spend in idleness or vicious amusements." Forced to maintain the production schedules set by the manufacturer and to cut costs where possible, supervisors lengthened the workday to obtain additional labor from hands.

To increase production further, the stretch-out and the speedup were intensified. Slater crowded more and more machines into already cramped spinning, carding, and weaving rooms and assigned additional machines to each worker. In the weaving department, for example, the number of looms attended by each weaver was increased steadily from two to three to four and then to six. Not only did the hands operate more machines, but the machines were run at higher speeds. Initially the speedup was management's response to the pressure of weavers who worked on a piece-rate basis (approximately 20 cents a cut for weaving 4-by-4 sheeting and shirting), who could increase their earnings only by producing more cloth. In 1837 Alexander Hodges complained to the head office: "The weavers are being uneasy about the speed being slow and some of the new ones will leave. I think we had better put on a little in order to keep the best of them nothing short of this will answer as the mills in this vicinity have advanced the prices." Soon, however, the speedup became a method to increase production. Writing to Union Mills in 1855, Fletcher confided, "As soon as the supply of good weavers can be obtained, . . . the increased speed of looms will show itself by increased quantity." Piece rates ramained constant at the earlier level. The speedup and stretch-out were introduced into almost every room in the factory, without an appreciable increase in pay. . . .

Supply and demand factors, new technology, education laws, and factory acts worked together by the 1850s to transform the labor force employed at Samuel Slater and Sons. The route pursued by the firm led toward an autonomous worker, one who was cut off from his or her family and looked to the factory system for opportunity, support, and survival. The labor force had been streamlined; the family unit, tied to a firm social base, was replaced by an individual tied to the wage economy.

 ## FOR FURTHER STUDY

1. Older traditions emphasized the importance of the family, parental authority, and the differences between men's and women's work. How did early industrialists such as Slater attempt to reconcile the new factory system with these preindustrial traditions?

2. Explain how the ethical and moral values of Protestant Christianity were related to the goals of industrial management.

3. How did the Slater Company break down traditional prerogatives of labor and older patterns of parental control?

4. In another country or another period, the expansion of the available labor force by the introduction of women, children, and immigrants might not have resulted in a general degradation of the position of all labor. What, in the position of labor in the early nineteenth century or in the general state of the Industrial Revolution at that time, might account for the fact that such degradation did happen in the United States?

5. What similarities and differences are there in the lot of workers in the early nineteenth century and in the present with respect to: their ability to bargain to improve their positions; the training necessary for their jobs; their mobility; their relationship to their employers; their security?

FOR FURTHER READING

The history of American workers and their working conditions is well researched. One perennial classic that gives an excellent picture of industrial conditions is Norman Ware's *The Industrial Worker, 1840–1860* (1964). A more recent analysis of skilled craftsmen is W. J. Rorahbaugh, *The Craft Apprentice: From Franklin to the Machine Age in America* (1986). New England has received most of the attention because it was the center of American industry for much of the antebellum period. Important studies include David A. Zonderman, *Aspirations and Anxieties: New England Workers and the Mechanized Factory System, 1815–1850* (1992), and Steven Dunwell, *The Run of the Mill* (1978), which shows factories through photographs and illustrations. More specialized studies of towns built exclu-sively for industry include Thomas Dublin, *Women at Work: The Transformation of Work and Community in Lowell, Massachusetts, 1826–1860* (1979), Anthony F. C. Wallace, *Rockdale: The Growth of an American Village in the Early Industrial Revolution* (1978), and Jonathan Prude, *The Coming of Industrial Order: Town and Factory Life in Rural Massachusetts, 1810–1860* (1983). Studies of larger cities include Bruce Laurie, *Working People of Philadelphia, 1800–1850* (1980), Sean Wilentz, *Chants Democratic: New York City and the Rise of the American Working Class, 1788–1850* (1984), and Steven J. Ross, *Workers on the Edge: Work, Leisure, and Politics in Cincinnati, 1788–1890* (1985).

Workers had to function within the changing American economy during the antebel-lum period. Several overviews include Thomas C. Cochran, *Frontiers of Change: Early Industrialism in American* (1981), Elisha P. Douglass, *The Coming of Age of American Busi-ness . . . 1600–1900* (1971), and Douglass C. North, *Economic Growth of the United States, 1790–1860* (1966). For inventors see *The Ingenious Yankees* (1975) by Joseph and Frances Gies. Technological changes inspired much of the early industrial revolution, as you can see in David A. Hounshell, *From the American System to Mass Production, 1800–1932: The Development of Manufacturing Technology in the United States* (1984), Nathan Rosenberg, *Technology and American Economic Growth* (1973), and David F. Hawke, *Nuts and Bolts of the Past: American Technology, 1776–1860* (1988). For one of the pioneers of American indus-try see Barbara M. Tucker, *Samuel Slater and the Origins of the American Textile Industry, 1790–1860* (1984).

A good general work on American economic development is Gilbert C. Fite and Jim E. Reese, *An Economic History of the United States,* 3rd ed. (1973).

CHAPTER 11

The Philbrook Museum of Art, Tulsa, OK, Museum Purchase (1966.11.2)

This painting, titled "The Endless Trail," (detail) by Native American artist Jerome Tiger starkly portrays the Cherokee tribe during their forced march west from their ancient homeland.

TRAIL OF TEARS

DALE VAN EVERY

*I*n the Declaration of Independence, Jefferson wrote that "all men are created equal" and are divinely endowed with the rights of life, liberty, and the pursuit of happiness. The members of the Continental Congress who signed their names to that proclamation were concerned with the rights of the colonists in relation to the governing power of England. Few of them considered these ringing phrases as guaranteeing social or political rights to minorities in American society. Some few voices were raised to suggest that women, blacks, and Native Americans might have a greater cause to revolt than did the planters, lawyers, and merchants who led the revolution against the authority of King George III. Throughout much of American history, various national, racial, and religious groups have been treated as less than equal.

The Age of Reform exhibited some striking contrasts in American sentiment. In many respects, it is a most revealing period for judging both the achievements and the failures of the American people in living up to the philosophy expressed in the Declaration. The 1830s witnessed the first great period of American social reform, with scores of organizations founded to assist the handicapped and the unfortunate. But it is also a decade that, one might say, lives in historical infamy, because Native American tribes were removed from their ancient homelands, as whites coveted and took over their lands.

In the selection that follows, Dale Van Every suggests that this is the ultimate catastrophe that can befall a people. Being torn from the land of one's birth, losing most or all of one's belongings, being forced to find a livelihood as best one can in an unfamiliar country, and losing one's very sense of identity are experiences we can hardly comprehend. The story of the removal of the Civilized Tribes of the southeastern United States—the Creeks, Chickasaws, Choctaws, Seminoles, and Cherokees—to new territories beyond the Mississippi River, and the numerous casualties they suffered along the "Trail of Tears," is one of the most famous and tragic in American history. In the North, the same story was repeated with different characters on a somewhat smaller

155

scale. Whatever the Declaration of Independence meant to white, male Americans in the early nineteenth century, it must have appeared to be a bitter mockery to the Native Americans who were forced out of their homes by this cruel invasion.

History records the sufferings of innumerable peoples whose country was overrun and possessed by alien invaders. There have been relatively fewer recorded occasions, as in the instance of the Babylonian Captivity of the Jews, of an entire people being compelled to abandon their country. This has been universally regarded as the ultimate catastrophe that can befall a people inasmuch as it deprives them of the roots which sustain their identity. Upon the exiles has been pronounced a sentence that by its nature denies all hope of reprieve or relief. To Indians, with their inherited conception of the land of their birth as the repository of those spiritual links to their ancestors which were holy and therefore indissoluble, the prospect of expulsion was clothed with added dreads beyond human evaluation.

The threat was in all its aspects so monstrous that in the spring of 1838 the bewildered masses of the Cherokee people, homeless, hungry, destitute, still remained incredulous that so fearful a fate could actually impend. Outrageously as they had been harassed for the past ten years by Georgia and Alabama white men, they still clung to their trust that most white men wished them well. This was a confidence instilled in them by the reports of John Ross [a respected Cherokee chief] who had been made more conversant with the apparent truth by his wide travels across the immense white nation stretching beyond the Cherokee horizon. They had been further prepared to accept his judgment on the inherent goodness of the white race by their own experience with the many white men who had lived among them as teachers, missionaries and counselors, sharing their struggles and tribulations. Their more recent experience with [General John] Wool and his officers and with [General R. G.] Dunlap and his Tennesseans had strengthened their impression that the white race could not be wholly committed to their destruction.

Ross was still in Washington engaged in a final frantic effort, with some dawning hope of success, to wring from the administration a temporary postponement of removal. His followers were continuing to obey his injunction that they persist in their nonviolent resistance. Most continued to refuse even to give their names or a list of their belongings to the agents commissioned to organize the details of the migration. May 23, two years from the date of the President's proclamation of

Adaptation of text from chapter eighteen, from *Disinherited: The Lost Birthright of the American Indian* by Dale Van Every. Copyright © 1966 by Dale Van Every. Reprinted by permission of HarperCollins Publishers Inc.

the Senate's ratification of the treaty, was the day, as all had for months been warned, when their residence in the east would become illegal but they still could not believe that a development so frightful could be given reality by that day's sunrise. Even after five regiments of regulars and 4,000 militia and volunteers from adjacent states began pouring into their country they still could not believe.

Major General [Winfield] Scott arrived May 8 to take command of the military operation. His May 10, 1838 address to the Cherokee people proclaimed the terrible reality in terms no Cherokee could longer mistake:

> Cherokees—The President of the United States has sent me with a powerful army, to cause you, in obedience to the treaty of 1835, to join that part of your people who are already established in prosperity on the other side of the Mississippi. Unhappily, the two years which were allowed for the purpose, you have suffered to pass away without following, and without making preparations to follow, and now, or by the time this solemn *address* shall reach your distant settlements, the emigration must be commenced in haste, but, I hope, without disorder. I have no power, by granting a farther delay, to correct the error that you have committed. The full moon of May is already on the wane, and before another shall have passed away, every Cherokee man, woman, and child . . . must be in motion to join their brethren in the far West. . . . My troops already occupy many positions in the country that you are to abandon, and thousands and thousands are approaching from every quarter, to tender resistance and escape alike hopeless. . . . Chiefs, head men, and warriors—Will you then, by resistance, compel us to resort to arms? God forbid. Or will you, by flight, seek to hide yourself in mountains and forests, and thus oblige us to hunt you down? Remember that, in pursuit, it may be impossible to avoid conflicts. The blood of the white man, or the blood of the red man, may be spilt, and if spilt, however accidentally, it may be impossible for the discreet and humane among you, or among us, to prevent a general war and carnage. Think of this, my Cherokee brethren. I am an old warrior, and have been present at many a scene of slaughter; but spare me, I beseech you, the horror of witnessing the destruction of the Cherokees.

Scott sincerely hoped that the enforced removal could be accomplished not only without bloodshed but without undue hardship inflicted upon the unfortunate thousands being ejected at bayonet's point from their homes. He had been impressed by Ross during conferences with him in Washington and like most professional soldiers of his time had developed a genuine regard for Indians. In his May 17 general orders to his troops he sternly admonished them to practice restraint:

> Considering the number and temper of the mass to be removed together with the extent and fastnesses of the country occupied, it will readily occur that simple indiscretions, acts of harshness, and cruelty on the part of our troops, may lead, step by step, to delays, to impatience, and exasperation, and, in the end, to a general war and carnage; a result, in the case of these particular Indians, utterly abhorrent to the generous sympathies of the whole American people. Every possible kindness, compatible with the necessity of removal, must, therefore, be shown by the troops; and if, in the ranks, a despicable individual should be found capable of inflicting a wanton injury or insult on any Cherokee man, woman, or child, it is hereby made the special duty of the nearest good officer or man instantly to interpose, and to seize and consign

the guilty wretch to the severest penalty of the laws. The major-general is fully persuaded that this injunction will not be neglected by the brave men under his command, who cannot be otherwise than jealous of their honor and that of their country.

Scott's intentions were humane but the larger portion of his army were state levies unaccustomed to discipline and without his professional susceptibilities. The nature of the operation required the army's dispersion in scattered detachments over a wide area. Most of the Cherokee to be removed were inhabitants of Georgia and their apprehension was conducted by Georgia militia who had long as a matter of policy been habituated to dealing harshly with Indians. Prison stockades had been erected at assembly and embarkation points in which the Cherokee were to be herded and confined while awaiting transportation west. There was little or no likelihood of attempted resistance. Most had been disarmed during Wool's regime and the irresistible military power that had been brought to bear was self-evident. The classic account of what next transpired is that recorded by James Mooney. His contribution to the Bureau of American Ethnology, eventually published in the 19th Annual Report in 1900 under the title *Myths of the Cherokee,* included a history of the Cherokee based upon years of field work. His narrative of the 1838 expulsion was drawn from personal interviews with survivors, white officers as well as Cherokee victims, and had therefore much of the vitality of an eyewitness report:

> The history of this Cherokee removal of 1838, as gleaned by the author from the lips of actors in the tragedy, may well exceed in weight of grief and pathos any other passage in American history. Even the much-sung exile of the Acadians falls far behind it in its sum of death and misery. Under Scott's order the troops were disposed at various points throughout the Cherokee country, where stockade forts were erected for gathering in and holding the Indians preparatory to removal. From these, squads of troops were sent to search out with rifle and bayonet every small cabin hidden away in the coves or by the sides of mountain streams, to seize and bring in as prisoners all the occupants, however or wherever they might be found. Families at dinner were startled by the sudden gleam of bayonets in the doorway and rose up to be driven with blows and oaths along the weary miles of trail that led to the stockade. Men were seized in their fields or going along the road, women were taken from their wheels and children from their play. In many cases, on turning for one last look as they crossed the ridge, they saw their homes in flames, fired by the lawless rabble that followed on the heels of the soldiers to loot and pillage. So keen were these outlaws on the scent that in some instances they were driving off the cattle and other stock of the Indians almost before the soldiers had fairly started their owners in the other direction. Systematic hunts were made by the same men for Indian graves, to rob them of the silver pendants and other valuables deposited with the dead. A Georgia volunteer, afterward a colonel in the confederate service, said: "I fought through the civil war and have seen men shot to pieces and slaughtered by thousands, but the Cherokee removal was the cruelest work I ever knew." To prevent escape the soldiers had been ordered to approach and surround each house, so far as possible, so as to come upon the occupants without warning. One old patriarch, when thus surprised, calmly called his children and grandchildren around him, and, kneeling down, bid them pray with him in their own language, while the astonished onlookers looked on

in silence. Then rising he led the way into exile. A woman, on finding the house surrounded, went to the door and called up the chickens to be fed for the last time, after which, taking her infant on her back and her two other children by the hand, she followed her husband with the soldiers.

Within days nearly 17,000 Cherokee had been crowded into the stockades. Sanitation measures were inadequate in those makeshift concentration camps. Indian families, accustomed to a more spacious and isolated existence, were unable to adapt to the necessities of this mass imprisonment. Hundreds of the inmates sickened. The Indian was by his nature peculiarly susceptible to the depressions produced by confinement. Many lost any will to live and perceiving no glimmer of hope, resigned themselves to death. Those who had become converts found some comfort in the ministrations of their white and native pastors. In every stockade hymn singings and prayer meetings were almost continuous.

All physical preparations had been carefully planned in advance by the federal authorities in charge of the migration so that little time might be lost in getting the movement under way. In the first and second weeks of June two detachments of some 800 exiles were driven aboard the waiting fleets of steamboats, keelboats and flatboats for the descent of the Tennessee. They passed down the storied waterway by the same route taken by the first white settlers of middle Tennessee under John Donelson in 1780. In the shadow of Lookout Mountain they could survey the wilderness vastnesses from which for 20 years bands of their immediate forebears had sallied to devastate the white frontier, some of them commanded by war chiefs who had lived to be condemned to this exile. Then, at Muscle Shoals there came an ironic contrast between the past and the future as Indians being driven from their ancient homeland were committed to transportation by the white man's newest invention. They disembarked from their boats to clamber, momentarily diverted, aboard the cars drawn by the two puffing little locomotives of the railroad recently constructed to move freight and passengers around the rapids. Returning to other boats, they resumed their seemingly interminable journey in the debilitating heat of an increasingly oppressive summer. The attendant army officers, however sympathetic, were helpless against the waves of illnesses. Scott, moving new contingents toward embarkation, was appalled by the reports he received of the mounting death rate among those who had already been dispatched.

The troops assembled for Cherokee expulsion had been by considered governmental design so numerous as to present a show of military power so overwhelming as to provide no faintest invitation to Indian resistance. By the army's first pounce more than nine tenths of the population had been rounded up and driven into the stockades. There remained only a handful of the wilder and more primitive residents of the higher mountains still at large. This handful, however, represented a problem causing Scott serious concern. Were they provoked to resist they might among their remote and cloudwreathed peaks prove as difficult to apprehend as were the Seminole in their swamps. From this tactical threat sprang the one heroic action to gleam across the otherwise unrelieved despondency of the removal scene.

Tsali was an hitherto undistinguished mountain Cherokee who suddenly soared to an eminence in Cherokee annals comparable to the homage accorded an Attakullaculla, an Old Tassel, a Sequoyah or a John Ross. The stories of his inspired exploit, drawn from eyewitnesses, survivors and references in contemporary official records, vary in detail and have become encrusted by legend but coincide in most essentials. According to the more generally accepted version, a young Cherokee woman upon being assaulted by two soldiers killed both with a hatchet. Tsali hid the weapon under his shirt and assumed responsibility for his kinswoman's act. Scott could not permit the death of his soldiers to remain unpunished and served notice on the band of mountain Cherokee of which Tsali was a member that a scapegoat must be produced. The band felt that it had a reasonable chance to elude pursuit indefinitely but its councils were impressed by the advice of a white trader, William Thomas, a friend of his native customers in the notable tradition of Ludovic Grant, Alexander Cameron and John McDonald. Thomas pointed out the advantage that could be taken of Scott's demand. Tsali was prepared to offer his life for his people. His fellow tribesmen thereupon notified Scott that he would be turned over to American justice in return for American permission to remain unmolested in their mountains. Scott, eager to escape the uncertainties of a guerrilla campaign in so difficult a terrain, agreed to recommend this course to Washington. Tsali was brought in, the voluntary prisoner of his compatriots. His Cherokee custodians were required to serve as the firing squad by which he, his brother and his eldest son were executed. The story became one of the few Indian stories with a happy ending. Thomas continued for years to interest himself in the prolonged negotiations with the governments of the United States and North Carolina which eventually resulted in federal and state recognition of Cherokee title to their mountain holdings. Tsali's sacrifice had permitted this fraction of the nation to become the remnant of the East Cherokee [and] to cling to their homeland where they still are colorful inhabitants of the North Carolina mountains.

Aside from the Tsali episode the roundup of the Cherokee proceeded without interruption. By June 18 General Charles Floyd, commanding the Georgia militia engaged in it, was able to report to his governor that no Cherokee remained on the soil of Georgia except as a prisoner in a stockade. Scott was able to discharge his volunteers June 17 and two days later to dispatch three of his five regular regiments to sectors where military needs were more pressing, two to the Canadian border and one to Florida.

Meanwhile so many migrants were dying in the drought and heat to which the initial removal was subjected that Scott was constrained to lighten the inexorable pressures. The Cherokee Council, which though technically illegal still spoke for the Cherokee people, begged for a postponement to the more healthful weather of autumn. Scott agreed. In July Ross returned and in conferences with Scott worked out a further agreement under which the Cherokee would cease passive resistance and under his supervision undertake a voluntary migration as soon as weather permitted. Scott was glad to be relieved of further need to use military force. The administration was glad to be offered some defense against the storm of northern criticism. Even Georgia made no serious protest, inasmuch as the Cherokee had already been removed from their land to stockades and there remained no questioning of the state's sovereignty. The one remonstrance, aside from the complaints of contractors, was voiced by the aging [Andrew] Jackson from his retirement at The Hermitage in a letter of August 23, 1838 to Felix Grundy, Attorney General of the United States:

> . . . The contract with Ross must be arrested, or you may rely upon it, the expense and other evils will shake the popularity of the administration to its center. What madness and folly to have anything to do with Ross, when the agent was proceeding well with the removal. . . . The time and circumstances under which Gen'l Scott made this contract shows that he is no economist, or is, *sub rosa,* in league with [Henry] Clay & Co. to bring disgrace on the administration. The evil is done. It behooves Mr. [President Martin] Van Buren to act with energy to throw it off his shoulders. I enclose a letter to you under cover, unsealed, which you may read, seal, and deliver to him, that you may aid him with your views in getting out of this real difficulty.

> Your friend in haste
Andrew Jackson

> P.S. I am so feeble I can scarcely wield my pen, but friendship dictates it & the subject excites me. Why is it that the scamp Ross is not banished from the notice of the administration?

Ross, having at last recognized the inevitable, gave to his preparations for the voluntary removal the same driving energy and attention to detail he had until then devoted to resisting removal. All phases of the organization of the national effort were gathered into his hands. All financial arrangements were under his supervision, including the disbursement of the basic federal subsistence allowance of 16 cents a day for each person and 40 cents a day for each horse. For convenience in management en route the 13,000 Cherokee remaining in the stockades were divided into detachments of roughly a thousand to head each of which he appointed a Cherokee commander. At a final meeting of the Cherokee Council it was provided that the constitution and laws of the Nation should be considered equally valid in the west.

The first detachment set out October 1, 1838 on the dreaded journey over the route which in Cherokee memory became known as The Trail of Tears. The last started November 4. The improvement in weather awaited during the tedious summer months in the stockades did not materialize. The spring migration had been cursed by oppressive heat and drought. The fall migration encountered deluges of rain followed by excessive cold. To the hundreds of deaths from heat-induced diseases were now added new hundreds of deaths from prolonged exposure.

The most vivid general account of the 1838 migration is again that of James Mooney, assembled from the recollections of participants:

> . . . in October, 1838, the long procession of exiles was set in motion. A very few went by the river route; the rest, nearly all of the 13,000, went overland. Crossing to the north side of the Hiwassee at a ferry above Gunstocker creek, they proceeded down

along the river, the sick, the old people, and the smaller children, with the blankets, cooking pots, and other belongings in wagons, the rest on foot or on horses. The number of wagons was 645. It was like the march of an army, regiment after regiment, the wagons in the center, the officers along the line and the horsemen on the flanks and at the rear. Tennessee river was crossed at Tucker (?) ferry, a short distance above Jollys island, at the mouth of the Hiwassee. Thence the route lay south of Pikeville, through McMinnville and on to Nashville, where the Cumberland was crossed. Then they went on to Hopkinsville, Kentucky, where the noted chief Whitepath, in charge of a detachment, sickened and died. His people buried him by the roadside, with a box over the grave and poles with streamers around it, that the others coming on behind might note the spot and remember him. Somewhere also along that march of death—for the exiles died by tens and twenties every day of the journey—the devoted wife of John Ross sank down, leaving him to go on with the bitter pain of bereavement added to heartbreak at the ruin of his nation. The Ohio was crossed at a ferry near the mouth of the Cumberland, and the army passed on through southern Illinois until the great Mississippi was reached opposite Cape Girardeau, Missouri. It was now the middle of winter, with the river running full of ice, so that several detachments were obliged to wait some time on the eastern bank for the channel to become clear. In talking with old men and women at Tahlequah the author found that the lapse of over half a century had not sufficed to wipe out the memory of the miseries of that halt beside the frozen river, with hundreds of sick and dying penned up in wagons or stretched upon the ground, with only a blanket overhead to keep out the January blast. The crossing was made at last in two divisions, at Cape Girardeau and at Green's Ferry, a short distance below, whence the march was made on through Missouri to Indian Territory, the later detachments making a northerly circuit by Springfield, because those who had gone before had killed off all the game along the direct route. At last their destination was reached. They had started in October, 1838, and it was now March, 1839, the journey having occupied barely six months of the hardest part of the year.

President Van Buren in his December 1838 message to Congress announced the administration's view of the event:

> . . . It affords me sincere pleasure to apprise the Congress of the entire removal of the Cherokee Nation of Indians to their new homes west of the Mississippi. The measures authorized by Congress at its last session have had the happiest effects. By an agreement concluded with them by the commanding general in that country, their removal has been principally under the conduct of their own chiefs, and they have emigrated without any apparent reluctance.

A traveler who had encountered the Indians en route was moved by the President's words to write his own eyewitness report which was published in the January 26, 1839 *New York Observer* under the heading "A Native of Maine, traveling in the Western Country":

> . . . On Tuesday evening we fell in with a detachment of the poor Cherokee Indians . . . about eleven hundred Indians—sixty wagons—six hundred horses, and perhaps forty pairs of oxen. We found them in the forest camped for the night by the road side . . . under a severe fall of rain accompanied by heavy wind. With their canvas for a shield from the inclemency of the weather, and the cold wet ground for a resting

place, after the fatigue of the day, they spent the night . . . many of the aged Indians were suffering extremely from the fatigue of the journey, and the ill health conse- quent upon it . . . several were then quite ill, and one aged man we were informed was then in the last struggles of death. . . . The last detachment which we passed on the 7th embraced rising two thousands Indians with horses and mules in proportion. The forward part of the train we found just pitching their tents for the night, and notwithstanding some thirty or forty wagons were already stationed, we found the road literally filled with the procession for about three miles in length. The sick and feeble were carried in wagons—about as comfortable for traveling as a New England ox cart with a covering over it—a great many ride on horseback and multitudes go on foot—even aged females, apparently nearly ready to drop into the grave, were traveling with heavy burdens attached to the back—on the sometimes frozen ground, and sometimes muddy streets, with no covering for the feet except what na- ture had given them. . . . We learned from the inhabitants on the road where the Indians passed, that they buried fourteen or fifteen at every stopping place, and they make a journey of ten miles per day only on an average. One fact which to my own mind seemed a lesson indeed to the American nation is, that they will not travel on the Sabbath. . . . The Indians as a whole carry on their countenances every thing but the appearance of happiness. Some carry a downcast dejected look bordering upon the appearance of despair others a wild frantic appearance as if about to burst the chains of nature and pounce like a tiger upon their enemies. . . . When I past [sic] the last detachment of those suffering exiles and thought that my native coun- trymen had thus expelled them from their native soil and their much-loved homes, and that too in this inclement season of the year in all their suffering, I turned from the sight with feelings which language cannot express. . . . I felt that I would not en- counter the secret silent prayer of one of these sufferers armed with the energy that faith and hope would give it (if there be a God who avenges the wrongs of the in- jured) for all the lands of Georgia. . . . When I read in the President's message that he was happy to inform the Senate that the Cherokees were peaceably and without reluctance removed—and remember that it was on the third day of December when not one of the detachments had reached their destination; and that a large majority had not made even half their journey when he made that declaration, I thought I wished the President could have been there that very day in Kentucky with myself, and have seen the comfort and the willingness with which the Cherokees were mak- ing their journey.

The first migrants reached their destination on the plains beyond the western border of Arkansas January 4, 1839. Other contingents continued to straggle in until late in March. Examination of all available records by Grant Foreman, out- standing authority on Indian removal, led him to conclude 4,000 Cherokee had died either during confinement in the stockades or on their 800-mile journey west.

While the Cherokee were traversing their Trail of Tears their fellow southern Indians were committed to afflictions as dismal. The processes of removal were grinding out the cumulative calamities that had been visited upon a race by gov- ernmental fiat.

The Chickasaw had at length embarked upon their self-governed migration. They were the aristocrats of the Indian world, long noted for the prowess of their warriors, the beauty of their women and the speed of their horses. They had bargained shrewdly until they had wrung every possible advantage from federal authorities, including uninterrupted control over their affairs and a good price for their lands in western Tennessee and northwestern Mississippi. When finally they started west it was a movement under their own leadership undertaken at a time of their own choosing after repeated inspections of their new territory and the route to it by their own representatives. They traveled in comfort, well supplied with equipment, food and money. It might have been expected that were removal ever to be conducted under acceptable conditions it might prove so in their case. But it did not. Their relative prosperity became one of the major causes of their undoing. Sensing unusual profits, contractors gathered stockpiles of supplies along the way in such quantities that the food spoiled before it could be eaten. The travelers were charged exorbitantly for transportation and their every other requirement. They picked up smallpox en route and the disease reached epidemic proportions after their arrival. Most had arrived too late to get in an 1838 crop and they were soon as hungry as their poorer fellow colonists. The move west had made plaintive beggars of the once proud and warlike Chickasaw.

Nearly 2,000 Seminole, rounded up by various devices, pseudoagreements and military pressures, were also on the way west in 1838. Having suffered so much more than other migrants before their start, they continued to suffer more en route. Many had scarcely emerged from their swampland refuges before they were crowded, naked and undernourished, aboard ship. Others had already endured long periods of imprisonment by which they had been weakened. Most were detained for weeks and months en route in noisome concentration camps in Tampa, Mobile and New Orleans. In addition to all their other privations and afflictions they were continually harassed at every stop and in every new state jurisdiction by the claims of slave dealers to the ownership of Seminole prisoners who showed evidence of Negro blood. A considerable proportion of Seminole were Negroes who had for generations been considered members of the tribe and even though they were closely guarded prisoners each group of exiles fiercely resisted every attempt to single out any of their number for delivery into slavery. The problem of identification had been complicated by the flight to the Seminole of many actual slaves during the war. Some of the slave traders' claims were thus clothed with a species of legitimacy which made adjudication of every dispute more difficult. As one controversial example, among the Seminole prisoners of war taken by the Creek auxiliaries in 1837 had been 90 black Seminole whom they had sold to traders. In all these disputes federal and state authorities, except for the attendant army officers, in their anxiety to expedite the removal tended to support the traders' claims to an extent that provoked a congressional investigation. Meanwhile, in Florida the war went on, with American troops now under the command of Brigadier General Zachary Taylor, later President of the United States, continuing their attempts to run to earth the some 2,000 Seminole still in hiding.

The year 1838 also witnessed the initiation of a companion Indian removal in an adjoining country. Bowl's band of Cherokee, the first recorded migrants who had fled their homelands in 1794, had eventually settled on the Texas side of the Red River in what was then Mexican territory. Joined by other Cherokee and other Indians, the colony had increased to some 8,000. At the outbreak of the Texas revolution Sam Houston had negotiated a treaty of friendship with Bowl's Cherokee which saved the Americans in Texas from possible attack by Indians at the precarious moment they were being assaulted by Santa Anna in return for a Texan recognition of Cherokee title to the land on which they had settled. But in 1838 Mirabeau Lamar, upon succeeding Houston as President of Texas, immediately proclaimed his intention of expelling all Indians from the republic. In the ensuing 1839 campaign the aged Bowl was killed, still clutching the tin box containing the documents and deeds relating to the 1836 treaty of friendship with Texas. The Texas Cherokee were driven across the Red River to share the fortunes of the West and newly arrived East Cherokee on the upper Arkansas.

Indian removal had now been accomplished. Aside from a few scattered remnants, such as the Seminole fugitives in the Florida swamps, the few mountain Cherokee in North Carolina, the Choctaw residue in Mississippi and an occasional tiny enclave in the north, every Indian nation which had originally occupied the immense expanse of woodland extending across the eastern half of the United States had been compelled to seek new homes on the plains beyond that woodland's western margin. It had required a persisting effort over a period of 15 years, distinguished not only by the sufferings inflicted upon Indians but by the virulent disagreements excited among Americans, to give effect to the outwardly plausible policy announced by [James] Monroe and [John] Calhoun in 1825. Removal had been a contemporary success in the sense that the national government had proved able to impose its will and the states concerned had been rid of unwanted Indian inhabitants. But for the Indians and for the larger interests of the United States it had been a deplorable failure. The opportunity for Indians to become useful and valued members of American society, an achievement many had seemed on the verge of attaining in 1825, had been heedlessly postponed for more than a century.

Most informed Indians had long realized that such an assimilation represented the one lingering hope that Indians might ever regain comfort and security. The mass of Indians, less aware of the economic and political realities, had as long clung despairingly to the more appealing hope that they might yet contrive some escape from the white incubus. Removal dealt crushing blows to both hopes. In the west progressive Indians were compelled to begin again, under far greater handicaps, the painful climb toward citizenship and all Indians were subjected to white exactions more distracting than any they had known in the east. It was only after decades of miraculously patient struggle that Indians were finally to gain recognition of the principle that the rights of the conquered are even more precious than the prerogatives of their conquerors.

During the three centuries Indians had been retreating before the inexorable advance of alien invaders they had been bitterly conscious that they were suffering greater deprivations than the loss of their lands and lives. Their entire way of life, their whole world as they had known it, was in the course of obliteration. They understood, as could nobody else, by how wide a margin their post-invasion opportunities to pursue happiness failed to match the opportunities they had known before invasion. There was little enough comfort in the reflection that these opportunities were being denied them by a force physically too strong for them to resist.

In their despair Indians had sought consolation in resort to the supernatural. Native prophets, such as those who had inspired the followers of Pontiac and Tecumseh, had emerged again and again to preach the doctrine of original blessedness. They had exhorted Indians to eschew every compromise with white influence, especially by forswearing the use of white tools, weapons and alcohol, so that by a return to their ancient purity they might regain the strength to regain their former freedoms. These movements had been frustrated by their adherents' realization that obedience left Indians even more defenseless than before. By the time of the removal Indians were increasingly addicted to more extravagant religious phantasies. A favorite conceit, intermittently erupting for generation after generation until its final resurgence as the Ghost Dance excitement among the Plains Indians in the late 1880's, envisioned the evocation, by appropriate prayers, dances and rites, of the innumerable spirits of all Indian dead who would return to earth as a mighty host capable of expelling the white invaders and thus restoring the land of peace and plenty Indians had once enjoyed.

Even so superior an intellect as Sequoyah's was subject to wishful fancies. He had from his youth believed that the one Indian hope to retain their identity as a people was to withdraw from white contamination. He had himself moved west nearly 20 years before removal and all his life had sought by advice and example to persuade Indians to shun intercourse with whites. In his declining years he became obsessed with the possibility that the Lost Cherokee, reputed by tribal legend to have disappeared into the farthest west in the forgotten past, still lived in innocence, freedom and security in some distant land. In his frail old age, still in pursuit of this relic of the Indian golden age, he set out on a two-year journey in search of a remote Cherokee colony reported to have found sanctuary in the mountains of Mexico. His 1843 death in a Mexican desert was giving ultimate poignancy to the discovery all Indians were being required to make. For them there was no way back. There was only the way ahead.

FOR FURTHER STUDY

1. Describe where each of the tribes discussed in this essay—the Cherokee, Seminole, and Chickasaw—lived before removal and how each of these nations reacted to the forced removal.

2. What problems did they face with respect to weather, supplies, health, and transportation on the trail west?

3. How did the sentiment of General Scott, who was directly responsible for supervising the Indian removal, differ from that of Andrew Jackson? How does a knowledge of the politics of the period help in understanding the views expressed in Jackson's letter?

4. Discuss the deeper, psychological impact of removal on the tribes. Explain what factors in the nineteenth century made it difficult to resist removal.

5. What differences can you think of between the removal of the Native Americans in this period and the forced removal of Japanese-Americans from their homes on the Pacific coast to concentration centers during World War II?

FOR FURTHER READING

The recent work of John Ehle, *Trail of Tears: The Rise and Fall of the Cherokee Nation* (1988) is both readable and well researched. Four other works deal directly with tribes involved in the removal. See William G. McLoughlin, *Cherokees and Missionaries, 1789–1839* (1984) and his *Cherokee Renaissance in the New Republic* (1987), Michael D. Green, *The Politics of Indian Removal: Creek Government and Society in Crisis* (1982), and a more general study by John R. Finger, *The Eastern Band of Cherokees, 1819–1900* (1984). Two other treatments are Arthur H. De Rosier, Jr., *The Removal of the Choctaw Indians* (1970), and Gloria Jahoda, *The Trail of Tears* (1975). Several discussions of white attitudes and federal policy are helpful in understanding these events. See Reginald Horsman, *Expansion and American Indian Policy, 1783–1812* (1967), and Bernard Sheehan, *Seeds of Extinction: Jeffersonian Philanthropy and the American Indian* (1973). For policy during Jackson's administration see Ronald N. Satz, *American Indian Policy in the Jacksonian Era* (1975), and Michael P. Rogin, *Fathers and Children: Andrew Jackson and the Subjugation of the American Indian* (1975). Another work that covers Native-white relations is Wilbur R. Jacobs, *Dispossessing the American Indian* (1972).

The best general history is Wilcomb E. Washburn, *The Indian in America* (1975).

Jerome B. Thompson's "A 'Pic Nick' in the Woods of New England," (detail) (c. 1850) is a rather idealized portrayal of a large, affectionate family group.

THE AFFECTIONATE FAMILY

STEVEN MINTZ AND SUSAN KELLOGG

$\mathcal{T}$he third essay in this volume, by Lyle Koehler, describes marital relationships in seventeenth-century New England. By the nineteenth century, very different ideas of child rearing were developing, as were changes in the roles and authority of husband and wife. In the earlier period, men spent much of their time as farmers or craftsmen in the home, and women made important contributions to family life. The father-husband, however, was the unquestioned head of the household. In the later period, children came to be seen as precious individuals, rather than primarily as economic assets to parents, so that love and support rather than only discipline were seen as parental duties.

As men increasingly went out of the home to earn a livelihood, separate spheres developed for men and women. The popular thinking of the "cult of true womanhood" suggested that women devote all of their time and strength to providing a cultivated retreat in the home for husbands and children. Womanly virtues included sexual innocence, healing the sick, teaching morality, and elevating the rougher nature of man. To write or lecture or engage in political causes was unfeminine. While some women found an increased independence and sense of authority in ruling the home, others felt constricted, and some suffered severe psychological and medical problems.

Many exceptional women exercised positions of leadership in the reforms of the Jacksonian period, and thousands of them became involved locally in antislavery activities, the temperance movement, and other crusades. As they did so, they gained confidence in themselves, skill in organizing, and an awareness of the inequality of their status. Women protested their condition at the famous Seneca Falls Convention in 1848 and fought for changes in the law and the practice on property ownership, divorce, custody of children, and a host of other subjects. They also entered new fields, including journalism, medicine, teaching, and industry. Yet, most American women continued to see their roles as those of wives and mothers. The following essay by Steven Mintz and Susan Kellogg is taken from their book titled *Domestic*

169

Revolutions. Not all revolutions are violent upheavals that overthrow governments; the one in the family described here might better be called an evolution, since changes in cherished institutions such as the family tend to be gradual. The contrast of the modern family with that described by Koehler is, however, certainly dramatic.

Between 1770 and 1830, a new kind of middle-class family appeared. The democratic family, as Alexis de Tocqueville called it, was characterized by a form of marriage that emphasized companionship and mutual affection, by a more intense concern on the part of parents with the proper upbringing of children, and by a new division of sex roles, according to which the husband was to be the family's breadwinner and the wife was to specialize in child rearing and homemaking. Mutual affection and a sense of duty provided the basis for the democratic family's existence.

Tocqueville shared the view of many foreign observers that the distinguishing characteristic of the American family was its isolation and detachment from society as a whole. By the 1830s Americans had come to define the family as essentially a private place, distinct from the public sphere of life. It was a shelter and a refuge, a contrast to the outside world.

During the seventeenth century, the family had been seen as the foundation of the social order and the center of institutional life. It was "a little church," "a little commonwealth," "a school," the cornerstone of church and state and a microcosm of the larger society. This conception of the family reflected the fact that colonial conditions had broadened the family's functions and responsibilities. Not only was the colonial family responsible for the care of children, it was also the basic unit of economic production, the center of religious observance, and the institution charged with primary responsibility for education and for the care of the ill and the elderly.

By the beginning of the nineteenth century, a radically new definition of the family had emerged. Instead of being viewed as an integral component of the network of public institutions, the family was beginning to be seen as a private retreat. The term "family" generally referred not to household or kin group but to the smaller and more isolated nuclear, or conjugal, family—the unit made up of the father, mother, and their children. It was a place for virtues and emotions threatened by the aggressive and competitive spirit of commerce, a place where women and children were secure and where men could escape from the stresses of business and recover their humanity.

The family, which seventeenth-century colonists believed to be governed by the same principles of hierarchy and subordination as the community at large, was, according to a flood of early-nineteenth-century books and articles celebrating the sanctity of hearth and home, governed by values fundamentally different from those that held sway in the outside world. The values of independence, self-reliance, and ambition were appropriate for the marketplace and government, but within the home, a wholly different set of values reigned supreme: love, mutuality, companionship, selflessness, sacrifice, and self-denial. No longer a microcosm of the larger society, the family was now a counterweight to acquisitive values and a refuge from materialistic corruptions.

The new attitude toward the family was a reflection of a more general eighteenth-century shift in sensibility that sentimentalized the home as a bastion of harmony and higher moral and spiritual values. It was also a reaction to the nation's rapid material and geographic expansion, which led men and women to a place a high premium upon the family, which worked for order and cohesion amidst vast social and economic change. An increasingly commercial and market-oriented economy demanded a new work discipline that required less emotionality on the job and more impersonal relations with other workers or customers. The home became the primary arena for feelings of affection, vulnerability, and belonging. . . .

The burgeoning literature on the family explicitly rejected the older conception of marriage as an economic transaction between two families based on property considerations in favor of marriage as an emotional bond between two individuals. As such, neither parental permission nor parental approval were prerequisites for a happy marriage. Rather than choosing spouses on economic grounds, young people were told to select their marriage partners on the more secure basis of love and compatibility. In a survey of all extant colonial magazines published during the thirty years preceding the Revolution, one issue out of four contained at least one reference to "romantic love" as the proper basis of marriage; during the next twenty years, the number of references to romantic love would triple. Affection, compatibility, and reciprocated love, readers were told, were the only lasting adhesives that would bind spouses together. Personal happiness, not wealth or a desire to please parents, should be the primary motive behind decisions to marry. Indeed, so great was the emphasis attached to personal happiness that more than one pre-Revolutionary author advised young women that they should reject any feelings of "obligation" to be married if these should conflict with their desire for personal happiness. . . .

A new attitude toward children was an essential element in the emerging mid-eighteenth-century conception of the family. . . . Even before the Revolution, parents were advised to train their children in independence. While still young and malleable, they had to develop a capacity for self-reliance, self-assessment, and self-direction, in the hope that this would prepare them for a world in which they would have to make independent choices of a career, of friends, and of a spouse. Childhood, previously conceived of as a period of submission to authority, was increasingly viewed as a period of growth, development, and preparation for adulthood.

There can be no doubt that many pre-Revolutionary families failed to conform to this new "individualistic" ideal of family life. Private behavior frequently diverged from the models set forth in the prescriptive literature. In fact, Benjamin Franklin, the printer, revolutionary, diplomat, and experimenter in electricity whose aphorisms in *Poor Richard's Almanack* have served as guides to moral virtue for countless Americans, fathered an illegitimate son, took a common-law wife, lived apart from her for fifteen years of their marriage, and apparently dallied with other women. His marriage was not based on affection and mutual respect. He quite openly described his relationship with his wife as little more than a marriage of convenience that provided a channel for his sexual appetites, "that hard-to-be-governed passion of youth that had hurried me into intrigues with low women that fell in my way which were attended with great expense and . . . a continual risk to my health by a distemper which of all things I dreaded." Emotional distance characterized his relations with his children as well as his wife. He refused to attend the marriage of either his son or daughter after they had chosen marriage partners over his objections, saw his son just once during a period of thirty years, and failed to return from Europe to visit his dying wife.

Yet there can be little doubt that the long-term historical trend was in the direction of increasing affection and equality between husbands and wives and parents and children. During the early nineteenth century, life became more domestic than it had been in the past. In many pious households, the day began with the family gathering for prayers and Bible readings. In the evening, many families reassembled to read aloud from the Bible, novels, or family magazines. On the Sabbath, families attended church together. By the mid-nineteenth century, the family vacation had appeared, as did a series of new family oriented celebrations, such as the birthday party, Christmas, and Thanksgiving. The birthday cake, the Christmas tree, Christmas presents, Christmas caroling, and the Thanksgiving turkey were all manifestations of the reorientation of daily life around the family. Heaven itself was increasingly described as a "home" where family members would be eternally united after death.

Along with a growing emphasis on domesticity, a new attitude toward marriage was characteristic of the nineteenth-century family. By the middle of the nineteenth century, the marriage ceremony was treated with greater solemnity than had been the case earlier. Church weddings became more common and more elaborate, and bridegrooms began to signify the permanence of their love by bestowing wedding rings on their brides. Within marriage, there was a marked decline in the formality and deference that had characterized relations between husbands and wives earlier in the eighteenth century. By the end of the eighteenth century, many spouses had abandoned the earlier practice of addressing each other as "Mister" and "Mistress." Fewer husbands addressed their spouses with phrases like "dear Child," which betokened patriarchal authority, and wives became more likely to address their husbands by their first names or to use pet names. In their correspondence a growing number of husbands openly sought out their spouses' advice and admitted that they loved and missed their wives.

Relations between parents and children also became somewhat less harsh and distant. By the beginning of the nineteenth century, there is significant evidence that children were increasingly being viewed as distinct individuals with unique needs. Instead of referring to an infant as "it" or "the baby" or "the little stranger," parents began to refer to newborns by their first names. Stiffly posed portraits depicting children as miniature adults gave way to more romantic depictions of childhood, emphasizing children's playfulness and innocence. Furniture specifically designed for children, painted in pastel colors and decorated with pictures of animals or figures from nursery rhymes, began to be widely produced, reflecting the popular notion of childhood as a time of innocence and playfulness. A declining number of affluent mothers put their newborns out to wet nurses, while the custom of naming newborns after recently deceased siblings disappeared. The appearance of a profusion of toys and books specifically intended for children highlighted the new focus on, and respect for, the child.

The early-nineteenth-century spread of a new conception of the family as a private and protected place was closely tied to a broad process of social and economic change that transformed the economic functions of the family. This economic process is usually termed "industrialization," but in fact, changes in the family's economic roles were already under way several decades before the significant growth of factories. This process would eventually deprive married women of earlier "productive" roles and transform them into housewives, prolong the length of childhood and produce a new stage of youth called "adolescence," and create the demographic transition through which families began to reduce their birthrates.

Throughout the seventeenth and eighteenth centuries, more than 90 percent of the population lived on farms, and most farm households were largely self-sufficient. Craftsmen with specialized skills produced the small number of items difficult to make at home, such as hats, iron implements, men's clothing, saddles, and shoes, but most other necessities were produced in the home. Families, sometimes assisted by neighbors, erected their own houses, produced their own food, made their own furniture, dipped their own candles, tanned their own leather, spun their own wool, manufactured their own cloth, and sewed their own garments, but not men's. Even in the Chesapeake and Southern colonies, where from an early date many farms and plantations produced such cash crops as indigo and tobacco, most households were largely self-sufficient in the production of food and clothing.

Inside the home, the husband, the wife, and their older children were all expected to play important productive roles. Typically a father and his elder sons took charge of the fields, while a wife and her daughters took care of dairy cows, the poultry, and spinning, knitting, weaving, and fabricating clothing. The wives of urban craftsmen might also manage the shop, keep accounts, and supervise apprentices. Because production was integrated with familial activity, servants, apprentices, and paid laborers usually lived in their master's house. . . .

By the middle of the nineteenth century, the older pattern in which husbands, wives, and children worked together as participants in a common economic enterprise had been replaced by a new domestic division of labor. The middle-class husband was expected to be the breadwinner for the family. Instead of participating in domestic industries, the middle-class wife was expected to devote herself full-time to keeping house and raising children. Psychologically the daily lives of men and women became more separate and specialized. For a growing number of men, the place of work shifted away from the farm or household to counting houses, mills, factories, shops, and offices, where work was defined by wages and a clearly demarcated working day. Women's work, in contrast, was unpaid, unsupervised, and task-oriented. It took place in a segregated sphere of domesticity, which became dissociated from the masculine, more literally productive world of income-earning work. As a result, work and family life came to be viewed as two distinct and separate endeavors. . . .

Of all the images associated with the nineteenth-century American family, none has proved stronger or longer-lasting than the picture of the bewhiskered Victorian father presiding over his dutiful wife and submissive children. Here, many believe, was a time when fathers were Fathers, women were glorified as Victorian housewives and mothers, and children were to be seen but not heard. In fact, the realities of nineteenth-century family life were much more complicated than any stereotype would allow, varying according to class, ethnic group, and region. And yet, like many stereotypes, the public image of the nineteenth-century family—the father as breadwinner, the wife as full-time housewife and mother, the children as dependents—was based on a kernel of reality.

During the late-eighteenth and early-nineteenth centuries, roles within the family were sharply redefined to meet the radically altered requirements of the workplace. The model husband and father was solely responsible for earning the family's livelihood; he was expected to earn the income that supported the family and to provide for his wife and children after his death. The ideal wife and mother devoted her life exclusively to domestic tasks; she was expected to run an efficient household, provide a cultured atmosphere within the home, rear moral sons and daughters, display social grace on public occasions, and offer her husband emotional support. And children, particularly in urban, middle-class homes, were expected to be dutiful dependents who were to devote their childhood and adolescence to learning the skills necessary for the demands of adulthood.

Alexis de Tocqueville likened the differentiation of roles within the family to the broader process of specialization and differentiation taking place in the economy as a whole. In the economic sphere, specialization maximized efficiency and productivity. In the domestic sphere, role differentiation also served the function of efficiency; each family member had a proper "place" that was appropriate to his or her age and gender and contributed in his or her own way to the family's effective functioning. The father earned income outside the family, the wife ran the domestic sphere, and children might help around the house or supplement the family's income by taking on odd jobs. As in a factory, the roles assigned to each family member were interdependent, distinct but complementary.

Today many people believe that the division of roles in the nineteenth-century family represents an ideal. But even in the nineteenth century, the family roles of father, mother, and child were already characterized by a series of latent tensions. Although the democratic family was idealized as a place of peace and a haven from the strains of modern life, it was not immune to internal stress and conflict. From its inception in the latter part of the eighteenth century, the family's roles were characterized by a series of underlying contradictions.

In sharp contrast with the contemporary image of the early-nineteenth-century father as the patriarchal head of his household, nineteenth-century observers emphasized the relative weakness of paternal authority in America. Foreign travelers and native commentators shared the opinion that the paternal role was characterized by an informality and permissiveness unknown in contemporary Europe or in America itself earlier in time.

During the seventeenth century, it had been an almost unquestioned premise that the father, as head of his household, had a right to expect respect and obedience from his wife and children. A father's authority over his family, servants, and apprentices was simply one link in the great chain of being, the line of authority descending from God. Fatherhood was associated with sovereignty. A king was the father of his country, individual communities were governed by town fathers, and God was the father of all his children. This ideal of patriarchal authority found vivid expression in the realm of law. The prevailing attitude was that a father had an absolute right to custody of and guardianship over his offspring and legal control over the property and earnings of his dependents.

The centrality of the father's position within the colonial household was reflected in child-rearing manuals, which—up until the middle of the eighteenth century—were addressed to fathers and not to mothers, and also in family portraits, which, prior to 1775, uniformly showed the father standing above his seated family.

By the middle of the nineteenth century, the scope of the father's authority had, to a limited degree, been constricted—a transition clearly evident in art, with family portraits, for the first time, showing all family members on the same plane, and in child-rearing manuals, which began to be addressed to mothers, not to fathers. In the realm of law, the father's prerogatives began to be restricted as well. As early as the 1820s, married women began to gain legal control over their own personal property and earnings and the right to enter into legal contracts and to bring lawsuits. A number of states gave courts discretion to grant mothers custody of younger children. The father's role within the household was also circumscribed. Fathers increasingly were expected to acquiesce in the early independence of their sons, and child-rearing experts openly criticized those who persisted in meddling in their children's lives after they had grown up.

The ability of a father to transmit his "status position" to his children declined. By the early nineteenth century, families were finding it increasingly difficult to pass on their status by bequeathing land or a family craft to their offspring. The practice of partible inheritance, in which the paternal estate was divided into equal portions for all the children, made it difficult for farm or artisan families to pass on farms or family shops over time. An increase in opportunities for nonagricultural work, and the replacement of land as a primary medium of value by more portable forms of capital, further reduced the dependence of grown sons upon their parents.

As the father's economic role changed, a new set of images of fatherhood began to emerge. Instead of referring to a father's sovereign right to rule his household, the late-eighteenth- and early-nineteenth-century literature on the family spoke about a father's paternal duties. Foremost among these was responsibility for his family's economic well-being. But a father was expected to be more than an economic provider. He also had a duty to provide love and affection to his wife and moral and religious training to his children, and he had ultimate responsibility for putting down disobedience or disrespect on the part of his offspring. The father's authority, which had once rested on control of land and craft skills, had become increasingly symbolic. Where the mother represented nurturance, selflessness, and devotion to others, the father was the symbol of public and external conceptions of authority. He was referred to as a "moral force" or a "governor" because his role was to prepare a child for a life of disciplined independence.

The early nineteenth century witnessed a radical redefinition of women's roles. A profusion of women's magazines, novels, poems, and sermons glorified the American woman as purer than man, more given to sacrifice and service to others, and untainted by the competitive struggle for wealth and power. This set of ideas, known as the "cult of true womanhood," extolled the American wife and mother as the personification of four primary virtues: piety, submissiveness, purity, and domesticity. A torrent of articles with titles such as "Woman, Man's Best Friend" and "The Wife, Source of Comfort and Spring of Joy" depicted women as inherently more virtuous and less selfish than men. This conception of womanhood was sharply at odds with the image that had held sway earlier. Well into the eighteenth century, womanhood was associated with deviousness, sexual voraciousness, emotional inconstancy, and physical and intellectual inferiority. Now, in a sudden reversal of opinion, there was a growing consensus that only women, through their uplifting influence over the home and children, could be a source of moral values and a counterforce to commercialism and self-interest. . . .

. . . A growing number of women achieved leadership positions organizing religious revivals, engaging in missionary work, establishing orphanages and almshouses, and editing religious publications. Many middle-class women achieved a public voice in such reform movements as temperance and antislavery and succeeded in communicating with a wider public as journalists and authors. Rising living standards, increased access to education, and unprecedented opportunities to work outside the home increased women's expectations for self-fulfillment and contributed to a new outlook on marriage.

Tocqueville and other European commentators were struck by a seeming paradox in American women's lives: Compared to their European counterparts, young American women experienced a high degree of independence and freedom. They had a much greater opportunity to attend school, to earn an independent income, to travel without a chaperone, and to choose a spouse free from parental interference. But the lives of American wives seemed more restricted. Their daily lives were largely circumscribed "within the narrow circle of domestic interests and duties" beyond which they were forbidden to step. European travelers were struck by the rigid social division between married men and women; they noted, for example, that at social gatherings women were compelled by public opinion to separate from men after dinner.

The discrepancy between the relative independence of girlhood and the "extreme dependence" and heavy duties of wifehood would exert a direct effect on women's attitudes toward marriage. During the colonial period, marriage was regarded as a social obligation and an economic necessity, and few women or men failed to marry. But beginning in the mid-eighteenth century, the number of unmarried men and women increased and a growing number of women elected to remain single. Marriage became a far more deliberate act than it had been in the past. It was an enormous responsibility. As Catharine Beecher, an early-nineteenth-century educator and author of the nation's most popular book on household management, put it, "the success of democratic institutions" depended "upon the intellectual and moral character of the mass of people," and "the formation of the moral and intellectual character of the young is committed mainly to the female hand. The mother forms the character of the future man . . . the wife sways the heart, whose energies may turn for good or for evil the destinies of a nation."

As new emotional and psychological expectations arose about marriage, marriage became a more difficult transition point than it had been in the past. The transition from the role of girl to the role of wife was so difficult that many young women experienced a "marriage trauma" before taking or failing to take the step. Many prospective brides who did eventually marry hesitated to leave the relative independence they had enjoyed in girlhood. In their correspondence many young women expressed fears about the loss of their liberty—often linking marriage with death or loss of self—and foreboding about the dangers of childbearing—often omitting children from their fantasies of an ideal marriage.

After marriage a growing number of women expected to take a more active role in running the household than their mothers or grandmothers had and expected their husbands to be more than providers. Congeniality, companionship, and affection assumed a greater importance within marriage. Novelist Harriet Beecher Stowe, for example, chastised her husband repeatedly for hiding himself behind his daily newspapers and failing to pay sufficient attention to her needs, problems, and interests. . . .

By 1830 a new conception of childhood began to emerge. The earlier pattern of children temporarily leaving and returning home began to give way to a lengthening period of residence within the parental household. Instead of sending their children off to work as servants or apprentices at the age of eight or nine or permitting their children to be hired out for months at a time, a growing number of parents, particularly in the Northeastern middle class, began to keep their sons and daughters home well into their teens and even their twenties. As the economic role of children began to shift from producer to consumer, childhood began to be viewed as a distinct stage of growth and development in which a young person was prepared for eventual emergence into adulthood.

Techniques of child rearing changed too. There was a growing consensus that the object of child rearing was not to break a child's will through intense moral or physical pressure but to shape his or her character in preparation for the temptations of life. The primary purpose of child rearing became the internalization of moral prohibitions, behavioral standards, and a capacity for self-government that would prepare a child for the outside world. According to innumerable guidebooks, tracts, and domestic novels dealing with the "art and responsibility of family government," the formation of character was best achieved not through physical punishment or rigorous instruction in moral and religious precepts, but by emotional nurture, parental love, and the force of parental example. Obedience remained a primary goal, but a growing number of experts believed that techniques designed to provoke guilt, such as confining children to their rooms, withholding love, or expressing parental disapproval, would be more effective in securing obedience than would physical punishment. As one popular writer put it, "Whatever the privation or other token of your displeasure may be, the delinquent must, if possible, be made to feel, that he has brought it upon himself. . . . " This writer considered exclusion of a child from the parents' presence an excellent way to teach him or her to assess the consequences of acts and to suppress instinctual desires, especially when accompanied by some such remark as "Much as I love you, I cannot bear to see you, till you are sorry for what you have done, and will promise amendment."

According to a growing number of writers, child rearing was a task for which women are uniquely suited. A reason for the shift from father to mother as primary parent was the belief that children were more effectively governed by persuasion than coercion and by rewards than by punishments (a belief that ties in with the growing conviction among laissez faire economists that laborers could be encouraged to work harder by rewarding rather than penalizing them). Women were perceived as more likely than men to entice obedience from their offspring. Physical discipline or corporal punishment, the province of fathers, was increasingly viewed as producing at best outward conformity; at worst it provoked obstinacy or a sense of bitterness. But persuasion held out the hope of bringing about a basic change in a child's character. The emphasis placed on moral influence tended to enhance the maternal role in child rearing, since mothers were believed to have a special talent for instilling self-control. Whereas paternal authority was associated with force and fear, female influence connoted love and affection. . . .

As more and more young people over the age of fourteen remained at home with their parents, emotional and psychological stresses, previously little noted, became more common in the middle-class home. Foremost among these were adolescent struggles with their parents. Middle-class children saw their financial dependence on their parents prolonged and intensified, in part because of an increase in the duration of formal schooling and in part because of rising living standards, which greatly increased parental expenditures on children's upbringing. Although a child might be anxious for the responsibilities of adulthood, he or she remained subordinate to the parents. While lengthened residence within the parental home provided a basis for increased emotional intimacy between parents and children, it could also be a source of potential strain.

By the middle of the nineteenth century, childhood and adolescence were beginning to be defined in terms recognizable today—special stages of life, with their own unique needs and developmental problems. Emotionally and financially, middle-class children were dependent much longer on their parents than had been their eighteenth-century counterparts, and yet, at the same time, they were also spending larger and larger portions of their daily lives away from adults in specialized age-segregated institutions like Sunday schools and common schools. Adulthood and childhood had been sharply differentiated into two radically separate times of life. . . .

The new domestic ideology was also recognized in legal changes involving child custody in divorces. English common law, on which most American law was based, had given fathers almost unlimited rights to the custody of their children, but by the 1820s in the United States, the growing stress on the special child-rearing abilities of women led judges in all parts of the country to limit fathers' custody rights. In determining custody, courts began to look at the "happiness and welfare" of the child and the "fitness" and "competence" of the parents. As early as 1860, a number of states had adopted the "tender year" rule, according to which children who were below the age of puberty were placed in their mother's care unless she proved unworthy of that responsibility.

Banners, barricades, and bayonets are often thought of as the stuff of revolutions, but sometimes the most important revolutions take place more quietly—and so successfully that when they are over, few even realize that they ever took place. Such was the transformation that took place in American family life between 1770 and 1830—as profound and far-reaching as the political revolution then reshaping American politics. This period witnessed the emergence of new patterns of marriage, based primarily on companionship and affection; a new division of domestic roles that assigned the wife to care full-time for the children and to maintain the home; a new conception of childhood that looked at children not as small adults but as special creatures who needed attention, love, and time to mature; and a growing acceptance of birth control in order to produce fewer children.

In many respects the new patterns of middle-class family life that emerged in the late-eighteenth and early-nineteenth centuries represented a clear advance over family life in the past. A marked decline in childhood and adulthood mortality meant that family life was much less likely to be disrupted by the premature death of a child or a parent. Lower birthrates meant that parents were able to invest more material resources and emotional energies in their offspring. Rising living standards and a shrinking family size allowed many middle-class women to raise their expectations for self-fulfillment.

There can also be little doubt that the new patterns of family life were well adapted to the changing conditions of society. The inward-turning, child-centered middle-class family was well matched to the object of teaching children the complex tasks demanded by an increasingly urban and commercial society. Within the home, parents would instill skills that children would need as adults: qualities of independence and self-direction, a capacity for self-discipline, an ability to suppress instinctual desires, and sensitivity to the needs and feelings of others. The sharp separation of the husband's and wife's roles fitted well with the process of economic specialization that was separating "domestic" and "productive" tasks and taking production and the father out of the home. Finally, this new style of family was well suited to providing men with an emotional haven from the world of work.

And yet, for all its many benefits, this new style of family life also involved certain costs. The patterns of family life that began to appear in the late eighteenth century often proved in practice to be a source of conflict and personal unhappiness. One underlying source of strain lay in the disparity between women's rising expectations for self-fulfillment and the isolation of married women within a separate domestic sphere. Young women were raised in a society that placed a high value on independence. Growing numbers of women attended school, earned independent incomes as mill girls, teachers, and household servants, and were allowed to manage courtship largely free of parental interference. On marriage, however, a woman was expected to "sacrifice . . . her pleasures to her duties" and derive her deepest satisfactions from homemaking and childbearing and rearing. The latent contradiction between woman's preparation for self-fulfillment and her role as the family's key nurturing figure often resulted in enormous personal tension, sometimes manifested in the classic nineteenth-century neurosis of hysteria. . . .

FOR FURTHER STUDY

1. What changes do you see in the status of women, in male-female relationships, and in child rearing in the nineteenth century as compared to the period described by Lyle Koehler in his essay on colonial New England (Reading 3)?

2. The seventeenth-century family served a number of different functions. Describe these functions and explain how they changed by the nineteenth century.

3. How did changes in economic life affect the family as a whole and the position of father, mother, and children?

4. In our time, most men and an increasingly large number of women spend most of their days outside the home, while children's time is largely occupied by school, athletics, and other activities external to the home. How has this affected parent-child relations?

5. Mintz and Kellogg describe the middle- and upper-class family. Other articles in this volume describe family life in other periods or among different classes. Consider writing an essay comparing the family described in this essay with family life as treated in the readings by Koehler (Reading 3), Faragher (Reading 14), and Owens (Reading 15).

FOR FURTHER READING

The most important transition in American family history occurred in the first portion of the nineteenth century, when the size of American families began to decline. Many other changes still with us today began in the antebellum period. Carl N. Degler summarizes the changes in *At Odds: Women and the Family in America from the Revolution to the Present* (1980). For relationships between men and women see Ellen K. Rothman, *Hands and Hearts: A History of Courtship in America* (1987). Nancy Cott's *The Bonds of True Womanhood: "Woman's Sphere" in New England, 1780–1835* (1977) is an important work. We knew little about southern women or Mid-Atlantic women until the studies of Susan Lebsock, *The Free Women of Petersburg: Status and Culture in a Southern Town, 1784–1860* (1984), Sally G. McMillan, *Southern Black and White Women in the Old South* (1990), Catherine Clinton, *The Plantation Mistress: Woman's World in the Old South* (1982), and Joan Jensen, *Loosening the Bonds: Mid-Atlantic Farm Women* (1987). Mary Ryan combined the study of family and community in *Cradle of the Middle Class: The Family in Oneida County, New York, 1790–1865* (1983). One of the chief advocates of domesticity is studied in Kathryn Kish Sklar's *Catherine Beecher: A Study of American Domesticity* (1973).

A number of works discuss various aspects of family life. James C. Mohr analyzes nineteenth-century public policy in *Abortion in America: The Origins and Evolution of National Policy, 1800–1900* (1978). Joseph F. Kett considers the teenage years in *Rites of Passage: Adolescence in America, 1790 to the Present* (1977). N. Ray Hiner and Joseph M. Hawes include articles on childhood in *Growing Up in America: Children in Historical Perspective* (1985). David H. Fischer has attempted a broad survey of social attitudes in his *Growing Old in America* (1977). Studies of education are Carl Kaestle, *Pillars of the Republic: Common Schools and American Society, 1780–1860* (1983), and Lawrence Cremin, *American Education: The National Experience, 1783–1876* (1980). Two works that discuss social policy and family law are Stephanie Coontz, *The Social Origins of Private Life: A History of American Families, 1600–1900* (1988), and Michael Grossberg, *Governing the Hearth: Law and Family in Nineteenth-Century America* (1986).

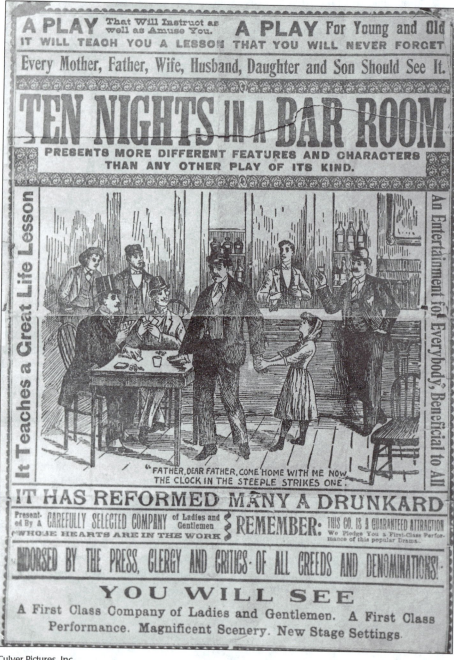

This advertisement for a theatrical version of Arthur's famous work shows the popularity of the campaign against drinking.

GETTING RID OF DEMON ALCOHOL

RONALD G. WALTERS

*T*oday we are constantly bombarded with messages about what is wrong with us and our society. Vices like smoking, drugs, and drinking create many problems which society is forced to confront. If only we could change all that— act better, eat right, and behave ourselves maybe America would be better. Many people think we need to shape up, or our lives and the lives of our children will be harmed forever.

It was just these kind of hopes and warnings which filled the air in the pre–Civil War era. Many Americans thought if they could only correct the worst vices, America would reach its true potential. On the other hand, left unchecked these vices would bring destruction and the end of the United States. Thus, many were driven to try to help this country, which Abraham Lincoln called the last best hope for mankind.

The list of perceived vices which plagued American society from 1815 to 1860 was a long one: immorality, slavery, mistreatment of women, of the insane, and of prisoners, and the influence of alcohol were among the most important. Some people also were led to experiment with new diets, and with quack medical remedies, and some founded utopian communities to either escape from the corrupt world or to provide a model of how people could and should live.

We will read about temperance, a term which includes any attempt to reduce or eliminate alcohol consumption. Americans drank a great deal in the first half of the nineteenth century. They thought it was good for their health, and often drank before noon and at virtually any political or social gathering. In fact, by 1820 American adults drank an average of seven gallons of alcohol per year—two and one half times more than adults drink today.

Ronald Walters' essay traces the various changes in the movement to curb alcohol consumption from its formation until the Civil War. Surprisingly, temperance attracted more people than antislavery. Notice that the changes include two steps. First, a shift from advising people not to drink certain kinds of alcohol to teetotalism, which required a pledge of total abstinence. The next step was the creation of groups led by reformed drunkards. But the most important lesson of the movement was that it could wield enough political clout to actually change state law and the behavior of Americans. In a sense it hinted that slavery reform required a political solution as well.

William Cobbett, an Englishman who closely observed drinking habits in the United States and Britain, lamented in 1819 that "Americans preserve their gravity and quietness and good-humour even in their drink." He believed it "far better for them to be as noisy and quarrelsome as the English drunkards; for then the odiousness of the vice would be more visible, and the vice itself might become less frequent." He was on to something. Drunkenness is partly what people make it. Even in such closely related societies as America and England, there are great differences in how individuals act when they drink, in what groups commonly drink, and in where, when, and why they do it. Equally important, cultures, classes, and generations vary in how they define "excessive" drinking and in the moral judgments they pass upon it. Although many late-twentieth-century Americans regard alcoholism as a disease rather than as the moral failing their ancestors believed it to be, drinking nonetheless has a history and takes place in social and cultural settings. And so do efforts to reform the drinker and eliminate the source of his trouble.

At the time Cobbett wrote, alcohol was an acceptable part of life in the United States. "You cannot go into hardly any man's house," he lamented, "without being asked to drink wine, or spirits, even in the morning." Men put down beer or harder beverages to fortify themselves for work, to be sociable, or out of habit. Rum was a staple of New England trade, and farmers in the West converted their grain to whiskey, a less bulky commodity to transport to market and a convenient medium of barter in a currency-poor region. There are stories of frontier clergymen paid with jugs of the local product; even New England ministers, the most priggish in the land, were not opposed to taking a drop or two. Alcohol was everywhere, whether used for commerce or for conviviality, and few people were much disturbed by it. That, however, was beginning to change not long before Cobbett put his critical words to paper.

 There had been scattered protests against alcohol in the late eighteenth century, primarily from religious groups such as the Quakers and, especially, the Methodists, who after 1780 were among the more strident opponents of hard liquor. But the most distinguished and persistent early temperance advocate was neither a clergyman nor a Methodist. He was a physician, Dr. Benjamin Rush, signer of the Declaration of Independence and a major figure in the histories of medicine and reform alike. In 1784 he published *An Inquiry into the Effects of Spirituous Liquors on the Human Body and Mind*. Rush accepted the notion that beer, cider, and wine were good for health and well-being, but he put his prestige behind the argument that distilled beverages led to physical, mental, and moral destruction. Rush's *Inquiry* continued to be quoted, reprinted, and plagiarized into the middle of the nineteenth century. He generated sentiment against liquor, both by his writings and through personal appeals to influential people; but anti-alcohol organizations were slow in coming.

• • •

By the mid-1830s prospects looked bright. There was still opposition, even within the churches, but much of the weaponry of evangelical Protestantism was in the service of the cause. Temperance had many of the high and mighty behind it and the message seemed to be filtering down to workingmen, groups of whom began taking the pledge. In common with conservative temperance reformers, they, too, had come to see drinking as a cause of poverty. There was a national organization, many newspapers in support, no shortage of pamphlets, and grassroots enthusiasm.

Arguments in favor of temperance had also come to maturity. Several lines of attack developed by the 1830s and persisted throughout the century with slight shifts and alterations. One appeal was personal and threatening. "The Holy Spirit," according to a circular, "will not visit, much less dwell with him who is under the polluting, debasing effects of intoxicating drink." Intemperance, in short, led to hell. In a more secular vein, temperance propagandists pictured alcohol as a form of tyranny, resembling slavery in depriving people of the ability to act as autonomous, morally responsible creatures.

If damnation and loss of self-control were not threatening enough, there were other temperance themes. Facts and figures demonstrated that alcohol produced insanity, poverty, and crime. By devastating families, it robbed society of a crucial institution and sent innocent women and children out into the cruel world, their lives destroyed by the husbands and fathers who were supposed to be their protectors. Everyone would gain by banishing alcohol, from the ex-drunkard to the hardworking taxpayer bearing the financial costs of crime and indigence. Temperance propagandists also played upon a powerful blend of patriotism and middle-class dismay at Jacksonian politics. They conjured visions of rum-soaked debtors using their votes to take charge of the country (a credible notion, given the realities of antebellum electioneering). The Reverend Heman Humphrey warned in 1828 that "if the emblems of liberty are ever to be torn from our banner—if her statues are to be hurled from their pedestals—if the car of a despot is to be driven over our suppliant bodies, it will be by aid of strong drink." Temperance advocates (including Abraham Lincoln in the 1840s) sometimes claimed that drunkenness was a worse national evil than slavery and that doing away with alcohol would uplift America, Americans, and the world.

Although they were often among the more conservative antebellum reformers on social matters, anti-alcohol crusaders were not blue-nosed reactionaries, as latter-day critics made them seem. They had a sense of progress and of the nation's potential. As they saw it, prosperity, godliness, and political freedom were the fruits of sobriety. Poverty, damnation, and tyranny were the consequences of intemperance.

Between 1835 and 1840 the temperance movement became a victim of its logic, which led to ever more extreme assaults on alcohol. Beecher and the American Temperance Society worked to destroy the notion that moderate drinking was tolerable. They were not entirely successful, although the pledge after 1825 usually required abstaining from "ardent spirits," which could be interpreted to exempt fermented ones such as wine and beer. Yet the sin was supposed to be in the alcohol, not in distilling, and one could get as drunk on beer as on an "ardent spirit" such as whiskey. By 1836 a large faction, which included Beecher and Justin Edwards, pressed the American Temperance Union to adopt a "teetotal" pledge, binding signers to abstain from any alcohol. That view prevailed, but it cost the union some auxiliaries and continued to meet resistance from people who believed that wine and beer were healthful as well as useful in weaning tipplers from harder drink. The teetotal position had in its favor the moral purity, or "ultraism," many antebellum reformers insisted upon; yet it raised further problems. What about communion wine? Was it sinful? Some people thought so. Others, equally pious, read the Bible differently.

Not that teetotalism exhausted opportunities for temperance reformers to quarrel. Like abolitionists, they disagreed among themselves on the role of women in the movement. Unlike abolitionists, they often did not press the issue: some societies separated the sexes into different organizations, others included both. More divisive was the question of whether temperance meant going beyond trying to convert individuals. In his sermons of 1825 Beecher had raised the possibility of legislation to stop the making and selling of liquor. The matter was openly debated in the Philadelphia convention of 1833 and it continued to be for years afterward.

Battles over such questions split organizations. The most socially prominent leaders had begun to drift away in reaction against teetotalism, and there was a general decline in membership by 1836. The movement was in the doldrums by the time the financial panic of 1837 cut further into its resources, as it did for reform in general. Within three years, however, temperance revived, although changed. The new inspiration did not come from New England or evangelical reform.

• • •

The setting was Chase's Tavern in Baltimore and the unlikely heroes of the piece were six friends, later to describe themselves as ex-drunkards. Their story was the stuff of which legends are made. They met on the night of April 2, 1840, with anything but sobriety on their minds. Tavern humor being what it was, they delegated a "committee" to attend a nearby temperance lecture, presumably to know their enemy. The committee report, duly delivered, was unexpectedly persuasive. The six swore off intoxicants and formed an organization, called the Washington Temperance Society in honor of the first President (a drinker but a virtuous man nonetheless). By Christmas there were a thousand Washingtonians in Baltimore, and before a year passed, the society established a beachhead in New York City. At the end of three years supporters claimed—with more enthusiasm than accuracy—pledges from 600,000 intemperate men, 100,000 of them formerly habitual drunkards.

Existing temperance organizations first greeted the Washingtonians as allies, but tensions soon appeared and were based on more than competition for members. Several things separated the new phase of the movement from the old. The first anti-alcohol societies had been dominated by clergy and wealthy evangelical laymen. The Washingtonians had help from ministers and many of their methods derived from revivalism, but their leaders were neither clergy nor men of social prominence. Of their two greatest lecturers, one had been a hatter and the other a bookbinder and minstrel. Such men were uninterested in theological niceties; occasionally they were hostile to the formal trappings of religion, much to the disgust of American Temperance Union officials.

An equally crucial difference between Washingtonians and their predecessors had to do with the people they tried to reach. Older temperance societies had not been eager to deal with drunkards. The Massachusetts Society for the Suppression of Intemperance was candid about its position. "The design of this institution," it admitted in 1814, "is . . . not so much to wrest the fatal cup from those who are already brutalized and ruined, as to keep sober those who are sober." In contrast, the Washington Society's chief goal was getting tipplers to pledge total abstinence. Not every member was an ex-alcoholic, but many were, and almost all were workingmen or from the lower ranks of society.

Temperance would never be the same after the Washingtonians. Before 1840 anti-alcohol crusaders had used a fair number of devices, ranging from sermons and pamphlets to temperance hotels for the sober-minded traveler. Leaders of such organizations as the American Temperance Union, nevertheless, primarily worked through religious groups, engaged in fairly logical discourse, corresponded with like-minded people elsewhere in the United States and Britain, and held meetings which, despite sharp debates, were reasonably staid. The Washingtonians adopted many of the same instruments of reform—they also gave lectures, published newspapers, and had conventions. There the resemblance ended. Like their clientele, the Washingtonians' behavior and tactics were not genteel.

Using wit, pathos, and the language of common folk, their orators moved audiences to tears, laughter, and signing the pledge. More unusual, they gave accounts of their own careers as drunkards and demanded similar confessions from the audience, a practice older temperance reformers found vulgar. The Washingtonians also sponsored picnics, parades, and fairs, techniques they learned from political parties and, probably, from abolitionists. They used the streets and public space more effectively than earlier temperance reformers, as when they staged spectacles like a giant day-long parade in Boston in 1844, addressed by the governor of the state, a temperance man. It was an easy step to move from that sort of festivity to popular entertainment, a transformation represented in the work of Timothy Shay Arthur. Already a believer in temperance by 1840, Arthur was inspired by the Washingtonians to write fiction for the cause. He was not the first or the last to do so, but his output was formidable and easily translated into stage productions. His enduring reputation rests upon the anti-alcohol equivalent of *Uncle Tom's Cabin,* entitled *Ten Nights in a Bar-Room* (1854), a novel, a widely produced melodrama, and, for a time in the mid-twentieth century, a staple of dinner-theaters playing it as parody. In the 1840s, however, Arthur's work was emblematic of the inventiveness of antebellum reformers in taking advantage of new opportunities in communications and popular culture. A considerable distance separated Benjamin Rush's scientific critique of alcohol from temperance as theater.

The Washingtonian movement, however, was past its prime when Joe Morgan, the fictional hero of *Ten Nights,* first took the pledge. The Washingtonians could not control their auxiliaries—the typical fate of national organizations in the antebellum period. Growth was as haphazard as it was swift and there was not enough central direction to sustain local societies. Despite their flair for parades and picnics, the Washingtonians had trouble figuring out what to do once the pledge was taken, the confession made, and the first enthusiasm gone. People lost interest or joined newer organizations. The Washingtonians also suffered from putting too much faith in men who were better at swearing off alcohol than staying off it. One lecturer disappeared for nearly a week in New York City, only to be found sobering up in a bawdy house. Such episodes, combined with institutional weakness, personality conflicts, and disagreements over issues, led to the quick decline of the Washingtonians. Within a few years most auxiliaries vanished.

Their influence lingered. The American Temperance Union and other, older organizations took on some of the Washingtonians' fervor, although they found the public confession and the use of popular entertainment hard to swallow. Thanks to the Washingtonians, the drunkard received more attention than he had in the past and efforts were made to broaden the movement still further, even to extend it to anti-liquor Catholics, with whom there had been no real chance for cooperation so long as evangelicals dominated temperance. The Washingtonians, on the other hand, were not especially concerned about religion and in their public festivities they embraced organizations like the St. Mary's Mutual Benevolent Total Abstinence Society, a Catholic participant in the Boston parade of 1844. The most ardent recruiting of Catholics would come later, in a lecture tour by Father Theobald Mathew, an Irish priest, in 1849; but the Washingtonians had helped prepare the way by separating temperance from Protestant sectarianism.

The Washingtonians were valuable to the cause in their failure as well as for their innovations. Several societies begun after 1840 remedied weaknesses in the Washingtonian movement. The majority of these new organizations were similarly nonsectarian, committed to total abstinence, and aimed at common people, but they had the sturdy institutional structure the Washingtonians lacked. The Sons of Temperance, begun in 1843, was among the most important, although there were others of consequence, including the Independent Order of Good Templars (1852), which admitted women as full members (a few lodges also admitted African Americans). With an elaborate hierarchy and centralized control, the Sons recruited a quarter of a million dues-paying brethren by 1850. (There was an independent women's organization, the Daughters of Temperance.) They exercised discipline over those who took their pledge, adopted the air of the secret fraternal orders then popular in America, and offered important forms of mutual assistance—all things that secured the loyalty of members to a degree unapproached by the Washingtonians.

The magnetism of secular groups like the Washingtonians and the Sons does not mean that religious campaigns against alcohol ended in the 1840s. The evangelical tradition persisted in the American Temperance Union, in churches, and in later organizations like the Woman's Christian Temperance Union (1874). They, too, learned from the Washingtonians, particularly from their tactics, some of which, like the public confession, fit well with the modes of revivalism popular among lower-middle-class folk. Even the use of popular culture, begun in the Washingtonian phase of the movement, had its impact on later evangelical temperance crusaders. At the century's end Carry Nation's assaults on Kansas saloons were as theatrical as anything written by Timothy Shay Arthur. (She, along with her bar-smashing hatchet, became a sideshow attraction at country fairs.)

One important new tactic in the 1840s the Washingtonians neither initiated nor accepted with enthusiasm. It was political action of the sort Lyman Beecher and others proposed two decades earlier. In 1833 a group of lawmakers and public officials formed the Congressional Temperance Society. Their avowed purpose was not to legislate alcohol out of existence but rather to provide a sterling moral example, as politicians rarely did. Yet the appearance of such a society was a sign that an influential anti-alcohol faction might possibly be put together in Congress. Its first president, Lewis Cass, had already used his political position as Secretary of War to remove liquor from the Army's rations. In 1833 the political question also surfaced within the convention that created the American Temperance Union. Gerrit Smith, an abolitionist later involved in the Liberty Party, introduced a controversial resolution declaring that "the traffic in ardent spirits" was "morally wrong" and that "the inhabitants of cities, towns, and other local communities, should be permitted by law to prohibit the said traffic within their respective jurisdictions." This was a direct statement of the prohibitionist position that characterized the movement by the end of the nineteenth century. The resolution passed.

In the 1830s and 1840s, however, many temperance people had their doubts about prohibition. Some feared casting aspersions on liquor dealers, a few of whom they thought to be pious, if misguided. There was also a feeling, common to many reformers, that electioneering appealed to base instincts and put expediency above virtue. Political action, furthermore, raised issues in temperance similar to ones that divided abolitionists. In particular, it compromised a commitment to "moral suasion" and the evangelical belief that true goodness could flow only from a converted heart. People had to want to behave properly, so the argument ran, and that came from enlightenment, not force. It took soul-searching for many temperance advocates to accept coercion, in the form of legislation, as a legitimate means of reform.

Still, prohibitionists had arguments in their favor. The liquor trade was licensed by the government and people were under no obligation to let their government license sin. Besides, most reformers agreed that if the public was godly, decent laws would follow as a matter of course. Prohibitionists felt that the process could be speeded up if temperance men engaged in political action, which would serve as a form of propaganda, and if alcohol, which corrupted many voters, were removed from the picture. That view gained renewed force in the 1840s and 1850s as reformers fretted about immigrants and their political power. A final argument—although few cared to put it so bluntly—was that prohibition promised to be successful.

Beginning in the 1830s, temperance voters agreed not to cast ballots for heavy drinkers, breaking the chains of party loyalty if need be. They also sought local option legislation, which gave communities the power to stop the traffic in liquor within their jurisdictions. The first statewide victory for temperance came in 1838, with a Massachusetts law banning the sale of distilled spirits in amounts of less than fifteen gallons, an act that removed hard beverages from taverns and kept them away from poor people, who could not afford such a quantity. The statute inspired civil disobedience from "rum-sellers" and much agitation for and against, during which many temperance people who had opposed political action fell into line behind the law. It was repealed in 1840, when Massachusetts prohibitionists shifted their attention to the towns, persuading about a hundred of them to go dry by 1845. In 1839 Mississippi passed a law like Massachusetts', although more modest. It forbade the sale of less than a gallon of liquor. After intensive lobbying on both sides, New York voters presented prohibitionists with a massive victory in 1846 and a defeat the following year. The U.S. Supreme Court gave the movement a boost in 1846 by deciding in favor of the right of states to deny licenses to sell distilled spirits. Reformers were not always so lucky in politics—a disastrous campaign set the cause in Georgia back almost a generation—but temperance battles at the ballot box and in the courts were fierce by the mid-1840s. By that time Maine had begun to lead the nation.

Much of what happened in Maine was due to two circumstances. The first was a strong antislavery movement. Abolitionists joined the fray, and their experience in building organizations and producing propaganda significantly increased temperance firepower in Maine. Prohibitionists had a second advantage in Neal Dow, a wealthy merchant and an ex-Quaker. Born in 1804, he converted to temperance in 1827 after exposure to Beecher and to Justin Edwards of the old American Temperance Society. By the early 1830s Dow was a total abstinence man and before the decade was out he took his principles into politics.

At about the time Massachusetts experimented with its fifteen-gallon law, Maine's legislature considered, then tabled, similar legislation. Meanwhile, Dow tried to move public opinion in Portland, his hometown. He and a coalition of groups, the Washingtonians among them, succeeded in 1842, when the Portland electorate voted by an almost two-to-one margin to stop the sale of alcohol. The ban was evaded and temperance men, led by Dow, agitated for statewide, and presumably more effective, legislation. In 1846 they got almost what they wanted: a law forbidding the sale of intoxicating beverages in less than twenty-eight-gallon lots. Enforcement, however, was the responsibility of town selectmen, who often looked the other way at infractions. Partly to remedy the situation, Dow ran for mayor of Portland; in 1851 he won. His office magnified his influence, and within a few months Dow and his supporters prodded the legislature into passing the so-called Maine Law of 1851. It prohibited the sale and manufacture of intoxicating beverages within the state.

Dow went on to have a long career in public life, although little of it in office. He was a tireless campaigner for prohibition in other states, as well as in Maine; he was a nativist, an abolitionist, a Republican, and, in the Civil War, the colonel of a regiment as sober as he could make it. His handiwork, the Maine Law, had even more impact. After its passage the American Temperance Union swung around to endorse prohibition. Within four years, thirteen states had their own versions of it and there were narrow defeats in others. By 1855 all of New England was dry; so, too, were New York and large parts of the Midwest. Those triumphs were swift and encouraging to prohibitionists, but temperance had achieved quieter, perhaps more impressive, objectives well before Maine saw the light. Per capita consumption of alcohol declined sharply between 1830 and 1850; and large parts of several states were dry before 1851 as the result of local-option laws.

Statewide prohibition legislation in the 1850s, however, was usually not well enough drafted or defended to survive court challenges. By the Civil War, Maine Laws had virtually disappeared outside New England, gone but, as it turned out, not forgotten.

Temperance politicking in the 1840s and 1850s had a testy but reciprocal relationship with the electioneering style of the day. On the one hand, temperance was a protest against the demagoguery of Jacksonian office seekers. It reeked with contempt for the besotted rabble and those (usually Democrats) who sought votes by praising the "people," attacking the "aristocracy," and ignoring moral issues. On the other hand, some temperance campaigners learned lessons from such politicians and ended up teaching them a few. Rather than reviling the masses for not electing their betters—the self-destructive course of Federalists in the early 1800s—anti-alcohol politicians worked hard to make a majority. They perfected their own brand of demagoguery, with lurid propaganda against drink and "conspiracies" by "rumsellers." Realizing the effectiveness of public spectacles, they followed the Washingtonians in imitating the parades and picnics of conventional party politics. They held cold-water Fourth of July festivities to cloak their cause in the mantle of patriotism, as well as to keep their supporters away from the standard celebrations, with their deadly combination of alcohol and oratory.

In numerous local elections throughout the nineteenth and early twentieth centuries alcohol mattered more than the national issues of the day. At times it fractured parties; at other times it formed a sharp division between them, as when wet Democrats ran against dry Republicans. In most instances temperance mingled with religion and ethnicity, and it easily fused with other political crusades—with anti-Masonry, nativism, antislavery, the Republican Party, and even woman's rights. Yet the crusade against alcohol had a vitality of its own, separate from the fortunes of any party or any other cause, which is partly why it stayed alive so long in American politics. More than antislavery, it convinced reformers not to rely exclusively upon moral suasion. The fifteen-gallon and Maine laws were proof that vices might be legislated away more easily than sinners could be converted. By the end of the antebellum period, moral issues—prohibition prime among them—shaped party affiliations and how Americans voted.

Besides venturing into politics, temperance made its way south of the Mason-Dixon line; in 1841 77 percent of the nation's distilleries could be found there. Although strongest in the usual havens for reform—New England, New York, and the Midwest—temperance was among the least sectional of the antebellum crusades. That is not accurately reflected in statistics from the 1830s, which underestimate the appeal of the cause in the South. Many Southerners were repulsed by the antislavery activities of American Temperance Union leaders like Arthur Tappan and Gerrit Smith; they often pursued an independent course, worked within their churches, or responded more enthusiastically to the organizations created in the 1840s, particularly the Washingtonians and the Sons of Temperance. In rural as well as urban areas throughout the South, temperance organizations of one sort or another popped up, inspired by a local clergyman, a traveling lecturer, or a few neighborhood enthusiasts.

Temperance also made considerable headway in the West. In 1861 a woman in Eugene, Oregon, assured an absent friend that the local society "is prospering finely since you left. Nearly all the drunkards in town have joined." (She added, however, that "most of them are now about as temperate as before they signed the pledge.") Even California, in the rowdiest period in its history, had a strong anti-alcohol movement. A visitor to San Francisco in 1853 could avoid the city's flesh-pots by staying at Hillman's Temperance House, with sixty rooms for lodgers and capable of serving two hundred teetotaling diners. At the same time, the Sons of Temperance claimed thirty chapters in the state, including an Oriental Division. In part because of politicking by the Sons, California had a vote on a "Maine Law" of its own in 1855. Although opinion ran against it by about a five-to-four margin, the gold-mining districts turned out narrowly in favor of the measure. That is impressive because of the rough-and-ready reputation of the Mother Lode country and because women, often the mainstay of temperance agitation, were outnumbered by men ten or twelve to one in the area. Thanks to the Sons, the Methodists, and a desire for law, order, and respectability, more than eleven thousand men in the mining counties went on record in favor of banishing alcoholic beverages.

Temperance crossed racial lines as easily as geographic ones. Anti-alcohol sentiment appeared in free African American communities by the end of the eighteenth century. Organized efforts began in the late 1820s, when temperance societies for blacks appeared in New Haven and New York, with others following shortly thereafter in Brooklyn, Baltimore, Boston, and elsewhere. The Boston organization, founded in 1833, had a female auxiliary, and like their white sisters, African American women were tireless and effective advocates of temperance.

For the remainder of the antebellum period, the message continued to be spread through a variety of black-run organizations, some, such as the New England Colored Temperance Society (founded in 1836), specifically focused on drinking. Other means of promoting the cause, such as black conventions, churches, and newspapers, mingled antialcohol messages with commitment to a wider range of reforms. Leadership often came from men and women like J. W. C. Pennington, Samuel Ringgold Ward, Sarah Parker Remond, Frederick Douglass, and others who were also important black antislavery activists. In common with abolitionism, moreover, the African American crusade against intemperance often ran parallel to, and cooperated with, white efforts, but by the 1840s it, too, increasingly pursued an independent agenda.

To a greater degree than white temperance crusaders, black ones refused to separate their cause from a broader platform of social reform and racial uplift. Where "slavery to drink" might be a powerful metaphor for whites, for African Americans the connections between alcoholism and bondage were far more complex and deeply felt. By the late 1830s black reformers such as Lewis Woodson presented drinking as both a tool of slavery—as when masters "rewarded" their bondsmen with rations of alcohol—and as its own form of slavery, threatening to sap free black communities of resources that should be devoted to education, to fighting injustice, and to acquiring economic power. While black temperance reformers are open to the same charge as their white counterparts, namely, that they sought "social control" and the imposition of middle-class values on their poorer brethren, their branch of the movement rested on a stronger sense of community—of a more powerful bond—linking the fate of the reformer, the drinker, and racial progress. Although the evidence is fragmentary and indirect, it further suggests that African American efforts, like white ones, had an effect. In that hub of reform activity, Philadelphia, for instance, black arrests for drunkenness after 1860, as well as other indicators of alcoholism, were significantly lower than for whites.

The most intriguing question is what made temperance so attractive to such a diverse collection of people, men and women, Northerners, Southerners, and Westerners, urban and rural, rich and poor, black and white. The easy answer (and there is much to it) is that America had a drinking problem. Reliable figures are difficult to come by, but it seems that per capita consumption of alcohol was higher around 1810 than in the supposedly hard-drinking 1970s. One authority aptly describes the estimates for early-nineteenth-century drinking as "staggering." (By 1850 the use of alcohol declined to a rate perhaps lower than late-twentieth-century consumption, testimony to the effectiveness of reform.) Yet temperance was more than a response to rampant intoxication. The real rise in drunkenness must have gone back to the last half of the eighteenth century, when Americans improved their ability to make rum and whiskey, and more than a generation before the first anti-alcohol society was formed. Much the same thing happened in England, where gin put its baneful stamp upon the working classes long before temperance organizations materialized.

It took social and cultural pressures, combined with that prior increase in intoxication, to make some Americans see alcohol as a problem and temperance as a solution. For the gentlemen and clergy prominent in the early movement, the reform was a badge of their own respectability and of their disapproval of the behavior of poor people, set loose from traditional moral controls by economic and religious changes. Temperance presumably would reduce the nastiness of life in the burgeoning cities, elevate the tone of politics, and help preserve the old moral order. Changes in the nature of work, moreover, made it desirable for employers that the labor force have the discipline to stay in factories for long hours rather than pursue the traditional course of artisans, who enjoyed independence, conviviality, and tippling. Those moral, social, and economic calculations swayed some early temperance advocates, especially members of elites. For evangelicals, there was also the millennialistic and perfectionist hope for human progress and the creation of a nation of free moral agents.

If temperance sometimes seemed aimed by elites at poorer folk, the latter also found the movement compelling. For some it offered a prescription for respectability and success: a temperate, disciplined lifestyle and steady habits promised, and sometimes delivered, economic and emotional rewards. Men with a taste for liquor had even more straightforward reasons for joining, particularly after 1840, when the Washingtonians began to seek them out: temperance provided self-discipline, moral support, and a way of gaining control over a destructive impulse. It gave order to disorderly lives.

Temperance also provided a stage on which gender conflicts and anxieties could play and sometimes come to resolution, especially after 1840. The thousands of women attracted to the crusade found a public role that was less threatening to the social order than antislavery, woman's rights, and communitarianism. If anything, it claimed to defend the status quo against the forces of dissipation and to strengthen that bulwark of antebellum society, the family. Even though temperance attracted militant feminists, its respectability made it equally acceptable to conservative women who feared or rejected radical agitation but who nevertheless sought a place in public life.

Temperance could also be a reproach to males and a critique of their domination of women. Anti-alcohol propaganda, like the sentimental fiction American females read and wrote, consisted of a catalogue of the awful sufferings men inflicted upon their loved ones. It was almost always the father (or son, or brother) who brought grief to his wife (or mother, or sister) and his innocent children. If he was redeemed, it was often through the agency of a woman (or child, or both) whose natural goodness exorcized the demon rum. These melodramas had a ring of truth—American men were capable of swinish behavior—but such stories also sound like acts of protest by women, not simply against alcohol but also against the male world that glorified them, confined them to the home, and failed to live by its own preachings.

That simply makes more curious the matter of what drove thousands of reasonably sober men to sign the pledge after 1840. The evidence is fragmentary, but it gives some hints in their ages, which appear to have clustered in the early twenties, and in their occupations. Many belonged on the fringes of respectability, working in the lesser professions (including teaching), as petty entrepreneurs, or as artisans in skilled trades such as carpentry. These were men making their way in the world (upward, they hoped). An image of propriety could be very important in increasing their prospects. If that were not a consideration, self-control, which temperance required, was a valuable virtue for people whose success in an expanding economy depended on thrift and hard work. As we shall see, there were other crusades—notably health reform—offering much the same thing to youth wandering through the opportunities and temptations of antebellum America. In addition, temperance had counterfeminist as well as feminist implications. Organizations such as the Washingtonians and Sons of Temperance offered male camaraderie in an alternative to the saloon and reaffirmed patriarchal relationships by asserting the importance of the male as breadwinner and protector.

Whatever psychological and emotional needs they fulfilled, temperance organizations provided important services. The Sons of Temperance were especially strong in that respect, having as one of their primary objectives "mutual assistance in cases of sickness." In fact, they offered life, as well as health, insurance, and the San Francisco branch (and perhaps others) acted as an employment agency, posting the names of members who needed work. Those were no mean advantages in days when the government did little to help the ill, destitute, and unemployed. Post-1840 temperance societies also provided opportunities for sociability. The Sons of Temperance, with their rituals and regalia, satisfied the same impulses that drew American males into lodges like the Odd Fellows and countless similar voluntary organizations in antebellum America. Throughout the year there were various excuses for getting together—picnics, fairs, and Fourth of July celebrations. These were fine places to enjoy companionship and for decent women and men to court.(A North Carolinian described a neighborhood zealot as "a young widower" who "wanted a wife—and he spoke to show how well he could speak rather than for any immediate practical effect in advertising the cause of temperance.") Besides saving drunkards, the movement redeemed the uncertainty and loneliness of life in antebellum America. Only when it did that could it become a genuine substitute for the solace of alcohol.

Despite the social and practical advantages of belonging to anti-alcohol organizations, interest waxed and waned, both over time and over the course of individual lives. Members acquired families and ceased to participate actively; brethren fell from grace, some to be forgiven, some to fall again. But at the core of the movement were dedicated people who carried it through the years. They were a diverse lot: reformers who saw conquest of alcohol as an important part of some broader program; religious men and women who felt abstinence was a divine command; and those who knew from personal experience the evils of strong drink.

• • •

FOR FURTHER STUDY

1. What arguments were used to convince people to join temperance groups? Why did some advocate teetotalism?

2. What was different about the Chase Tavern group and Timothy Shay Arthur in the Washingtonian movement? Include audience, tactics, and success.

3. Trace the attempts to limit the sale of alcohol and describe the Maine law and its effectiveness.

4. How was temperance successful in the South, the West, and among African Americans?

5. Given the history of the temperance movement list at least three of its successes and three of its failures.

FOR FURTHER READING

Another synthesis of the entire reform era is Steven Mintz, *Moralists and Modernizers: America's Pre-Civil War Reformers* (1995). See also Lewis Perry, *Boats Against the Current: American Culture Between the Revolution and Modernity, 1820–1860* (1993) and Robert H. Abzug, *Cosmos Crumbling* (1994). For drinking in particular see W. J. Rorbaugh, *The Alcoholic Republic* (1979) and Edward Lender and James Kirby, *Drinking in America: A History* (1987). For temperance see Ian R. Tyrell, *Sobering Up: From Temperance to Prohibition in Antebellum America* (1979), Jack S. Blocker, *American Temperance Movements: Cycles of Reform* (1989). For the important role women played see Barbara Leslie Epstein, *The Politics of Domesticity: Women, Evangelism, and Temperance in Nineteenth-century America* (1981).

PART IV

INDUSTRIAL NORTH AND PLANTER SOUTH

$\mathcal{I}$n our time, more than in any earlier period, the American people are a single people. They drive the same cars, use the same products, eat much the same food, and wear the same styles—whether they live in California or New England. With slight differences, their values and their popular culture—on the screen, on radio, on television, and in national magazines—are identical in Atlanta, Georgia, and Minneapolis, Minnesota. The homogeneity of modern American society obscures the fact that differences among classes, nationalities, and sections of the country played a prominent role in earlier American history. The strong nationalistic sentiments of the first three decades of the nineteenth century faded rapidly after 1830. Always somewhat distinct in language, politics, and social life, the North and South saw their respective economic interests as being in conflict. Both hoped for the support of what was rapidly emerging as a third distinct section, the Trans-Appalachian West. Moreover, industrialization and urbanization constantly changed the Northeast. In mines and factory towns, on canal and railroad projects, the strange tongues of numerous European nationalities could be heard. In contrast, the South was largely untouched by industrial and urban growth that would eventually characterize the entire country. Few immigrants went south, and slavery, with all its social as well as economic implications, swept westward from the South Atlantic states into Mississippi, Alabama, and other newly opened cotton lands.

The West was less clearly defined than the North or South; indeed, what was the West was ever-changing as the line of settlement passed from western New York to Ohio, Iowa, and beyond. What we now call the Midwest was a region of non-slaveholding farmers, many of them Scandinavians and Germans who had come directly west from the port of entry; others had moved west from the old northeastern states. Though the family farm was the ideal, midwestern agriculture was increasingly being drawn into the country's commercial and industrial growth.

The first article in this section describes midwestern agriculture, with special attention to the lives of farm women whose contributions were essential to family survival. The second selection provides a graphic picture of slavery, the institution that was more important than any other in setting the South apart. Though the vast majority of Americans lived in rural areas, many new immigrants settled in cities. The third reading describes why some left Europe and the problems they faced in the "promised land." The rapid urban growth and dislocation of so many people led to social conflict. The last reading describes the repeated riots and violence that occurred as different ethnic, religious, and racial groups confronted each other.

CHAPTER 14

Kansas State Historical Society

*While middle-class women were idealized and placed on a pedestal by the "cult of domesticity,"
farm women worked as hard and as unceasingly as men to ensure the survival of farm families.*

THE MIDWESTERN FARM

JOHN M. FARAGHER

*I*n 1790, shortly after Washington assumed the presidency, the United States census recorded a national population of 3,929,214, of whom only 51,000 lived in the North Central part of the country. By 1820, the country's population had nearly tripled to 9,638,453, but the Midwest, or North Central, region had grown even more dramatically to 859,000 persons. Thirty years later, the respective figures were 23,191,876 for the country as a whole and 5,404,000 in the North Central states. By 1850, the United States was becoming a major manufacturing and commercial center with a growing urban population that had to be fed. The internal migration of people that had been a trickle at the end of the Revolutionary War assumed the dimensions of a flood tide between 1820 and 1860. The New South supplied cotton, sugar, and cattle, while the Midwest became the nation's wheat and corn belt.

In the eighteenth century, the small, self-sufficient farm of 40 to 200 acres had been typical of northern agriculture. Worked entirely by family labor, there was a limit to the number of acres that could be cultivated because of the primitive farming methods of the time. In the nineteenth century, farm families were drawn increasingly into commercial agriculture. A reliable market for basic crops could be found in the East, and new transportation developments and the invention of threshers and other machines enabled midwestern farmers to meet the demand of the growing population.

Successful farming depended on the contributions of men, women, and children. The following essay by John M. Faragher indicates how varied and crucial the work of farm women was. In towns and cities, the lives of men and women were played out in separate spheres. Men spent much of their time outside the home, in offices and factories, to provide family needs. A "cult of domesticity" suggested that women's proper place was in the home, providing a civilized refuge for men and rearing children. Increasingly, women became consumers, patronizing the glowing department store palaces, rather than producers who grew the family's food, made its candles, and wove its clothing. Farm women could not afford the luxury of such leisure. Faragher provides a view of the isolation and work of men and women on midwestern farms and an understanding of how family farms were changed by America's commercial and industrial growth.

Farming in the antebellum Midwest was part of a way of life that stretched back through the centuries, a way of life on the verge of a fundamental reordering. Families were at the center of this rural political economy; working lives were regulated principally through families. Work was organized by a domestic division of labor, roles and routines were set by family patterns, production decisions determined by a calculus of family needs. This traditional way of life was very different from our own, and we would do well to base our understanding of men and women emigrants on a detailed look at their lives on the farm. . . .

. . . As the eastern seaboard became more a part of the Atlantic market, a new regional division of labor occurred, and commercial centers provided lucrative markets for farm products. Seventeenth-century opinion had stressed and valued self-sufficient farming and the closed circle of family labor. Farmers clung to these old attitudes tenaciously, but commercial values stressing economic rationality in market terms were more salient under the changed circumstances. Farming moved increasingly toward commercialization and specialization to meet the market demands of nascent urban communities. The view of farming as a business rather than a way of life was ascendant, if not dominant, in the Northeast by the first years of the nineteenth century.

Those who emigrated to the geographic and social periphery of the nation, on the other hand, met a different set of conditions. The move itself usually required some years of rather primitive living, but even after the early hunting-farming stage of pioneering had passed, the dominant fact of life in the Midwest was the isolation of farmers from the commerce of the East. Full entry of midwestern agriculture into the growing urban-industrial economy required effective transportation links with urban markets. The absence of transportation and market demands, R. Carlyle Buley notes in his seminal history of the early Midwest, "contributed to the practice of a self-sufficient domestic economy which in many regions by 1840 reached a high degree of development. . . ."

During the second quarter of the century the hopes and expectations of midwestern farmers paved the way for the changes introduced by the railroads; these finally solved the transportation problem and brought the Midwest fully into the market. The decisive moment of change came in the mid-1850s. As far as future developments were concerned, the nascent commercial trends and structures were unquestionably the most important aspects of the years before 1850, and his-

---

torians emphasize them most. But we are concerned here with the actual way of life of the majority of farm families in the Midwest. Until the Civil War (and the period of overland emigration to the Pacific Coast was mostly antebellum), most midwesterners lived by the traditional means of family self-sufficiency, whatever their aspirations. Before the Civil War, as Paul Gates observes, most midwestern farmers were isolated from commercial opportunities and practiced diversified, home-consumption farming. With some exceptions the overland emigrants were coming from an essentially self-sufficient agricultural system.

The general shift to commercialism that began in the Midwest during the 1850s was accompanied by a revolution in farm technology. The steel plow, drill, reaper, mower, and thresher, although inventions of the 1830s, became commonly available during the fifties and were only fully utilized in response to the huge market demands, labor shortages, and high prices of the Civil War. This technology facilitated commercial production by cutting labor costs and shifting farming to a capital-intensive basis, allowing for specialization in highly marketable grain crops, and incidentally facilitating agriculture's entry into the credit market, since most farmers were forced to borrow heavily to finance their investments in machinery. The interdependence of commercial production and improved technology reminds us that until the Civil War the self-sufficiency of midwestern farmers was in large measure a feature of the means of production: hand power did not provide the average midwestern farm family with enough productivity to turn to strict commercialism.

The technology of most midwestern farms, then, was a traditional force, tying men and women to the hand-power heritage. The essential tools of the farm—the ones the overland emigrants carried in their wagons—were the chopping ax, broadax, frow, auger, and plane. Farmers used these tools to manufacture their own farm implements—hoes, rakes, sickles, scythes, cradles, flails, and plows—resorting to the blacksmith for ironwork. Except for the cradle, which came into wide use west of the Alleghenies during the mid-1830s, the home production of these same hand implements had been a constant of farm life for centuries.

Hand technology set upper limits on the number of acres that a family could cultivate in a season; the only way productivity could be increased beyond that limit was by adding field hands. Working at maximum output, a farm family with two economically active males could utilize perhaps fifty acres of growing land with the traditional technology. Of these, perhaps one acre was devoted to the home garden, a score to small grain crops, the remainder to corn. In order simply to survive, a family required at least half an acre for the garden, the same for grain, and some ten acres in corn. Corn was the most essential; according to one observer, "it affords the means of subsistence to every living thing about his place." Before the 1850s the majority of midwestern families fell between these limits: most families lived on farms with forty to fifty improved acres.

As to livestock, an ox, or preferably a yoke of oxen, was essential, although when first starting out some families made do working a cow. Cows were necessary for milk and its products, however, and working them as draft animals negatively affected dairy production. A few sheep of mongrel breeds were necessary for wool, but mutton was almost never eaten. Geese and ducks were sometimes butchered, but they were valued most for their down. A family's meat supply was provided by the ever-present brood of chickens and the herd of swine, a dozen or more being necessary for a medium-sized family. These animals were frequently unsheltered, although on the better farms cattle might have a lean-to shelter for winter. As late as 1850 farmers throughout the Midwest were reportedly in the habit of letting cattle and hogs forage on available grass and mast. When butchering time came hogs were rounded up for the kill.

A farm family could gradually increase its level of consumption by clearing, draining, and preparing more land, and by increasing the size and improving the breed of its livestock. Then there came a limit, when the level of technology was a fetter on further expansion without resort to hired labor. The limit came, however, after the level of consumption had been raised to the level of contemporary comfort. "A backwoods farm," wrote an English observer, "produces everything wanted for the table, except coffee and rice and salt and spices." To the list of supplementals could be added occasional dry goods, shoes, and metal for farm implements. A self-sufficient family could produce enough for its annual table, along with a small trading surplus, but the task required the close attention of men and women to the needs of the land and the demands of the seasons.

The dominant paradigm of farm life was the cycle: the recurrence of the days and seasons, the process of growth and reproduction. Handpower technology did not deceive men into thinking they could overcome nature; their goal was to harmonize man's needs with natural forces as best they could. The length of the working day, for example, was largely determined by the hours of sunlight. Candles and grease lamps were common but expensive, and the hearth's flickering light was too dim for more than a little work after dark. So most work was largely confined to daylight: up and at work by dawn, nights for sleeping. And in keeping with this daily round, midwesterners told time by the movements of the sun, not the clock. There was a variety of time phrases so rich they nearly matched the clock in refinement; the hours before sunrise, for example, were distinguished thus: long before day, just before day, just comin' day, just about daylight, good light, before sunup, about sunup, and, finally, sunup. Each period of the day was similarly divided. . . .

The cycle of the seasons encouraged a traditional view of work as well. Work was the expenditure of human energy to meet given tasks. When wheat was ready for harvesting, for example, men would readily work fifteen-hour days to bring it in before the precious grain was shed on the ground. On the other hand, when seasonal demands slackened, as in winter, a man might quit early without qualms, and few worried when a winter storm closed in the family for a few days. The persistent pace of modern labor, measured not by natural cycles but by the clock, was almost unknown to midwesterners. By the same token, work was understood not as the opposite of leisure but as life's requirement for all creatures, regardless of sex or age. Men, women, and children would share life's burdens. "The rule was," William Howells remembered of his farm life, "that whoever had the strength to work, took hold and helped."

The common work of the farm was, then, divided among family members, but the principal division of work was by sex. Men and women worked in different areas, skilled at different tasks, prepared and trained for their work in different ways. In an economy based on the family unit, women and men in midwestern society achieved common goals by doing different jobs. . . .

The functional principles of the general divisions of work by sex on the midwestern farm were quite clear and quite strict in application. In only a few areas did the work of men and women overlap. Most clearly, men were occupied with the heaviest work. First, they had responsibility for work with the broadax. If the family was taking up new wooded ground—as many Oregon emigrants would be doing, for example—the land had to be cleared. Frequently a farmer would gird the trees with his ax the first season to kill foliage, felling trees and removing stumps in the following winters. Logrolling, when the men of the neighborhood joined together to clear a field belonging to one of them, was a common late-winter social event for men. Construction, including making fences, was also a male job, as was the ongoing work in the family woodlot. Wood was chopped, hauled and stacked, or dumped near the house.

Men also controlled work with the plow. For new land a breaking plow, drawn by several yoke of oxen, was often needed, especially in prairie sod. Working improved acres was easier, but still hard, heavy work. And within the limitations of available labor and marketability, men were usually itching to put new land to the plow, so the plow was associated with work of the heaviest sort and understood to be male. Work in the cleared and plowed fields, where grain or corn grew, also fell to male control and supervision. Men plowed in spring or winter, sowed their wheat broadcast (until the 1850s), and planted their corn in hills. Men and boys harrowed and weeded until harvest, when they picked the corn together and cooperated in bringing in the wheat, men cradling and boys binding. Field-work kept men extremely busy. Two mature men of fifty acres of corn and wheat land spent three-quarters of the whole growing season plowing, planting, and havesting, exclusive of any other work.

There was plenty of other work to do. Men were responsible for upkeep and repair of tools, implements, and wagons and care of the draft animals, the oxen, mules, or horses. Hogs and sheep, both pretty much allowed to roam, were herded, fed, and tended by men and boys. Finally, men were responsible for cleanup and maintenance of the barn, barnyard, fields, and woodlot. This meant ditching and trenching, innumerable repairs on all the things that could—and did—break, laying down straws and hay, and hauling manure.

Less important in fact, but work which nonetheless played an important role in male thinking, was hunting. For the early pioneers game provided most of the protein in the family diet. By mid-century those pioneer days had passed in the Midwest. But the rifle remained in its central place over the door or mantle long after the emergencies that might call it out had gone the way of the forests. Hunting remained, if only as an autumn sport or shooting match, a central aspect of male identity. "Even farmers," says Buley, "at certain seasons felt a peculiar restlessness." The hunting legacy had one practical consequence for male work loads: men had primary responsibility for slaughtering and butchering large farm animals. Indeed, when hogs ran wild, they were sometimes picked off by rifle shot.

Hunting was the male activity that most embodied men's self-conceived role—keystone of the hearth, defender of the household, and main provider.

In fact, women were more centrally involved in providing subsistence for the farm family than men. Nearly all the kinds of food consumed by farm families were direct products of women's work in growing, collecting, and butchering. An acre or so of improved land near the house was set aside for the domestic garden. After husbands had plowed the plot, farm women planted their gardens. Housewives began by setting out onions and potatoes in early April, following up later that month by planting lettuce, beets, parsnips, turnips, and carrots in the garden, tomatoes and cabbages in window boxes indoors. When danger of late frosts had passed, the seedlings were moved outside and set out along with May plantings of cucumbers, melons, pumpkins, and beans. Women also frequently laid down a patch of buckwheat and a garden of kitchen and medicinal herbs—sage, peppers, thyme, mint, mustard, horseradish, tansy, and others.

The garden required daily attention. At first the seedlings needed hand watering. Then crops required cultivation, and the everlasting battle against weeds began. Garden harvesting could commence in late April and was a daily chore throughout the summer, supplying fresh vegetables for the family table.

Wives and daughters were also traditionally responsible for the care of henhouse and dairy. After a dormant winter poultry came alive in the spring. The farm-wise woman carefully kept enough chickens to produce both eggs for the kitchen and to set hens for a new flock of spring roasters. From late spring to late fall the family feasted regularly on fresh-killed rooster, selected and usually butchered by the housewife. Daughters and young boys gathered the eggs that were another mainstay of the summer diet. Women's responsibility for the henhouse extended even to cleaning out the manure by the bucket load.

Cows were sheltered in whatever served as a barn, and men's general supervision there relieved women of having to shovel the stalls. But women milked, tended, and fed the animals. The milking and the manufacture of butter and cheese was one of their central tasks. Cows were milked first thing in the morning and the last thing at night; housewives supervised the milking but parceled the job out to children as soon as they were able. Boys, however, with their father's sanction would rebel from milking; "the western people of the early days entertained a supreme contempt for a man who attended to the milking." Making good butter was a matter of pride among farm women. The churn had to be operated with patience and persistence if the butter was to come.

> Come butter, come;
> Come butter, come;
> Little Johnny's at the gate,
> Waiting for his buttered cake.
> Come butter, come.

The meter marked the up and down of the churn. When it had come, the butter was packed into homemade, hand-decorated molds, and pounds of it consumed each week. Cheesemaking was less general; ripened cheeses were the product of a minority. Nearly all women, however, were trained in the manufacture of cottage cheese and farmer's cheese. Dairy production was especially important to the household and central to the definition of women's work. In 1839 a Springfield, Illinois, newspaper reprinted with horror a report that New England women were pressuring their husbands to take over the milking.

There were some areas of food production where women's and men's operations overlapped, but these were the exceptions. When hogs were butchered in fall, men from several farms might work together; it was mainly when it became necessary to supplement the meat supply that women helped men to slaughter and dress the animal. In any event, women were always a part of the butchering, there to chop the scraps and odd pieces into sausage, prepare the hams for curing, and cook the ribs immediately. At other social and almost ritual occasions of food preparation—making cider or apple butter, rendering maple sugar—men and women regularly worked side by side. All of the work of the orchard was often a joint project.

The sexes also sometimes combined their energies during planting. If not preoccupied with field planting, men might help to set out garden seed. More likely, however, field planting would fall behind the schedule set by zodiac or moon, and men called their womenfolk out to help. Women most often assisted in the cornfield. "Tarpley made a furrow with a single-shovel plow drawn by one horse," Iowa farm woman Elmira Taylor remembered of the 1860s. "I followed with a bag of seed corn and dropped two grains of seed each step forward." A farmer with no sons worked his daughters in the fields at planting time without a second thought.

Food preparation was, of course, women's work, and by all reports midwestern men kept women busy by consuming great quantities at mealtime. Wives were responsible for preparing three heavy meals a day; most farm wives spent their entire mornings cooking and tried to save afternoons for other work. Included in the daily midwestern diet were two kinds of meat, eggs, cheese, butter, cream (especially in gravies), corn in one or more forms, two kinds of bread, three or four different vegetables from the garden or from storage, several kinds of jellies, preserves, and relishes, cake or pie, and milk, coffee, and tea. Making butter and cheese were only two of the innumerable feminine skills needed to set the farm table. . . .

Women cooked on the open hearth, directly over the coals; it was low, backbreaking work that went on forever; a pot of corn mush took from two to six hours with nearly constant stirring. Cast-iron, wood-burning cook stoves were available in Illinois in the mid–1840s, and by 1860 most midwestern women had been given the opportunity to stand and cook. The next great improvement in domestic technology was the general introduction of running water in close proximity to the kitchen. But throughout the antebellum Midwest, water had to be carried to the house, sometimes from quite a distance, and that invariably was women's work. Domestic work—housecleaning, care of the bedding, all the kitchen work, in addition to responsibility for decorating and adding a "woman's touch"— was a demanding task under the best of circumstances, and farms offered far from the best. The yard between the kitchen and barn was always covered with enough dung to attract hordes of summer houseflies. In those days before screen doors kitchens were infested; men and women alike ignored the pests. In wet months the yard was a mess of mud, dung, and cast-off water, constantly tracked into the house. A cleanly wife had to be a constant worker.

A farmer was said to be a jack-of-all-trades. But women's work outdistanced men's in the sheer variety of tasks performed. In addition to their production of food, women had complete responsibility for all manufacture, care, and repair of family clothing. During the first half of the nineteenth century, domestic manufacture gave way to industrial production of thread and cloth, but in the Midwest, from 1840 to 1860, while home manufactures declined, they remained an important activity for women. On the Taylor homestead in southeastern Iowa, for example, the assessed valuation of household manufactures declined from $73 in 1850 to $50 in 1860, but this marked a decline, not an end, to the use of the wheel and loom: in 1861 Elmira Taylor spun her own wool, took it to a mill to be carded, and wove it into cloth throughout the winter on her mother-in-law's loom.

. . . Wool had first to be carded into lean bunches, then spun on the great wheel; the spinner paced back and forth, whirling the wheel with her right hand, manipulating the wool and guiding the yarn on the spindle with her left. Two miles of yarn, enough for two to four yards of woven wool, required pacing over four miles, a full day's work. An excellent spinner, sitting at the smaller flax wheel, could spin a mile of linen thread in a day.

The yarn was woven into wool and linen cloth or more commonly combined into durable linsey-woolsey on homemade looms. If cotton was available it was woven with wool warp to make jean. The giant loom dominated cramped living quarters when in use; it was knocked down and put away when weaving was completed. The cloth still had to be shrunk and sized (fulled)—a job usually put out to the fulling mill if one were nearby—and dyed, sometimes from home dyes, but increasingly with commercial dyes bought at local stores. Nearly all farm clothing was cut from this cloth. Coarser tow cloth, made from the short-fiber, darker parts of the flax, was used for toweling, bandage, menstrual cloth, rags, or rough field clothing. Pillows and mattresses were made of tow and stuffed with the down women collected from the geese and ducks in their charge. The finest homespun, the pure linen bleached scores of times till it reached its characteristic color, was reserved for coverlets, tablecloths, appliqué, and stitchery. For their annual clothing a family of four would require a minimum of forty yards of cloth, or at least two full weeks at the wheel and loom for an experienced housewife. This work was, of course, spread throughout the available time, and one could expect to find women spinning or weaving at almost any time of the day, at every season of the year. . . .

Every wife was a tailor, fitting and cutting cloth for her own slip-on dresses and those of her daughter, her son's and husband's blouses and pantaloons, and the tow shirts of the younger ones. If there was "boughten" cloth available—cotton or woolen broadcloth, gingham or calico—it was used for dress-up clothing, home-tailored of course. Socks, mittens, and caps were knit for winter wear, but every adult went sockless and children barefoot in the summer. Underclothes were not manufactured or worn, for they were considered an unnecessary extravagance. . . .

On a more mundane level, clothes had to be washed, and women made their own soap for both the clothes and the family who wore them. Women loaded hardwood ashes into the ash hopper, poured water over and collected the lye in the trough below. They boiled kitchen fats and grease, added the lye, and if everything was going well the soap would "come" after long, hot hours of stirring. They poured the hot soap into molds or tubs and stored it. Soapmaking was a big, all-day job, done only two or three times a year. Monday, by all accounts, was the universal wash-day. Rainwater was used for washing, or alternately a little lye was added to soften well water. The water was heated in the washtub over hearth or stove, soap added, and clothes were pounded against a washboard, then rinsed, wrung out by hand, and hung. The lye, harsh soap, and hot water chapped and cracked the skin; women's hands would often break open and bleed into the tub. In the winter, the clothes were hung outside where sore, wet hands would freeze painfully, or inside, draped over chairs or lines, steaming up the windows and turning the whole place clammy. Ironing and mending were also allocated one day each week.

To women fell a final task. Women bore the children and nursed them for at least the first few months, and in this they worked completely alone. Even after weaning, farm women remained solely responsible for the supervision of young children; both boys and girls were under their mother's supervision until the boys were old enough to help with the fieldwork, at about ten years, at which time they came under their fa-ther's guidance. Girls, of course, remained apprenticed to the housewife's craft. Farm mothers put their charges to work "almost as soon as they could walk," and al-though they could not contribute materially until they were five or six, the correct work attitude had by then been instilled. There was plenty that children could do around the garden, dairy, and henhouse; they watered, fed the animals, collected eggs, milked, hauled water, weeded, and performed innumerable other chores that housewives could never have finished but for the work of their children. . . .

Let us translate abstract fertility into the real terms of farm women's lives: child-bearing had to be a dominant fact. Over half the emigrant women gave birth to their first child within their first year of marriage, another quarter the second year, and fully 98 percent by the end of the third. Thereafter a mean of 29.0 months intervened between births throughout a woman's twenties and thirties. For their most vital years farm women lived under the dictatorial rule of yet an-other cycle, a two-and-a-half-year cycle of childbirth, of which nineteen or twenty months were spent in advanced pregnancy, infant care, and nursing. Until her late thirties, a woman could expect little respite from the physical and emotional wear and tear of nearly constant pregnancy or suckling.

Given the already burdensome tasks of women's work, the additional responsi-bilities of the children were next to intolerable. Women must have searched for some way of limiting the burden. It is possible that mothers introduced their ba-bies to supplemental feeding quite early and encouraged children's indepen-dence in order to free themselves from the restrictions of nursing, which had to seriously limit their capacity to work. There is almost no mention of child-feeding practices in the literature, but there are some indirect indications that babies were soon consuming "bread, corn, biscuits and pot-likker" right along with their parents. On the other hand, there was a prevalent old wives' notion that pro-longed nursing was a protection against conception. To achieve a twenty-nine-month cycle without practicing some form of self-conscious family limitation, women would have had to nurse for at least a year.

Short of family planning, there was no easy choice for women in the attempt to reduce the burden of child care. Other groups had practiced family limitation before this time, but the need for labor may have been a mitigating factor here. It comes as no surprise, then, that as soon as it was possible, children were pretty much allowed and encouraged to shift for themselves, to grow as they might, with relatively little parental or maternal involvement in the process. We will find children little mentioned in overland diaries and reminiscences.

By no means were men the "breadwinners" of this economy. Both women and men actively participated in the production of family subsistence. Indeed, women were engaged in from one-third to one-half of all the food production of the farm, the proportions varying with regional and individual differences. Of the farm staples—meat, milk, corn, pumpkins, beans, and potatoes—women produced the greater number as a product of their portion of the division of labor. Women were also likely to be found helping men with their portion at peak planting time. To this must be added the extremely important work of clothing manufacture, all the household work, and the care of the children. To be sure, men and women alike worked hard to make their farms produce. But one cannot avoid being struck by the enormousness of women's work load. . . .

. . . The true inequity in the division of labor was clearly expressed in the aphorism, "A man may work from sun to sun, but a woman's work is never done." The phrase has a hollow ring to us today, but it was no joke to farm women, who by all accounts worked two or three hours more each day than the men, often spinning, weaving, or knitting late into the dark evening hours.

There are some areas of women's participation in farm life that suggest a higher status. Cross-cultural studies indicate that the responsibility for exchanging goods and services with persons outside the family tends to confer family power and prestige. "The relative power of women is increased if women both contributed to subsistence *and also* have opportunities for extra domestic distribution and exchange of valued goods and services." In the Midwest, the products of dairy, henhouse, garden, and loom were often the only commodities successfully exchanged for other family necessities. Powder, glass, dyes, crockery, coffee, tea, store cloth, metal utensils, and sugar were bought on credit from the local merchant; butter, cheese, eggs, vegetables, homespun, and whiskey were the main items offered in trade to pay the tab.

However, while it was true that women traded, the proceeds were not credited to them individually, but to the family in general. Commodity exchange in corn and grain surpluses, on the other hand, was most frequently used for male economic pursuits: paying off the farm mortgage, speculating in new lands, and as innovations in technology became available, experimenting with new farm equipment. Men's product was for male use; women's product was for the family. It has been claimed that "there was no doubt of her equality in those days because she showed herself equally capable in all the tasks of their life together, and she was proud to know that this was true. Her position and dignity and age-old strength was that of the real help-mate in everything that touched the welfare of the family and the home." From a modern perspective equal work may seem a first step toward sexual equality, but the question of power is not only a question of what people do but also of the recognition they are granted for what they do and the authority that recognition confers. There is little evidence to suggest that men, for their part, gave women's work a second thought. That it was a woman's lot to work that hard was simply taken for granted. . . .

FOR FURTHER STUDY

1. Explain how the Industrial Revolution and commercial growth affected midwestern farming.

2. In our time, distinctions have been softened between what is properly men's and women's work. What made such gender distinctions much more important in the nineteenth century, and what in our times have been the forces that have modified them? Are there gender differences between men and women, other than biological, that apply to all time periods or are most of them culturally induced?

3. Some writers have suggested that women should be paid a fair wage for housework and the other contributions described by Faragher. What arguments might be advanced for and against such a proposition?

4. How does the life and work of a woman today differ from that of the women described in the essay? In what ways are they similar?

FOR FURTHER READING

We know much more about women, especially working-class women, in American history now than we did twenty years ago. Works dealing with the life of women moving west are Sandra L. Myres, *Westering Women and the Frontier Experience, 1800–1915* (1982), Glenda Riley, *Frontierswomen: The Iowa Experience* (1981), and Walter O. Meara, *Daughters of the Country: The Women of Fur Traders and Mountain Men* (1968). Domestic servants, both native and immigrant, worked in wealthy houses, as discussed by Faye E. Dudden in *Serving Women: Household Service in Nineteenth-Century America* (1983), and Daniel Sutherland, *Americans and Their Servants: Domestic Service in the United States from 1800 to 1920* (1981). There are studies of women in different regions, such as Anne F. Scott, *The Southern Lady: From Pedestal to Politics, 1830–1930* (1970), Catherine Clinton, *The Plantation Mistress: Woman's World in the Old South* (1982), and Marilyn F. Motz, *True Sisterhood: Michigan Women and Their Kin, 1820–1920* (1983). For a variety of reasons, many women chose to remain single; their lives are studied in Lee V. Chambers-Schiller, *Liberty a Better Husband: Single Women in America . . . , 1780–1840* (1984). Other works studying professional women include Barbara J. Harris, *Beyond Her Sphere: Women and the Professions in American History* (1978), Barbara J. Berg, *The Remembered Gate: Origins of American Feminism . . . , 1800–1860* (1978), and Susan Conrad, *Perish the Thought: Intellectual Women in Romantic America, 1830–1860* (1976). Catherine Clinton, *The Other Civil War: American Women in the Nineteenth Century* (1984), and Sara M. Evans, *Born for Liberty: A History of Women in America* (1989), are two good surveys of women's history.

Rural life has recently received much attention in Don H. Doyle, *The Social Order of a Frontier Community: Jacksonville, Illinois, 1825–1870* (1978), John Mack Faragher, *Sugar Creek: Life on the Illinois Prairie* (1986), and Hal S. Barron, *Those Who Stayed Behind: Rural Society in Nineteenth-Century New England* (1984).

CHAPTER 15

Library of Congress

This photograph of four generations of a southern slave family suggests the ability of slave families to survive in the face of overwhelming obstacles.

THE AFRICAN-AMERICAN FAMILY

LESLIE H. OWENS

By 1800 slavery had been eliminated in the North, and in 1808 Congress banned the further importation of slaves from Africa. Although some illegal importation continued, other factors primarily accounted for the extraordinary elaboration and expansion of slavery in the nineteenth century. One such factor was the invention of the cotton gin, which allowed the quick cleaning of as much cotton as slaves could pick. A second contributing cause was the opening of rich new lands beyond the Appalachians, which created a market for slaves and gave rise to the domestic slave trade within the United States. Between 1820 and 1860, the slave population of the state of Mississippi alone increased from fewer than 35,000 to more than 435,000. In short, southern planters found slavery economically profitable. There was also a high birth rate among African Americans, and by the eve of the Civil War nearly four million African Americans lived as permanent, hereditary slaves. Forming the chief labor force from the tobacco fields of Virginia to the cotton fields of Alabama, African Americans were crucial to southern agriculture and the southern economy. These chattels, bought and sold like livestock, were an easily marketable property that could bring ready cash to the slaveowner.

But slavery was more than a key feature of southern economic life. Its influence was all-pervasive, affecting law, education, social class, sexual mores, and other aspects of life. No one in the South escaped the influence of slavery and racism, neither slave nor slaveowner, free black or nonslaveholding white. Wilbur J. Cash has written, "Negro entered into white man as profoundly as white man entered into Negro—subtly influencing every gesture, every word, every emotion and idea, every attitude."

Few things were influenced more radically than the African-American family. Today, much is made of the growing instability or breakdown of the American family. The daily press has become a record of divorce, juvenile delinquency, alcohol and drug abuse, wifebeating, and parent-child hostilities so extreme that murder is sometimes the outcome. Imagine, then, what might happen to a family under these conditions: a mother and her children might have to watch the father being whipped; a mother-wife might be forced to have sexual relations with a stranger who invades the family cabin; the children might be sold at the age of ten or twelve to a distant owner, never to see their parents again. Such were the possibilities for the African-American family under slavery, and some people have suggested that such experiences scarred the African-American family to the present day.

A full understanding of the African American, or any other, family can be gained only by comparisons with families in other periods and societies. Recently, historians have devoted considerable energy to studying the family as a social institution in periods ranging from ancient China to medieval France to contemporary America. They have come to new conclusions as to the role of the Industrial Revolution in affecting the family, how pervasive single-parent households were in earlier periods, and whether or not the "nuclear" family—consisting of parents and children only, rather than broadly extended kin relationships—is a typically modern form. Leslie H. Owens's book *This Species of Property* is an excellent study of slave life and culture, and his chapter on the African-American family is especially poignant. Despite their enslavement and the breakup of families owing to the slave trade, African Americans had a strong sense of family ties and family affection. Many slaves who attempted to escape seem to have been trying to get back to their families, and after the Civil War, thousands of ex-slaves solidified their informal alliances with marriage licenses and wedding ceremonies.

Few aspects of the slave's bondage have come in for as much speculative writing as the impact of slavery upon the slave family. Researchers in many disciplines have argued that bondage rent asunder this most basic of American institutions, injured black identity, and left scars to haunt black Americans down to our day. But all this needs further examination.

Planters usually evidenced concern and not a little ambivalence, as several historians have preferred to put it, when reaching the decision to split up a black household. The practice was in sharp contrast to what many felt to be right, though planters consistently overcame nagging doubts. An agent representing John McDonogh of Louisiana complained to him that a slave trader "refused to give me a little negro boy and girl belonging to the Mulattresses, claiming that he could not separate the families." He added bluntly, "It was a poor reason." It can-

From *This Species of Property: Slave Life and Culture in the Old South,* by Leslie Howard Owens. Copyright © 1977 by Oxford University Press, Inc. Used by permission of Oxford University Press, Inc.

not be denied that the slave family took a tremendous beating; its members were sold to satisfy creditors and purchased to increase personal wealth. . . .

To avoid the public disapproval that increasingly attached to putting slaves on the auction block, some masters sold their bondsmen privately. For the slave, however, the impact remained the same, and scenes of mothers crying because they would never see their children again are more than products of historical imagination. George Tucker, a nineteenth-century Virginia novelist, offended many of his southern readers by writing, "One not accustomed to this spectacle [an auction] is extremely shocked to see beings, of the same species with himself, set up for sale to the highest bidder, like horses or cattle; and even to those who have become accustomed to it, it is disagreeable."

Historically, the auction block has both real and symbolic importance. The lyrics from a slave melody, "No more auction block! No more, no more," capture both meanings. For slaves it meant a parting—often final—from relatives and friends. Unable to face such doubtful futures some ran off or mutilated or killed themselves. To curb such occurrences planters sometimes gave only a day's or even just a few hours' notice to bondsmen selected for selling and then guarded them closely or locked them up. One master, no doubt guilty of understatement, conceded that his "Negroes will probably be somewhat distressed at being sold." He therefore advised his son, "You must say what you can to reconcile them."

Slave traders held auctions, advertised well in advance, several times during each year in local towns and cities. A great throng of slaveholders or potential slaveholders attended each session, accompanied sometimes by their wives, who might be clad in stylish dresses. It was, at the larger slave auctions, a time of gala social functions running through the day into late evening. The traders sponsored most of these events and invited planters up to their hotel rooms for pre-auction drinks and casual conversation. There was much imbibing and not a little carousing. Gangs of youths roamed the streets shouting names at free blacks, perhaps indicating a desire to see them returned to bondage. All had a good time except members of the black community—slave and free.

Of course the bondsman's participation in the auction began much earlier than these social functions. His psychological preparation started at the moment his master told him that he was to be put on the market. Parents gathered children too young to understand their fate around them and told stories of going on a long trip and not seeing one another for a great while. It could easily be the infants and adolescents who were being put up for sale, for nearly "all traders dealt in those from 10 to 12 years of age and many advertised for those from 6, 7, 8, and 9." A Virginia agent wrote to a prospective buyer in 1850, "Boys and Girls are selling *best*." For this reason Harriet Tubman, the underground railroad heroine, recalled that while she was in bondage, "every time I saw a white man I was afraid of being carried away." The domestic trade, few would deny, was a basic reason for some bondsmen having only faint memories of their parents and of children growing up under the adoptive care of childless slaves and other foster parents. Frederick Douglass's well-known confession is emblematic: "I never saw my mother to know her as such, more than four or five times in my life. . . . I received the tidings of her death with much the same emotions I should have probably felt at the death of a stranger.". . .

   To soothe those slaves intended for auction planters sometimes explained their reasons for selling them, hoping to win their confidence. Dr. James Marion Sims of Alabama wrote to his wife about an impending sale: "Let them understand that it is impossible for us to keep them . . . already are there mortgages on some of them and there is no telling when they may be foreclosed. . . . Let them know too that it lacerates our hearts as much as it does theirs to be compelled to the course we suggest." Masters also promised not to allow reputedly cruel planters to purchase aggrieved bondsmen. Was this merely deception? In many cases it undoubtedly was. Yet there was not always cause to view a master's promises suspiciously, for some tried to keep their word. . . .

   The time finally came for slaves to travel to the auction. In preparation, masters plucked out some of the older slaves' gray hairs or painted them over with a blacking brush. This was an illegal practice, but nonetheless widely engaged in, and traders delighted in outsmarting one another and uncovering the hucksters' deceptions. Masters also had some slaves grease their bodies to make their muscles or a smiling face shine, but also to cover up recent or old marks of abuse. At the larger slave markets such as Richmond, Natchez, New Orleans, and Wilmington, North Carolina, bondsmen were placed in slave pens to await the arrival of auction day. The abolitionist James Redpath visited the one in Wilmington in the 1850's and reported it filled with slaves of both sexes. . . .

   The sale began as the auctioneer's voice boomed out over the crowd's noise: "Now gentlemen, who bids for Tom? . . . His only fault is that he has a great idea of his own reserved rights, to the neglect of those of his master." Several slaves were on the platform. The auctioneer commented on each one's relative value and merits, "and when the hammer at length falls, protests, in the usual phrase, that poor Sambo has been absolutely thrown away."

   An historian has written that many slaves were apparently unaffected by the auction experience "and were proud of the high prices that they brought." This would seem to be an oversimplification of how slaves actually felt. Many, though colorfully dressed, wore somber expressions on their faces. At the Charleston market Captain Basil Hall noted a puzzling air of indifference in the slaves' manner. And another observer, on a different occasion, remarked that "the poor victims did not seem to think hard of this matter, but regarded it as a matter of course." In reality, some slaves had simply resigned themselves to being sold, and saw little need for a display of emotion that might later bring them punishment.

   But it seems that many slaves determined ahead of time to take an active part in the direction of the bargaining. They looked over the buyers, as the buyers did them, and selected several preferable ones. Often their decision hinged upon a knowledge of the planter's wealth and the living conditions and work load he would subject them to. They learned the needed information by keeping alert, quizzing other slaves, and sometimes confronting purchasers directly with rather blunt questions. Some were deliberately offensive to small planters, believing that slaves owned by them lacked social status and also life's necessities. The slave John Parker explained: "I made up my mind I was going to select my owner so when any one came to inspect me I did not like, I answered all questions with a 'yes' and made myself disagreeable. So far as I was concerned the game was on, and I began to play it." William Hayden claimed that because of his "utter indifference and apparent independence" to the events around him when he was on sale at an auction in Natchez, Mississippi, many prospective "purchasers were at a loss to know if, in reality, I were a slave, and subject to the hammer." Slaves not as well attuned as Parker or Hayden to fine points of bargaining were less subtle. They might even kick or spit on buyers they did not like, and, according to the traveler E. S. Abdy, even shouted, "You may buy me . . . but I will never work for you." Such threats turned many buyers away, but others were willing to accept the risk, confident in their ability to handle any bondsman.

Another method employed by slaves was simply to complain of imaginary ailments to every buyer except the desired one. Prospective purchasers often believed these stories because of those real instances of doctored-up slaves whose masters sought to dupe the unsuspecting buyer. Female slaves acted the coquette, offending planters and the sensibilities of accompanying wives. They bickered and nagged at masters, convincing many that they would be a disruptive force in any work gang. They also made threats not to bear any children while owned by an undesirable master, and even to put infants that might be born to death. Only planters somewhat unfamiliar with slave management took these warnings lightly. For most, there was always a faint memory of a time on one's plantation or on a neighbor's when a slave had carried out an unheeded threat. . . .

But before a buyer sealed his purchase of a slave, he usually wanted to examine him physically. He looked at his teeth, limbs, and back, felt and poked muscles. Often buyers touched female slaves in most familiar ways, and the auctioneer and members of the crowd told obscene jokes. An English observer at Richmond noted, "I beheld with my own eyes a man . . . go and examine a poor African girl . . . grasping her arms and placing his course [*sic*] and on her bosom!" Many domestic slaves were unprepared emotionally for such examinations, and when they occurred many broke into tears, almost as if for the first time the full weight of their bondage pressed down upon them.

For more intimate examinations, a small yard was set aside. Slaves carried back there, according to the ex-slave Solomon Northup, were "stripped and inspected more minutely." Buyers looked for scars or signs of syphilitic ailments, for example, and examined the pelvic areas of females for purposes of speculation of their future as childbearers. The ordeal was especially difficult for husbands who were powerless to assist weeping wives. Yet bondsmen submitted reluctantly to such examinations if they provided the chance of being purchased by a preferred owner. Prospective buyers also compelled slaves to jump and dance as further proof that their limbs were operative. . . .

Because of the frequency of auction block scenes, the composition and stability of the slave family has been the subject of much confusion. Was the family in a state of constant disruption? And if this was commonly so, what impact did such disruption have upon the development of its members' identities and general mode of being?

The primacy of one's family relationships in shaping one's character is axiomatic among today's social theorists. Family members gain personal strength from being loved and trusted by one another, and the family unit serves as a shield against outside attacks and the feeling of emptiness that often comes from being alone. The principles are easy to understand, but the elusive nature of the slave family makes them difficult to apply. Even the concept "family" as it applies to slaves needs reconsideration. With regard to them we might view it as several overlapping concepts. Slavery made it essential that the slave family be a great deal more inclusive than its white counterpart. Its ranks included not only blood relatives but also "adopted" relatives. Few slaves seemed lacking in aunts or uncles, real or otherwise.

The odds against survival of the slave family intact were formidable. To begin with, marriage was not legally binding between slaves in any of the southern states. As late as 1855 there was a petition before the North Carolina Legislature requesting "that the parental relation . . . be acknowledged and protected by law; and that the separation of parents from their young children, say of twelve years and under, be strictly forbidden, under heavy pains and penalties." Though such memorials were frequent, legislators never heeded them, for their implementation would merely have served to increase the moral questions that bothered many slaveholders, as well as greatly restrict the domestic slave trade. In the main, masters dictated the rules governing slave unions. What they were not able to dictate, however, was the seriousness with which bondsmen took their vows. These a sizable majority stood by steadfastly. . . .

Once married, separations were usually not a matter of impulse on the slave's part. The domestic trade annulled an inestimable number of unions, but in the instance of voluntary separations some planters wanted to know the causes for the disunion and, in the case of James Henry Hammond of South Carolina, believed in disciplining the offenders. Slaves, nevertheless, have gained a reputation for licentiousness and immortality that is out of proportion, considering the circumstances under which they lived. There were, of course, slaves who had several wives or husbands. But ulterior motives of both slave and master often spawned these arrangements. One planter thus discouraged his slave Peter from marrying a woman on another plantation because of "temptations to get into the rascality or meanness." He perhaps suspected that such a marriage would lead to eventual disobedience by Peter should their judgments differ on when Peter might visit his proposed wife. And he probably feared Peter's performing some unauthorized errands. Yet other slaveholders sometimes reasoned that preventing a slave from taking a wife of his choice could lead to serious managerial problems with him. At any rate, slaves whose spouses died often remarried as soon as they could. The practice was not uncommon among planters and overseers as well. It was "very common among slaves themselves to talk of" marriage, wrote ex-slave William Wells Brown. What bothered him was that after marriage, "some masters, when they have sold the husband from the wife, compel her to take another" almost immediately, ignoring her personal feelings. . . .

Many past and present researchers have assumed that the slave family was a very loosely organized group whose primary cohesion was provided by women.

The black sociologist E. Franklin Frazier capsulized this interpretation in his 1939 study when he characterized the slave mother "as the mistress of the cabin and as the head of the family." Frazier also mentioned that the mother had a "more fundamental interest in her children" and was able to develop "a spirit of independence and a keen sense of her personal rights." His canonization of slave women catapulted them to the forefront of modern discussions about the slave family. Was he correct in his conclusion about the matriarchal structure of the family? His picture seems somehow too inflexible, for the slave family developed in ways which Frazier seems not to have imagined.

Under some conditions—when slave children were infants—southern laws provided that masters could not divide slave families. What these laws sought primarily to prevent was the separation of child from mother; the father might still be sold. Indeed, when planters spoke of slave families they often referred to husbandless women and their children. The logic rings familiar even today, in that when a husband and wife legally separate the wife normally obtains custody of the children. We seldom assume, however, that the husband has been a passive agent in the family. Why then should we assume this to be so in the case of the slave, when there is no significant precedent for such an assumption in the slave's African past or in many of his American associations? Of course, this is not to deny that a slave father was a great deal more helpless than a free father today.

A variety of circumstances determined the position of the slave mother as well as the father. If women were the heads of the households, they rarely gained that dominant status among slaves at large. Women worked side by side with men at nearly every task on the plantation, but there were certain duties considered women's work that men declined to do. Some male slaves refused to do washing for this reason. Cooking was usually the task of women, as was sewing and some forms of child care. Sometimes masters punished males by forcing them to work with women labor gangs in the fields or compelling them to wash the family's clothes and attend to housecleaning. So great was their shame before their fellows that many ran off and suffered the lash on their backs rather than submit to the discipline. Men clearly viewed certain chores as women's tasks, and female slaves largely respected the distinction. . . .

The often peculiar marriage and dating relations of bondsmen have caused many scholars to doubt their morality. Females have borne the brunt of unfavorable conjectures. Scores of mulatto children fathered by masters have been used to support arguments that bondswomen were indiscriminate in their selection of male sex partners. Added to this was the fact that in the "southern states the prostitutes of the communities are usually slaves, unless they are imported from the free states."

Motherhood in bondage provided extremely difficult tests of a slave's energies and identity. The slave had to play the role of wife and mother under circumstances that marred her effectiveness at each. Her plantation duties eroded the time she had to spend with husband and children. Distractions were infinite. This was akin to the condition that some planters' wives found themselves in, trapped in a continuous cycle of chores.

Slavery struck most directly at bonds of affection joining husband and wife. The slave trade occasionally separated slaves married only a few weeks. We may suppose that some slaves were reluctant to love anyone deeply under these circumstances. Yet most spent several years with one owner and one husband or wife, and came to know their fellow bondsmen well. Thus when slaves married it was often the consequence of courtship extending over some time. The resultant marriage was steeped in emotional attachment. "Our affection for each other was strong," wrote a slave of his marriage, "and this made us always apprehensive of a cruel parting." The slave Sam, like so many others, ran away from his Virginia master because he thought "it a hard case to be separated from his wife."

Planters understood such affections. "You have a woman hired in the neighborhood whose husband we own," began a letter to Colonel Barksdale of Virginia. His "name is Israel, he is our Blacksmith, and he seems to be so much attached to her we [would] like very much for her to be hired near him . . . would you sell the woman?" A sound marriage meant a better worker for the planter and often a sense of purpose for the slave.

But slavery compelled an uneven husband-wife relationship. A master could physically discipline either while the other stood by helpless, at least for the moment. Slaveowners worked both hard, and they often had little time left to enjoy each other's company in the evening. The relationship nonetheless had many interesting potentials. "A slave possessing nothing . . . except a wife and children, had all his affections concentrated upon them," wrote Francis Fedric. Occasionally, the marriage partners focused so much attention on each other that the slightest change in the routine of one tended to disrupt the other's habits. Sickness is a good example. Wives and husbands often insisted that they nurse each other back to health, fighting bitterly against efforts to force them into the fields when the possibility of a loved one dying existed. Slaveholders severely punished many and accused them of merely trying to escape duties—but discipline was seldom an effective deterrent. A planter could, of course, make arrangements for such times; expected that wives and husbands might be off work briefly or difficult to manage during days when important personal matters came up. Sometimes a sick husband would prolong his sickness by refusing to take medicine from any but the hands of his wife, whom he could also trust to find out if someone had "hexed" him. . . .

The arrival of children served in large measure to solidify the slave marriage. Yet some parents feared that slaveholders would mistreat offspring or sell them away. A few adults also refused to assume parental responsibilities. They married and had children, but declined or allowed others to take care of them, and were occasionally abusive parents. Still, most assumed parental ties eagerly and were, according to a Mississippi mistress, "all so proud of showing their children." While discussing the possible sale of a slave to an Annapolis slaveholder, Charles Ridgely wrote that she "is married in the neighborhood and has a family of young children, and would I think now be extremely unwilling to be separated from them."

In Africa "tribal customs and taboos tended to fix the mother's attitude toward her child before it was born," making children greatly appreciated, and such tendencies were not absent in American slaves. Few women probably did not want children, though they were aware they might not be able to devote the attention to them that would be required. The emotional outbursts of mothers following the deaths of infants, and their resistance to being parted from offspring, indicate that female slave attitudes in this regard were not markedly distinct from those of mothers worldwide.

In fact, many disruptions of the workday stemmed from slave parents requests to tend their children. Masters set aside a period during the day for the nursing of babies, but there was also frequent disciplining of bondswomen when they failed to return to their duties on schedule. Yet mothers repeatedly risked the lash in order to allow their body temperatures to cool down enough for effective milk nourishment. Still, Moses Grandy observed that overseers forced many to work in the field carrying full breasts of milk. "They therefore could not keep up with the other hands," and when this happened overseers whipped them "so that blood and milk flew mingled from their breasts." It does not appear that he was merely trying to achieve literary effect with this dramatic statement. But often mothers got their way, for it was difficult for a master to justify, either to his conscience or his hands, children found dead from want of care. The slave's human increase was also an owner's most valuable form of property. On many plantations masters periodically assigned one or two slaves to furnish the nursing needs of all infants. They also hired slaves to nurse their own offspring. . . .

In bondage, the varieties of adult family behavior served as the most significant models after which slave children patterned their own actions. We know that "where a variety of behavior or models is available, selection can be influenced either by affection and rewards, by punishment, or by awareness of what is appropriate." All these factors operated with peculiar force within and upon the slave family. J. W. C. Pennington, the fugitive blacksmith, experienced what he called a "want of parental care and attention." By way of explanation he added, "My parents were not able to give any attention to their children during the day." While this was not unusual, many parents did devote their evenings and weekends to family affairs—a first duty of which was to teach children the limits placed on their conduct. This was no simple task. . . .

For the young slave, family life was vastly important. His early years somehow slipped past with the idea probably seldom if ever occurring to him that he was but a piece of property. His main worries related to minor chores assigned to him at about age five or six by parents and master: and adult slaves at times bore much of the burden of these. Children also escaped much of the stigma of racial inferiority that whites attached to the personalities of their mothers and fathers. Concerning his childhood one slave reminisced, "let me say to you that my case were different from a great many of my colore so I never knew what the yoke of oppression was in the early part of my life." He was relatively carefree and innocent, he explained, until "the white boy . . . began to Raise his feathers and boast of the superiority which he had over me." . . .

It was not true that when black children learned to walk and then play with the master's children their "first lesson is to obey everything that has a white skin," as one bondsman claimed. Some masters' children learned this lesson the hard way when they tried to boss the little "niggers" about: "Every time they crossed me I jumped them," recalled one ex-slave about his white playmates.

Frequently the tendency among black and white children was towards a general equality. They played marbles together, and the slave children themselves spent many hours at this game: "My favorite game was marbles." They also played sheepmeat, a game of tag played with a ball of yarn that was thrown by one child at others running about the grounds. They enjoyed a great variety of childhood sports. Sir Charles Lyell, the English geologist, witnessed slave and white children playing, "evidently all associating on terms of equality." One slave narrator remembered too that he was very close to a son of his Virginia master: "I was his playmate and constant associate in childhood." He learned the alphabet and some of the elements of reading from him. "We were very fond of each other, and frequently slept together."

On large plantations communities of children were largely autonomous. Slave narratives relate that often one of the bondsman's earliest recollections of slavery was the sight of his mother or father being whipped or his brothers and sisters standing on the auction block. But this side of childhood can be overplayed. Fear did not perpetually pervade the environment. There are accounts of seeming childhood contentment which, though occasionally overdrawn by some interpreters, are to some measure accurate. The slaveholder did not constantly try to shape the character of slave children. There was little time for that. "The master, I think, does not often trouble himself with the government of these juvenile communities," observed a doctor from Kentucky. "He is not, therefore, an object of dread among them."

To a great extent, children learned to shape their behavior to the expectations of other slaves. A beginning lesson was to respect slave elders, particularly the aged. Tradition shaped this differential treatment. The child was, moreover, at the bottom of the hierarchy of both blacks and whites, while old slaves were in a manner the domestics of the slave quarters. Their functions were not unlike those of the slaves who ordered the master's children about and instructed them in etiquette. . . .

Some parents also saw initial work responsibilities, if properly performed, as an opportunity for their sons and daughters to escape the rigors of field labor. They encouraged their children to learn a trade if possible. A skill meant an opportunity to obtain preferred duties in later life. Masters wanted at least a few trained hands, chiefly as carpenters, for they increased the efficiency of the plantation as well as their own monetary value. John McDonogh of New Orleans hired a slave brickmason and later recommended him to a neighbor, suggesting that he might teach bricklaying to "two or three of your black boys" and "with two boys of 10 or 12 years of age to work with him in laying brick he will do all your buildings."

Occasionally, children's jobs required that they go through a prolonged or permanent separation from their families; but a determined parent was willing to accept this if it promised ultimately to provide an easier life for a son or daughter. The slave Julianna, age twelve, was the subject of a contract that engaged her services for six years. Her contractual master guaranteed "to teach her to sew, & bring her up to be a good seamstress, and a useful servant." The arrangement continued on a partially personal note: "In addition to the above I agree to allow

the said girl Julianna to go to Shirley [Plantation] . . . once each year to see her relations, & remain with them one week each year."

Bondsman Henry Bibb was especially aware of the shortened childhood of the
slave. "I was taken away from my mother," he wrote, "and hired out to labor for
various persons, eight or ten years in succession." Other hired-out children were
more fortunate than Bibb. Employed as families, as were "Great Jenny & her 3
youngest children," they partially escaped the emotional turmoil that accompanied separations. . . .

When the terms of bondage necessitated the division of families, parents often
sought the aid of masters to reunite them. Lucinda, who served as a washwoman
for a planter "nearly twelve years," asked him to hire her daughter Mary Jane from
a nearby planter. "To oblige her," wrote her owner to Mary Jane's master, "I will
become responsible for the amount, if you will let her have her daughter for the
sum of Thirty dollars," which Lucinda was apparently willing to repay by her earnings during the remainder of the year. In another case, the slave George approached his master R. Carter about his daughter Betty—"7 years old, motherless,
now at Colespoint-plantation—." In a letter to his overseer, Carter noted that
"George wishes Betty live at Aires, with his Wife who lives there." As if not to appear overly accommodating to George's wishes, Carter continued, "If Betty is not
useful where She now lives—I desire to indulge George . . . you will accordingly
permit him to take his daughter." At other times, slaves acted on their own to reunite themselves with loved ones. One runaway was persistent in this way: "She has
a husband, I think, at his [a neighbor's] house & tho' taken up by him the first
time came straight back to his house."

When a master abused or humiliated one member of a family, the rebuff rever-
berated throughout the slave household and beyond. An example appears in the
opening pages of the fugitive blacksmith's narrative. Following the whipping of
his father, J. W. C. Pennington remembered, "an open rupture" developed in his
family [against their master]. Each member felt deeply offended by the deed, for
they had always believed their conduct and faithfulness was exemplary. They
talked of their humiliation in the "nightly gatherings, and showed it in . . . daily
melancholy aspect."

Planters' ill-handling of slaves was only one of many factors that brought out
family consciousness. Bondsmen's misdeeds against other bondsmen sometimes
marked families for harassment and shame. A serious offense, such as stealing another's hunting catches, might lead to brief periods of social isolation, with members of the offending family finding themselves excluded from slave gatherings or
nightly ramblings. Bondsmen saw themselves as having their primary identification with a distinct family unit to which they had responsibility and which had responsibility to them.

However, the slave family was a unit with extensions. Quite frequently it seems to
have consisted of more than just parents and their natural children. It could include a number of blood or adopted relations—uncles, aunts, and cousins—who
lived on the same plantation or on nearby estates. Adults "claimed" parentless chil-

dren, and the slave community seldom neglected old slaves. Local bondsmen usually absorbed new arrivals on a plantation into a family setting and expected them to make a full contribution immediately. But can such a group really be called a family? Slaves considered it as such and treated adopted relatives with real affection.

The extended slave family frequently arose to augment or replace the regular family unit split up by slavery's misfortunes. There were deaths resulting from disease, accidents, and natural causes that left wives husbandless and children without parents. Then there were the family breakups caused by the slave trade. In an important, though not typical, exception, however, Robert Carter of Virginia agreed to sell his slaves to the Baltimore Company only "if the Company will purchase men their wives & children [ten families].". . .

In slave families wives seldom possessed greater financial stability than husbands, a circumstance that often gives rise to psychological problems in men of minority households in our day. Both worked at tasks that the slave culture did not stigmatize as menial, so there was no need for the male to feel a lack of importance in his family on that score. The power of masters to disrupt families at any time weakened male slaves' sense of responsibility and dignity, but they did not invariably see this as a slight to their manhood. Yet for the slave who experienced the breakup of his household there remained that indelible hurt, as perhaps exemplified by Charles Ball's father, who "never recovered from the effects of the shock" of losing a portion of his family and became "gloomy and morose." Whenever the slave family—natural or extended—was intact, however, and slave males were reliably performing their duties, they most likely did symbolize authority within the family structure.

Except for sales of its members, much of the time slaveholders left the slave family to its own devices. And though the slave trade drove blood relatives apart, bondsmen's common persecution brought many of them back together in extended family groupings which provided for many of the emotional needs whose satisfaction the regular family, had it remained untouched, might have rendered less vexatious. Under these conditions the personalities of bondsmen were certain to gain much strength.

FOR FURTHER STUDY

1. How would the following factors affect a slave's price on the auction block: age, sex, health, and attitude? What techniques were used by sellers to try to make a slave appear more valuable?

2. Summarize Owens's view of the role and attitudes of male and female parents in the African-American family under slavery. What evidence does he use to argue that slaves made clear distinctions in the roles of men and women, though both did the same kind of field labor?

3. What generalizations can be made about the attitudes of masters toward selling slaves, toward slave marriages, and toward breaking up families?

4. Many European and American white families were "nuclear"—consisting only of parents and children without grandparents or uncles and aunts living in the same household. Owens suggests that the African-American family was more "extended," with considerable respect for age and the care of parentless children by others. Why would you expect such features to have developed in southern slavery?

5. What factors in modern society have somewhat modified the differences among families with varied backgrounds? Think, for example, of a southern rural and a northern urban African-American family; a second-generation Slavic family; a Chinese-American family; an Italian Catholic family. Compare the differences you see today in such groups with those that existed several decades ago.

FOR FURTHER READING

The most recent survey of the peculiar institution is Peter Kolchin's *American Slavery, 1619–1877* (1993), which can be supplemented by the collection of essays in Lawrence B. Goodheart et al., eds., *Slavery in American Society*, rev. ed. (1993). These works replace the two earlier treatments by Ulrich B. Phillips—*American Negro Slavery* (1918) and *Life and Labor in the Old South* (1929), which portrays slaveowners as benign—and Kenneth Stampp, *The Peculiar Institution: Slavery in the Ante-Bellum South* (1956), which stresses the harshness of slavery. The most comprehensive discussion of slave life and culture is Eugene D. Genovese's *Roll, Jordan, Roll: The World the Slaves Made* (1974). Virtually every major conclusion about slavery was challenged in the highly controversial study by Robert W. Fogel and Stanley L. Engerman, *Time on the Cross*, 2 vols. (1974), followed recently by Fogel's *Without Consent or Contract: The Rise and Fall of American Slavery* (1989).

The impact of slavery on slave personality is considered in Stanley M. Elkins, *Slavery: A Problem in American Institutional and Intellectual Life*, rev. ed. (1976), and John W. Blassingame, *The Slave Community: Plantation Life in the Antebellum South*, rev. ed. (1979). Newer studies of the slave family include Herbert G. Gutman, *The Black Family in Slavery and Freedom, 1750–1925* (1976), and Ann Patton Malone, *Sweet Chariot: Slave Family and Household Structure in Nineteenth-Century Louisiana* (1992). For slave women see Deborah Gray White, *Ar'n't I a Woman?: Female Slaves in the Plantation South* (1985), and Elizabeth Fox-Genovese, *Within the Plantation Household: Black and White Women of the Old South* (1988).

For a study of rural communal life see Charles Joyner, *Down by the Riverside: A South Carolina Slave Community* (1984), and for slavery in cities see Claudia D. Goldin, *Urban Slavery in the American South, 1820–1860* (1976). Two interesting focused studies are the story of a slave who killed her abusive master and was tried for the offense, in Melton A. McLaurin, *Celia: A Slave* (1991), and a discussion of one slave plot, in Winthrop D. Jordan, *Tumult and Silence at Second Creek: An Inquiry into a Civil War Slave Conspiracy* (1993).

To experience slavery through the words of those who lived it see Paul D. Escott, *Slavery Remembered: A Record of Twentieth-Century Slave Narratives* (1979), and Charles L. Perdue, Jr., et al., *Weevils in the Wheat: Interviews with Virginia Ex-Slaves* (1976).

The best general survey of African-American history is John Hope Franklin and Alfred A. Moss., Jr., *From Slavery to Freedom: A History of American Negroes*, 7th ed. (1994).

CHAPTER 16

Museum of the City of New York, gift of Mrs. Robert M. Littlejohn, (33.169)

This Samuel Waugh painting, The Bay and Harbor of New York, *(detail), (c. 1855) shows Irish immigrants landing at Castle Garden, New York, full of hope and anxiety about their prospects in America.*

A NATION OF
IMMIGRANTS

DAVID A. GERBER

*I*mmigrants helped the American colonies and the new nation build a strong, reliable work force. In the colonial period most immigrants from Europe could not afford to pay their own way to North America and came as indentured servants, but after 1800 the need for indentured servants declined steadily until by the Civil War it had virtually disappeared. This change did not reduce the number of people who wanted to come to the United States, but it did change their conditions and prospects. After 1820 two developments combined to continue the flow of poor workers to American shores. First, a series of political and agricultural problems in Europe propelled people off the land their families had farmed for centuries and sent them looking for new places to work. Second, the developing American economy required thousands of unskilled workers to load and unload ships, to dig canals, and to work in factories.

The major migrant waves of the pre-Civil War period came from Germany and Ireland. These two areas were ravaged by war, political upheaval, and agricultural consolidation. Beginning in the second decade of the nineteenth century and continuing beyond midcentury, immigrants left for America and the promise of better opportunities. They found these opportunities in eastern seaports and the growing inland cities of the North and Midwest. Few went south because slaves supplied the labor there even when factory work was needed.

In the following selection from *The Making of an American Pluralism: Buffalo, New York, 1825–1850,* David Gerber discusses the Irish immigrant experience. Gerber captures Irish communal values and living conditions as well as the native-born American reaction to them. His conclusions, while drawn from one city, represent the typical experience of most Irish.

As you read, see if you think, like many historians of a generation ago, that the United States was a "melting pot" where the unique characteristics of each separate immigrant group blended with all other residents to create a distinct American nationality. Or do you believe, as Gerber does, that ethnic groups maintained enough of their separate identities to join a society of many cultures—a pluralistic society?

Life in Ireland was tightly circumscribed by British colonialism and rural exploitation and poverty. British colonial administration had long sought to suppress Roman Catholicism and the yearnings of the Catholic masses for national self-determination, and to keep the island's inhabitants powerless and ignorant. Moreover, colonial policy had long ago created a class of Protestant, Anglo-Irish landowners, whose privileges and estates were protected at the expense of the native rural population. A system of land tenure, based on the monopolization of the best lands, consigned small farmers to work, as population grew, ever smaller parcels of land, or to join the broadening ranks of a landless rural proletariat composed of laborers and tenants. The growing impoverishment of the masses not only set land-poor Irishmen against the Anglo-Irish landlords, but set Irish rural labor and renters against Irish yeomen smallholders, who also exploited desperate wage earners and cultivators. Class antagonisms were thus added to traditional regional rivalries as sources of division. The catastrophic Potato Famine of 1845–50 revealed the viciousness of these mechanisms of powerlessness, poverty, dependence, and fragmentation. A famine in the key food crop of the rural poor led to the death of perhaps a million and the emigration of a million and a half, and left the countryside a social ruin.

Within these historical constraints, the Irish developed a strong folk culture, which centered around family, kinship, commune, and church. Along with a secular ideology of national liberation, the folk culture served as a basis for a growing sense of Irish peoplehood. National solidarity helped counter internal sources of division, and it provided a basis for early nineteenth-century popular mobilizations for Catholic emancipation and against exploitation by the Anglo-Irish renter class.

Immigration, however, remained a more common strategy than confrontation. Perhaps a million Irish immigrated to the United States between 1815 and 1845, but many of them, especially in the early years, were Protestants whose skills, religion, and individualistic culture helped them gain both acceptance by Americans and socioeconomic mobility. Catholic immigration also increased in those years, but before the famine significantly sized Irish Catholic populations were found

---

only in eastern seaboard cities. There were few Irish Catholics in Buffalo before the late 1840s. . . .

Famine-era immigration then established the basis for both a sizeable Irish population and Irish ethnicity. Indeed in 1855, fully 56 percent (1,525) of the Irish household heads had arrived in 1850–51 alone. While the prefamine migration was comprised mostly of young, single men and women, the majority of famine emigrants were with their families. Some of these hard-pressed families went to destinations where they could get assistance from already resettled kin and friends. But many had no such chains to link them to destinations and to ease their passage. They were forced to adopt a strategy of serial migration, characterized by brief residence in several locations to earn money to travel in search of better situations. . . .

Even with the advantage of knowing English, the famine-era Irish had much going against them in America. They had few marketable skills, little education, and no money. Substantial social disorganization—poverty, crime, disease, alcoholism, and family dissolution—accompanied their resettlement in America. Such difficulties were exacerbated by strong rejection by American Protestants of their peasant ways and devout Catholicism, and by the harsh stereotypes that determined popular attitudes whenever the Irish came to mind. These obstacles limited the chances for individual lives and depressed the group's social position. The socioeconomic bases of Irish ethnicity would be quite weak, and the group's constricted range of opportunity would be too narrow to produce a stable, sizeable leadership beyond the ranks of the clergy, who were representives of the only abiding institution the Irish possessed.

Yet to view the 1840s and 1850s as Irish-America's "tragic era" falls short of the mark. The famine-era immigrants had useful social resources in their peasant culture and their religion. Family and kinship ties and a strong female role often survived the famine and served as bases for organizing the domestic economy of the individual household. As the foundation of a stable institution and a coherent morality and worldview, Catholicism proved an essential resource for group formation. So, too, did the group's Old World political and prepolitical experience, its long-established habits of solidarity in the face of external threat, and its emotional nationalism, which was informed by folk memories of oppression and resistance. In America, these Old World forms of identity and organization left a particularly deep impression upon the processes of Irish group formation, as would such New World experiences as political mobilizations in defense of the Catholic church, highly unified and strongly partisan participation in the Democratic party, and intermittent but intense labor struggles.

Irish immigrant life took form amidst the pressures of poverty. In 1855, 57 percent of Irish households resided in lakeshore and canal corridor slums, variously named "the Patch," "the Flats," "the Beach," "the Hook," and "Sandytown," of the First and Eighth wards. The First Ward, which was 62 percent foreign-born and mostly Irish, had more recently arrived immigrants. Thirty-nine percent of its people were not citizens, in the Eighth Ward, though 80 percent were foreign-born (also mostly Irish), only 13 percent were aliens and thus probably in the country under five years. . . . These residential patterns reflected both proximity to Irish workplaces and poverty. Along the canal corridor and near the docks one found the cheapest housing. Most of the better-off Irish workers lived in decrepit, small to medium-sized dwellings, which had been subdivided in order to accommodate several families. It was subdivision, rather than the presence of multiunit residences, such as tenements, that accounted for the fact that, while the largely German Sixth and Seventh wards averaged two and five residents per dwelling, respectively, in the Irish First and Eighth, the figures were ten and eighteen, respectively. Though they usually avoided this type of crowding, the poorest Irish often lived in huts no more than twelve feet to a side. These were located on the beach or just off the docks, and constructed of waste boards. Some lived aboard decommissioned canal boats that had been beached. In the densely packed dwellings of these shantytowns, where, said the *Courier* in 1851, one saw "the spectacle of a most squalid poverty hardly credible in this land of plenty," each dwelling constituted a fire hazard to the next. The tidal wave bearing storms that swept the lakes also decimated these neighborhoods. Few of these shacks were owned by their inhabitants. . . .

The Irish nonetheless attempted to fashion familiar living arrangements. As in the old country, they regularly kept pigs, poultry, and dairy cattle in and around their places of residence, as Dr. Burwell found when he attended a birth at a shack on the beach and found himself competing for floor space with the resident swine. In America, too, the animals were a precious asset, though they did nothing to improve the image of the Irish among Americans like Burwell. Irish families regularly supplemented their incomes selling milk in the city, a kind of working-class entrepreneurship through urban agriculture in which the East Side German even more frequently took part. Cows belonging to the Irish could graze freely during the summer in the rich bottomlands south of the central docks and in the wild places along the Niagara, but in the winter, along with the other beasts, they had to be consumed or sold—or admitted to the family circle.

However much culture and tradition shaped it, entrenchment of this way of life was ultimately a consequence of the particular niche in the local economy that Irish men occupied. Their lack of urban job experience and skills combined with the city's tremendous need for unskilled labor to guarantee them a secure foothold only in the secondary labor market. Mattis's sample of 5 percent of all Irish men taken from the 1855 state census establishes that 46 percent could state no regular occupation at all, another 20 percent described themselves as outdoor or general laborers with no fixed working place, and 2 percent said they were steadily employed, unskilled workers at a nameable workplace. Six percent were transport workers—principally teamsters, lake sailors, and canal boatmen—whose skill level was not high. Only 17 percent were skilled or semiskilled, 7 percent lower white-collar workers, and 2 percent owners of retail, wholesale, or industrial establishments. Lack of skills and experience, as well as capital, rather than discrimination, also conspired to impair occupational mobility. Occasionally, it is true, want ads in the local press did specifically express preferences for other than Irish workers, but Germans and even British and Canadian workers were also explicitly excluded at times in such advertisements. There is no evidence of a systematic, customary, or certainly of a legal prohibition against employing Irish workers in better positions. That locally the "NINA" ("No Irish Need Apply") syndrome, which was common along the eastern seaboard, was an individual, nativist idiosyncracy is attested to, under any circumstance, by the fact that such prohibitions exclusively appeared in advertisements for domestic servants. This was a field, however, in which Irish women had a secure foothold, and it was actually . . . a relatively bright spot in the Irish employment picture.

Unskilled labor was a significantly sized, diverse occupational cohort, but the Irish occupied an especially limiting functional location within it. Many Germans were unskilled laborers, too, more indeed in absolute numbers than the Irish. But the Germans were found largely in building construction, where opportunities for informal, on-the-job apprenticeship were common, because laborers mixed constantly with artisans and craftsmen during the working day. In contrast, Irish unskilled work was a dead end in terms of both skill acquisition and opportunities for mobility. . . .

There were formidable obstacles to making a living at outdoor, unskilled labor even in a booming port. The work was low-paying, seasonal, and without regular or predictable hours, which further limited earnings. "We discharge daily more or less men depending on daily needs," explained a contractor involved in canal enlargement in 1849. Joseph Dart has left records to illustrate this pattern. He hired a group of six Irishmen in 1846 to do excavating at his port properties. Over the course of approximately seven weeks of work, the two men for whom there are extant pay records averaged 2.4 and 1.9 days a week, at a rate of seventy-five cents a day. In the 1850s Erie Canal laborers could make a dollar a day, when working a full day, but like Dart's laborers, few actually were able to do so. In grain the "scoopers" were paid on a low, piece-rate basis according to the number of bushels offloaded. Even if one had to go from one job to another several times a day, work was plentiful. But labor was hardly in short supply, a fact which explains the very low wage rates, and, a few notable examples aside, the near impossibility of uniting men so desperate for work to struggle against low wage rates. The vast numbers of Irishmen looking for work about the port also explains the callousness of foremen in the face of the constant dangers of longshore work. Grain scoopers were often sucked along with grain as it moved, with tremendous force, through pipes conducting it from elevators to boats (or vice versa), and were asphyxiated in a dense mass of flying grain. In addition, as farm boys, many Irish longshoremen did not know how to swim. When they fell off a gangplank with a heavy load on their backs, drowning was predictable. Yet Irish life, like Irish labor, came cheap, and the attitude toward these accidents may well be summed up by an 1846 incident. When an Irishman fell into the water with a grain sack on his shoulders, reported the *Commercial Advertiser,* "Efforts to save the wheat were successful, but the same exertions were not made to save his life."

Seasonality, underemployment and subemployment forced Irish laborers and their families to adopt various occupational and domestic strategies for supplementing their incomes. Fundamental to the laborers' effort, both in winter and in occasional slack periods during the season of navigation, was a willingness to travel to distant sites to take jobs and to remain away for months if need be. Irish laborers were regularly hired by professional labor recruiters, who worked in cooperation with the Overseers of the Poor, the agent of the Commissioners of Immigration, and tavern and boardinghouse keepers to find men in need of work to lay down railroad track or to dig canals in southern New York State, Pennsylvania, and more distant points, such as Illinois. . . .

Working Irish women, whose knowledge of English enhanced their prospects in the market for service workers, were able routinely to find jobs in domestic and personal service. They worked as maids, laundresses and domestics in hotels, but most often were employed by affluent American families. The work involved close scrutiny by one's employer, having to be on call twenty-four hours a day, and in the case of the live-in servant, isolation from family and friends. No wonder it was unpopular among those like workingclass American girls, whose relative affluence allowed them to try to find something better. But the wages were no worse than those paid women in eastern factories, and were a good deal better where servants were in short supply. Moreover, there were such benefits as a private room, board, and Christmas bonus, and gifts of discarded clothing and other personal items from employers. Under any circumstance, there was little alternative source of employment for women. Without a significant textile and ready-made clothing industry of the type that absorbed female workers in the East, Buffalo could not offer women work outside domestic and personal service. What few industrial opportunities there were for those other than adult men went usually to boys, who worked as helpers and fabricators at petty, low-wage mechanical tasks in small shops.

Irish service work must be seen in the context of the domestic economy of the Old and New World Irish household, in which poverty compelled each member to engage in the struggle to make ends meet. Irish women were found in service both before and after marriage. In 1855 about 19 percent of Irish women were employed outside the home, 86 percent of them as service workers. Almost all of these employed women were young, unmarried girls. Some were solitary emigrants, and many of them hoped to earn money enough to send for family, or at least through periodic remittances to help maintain those in Ireland. Probably the majority, however, were the daughters of local families. Irish girls began leaving their families for service as early as age eleven, and by the years between eighteen and twenty-one, from 46 percent to 66 percent were in service. . . . Though by age twenty-two a majority of Irish girls were married, at ages twenty-eight and twenty-nine nearly one Irish woman in five was still in service and still no doubt continuing to make contributions to the family economy in Ireland or the United States. This pattern of long delayed or no marriage was considerably reinforced by Irish cultural values. The Irish did not look scornfully on an unmarried girl working, or generally on the single woman, and placed a high valuation on celibacy for both sexes.

A contrast to the pattern of single working girls and women is provided by the 6 percent of Irish women in service who were married, some no doubt keeping positions they had prior to being wed, but others taking up work after marriage. Yet the figure vastly underestimates the actual number of married Irish women who worked in service, since many women did service work in their own homes while caring for their own children and keeping house. Laundering on a pick-up-and-delivery basis was a specialty of Irish women. Irish women also took in roomers and boarders, who, related and unrelated, were to be found in 29 percent of Irish households in 1855. Irish women probably also superintended boarding and rooming arrangements at the sixty-odd Irish groceries and at dozens of Irish saloons, where young, single laborers often slept in the basements and in corners. The women cooked, cleaned, and sewed for boarders, and they also served liquor and waited on shoppers. Finally, though it was as much entrepreneurial as service work, Irish housewives peddled and delivered the milk given by their family dairy cows. By 1859 it was estimated that there were as many as forty First Ward family milk businesses, a large percentage of them Irish-owned.

The boarding of relatives and women's contributions to household income were part of a larger pattern of family and kin mutual support that had origins in the peasant villages of Ireland and underwent various transformations, like boarding, while taking root in the city. Support was obtained not only from kin who were boarders, but also from those relatives who lived nearby. In contrast to the Germans, only some 12.5 percent of whom had kin in Buffalo in 1855, approximately 25 percent of the Irish did, a sign of strong immigration chains. Half of these kin lived as boarders in the homes of relatives. The other half resided in the same working-class Irish neighborhoods of the First and Eighth wards. The value of localized kin ties beyond boarding is seen in the godparentage roles kin assumed when they sponsored an infant at baptism. The act of sponsorship contained the promise that should some disaster befall the biological parents, the child would be looked after. For the majority without local kin ties, friends were chosen to act as baptismal sponsors, an eventuality that probably took place less often in Ireland. These fictive kinship ties moved friendship one step beyond its usual obligations to the moral plane of familial mutualism.

Changes in family formation habits also were among the strategies developed for coping with poverty, and they were reinforced by patterns developing simultaneously in Ireland. The famine was a watershed in the history of the Irish peasant family system, marking the acceleration of the trend toward deferred marriage, lower birth rates, and increasing celibacy, which, along with emigration, were means for ending further parcelization of land holdings. The famine Irish in America had their own reasons for adopting these same patterns—the unpredictability of the urban job market for the unskilled male and the inability of male children to make as significant a material contribution as they had on the farm. The Old World situation was not irrelevant, however, for the chains the American

Irish established to the Old World linked them to those, many of whom they would bring to America, increasingly adopting the same patterns. This process of change began almost immediately upon resettlement with what appear to be conscious decisions to limit fertility. . . .

No family strategy could be broad enough in the context of poverty and occupational ghettoization to cover all contingencies. Moreover, for those without local kin or friends, these networks were absent. It is not surprising that individual and family disorganization was ever present among the Irish, and that it frequently became the basis of the view of them held by others, especially Americans. . . .

Certainly the crushing burdens of supporting a family on a laborer's occasional wages must have broken the spirit of many a man and led him to desert. As it was, the status in the family of these men was eroded in the act of resettlement. In contrast to their situation in Ireland, they had no skills or land to pass down to their sons, and they were often quite dependent on the money-making activities of wives and daughters. . . .

Irish men did experience a much greater tendency toward moral breakdown and a disorganized, self-defeating social existence. . . .

The Irish drank a great deal, and drinking was deeply integrated, both in Ireland and United States, into the structure of daily life. . . .

. . . In Ireland, whiskey was used as a substitute for food in times of famine and on Catholic feast days, when only one meal was permitted. Folk tradition prescribed it as medicine and tonic, and it was given to children as an inducement to good behavior. In lieu of warm clothing, it offered temporary relief from, not to mention a way of forgetting, the discomforts of the island's cold and damp winter climate. Illegal distillation, which was common in Ireland, provided supplements for peasant incomes, and offered a way of resisting British power by evading imports. Whiskey was at the center of social life from cradle to grave. It was a staple at christenings, weddings, and wakes. Much Irish social drinking, however, was sex segregated, for it took place in a culture characterized by rigid social separation of the sexes. The "shebeen," or rural drinking hut, was perhaps the only male retreat from crowded peasant cottages. Too, there was an element of male sport and competitiveness, as well as bonding, about the practice of "treating," by which one established a capacity to drink and to spend money.

In America whiskey was socially contextualized in many of the same ways. But it also came to enter the life of young, single men in additional, new ones. The lodging and boarding houses where these men lived and socialized were also often grocery-saloons. Here, too, while waiting around and drinking, many men were recruited daily for work by stevedores and contractors. These employers routinely provided Irish laborers on the canals and railroads with whiskey to keep them contented on the job and preoccupied in the evening at isolated, rural work sites. The cost of whiskey was often deducted from a man's pay.

Irish culture and American circumstances, therefore, both tended to legitimate drinking and to expand the opportunities in which it might take place. As a result, many men went down the road to impoverishment and lack of responsibility to those dependent on them, and ultimately to alcoholism and premature death. Almost as significant in deepening the difficulties with alcohol of the Irish as a group was the deeply felt desire of many Americans to use the law to regulate or to prohibit the use of spirits. These desires were a response to a concrete problem, and hardly exclusively an Irish one, for there were large numbers of intemperate Americans. But in moving the problem of liquor and its control to a legal plane, temperance could transform the Irish tippler, who saw nothing wrong with his behavior, into a law-breaker and pariah, and indirectly help to form a socially disruptive drinking culture. In so doing, temperance reinforced the solidaristic and alienated bases of Irish male drinking, and worsened the problem it wished to eradicate. Moreover, this complex interaction between the Irish drinker and society assisted in sealing upon the ethnic group its reputation for uncivilized behavior. . . .

The Irish thus displayed much evidence of antisocial behavior, but this is not to suggest that the American image of the Irish was simply based on objective analysis. Stereotypes are distortions, more often derived from fantasy and projection than reality. The ones attached to the Irish were intensely distorted and negative, and thus capable of doing great psychic violence to the immigrants and their American-born children. As such, stereotypes provided impetus for Irish ethnicization, for the group was an essential source of defense and security amidst rejection and hostility. . . .

Within a short time, the outlines of the stereotype of the typical Irish man, whom the American press called "Pat," emerged. Pat was ignorant yet cunning. He was feckless, lazy, self-indulgent, and drunken, priest-ridden and superstitious, and prone to violence. He and his kind lived like—and frequently with—pigs. As a laborer, he was a wily strategist. He avoided hard work and stole his employer's goods. He was shiftless; for how else could his frequent joblessness and stays in the poorhouse be accounted for? The *Commercial Advertiser* approved lower wages for the Irish, because, it said, "It is well-known the way the Irish generally work." Pat was a clever knave in his dealings with American power. As a defendant in court, he so confused the proceedings with garbled testimony that the desperate judge dismissed the charges just to be rid of him. On his own ground, however, Pat was the prototypical "Wild Irishman." Frequently drunk and looking for action, he sought amusement in riot and violence, and in the process mocked the manners and morals of respectable Americans and showed contempt for their authority.

Pat, in fact, had no morals; his manners and behavior proved that. Unlike Americans, he did not believe that he should stay home after church on Sunday in order to think about his relation to his maker. He did not appreciate those social superiors who told him he should. As early as 1835, when Alderman Lewis

Allen made the mistake of trying to break up Sabbath drinking and fighting on the docks, the assembled Pats took a respite from battling each other to chase the councilman from the scene. Pat's moral sense was blunted by priestcraft and those rituals of the church—confessions, offerings, and indulgences—that made him feel safe from the consequences of his behavior, while leading him to fear and respect no one but his priests. His relation to God was blighted by idolatry (did not Catholics venerate saints?) and by religious pageantry, which the *Christian Advocate* called the church's "emblazoned buffoonery." His understanding of civic obligation was perverted by both the demagogic rhetoric of Irish politicians and the secular teachings of nuns and priests in sectarian schools and in weekly sermons that left Pat putting church interests before the public good. Both priest and politician told Pat and his fellow immigrants to vote Democratic, so on election day, said the *Express* in 1856, out they came "in herds and droves . . . like sheep following a leader." They would vote, the paper was sure, "for a horse or an ox if it were on the Democratic ticket." That Pat should come to a bad end was no surprise to Americans. That he should do so surrounded by the symbols and people who had led him astray was appropriate. One may then imagine the reaction of Americans to the execution of twenty-four-year-old Lawrence Fogarty, an immigrant from Limerick, for the murder, while drunk, of an American. Surrounded by priests, crucifix in hand, he mounted the gallows and offered these last words: "I am an Irishman and a Catholic; I have lived and died a Catholic. And its little I thought as a child, I should come to this end." There were many Americans who could find a great deal of explanation in this statement.

Education or prosperity might round out some of the rough corners of Pat's character, but could not fundamentally alter him. As a priest, the Irish man was little more than a crafty power-seeker and none too honest. When in 1856 a national Irish convention met at Buffalo, at the initiation principally of priests, to contemplate emigration to the frontier to break free of urban poverty and nativist hostility, the *Commercial Advertiser,* like the anticlerical German *Demokrat,* could see nothing in it but the priests' desire to speculate in land. Irish politicians, said the *Republic* in 1853, were frequently "demogogues and self-interested wily men," who had no public vision beyond patronage and offices for family and friends, and were trying to freight American politics with such irrelevancies as their hatred of England and "their daydream nationality." When given a public trust, the Irish man proved irresponsible. As a policeman, for example, he was the cop on the beat who fell asleep in an empty lot and had his hat and nightstick removed by pranksters. (Commenting on one such incident, however, the *Commercial Advertiser* said that many of the Irish police were "even worse.") As an entrepreneur, the Irish man cut a poor figure, too. Local credit reporters described Irish shopkeepers as "careless" and "reckless" with money, inattentive to business, "keeping free and easy company," and frequently intemperate. ("Grog shop—with himself as best customer," it was said of one saloonkeeper.) The ethnic leadership that came out of this small class of shopkeepers and others inevitably found little favor among Americans. Liberals such as George Washington Johnson found Irish leadership priest-ridden, and detested its conservatism on abolition and social reform. American conservatives, ever fearful of disorder, were equally unen-thusiastic. After observing the major Irish organizations marching in the annual St. Patrick's Day parade in 1857, the *Commercial Advertiser* criticized the intoxica-tion and incompetence of the marchers and went on to question whether the Irish could ever hope to govern themselves in Ireland.

"Bridget," the Irish domestic, was Pat's female counterpart, and Americans could claim even more intimacy with her, because often she lived with them. She had many of Pat's defects, but a number of her own, too. In Hasia Diner's accu-rate depiction of the stereotype, Bridget "darted from one American kitchen to another, usually shattering the crockery as she went." She was "not very bright or dependable," and she was "a horrendous cook." When she was not breaking household valuables, she was stealing them and she regularly "toted" food from her mistress's kitchen to her mother's or sister's. She spent money at the market on "lollypops and red ribbons," said the *Commercial Advertiser,* and brought back, at her own slow pace, "inferior provisions." Her friends often came to the kitchen to be fed. Her cavorting at wakes left her too tired to work. Just when she was fi-nally properly trained, she quit—showing no gratitude to her mistress for instruc-tion in manners and for gifts of discarded clothing.

There were surely those Americans, like the Hawleys, who willed money to their faithful Bridget, whose experience was different. But most were deeply dis-content with Irish help. Some, like Nancy Spaulding, wife of a prominent lawyer and politician, reached the conclusion after their "girl" quit that they were "fully determined never to hire another,"—even while having to admit to themselves that there was really no other source of English-speaking help, since American women seldom did domestic work. Other Americans, including even Dr. Foote of the *Commercial Advertiser,* refused to give up on Bridget. They urged following the lead of some eastern cities and forming "a society for the encouragement of faith-ful domestics," a combination employment agency, referral service, mutual bene-fit society, and recreational organization that would also set standards for the wages and treatment of servants. This was never done, suggesting that either Americans had become resigned to making peace with Bridget on her terms, or they did not wish to be bound to improving her lot.

Like Pat, Bridget, whose views are probably less well-known, had her own opin-ion of the situation—and of her employer. She was very likely the daughter of im-migrants, a mere teenager who had begun life in a one-room peasant cottage. Along with Dr. Foote, she doubtless thought it unfair that her employer was "as-tonished that she did not at once understand the use of napkins, finger bowls, and dessert knives." Moreover, she awoke at dawn to a day of drudgery. She was isolated from her peers, and might well have felt she was watching her youth re-cede before her. While she gave much of her income to her family, her employers seemed to have unlimited wealth. Since they often bought in bulk, it was difficult for her to believe that they could possibly miss, let alone need, the bit of food she took home.

As Bridget mastered her circumstances, she changed, and her confusion and incompetence gave way to self-confidence. She took on those of her employer's standards that served her needs. She began simultaneously to see those needs differently, comparing her little room not to her ancestral hut, but to the commodious suite of her mistress's daughter. It was this confidence, which had at its heart a greater valuation of herself and her labor, that led Bridget to quit when aggrieved, or in response to a better opportunity. It was this confidence, too, that led her to come to judge her employers irreverently. Bridget, said Harriet Prescott Spofford, an insightful American chronicler of "the servant question" in a book addressed to the bourgeois mistress, "thinks you are an upstart, for your grandmother was perhaps a shoemaker's wife, and if you were overseas you would be a shoemaker's wife, too." Moreover, said Spofford, Bridget resented being asked "to try to do so much with so little [assistance]" about the house and kitchen, and thus, she "despises your ignorance, and is sure you would starve without her."

Bridget's understanding of her employer's nouveau riche status was not inaccurate, as her employers, in their better moments, would have been the first to admit. But there is a more important meaning to her perceptions. As in the Irish priest's assertion of the superiority, not mere equality, of Catholicism, the Irish parent's rejection of the public schools as inferior to diocesan ones, or the Irish politician's pride in besting Americans in the quest for power and place, Bridget's pride in her competence and toughness and her jaundiced view of her employers represents the emergent, positive side of Irish self-understanding in America. While the impetus to ethnicization was often a self-protective, reflexive turning away from hostility and contempt, it might also be, after time enough to evaluate oneself in the new homeland, something more: the embrace of a newly appreciated self for its endurance and strength, and an appreciation of the resiliency and richness of cultural resources brought from the Old World. Thus, ethnicization could be at once a celebration and a retreat. To understand it only as the latter risks failing to see the extent to which the immigrants might come to take pride in their accomplishments, if only at surviving. Yet to see it only as the former risks failing to see how desperate the social circumstances of those like the Irish could be. . . .

 ## FOR FURTHER STUDY

1. What conditions forced the Irish out of their homeland? Why and when did they come to Buffalo? Were they totally without traditions and community ties?

2. What living and working conditions did the Irish have in Buffalo? How much did their experience in Ireland determine these conditions and how much was determined by the American economy?

3. How did the Irish immigrants cope with underemployment of male members? What reasons did single Irish women have for taking outside jobs? Did this change when they married? How were Irish families able to remain close under these circumstances?

4. Describe the "Pat" and "Bridget" stereotypes of Irish Immigrants and comment on what impact they had on the Irish themselves and on others' views of the Irish.

5. What was positive about the process of "ethnicization" and the survival of the Irish?

FOR FURTHER READING

For a more detailed look at groups in Buffalo in the 1850s see Lawrence A. Glasco, *Ethnicity and Social Structure: Irish, Germans, and Native-Born of Buffalo, New York, 1850–1860* (1980).

The best comprehensive introduction to the Irish is the recent work of Kirby Miller, *Emigrants and Exiles: Ireland and the Irish Exodus to North America* (1985). For surveys of the Irish in America see Lawrence J. McCaffrey, *The Irish Diaspora in America* (1984), and Hasia R. Diner, *Erin's Daughters in America: Irish Immigrant Women in the Nineteenth Century* (1983). Oscar Handlin, *Boston's Immigrants,* rev. ed. (1968), is an excellent older study of one city. On Irish stereotypes in general see Dale T. Knobel, *Paddy and the Republic: Ethnicity and Nationality in Antebellum America* (1986), and on drinking in particular see Richard J. Stivers, *Hair of the Dog: Irish Drinking and American Stereotype* (1976).

Germans also came in large numbers to the United States before the Civil War. See Mack Walter, *Germany and the Emigration, 1816–1855* (1964). There is relatively little general work done on this important group, however see Frank Trommler and Joseph McVeigh, *America and the Germans, An Assessment of a Three-Hundred Year History,* vol. I, *Immigration, Language, and Ethnicity* (1985). German immigrants themselves tell their American experiences in Walter D. Kamphoefner, Wolfgang Helbich, and Ulrike Sommer, eds., *News from the Land of Freedom: German Immigrants Write Home* (1991).

J. P. Dolan looks at immigrant religion in *The Immigrant Church: New York's Irish and German Catholics, 1815–1865* (1975). Studies of urban immigrants include the older, excellent study by Robert Ernst, *Immigrant Life in New York City, 1825–1863* (1949), and the more recent work of Kathleen Neils Cozen, *Immigrant Milwaukee, 1836–1860: Accommodation and Community in a Frontier City* (1976). Mark Wyman traces migration to the Mississippi River Valley in *Immigrants in the Valley* (1983).

Immigration history has flourished recently because of the renewed interest in the contributions many groups made to the nation. Still, some older studies capture the flavor of the plight of immigrants. Oscar Handlin's Pulitzer Prize-winning *The Uprooted: The Epic Story of the Great Migrations That Made the American People,* rev. ed. (1973), and his collection of documents, *Immigration as a Factor in American History* (1969), are useful introductions. More recent popular views of the negative side of immigrant treatment can be found in Michael Novak, *The Rise of the Unmeltable Ethnics* (1972).

Philadelphia's 1844 anti-Catholic riot, which required calling in the state militia, suggests the crime and violence that plagued early nineteenth-century cities.

URBAN PROBLEMS

MICHAEL FELDBERG

*T*oday a vast majority of the United States population lives in sizeable towns and large cities. Along the Atlantic seaboard, farmlands near the great urban centers have been turned into housing developments at such a rate that the hundreds of miles between Washington, D.C., and Boston are becoming one great urban corridor. The American people have become so thoroughly an urban people that few are left who know the difference between timothy and alfalfa or who have any idea of what the farm implement known as a harrow does. In recent years, an increasing number of farm museums have developed, where city folks can go on a Sunday afternoon to look at weathered farm equipment and see live sheep and cattle. There is a considerable irony in all this, since during much of American history the country was predominantly rural and the American dream was the acquisition of one or two hundred acres one could farm for oneself.

In the eighteenth century, most centers of settlement were nothing more than tiny farming villages. Boston, the largest city in 1730, had 13,000 people; Philadelphia was second, with 11,500, and New York third, with 8,500. As late as 1790, the population of the largest American city, Philadelphia, numbered only 30,000. By 1860, it had risen to an incredible 565,000; New York was home to more than 800,000; and the relatively new, western metropolis of Cincinnati had 160,000 people. The extraordinary growth of cities in the nineteenth century brought new problems and required new policies and institutions to solve some of the older problems.

Epidemics of cholera and yellow fever swept American cities in the early nineteenth century, taking as many as 3,500 lives in a single year in New York. In the same city, hundreds of homeless poor, including orphaned children, roamed the streets begging, and tens of thousands of people lived in dark cellar holes and tenement buildings. Crime and gang violence became critical problems in the larger cities, as did supplying water, fire protection, and other services to these vast metropolitan areas. Singing the old refrain that the city is "a great place to visit, but I wouldn't want to live there," a visitor to New York in 1828 said that something about it made it "more a gratification to visit, than to abide."

Some of the urban problems were solved by private efforts, some by the development of professional government service departments to replace the earlier private fire-protection clubs. In 1860, for example, 79 private companies and 57 public works supplied water to the cities. Protection against crime and the devastating riots that swept American cities led to the creation of modern, trained police forces. The riots involved many different groups and issues, ranging from religious and ethnic hostilities to political warfare, economic competition for jobs, and abolitionist activity. The following essay by Michael Feldberg depicts crowd violence in Philadelphia in the 1840s.

Americans who remember the urban unrest of the 1960s can readily identify with the crisis of violence that gripped Jacksonian American cities. The 1830s, 1840s, and 1850s produced a constant stream of riots reminiscent of the "long hot summers" of the not-too-distant past. Jacksonian cities were torn by fighting between immigrants and native-born Americans, abolitionists and anti-abolitionists, free blacks and racist whites, volunteer firefighters and street gangs, Mormons and "Gentiles," even rival factions of Whigs and Democrats. And, like the 1960s, Jacksonian collective violence resulted in greatly enlarged and strengthened police forces better able to repress riots and disorders—either with or without death or injury to the rioters.

Yet there are some notable differences between the upheavals of the pre-Civil War decades and those of the 1960s. Compared with the death and devastation in Watts, Newark, or Detroit, Jacksonian rioting seems rather tame. Whereas a few major confrontations in the 1840s and 1850s took the lives of at least a dozen persons, deaths in Jacksonian rioting were a relatively rare occurrence. Certainly the property damage to Washington, D.C., after the assassination of Martin Luther King, Jr., or to Harlem during the New York Blackout of 1977, was unequaled by even the most destructive pre-Civil War violence.

In its own way, however, urban rioting posed for Jacksonian society a social and political crisis seemingly equal to that of the 1960s era of protest. To some contemporaries, violence in the 1830s and 1840s portended the possible destruction of American civilization. . . . As sober an analyst as Abraham Lincoln warned in 1837 that

> . . . there is even now something of an ill omen amongst us. . . . Accounts of outrages committed by mobs form the every-day news of the times. They have pervaded the

country from New England to Louisiana; they are neither peculiar to the eternal snows of the former nor the burning suns of the latter; they are not the creatures of climate, neither are they confined to the slaveholding or the non-slaveholding states. Alike they spring up among the pleasure-hunting master of Southern slaves, and the order-loving citizens of the land of steady habits. Whatever their causes be, it is common to the whole country.

Lincoln was not exaggerating the dimensions of the crisis. Historian Richard Maxwell Brown has counted thirty-five major riots in Baltimore, Philadelphia, New York, and Boston during the three decades from 1830 to 1860. Historian John C. Schneider found that "at least seventy percent of American cities with a population of twenty thousand or more by 1850 experienced some degree of major disorder in the 1830–1865 period." The abolitionist movement, which kept its own count of anti-abolition and racially motivated mobs, reported no less than 209 such incidents for the 1830s and 1840s alone. . . .

The historical significance of rioting in a given period should not be measured solely by its frequency or intensity. Collective violence should be judged in its broader social and political contexts as well; it must be seen as one of several forms of interaction that can occur among groups, or between groups and their government. We must look at the functions Jacksonian rioting served, the kinds of groups that employed it, and the success of those groups in using violence to attain their goals. In the Jacksonian context, collective violence was one means by which various groups attempted to control competition among themselves, or by which they responded to changes in their relative status, power, wealth, or political influence.

. . . Jacksonian collective violence stemmed from a number of sources: the racial and ethnic tensions of the period; the era's ideological climate; the inability of political systems and legal institutions to resolve group conflict by peaceable means; rapid urbanization and population changes; and economic and technological innovation. What distinguishes Jacksonian rioting from collective violence in other periods of American history is not its sources, however, but the frequency of its occurrence, its effectiveness, and the relative inability of public authorities to control or suppress it. Yet the very success achieved by private groups through rioting called forth forces that, by the 1850s, would change the balance of power between rioters and local peacekeeping officials and impose professional police systems on American cities. The epidemic of collective violence in Jacksonian cities ultimately undermined the American public's traditional resistance to the creation of effective urban police forces. By the time of the Civil War, most of the nation's important cities had established recognizably modern police departments. . . . The creation of urban police departments became the most enduring legacy of Jacksonian collective violence.

The great Philadelphia Native American Riots of 1844 were certainly among the most dramatic and violent episodes in pre-Civil War American history. In both their Kensington and Southwark phases, they present a capsule portrait of the sources, uses, and consequences of Jacksonian collective violence. Although they grew out of cultural and religious conflict between Philadelphia's Protestant nativists and Irish Catholic immigrants, the riots were the immediate result of a political controversy over the use of the Bible in the Philadelphia public schools. The fighting also reflected the social and political disorganization of Philadelphia and the weakness of its peacekeeping system. . . . Above all, the two phases of Philadelphia Native American Riots of 1844 illustrate the ease with which private groups in Jacksonian America employed collective violence as a tool for conducting social conflict and expressing political protest. The riots also reveal the difficulties public authorities faced when they tried to control group violence in the nation's rapidly changing cities.

By February 1844, Louisa Bedford had finally run out of patience. She was having a difficult enough time teaching elementary school in Kensington, a working-class suburb just north of Philadelphia. Now her job was made even more trying because of hard feelings between the parents of both her immigrant Irish Catholic students and her native-born Protestant students. . . . Two years earlier, in 1842, the Philadelphia County Board of School Controllers had ordered that the King James, or Protestant, version of Holy Scripture be used as a basic reading text in all Philadelphia public school classes. Upon hearing this, the Catholic Bishop of Philadelphia, the Reverend Francis Patrick Kenrick, asked that Catholic children be allowed to read the Douay, or authorized Catholic, version of Scripture, and that Catholic teachers not be compelled to read from the King James during reading exercises. The controllers denied Kenrick's request.

During the 1840s many American Protestants feared Catholicism because it seemed alien and anti-democratic. . . . Because of this widely held prejudice, the Philadelphia School Controllers were afraid to grant equal status to the Douay Bible by allowing it in the schools. . . . Yet to ease Bishop Kenrick's objections to an obvious injustice, the Board of School Controllers saw fit to offer a compromise solution: Catholic children could leave their classrooms while Bible-reading exercises were conducted, but the Douay version was still not to be admitted into the schools.

This compromise pleased almost no one. Catholics believed that the plan ignored this bishop's plea for justice and equality; evangelical Protestants felt that Catholic children should be compelled to read the King James version as an antidote to their "priestly dictated" and "popish" beliefs. The solution also failed to please teachers like Louisa Bedford, who could not tolerate the disruption caused by her Catholic students waiting noisily outside her door until the Bible-reading session was over. To remedy this situation, Bedford took actions which, in a short time, led to the great Philadelphia riots of 1844.

Louisa Bedford was a Protestant, although not a militant evangelical. Seriously committed to teaching the working-class children of Kensington to read and write, she resented the chaos caused by the controllers' policy. Thus when School Controller and Irish Catholic politician Hugh Clark was making his weekly tour of

Kensington's public schools, Bedford asked Clark if she could have a word with him. She explained her unhappiness to the politically astute Clark who, one suspects, was waiting for just such a moment. Clark then sympathetically offered an alternative to sending Catholic students out of her room: She could suspend *all* Bible reading in her class until such time as the School Controllers devised a better method for excusing Catholic students from the exercise. Clark volunteered to assume responsibility should she decide to follow this course. Bedford chose to accept Clark's offer and told her students that, for the time being, they would not have to do their Bible reading. Much to her relief, she turned to teaching other subjects.

. . . Word of Clark's decision to "kick the Bible out of the schools," as his enemies inaccurately described it, spread like wildfire throughout the city. Evangelical Protestants, most of them native-born Americans and the remainder immigrant Irish Protestants, had been organizing in Philadelphia for nearly a decade. The evangelicals were alarmed by what they believed to be the growing political and religious influence of Catholics, particularly Irish Catholic immigrants. Nativists, . . . those who openly opposed all "alien" elements such as Catholics, immigrants, Mormons, and others who did not conform to the dominant white Protestant religious and cultural values of the era, had especially feared the political activism of the Irish Catholic clergy. . . . Protestants concerned with the increasing influence of Catholics and immigrants in American life joined a new political movement known as the American Republican party, which had branches in Philadelphia, New York, Boston, Baltimore, and New Orleans. The American Republicans held rallies and ran candidates to oppose the influence of immigrants in local politics. . . .

For the most part, American Republican leadership in Philadelphia was composed of "middling" and "respectable" men: lawyers, doctors, clergymen, newspaper editors, shopkeepers, craftsmen, printers, barbers, dentists, and teachers. These individuals were neither numbered in the ranks of the city's traditional upper classes—wealthy merchants, bankers, manufacturers, and gentlemen farmers—nor drawn from the ranks of the struggling poor. Rather, these American Republicans had formerly provided the bulk of middle-class voters for the Whig and Democratic parties. With their wives they filled the pews of Philadelphia's Methodist, Baptist, and Presbyterian churches. By their own description they saw themselves as the "bone and sinew" of society, the hard-working silent majority who, while never independently wealthy and secure like the upper classes, would never allow themselves to fall to the level of the impoverished or degenerate immigrants.

Because they saw themselves as the nation's only "real" Americans, nativists could not stand to see their public schools, or the political system in general, "captured" by persons who spoke with a foreign accent—especially an Irish brogue. The social isolation of America's Irish immigrants and their continued loyalty to their native land particularly worried American nativists. They believed that the typical Irish immigrant would never become a loyal American citizen, freed of his allegiance to Ireland or to the Roman Catholic Church. They did not realize that the experiences of Irish Catholic immigrants with English-speaking Protestants had convinced the Irish to cling to their religion and to their nationalism. . . .

To maintain their solidarity, to resist integration into a Protestant-dominated society such as the one they had fled, the American Irish tended to cluster in self-imposed ghettos, to socialize in their own taverns, to attend mass in their own parish churches, and to meet in their own political and nationalist clubs. Such self-inflicted isolation upset Protestant American nativists, but the apparent political control that the Irish-born Catholic clergy seemed to exercise over their immigrant followers appeared to bother them even more. Nativists convinced one another that the American Irish voted overwhelmingly for the Democratic party, not because the Jacksonian political platform or personal style appealed to the newcomers, but because corrupt Roman Catholic priests "dictated" voting orders from Rome to their sheeplike parishioners. . . .

Philadelphia American Republicanism was closely allied with the most popular reform movement of the era, the temperance crusade. At its inception in the early 1800s, the American temperance movement was dedicated to persuading individuals to consume only moderate amounts of alcoholic beverages. In the 1840s, its national membership may have numbered over 100,000, and most of these members believed that all sales of drinking alcohol should be outlawed. Alcoholism had become closely associated with poverty, unemployment, crime, ill health, and broken families. Somewhat unfairly, it was also closely associated with urban immigrant communities; gin and rum with the Irish, beer with the Germans, and wine with the French and Italians. Since nativists considered immigrant groups, and especially the Irish, responsible for most of the nation's poverty, crime, and prostitution, their interest in temperance reflected their critical attitudes toward the lifestyles of America's urban immigrant populations.

It was unfair of nativists and temperance advocates to equate alcohol consumption primarily with immigrants. The nation's upper classes were the chief consumers of good French wines, port, sherry, and Madeira. Many native Protestant workingmen were paid a portion of their wages in a daily allowance of rum, and nearly every workshop and factory employed young boys to run out frequently for buckets of beer. Drinking to excess was a universal problem that crossed ethnic and class boundaries. The vast quantities of alcohol consumed in Jacksonian America convinced many temperance advocates, nativist and non-nativist alike, that an individual's mere verbal pledge to drink moderately was not enough to keep him from abusing alcohol, and temperance crusaders increasingly switched from a voluntarist to a prohibitionist position. They argued that only by outlawing the sale of liquor could its evil effects be controlled.

The conversion of Philadelphia's temperance movement to a prohibitionist stance was tied in important ways to the American Republican and evangelical Protestant movements of the era. Closing bars and rum shops could have important social and political implications for immigrant communities. Taverns were one of the focal points in working-class Irish and German neighborhoods, and they often served as social and political centers. Their patrons did not usually welcome native Protestant—or even other ethnic—outsiders, and many a Phila-delphia brawl was started when an unwitting stranger of the wrong ethnic back-ground violated the sanctity of a German or Irish saloon. Particularly in Irish neighborhoods, taverns became symbols of Irish-Catholic separatism and Irish im-migrant rejection of integration into wider American culture.

But nativists had political as well as cultural objections to the immigrants' fond-ness for alcoholic beverages. They argued that just as priests could control the consciences of immigrant Catholics through the religious doctrine of papal infal-libility, so could tavern owners manipulate the political loyalties of immigrants by trading liquor for votes. Nativist temperance advocates feared an unholy alliance between Catholic priests and ambitious tavern-owning politicians that would maintain the immigrants' dependence on the Church and the bottle. The battle against liquor, then, was in part a battle to preserve American political freedom from Catholic-sponsored conspiracies.

One person's reform, though, is another person's oppression, especially when the targets of the reform movement saw nothing wrong in their style of life or reli-gious values. Catholic and Irish community leaders believed strongly that the Constitution entitled community members to liberty of conscience in their reli-gion, freedom of association in their social contacts, freedom of thought in their political beliefs, and freedom of choice in their use of alcohol. The Catholic Archdiocese of Philadelphia organized its own voluntary temperance societies, but it strongly opposed any attempt to legislate away the individual's right to in-dulge in alcohol. And while it urged its parishioners to attend mass on Sunday, the Archdiocese resisted efforts to suppress popular amusements on the Sabbath. Most important, Bishop Kenrick personally resented the efforts of Protestant ac-tivists to "save" Catholic children by forcing them to read the King James Bible in the public schools.

Unfortunately for Bishop Kenrick and the rest of Philadelphia's Catholics, the school Bible issue stirred intense hatred in the "City of Brotherly Love." The city's nativists chose (deliberately or otherwise) to interpret Kenrick's request to grant equality to the Douay Bible as a demand that the King James Bible be *removed* from the public schools. . . .

Thus it is clear why Hugh Clark's suggestion to Louisa Bedford that she sus-pend Bible reading in her Kensington classroom caused such upheaval through-out Philadelphia. It was as if the bishop's alleged conspiracy had finally come out in the open. The first word of Clark's actions was carried by Henry Moore, a Methodist minister who burst into a prayer meeting at his Kensington church to inform the congregation that Clark had forced Miss Bedford against her will to "kick the Bible out of her classroom." Word spread rapidly throughout the city's nativist network, and Philadelphia's American Republican leaders and evangelical Protestant clergymen convened a series of mass rallies in mid-March to protest Catholic attempts to "trample our free Protestant institutions in the dust." At one rally more than 3,000 protestors gathered to hear an American Republican spokesman remind those who would "remove the Bible from the public schools" that, "when we remember that our Pilgrim Fathers landed on Plymouth Rock to establish the Protestant religion, free from persecution, we must contend that this was and always will be a Protestant country."

Their enthusiastic reception at the city-wide rallies encouraged the American Republicans to carry their crusade right to the lair of the beast, the very neighborhood that symbolized Irish Catholic solidarity in Philadelphia: Third Ward, Kensington. The community was long and widely recognized as immigrant Irish "turf." It was dominated by Irish handloom weavers, dock laborers, teamsters, and other semiskilled workers who held little love for their native Protestant neighbors in adjoining wards. The neighborhood had been the scene of several riots in recent years, including a series of attacks on railroad construction workers trying to lay tracks down Front Street and some violent attacks on nonunion weavers who were failing to honor a strike by their fellow "brothers of the loom." Perhaps the most notorious incident had occurred a few months earlier, when the striking weavers attacked and dispersed a sheriff's posse, beat the sheriff soundly, and had to be quelled by the state militia troops. It was in this neighborhood of militant and aggressive Irish immigrants that the American Republicans chose to hold a rally on Friday afternoon, May 3, 1844, and invite the general public to attend.

That Friday meeting might well have been calculated to provoke a fateful confrontation with Kensington's immigrant Irish. The American Republicans chose to hold their rally in a schoolyard at Second and Master streets. When the American Republican spokesmen began their speeches, they were heckled, booed, and pelted with rocks and garbage by a crowd of several hundred, and eventually driven from the speaker's platform they had erected earlier in the afternoon. Undaunted (and quite self-righteously), the party decided to reconvene the meeting in the schoolyard on Monday, May 6, and placarded the city with notices urging every American Republican loyalist to attend. This time a large crowd of 3,000 turned out. Around 3:00 P.M., while noted temperance lecturer and political nativist Lewis C. Levin was arousing the crowd's interest, a sudden rainstorm erupted and the crowd moved spontaneously in search of shelter toward the Nanny Goat Market.

Relocating the rally in the market proved catastrophic. The Nanny Goat Market was the hub of the Third Ward Irish community. An open-sided, block-long covered shed at Third and Master streets, the market house served as a shopping center, a meeting place, and a social center for local residents. When the noisy but peaceable nativists arrived, a group of thirty or so Irish locals was waiting there to greet them. One Irishman was heard to proclaim, "Keep the damned natives out of our market house; this ground don't belong to them, it's ours!" Lewis Levin tried to continue his speech from a vendor's stand but hecklers drowned him out. Pushing and shoving began, someone pulled a pistol, a rival dared him to shoot, he did, and panic erupted under the shed. The Irish residents fled to their nearby homes, but the nativists were trapped in the open-sided shed with few places to hide. A rain of gunfire poured down on them from surrounding buildings, most of it from the Hibernia Hose House, the headquarters of an Irish volunteer fire company. The first nativist killed in the shooting, nineteen-year-old George Schiffler, became a martyr to the cause. His name was soon immortalized when a nativist militia company, a volunteer fire company, and a fighting street gang each took his name as their own. In subsequent years the street gang known as the Schifflers would fight many battles with Philadelphia's Irish and Democratic street gangs and volunteer fire companies.

The initial advantage possessed by the Irish snipers was soon balanced by the arrival of approximately eighteen nativist reinforcements who brought rifles and shotguns with them. Protected by the fire of their own sharpshooters, nativists began making forays out of the Nanny Goat Market, breaking windows and doors of the houses from which gunfire had been coming and scattering the inhabitants. Several Irishmen were badly beaten and left for dead as others saw their homes and furniture wrecked by the furious nativists. Finally, after two hours of heavy fighting, Sheriff Morton McMichael and a posse of two hundred deputies arrived and the fighting subsided.

That night, when darkness descended on Kensington, nativists from every corner of Philadelphia found their way to the neighborhood around the Nanny Goat Market. Around 10:00 P.M. a crowd "collected in the vicinity of Franklin and Second streets," marched toward the Nanny Goat Market, and on the way "commenced breaking into the houses on both sides of the street, destroying the furniture, demolishing the windows, and rendering the houses completely uninhabitable." The crowd then arrived at the gates of the seminary of the Catholic Sisters of Charity and were threatening to burn it down when a group of Irish defenders "advanced from above and fired a volley of ball and buckshot into the crowd." One nativist attacker died instantly, a second lingered for a month before dying of a chest wound, and several others were injured. On this note, Monday night's fighting in Kensington drew to a close.

Philadelphians awakened Tuesday morning, May 7, to find their city plastered with printed calls to a rally protesting the murder of George Schiffler. The message ended with the inflammatory words, "LET EVERY MAN COME PREPARED TO DEFEND HIMSELF." That morning, the nativist press was filled with militant cries for revenge. The daily *Native American* proclaimed:

> Another St. Bartholomew's day has begun in the streets of Philadelphia. The bloody hand of the Pope has stretched forth to our destruction. Now we call on our fellow-citizens, who regard free institutions, whether they be native or adopted, to arm. Our liberties are to be fought for—let us not be slack in our preparation.

By 3:30 P.M. that Tuesday afternoon, more than 3,000 persons had gathered behind Independence Hall to hear speeches condemning Kensington's Irish. . . .

When the speeches were finished and the American Republicans called for the meeting to adjourn, a voice in the crowd shouted, "Adjourn to Kensington right now!" The crowd took up the call, marched in loose military fashion out of the meeting ground, and turned northward to Kensington. When they arrived in the neighborhood of Second and Master, the marchers found that many of Kensington's Irish had fled the neighborhood and taken their belongings with them. Other inhabitants simply waited at home with their loaded guns. This time, the nativist procession did not pause to convene a meeting and hear speeches, but immediately attacked the Hibernia Hose House. Armed defenders there and in some of the houses along the street immediately opened fire, and in the few moments of shooting four nativists lay dead and eleven others fell wounded. The remaining nativists with a stomach for a fight retreated to the Nanny Goat Market for shelter, and it seemed that the pattern of the day before would repeat itself. This time, however, the nativists changed their tactics. Rather than try to shoot it out with the well-concealed Irish, the nativists snuck out of the market building and set fire to each of the houses from which gunfire had been coming. This tactic proved successful as hidden Irish snipers came tumbling out of the flaming buildings. They made easy targets for nativist gunners, and only poor nativist marksmanship explains why no Irishmen were killed. It was not until 5:00 P.M., nearly an hour after the shooting started, that General [George] Cadwalader, previously unprepared, arrived with several militia companies to restore order in the neighborhood.

The use of fire struck panic in the hearts of the remaining Kensington Irish, and by Wednesday morning most of them had packed their possessions and gone elsewhere to stay with friends and relatives, or to camp in the woods on the outskirts of Philadelphia. The militia was left to guard their abandoned homes, but the outnumbered soldiers were inadequate for the task. Roving bands of nativists snuck from house to house in the vicinity of the Nanny Goat Market and set each on fire. The city's volunteer firefighters, mostly native-born Americans, had little enthusiasm for fighting the flames. In addition, after setting up a diversion to draw the militia away, a group of arsonists gained access to St. Michael's Roman Catholic Church, whose priest had been an outspoken foe of nativism, and set it to the torch. Flames rapidly devoured the wooden structure, and as the cross fell from the toppling steeple the crowd cheered loudly. Volunteer firefighters, arriving on the scene, determined that the gathering would never permit them to extinguish the fire, so they contented themselves with hosing down nearby buildings to keep the flames from spreading. Other rioters completed the day's work by ransacking two stores that had been selling ammunition to Irish marksmen, and eventually they invaded the home of Hugh Clark, the man whose decision to suspend Bible reading in Louisa Bedford's class had provided the pretext for the fighting. The invaders threw Clark's valuable books and furniture into the street and used them to start a bonfire. Finally, several hours after the arson had begun in Kensington, General Cadwalader and Sheriff McMichael arrived with reinforcements and brought the wandering rioters under control.

Thus blocked, the angry nativists simply transferred their field of activity to downtown Philadelphia. By 10:30 that Wednesday night, a huge crowd had gathered in front of St. Augustine's Roman Catholic Church in the heart of that city. Although the mayor stood on the building's front steps and pleaded with the crowd to disperse, his appeals went unheard. Someone knocked him down by heaving a stone against his chest, and a young boy managed to sneak past the constables at a rear door and set the church afire. Within half an hour the $45,000 brick structure was a total loss. As the steeple fell, the crowd cheered as it had done at St. Michael's. Again the volunteer fireman dared only hose down nearby buildings.

The burning of St. Augustine's marked the last major violence in the Kensington phase of the Native American Riots. Governor David R. Porter placed Philadelphia under martial law, and the chief commander of the Pennsylvania militia, General Robert Patterson, took complete command of the city's government. More than 2,000 soldiers from across the state patrolled the streets of Philadelphia, and General Patterson banned all meetings and demonstrations. . . .

Martial law remained in effect for a week without a serious confrontation between troops and civilians, after which civilian government was restored to Philadelphia. Thus ended the Kensington phase of the 1844 Native American Riots.

The Kensington Riots had been the worst in Philadelphia's history. At least six persons had been killed, and as many as fifty had been seriously injured. Property losses in the three days of violence were conservatively estimated at $250,000, not counting the cost of medical bills and lost time from work.

While unusually destructive, the Kensington riots were in other ways typical of collective violence in the Jacksonian period. First, despite the fact that there was gunfire and killing in the first two days of fighting, it appears that only a relatively small portion of combatants on either side was armed. There is no way for us to know how many Philadelphians owned firearms in 1844, although rifles for hunting seem to have been quite common, and ammunition was widely sold in shops around the city. One of the stores set aflame by the crowd in Kensington, Corr's Grocery, was burned because its proprietor had been supplying bullets to his Irish compatriots. Jacksonian cities seem to have had no legal regulations about who could own, sell, or distribute guns or ammunition. Yet the use of guns by rioters was rarely reported in contemporary newspaper accounts. Crowds usually fought by hurling rocks, paving stones, bricks, and garbage, or by wielding clubs, knives, and slingshots. As a result, it was the exception rather than the rule for pre-Civil War rioting to claim the lives of its victims, or for more than one or two persons to be killed in the course of even the most serious fighting. During the three days and nights of the Kensington riots, for example, only one Irishman was killed, and he was an innocent bystander.

Second, the pattern of damage to property in Kensington indicates that, like most Jacksonian crowds, the nativist rioters exercised a good deal of restraint in their attacks. Despite their anger over the school Bible issue, the ambush at the Nanny Goat Market, and the murders of Schiffler and the others, it was not until Wednesday, two days after the outbreak of fighting, that widespread destruction was inflicted on Irish property. Before then only a few houses that had served as shelters for Irish snipers were targeted for burning. Other houses were stoned or damaged, but these too were suspected of harboring Irish marksmen. Even the choice of targets on Wednesday, when widespread arson was employed, was hardly random: Hugh Clark's house, his brother's tavern, Corr's Grocery, and two Catholic churches. Some additional homes may have been deliberately burned, especially in the area around the Nanny Goat Market, but many others fell unintended victim to the spreading flames. Rioters even bypassed the home of one elderly Irishman when they found him inside, too ill to make his escape. However much their anger had been provoked, the nativist rioters never rampaged through Kensington randomly destroying property or retaliating against whoever fell to hand. There was in short, no orgy of irrational nativist fury. The rioters possessed clearly defined notions of what and who their targets ought to have been and why those targets deserved to suffer violence. While no one would argue that either the nativist or Irish rioters were acting dispassionately during the fighting, neither can one say that the rioters were insane, deranged, animalistic, or totally without sense or reason.

Third, the social composition of both sides in the Kensington riots was characteristic of that in many other Jacksonian riots. Contrary to many current stereotypes of rioters and looters, the Kensington combatants were not drawn from the poorest or most oppressed strata of Jacksonian society. The names of those injured or arrested, when traced to city directories, indicate that the rioters, frequently boys and young men in their twenties, were often employed as apprentice artisans, weavers, or laborers. They were not povertystricken outcasts, nor were they without a permanent residence. Many of the older men and women who participated on both sides were established members of their communities. Among the Irish there were property-owners, landlords, and employers who became as caught up in the heat of battle as their less affluent fellow immigrants. On the nativist side there were respectable American Republican lawyers, doctors, and dentists, as well as some constables and other elected officials. They fought alongside the youthful working-class members of nativist street gangs and volunteer fire companies notorious for their rowdy and combative behavior. What motivated rioters on both sides was not alienation, a sense of economic oppression, or a feeling of having "nothing to lose," but rather a deep commitment to their ethnic heritage and their political cause, intensified by their anger over the course of events that unfolded at the Nanny Goat Market. Tellingly, in three days of fighting and destruction, there was only one reported instance of looting. When rioters removed property from an Irish shop or Hugh Clark's home, it was to destroy it, not to keep it.

Fourth, the Kensington riots illustrate the intertwining of Jacksonian era collective violence with other, more peaceable forms of political and social behavior. The competition between immigrant Irish Catholics and native Protestant American Republicans began as a cultural controversy over the use of the Bible as a reading text in the public schools. It became a political issue when Hugh Clark convinced Louisa Bedford to remove the King James version from her class's daily lesson. After that, American Republicans began campaigning over the issue of "foreign interference" in the public schools, and when they carried this political campaign to Third Ward, Kensington, the debate changed from a clash of words to a clash of arms. . . . [T]he transition from cultural conflict to political conflict to physical conflict was all too frequent in Jacksonian group relations.

That the school Bible controversy shifted from a battle of petitions before the School Controllers to a battle of weapons in the streets of Kensington is stark testimony to the power of ethnic and religious issues to stir the passions of Philadelphians in 1844. It is also indicative, however, of the fifth and final factor common to most Jacksonian riots: the inability of public officials to prevent or suppress riots before they required the intervention of military troops. How strange it would seem today if, like Philadelphians on May 7, 1844, we awoke to find the walls, lampposts, and fences of our city or town plastered with calls for us to arm ourselves and attend a rally in order to seek revenge for the death of one of our fellow citizens. Then, once we arrived, we would find *no police officers* present to control the crowd or disarm its members. The current form of urban policing, in which uniformed officers actively patrol the streets searching out crime and disorder, and in which the police routinely patrol any political or protest rally prepared to disperse the crowd at the first sign of violence, was simply unknown in Jacksonian America.

"Preventive policing," as Jacksonians came to call it, was not introduced in Philadelphia until the 1850s. Like its sister cities Boston and New York, Philadelphia in 1844 still maintained public order through a system of constables, watchmen, and sheriff's posses whose origins dated back to the Middle Ages. . . .

. . . In the pre-Civil War era, city governments suffered from a shortage of manpower to police their citizens effectively. For various reasons, the majority of urban residents was not yet ready to surrender to local governments the tax monies or the authority needed to repress disorder and anti-social behavior. Jacksonian Americans seemed to possess a certain fatalism about the inevitability of periodic rioting—"intestine disorder," as it was known—and so cities and their residents simply learned to live with collective violence.

But neither the fatalistic outlook nor the weakness of public authorities was to survive the 1850s. By the eve of the Civil War, most of the nation's major cities had established preventive peacekeeping systems along lines still recognizable in today's urban police departments. With their introduction, collective disorder declined steadily in the 1850s and 1860s, and the 1870s was marked by a higher standard of urban public order than Jacksonians had ever imagined possible.

However dramatic their introduction, the police were not the only innovation that helped to pacify American cities by the time of the Civil War. By 1860, the northern industrial states had made public-school attendance compulsory for their youth. Public schools were meant to serve as nurseries for moral training and good citizenship. At the same time, the temperance movement stepped up its legal efforts to curb or eliminate liquor sales to the urban masses. In addition, having fought to a stalemate in the street, nativists and immigrants both channeled their competitive efforts into electoral politics, further diminishing the level of collective violence in the 1850s. Finally, other events such as the Mexican War of 1846–47 permitted a significant portion of America's urban street-fighting populations to vent their aggressive feelings on a common foreign foe, rather than each other. When reinforced by determined and street-wise police forces willing and able to carry out a mandate for civic order, these developments helped to make the 1850s a far less violent period than the 1830s and 1840s.

FOR FURTHER STUDY

1. In the colonial period, many crowd demonstrations and riots were to *support* local government, such as the Boston selectmen or colonial legislature, against British policies. In our time, many demonstrations *are against* constituted authority, as in black protests against police arrests or antiwar and antinuclear sit-ins. How would you characterize the Philadelphia riots in this respect?

2. Feldberg mentions several causes of collective violence: religious prejudice; ethnic hostility; job competition; threats to an established group's wealth, power, or status; and a struggle for political power. Which causes seem to you to have been the key factors in the riots he describes? Why was the violence directed against the Irish, but not against the German immigrants?

3. The riots took place largely on "Irish turf" in Kensington and Southwark, and in the relatively good weather of May. What might have been different if the nativists had held their rallies in their own neighborhoods, and in January? Were these factors of locale and timing also important in the riots of the 1960s and the Los Angeles riot of 1992?

4. Feldberg concludes that "the nativist rioters exercised a good deal of restraint in their attacks." In view of his description of the riots, do you agree with this conclusion? What does he mean by restraint in this context?

5. Do you see any differences between the kinds of people involved in riots in the 1840s and those involved in our time? Can one argue that rioting in the 1840s was provoked by the majority group in society, and that rioting today is more likely to be instigated by minority groups?

FOR FURTHER READING

The American city has always been an economic and cultural center. For the colonial period the works of Carl Bridenbaugh, *Cities in the Wilderness* (1938) and *Cities in Revolt* (1955), are still useful. For the first portion of the nineteenth century Richard C. Wade's *The Urban Frontier: The Rise of Western Cities, 1790–1830* (1957) is also a good introduction to western urban development. For Atlantic seaboard areas see David T. Gilchrist, ed., *The Growth of the Seaport Cities, 1790–1825* (1967).

The history of particular aspects of city life has received recent attention. See Melvin A. Adelman, *A Sporting Time: New York City and the Rise of Modern Athletics, 1820–1870* (1986), Stuart M. Blumin, *The Emergence of the Middle Class: Social Experience in the American City, 1760–1900* (1989), and Timothy J. Gilfoyle, *City of Eros: New York City, Prostitution, and the Commercialization of Sex, 1790–1920* (1992). An interesting study of ordinary people in Boston is Peter R. Knights, *Yankee Destinies: The Lives of Ordinary Nineteenth-Century Bostonians* (1991). Edward Pessen discusses the problems of power in the city in *Riches, Class, and Power Before the Civil War* (1973). Other studies of city life include Richard B. Scott, *Workers in the Metropolis: Class, Ethnicity, and Youth in Antebellum New York City* (1990), Allen F. Davis and Mark H. Haller, eds., *The Peoples of Philadelphia: A History of Ethnic Groups and Lower-Class Life, 1790–1940* (1973), and Stephan Thernstrom, *Poverty and Progress: Social Mobility in a Nineteenth-Century City* (1964). Two typical works on violence in particular cities are Roger Lane, *Roots of Violence in Black Philadelphia, 1860–1900* (1986), and Paul A. Gilje, *The Road to Mobocracy: Popular Disorder in New York City, 1763–1834* (1987). For a fascinating new approach to urban history see William Cronon, *Nature's Metropolis: Chicago and the Great West* (1991).

A general survey of urban history is Howard P. Chudacoff, *The Evolution of American Urban Society* (1975).

WESTERN *&* EXPANSION AND CIVIL WAR

At the time of the Treaty of Paris of 1783, the western and southern boundaries of the United States had been set at the Mississippi River and along the 31st parallel. By 1853, the country had added the huge territory of the Louisiana Purchase, acquired Florida from Spain, and swept westward over Texas, California, and Oregon into every square mile of territory that was to make up the continental United States. This breathtaking acquisition of territory involved American intrigue in Florida, revolution in Texas, a blustering threat of force in Oregon, and full-scale war against Mexico. Generally, however, the American people were in advance of their government. Rather than gold, land—to settle on or to speculate in—was the chief lure that drew Americans westward into lands beyond the borders of their own country. While natural barriers had to be crossed at great peril, the human impediments were viewed as obstacles to be conquered rather than included.

The acquisition of millions of acres of land beyond the Mississippi was one of the crucial factors which accentuated the sectional conflict begun in the 1830s. By the 1850s, the morality of slavery was the overriding issue in the minds of abolitionists. For most people of both the North and the South, however, a matter of more immediate concern was whether or not slavery would expand into the western territories. The slogan of the Free Soil party of the North embodied several aspects of sectional conflict: "Free Soil, Free Speech, Free Labor, and Free Men." This party's concern that labor and soil in the West be free points up the economic division of North and South. The other parts of the slogan-free speech and free men suggest, however, that the country was also divided by psychological and social differences.

By 1861, many national social institutions, including major religious denominations, had broken apart along sectional lines. By that time, many thousands of southerners saw the triumph of the northern Republican party in the 1860 election as not simply a political defeat but a threat to all southern institutions and to the southern way of life.

When we think of the westward movement, we usually imagine small parties struggling in near starvation and haunting loneliness as they cross the Great Plains. The first reading describes crowded conditions on the trails at the height of migration and the cooperation that eased the hardships. The second selection highlights the contributions Tejanos, Mexicans living in Texas, made to the early culture there. The third reading shows how soldiers on both sides in the Civil War fought for complicated and changing reasons. Their emotional commitment, especially in the last years of the war, suggests that American society had been torn asunder. The fourth reading shows the difficulties of living in those parts of the South occupied or close to the Union army and the fifth shows how these difficult times continued into reconstruction.

The reweaving of disparate threads into a new social fabric was to prove a long and trying process. Some of the difficulties that were involved are described in the essay on the Reconstruction period that concludes this volume.

CHAPTER 18

The Denver Public Library, Western History Collection

This photograph of pioneers on the trail westward illustrates their mode of travel and the way they clung to the fashions they were used to back in the east.

THE WAY WEST

JOHN D. UNRUH, JR.

$\mathscr{F}$ew movements in all of our history have captured the imagination as has the settlement of the great American West. The image of the sturdy pioneer, plodding beside a lumbering covered wagon, fighting off Indian attacks, fording swift streams, and finally looking out on the blue Pacific, has become enshrined in American folklore and on Hollywood celluloid. There is much in all of this that is sheer myth, but there is also much that is true.

The earliest openings of some American frontiers were accomplished by lone trappers and hunters who, because the game was there or because they weren't comfortable in more settled communities, turned their paths westward. Such men served as guides and added to the scant geographical knowledge of nineteenth-century America. But even in the fur trade, the single hunter was rapidly supplanted by the business organization, and it was John Jacob Astor's Pacific Fur Company that led thousands of other Americans to dream of the Oregon country.

In fact, settlement of the West in large numbers required careful planning, substantial equipment and supplies, organization, and community effort. Whether seeking gold in California, land in Oregon, or a religious Eden in Utah, the pioneers usually went west in a group. Leaders were chosen, supplies carefully assembled, and laws of the trail set down. But the fact that pioneer life primarily involved organized communities rather than lone scouts does not mean that struggle and hardship were any less a part of the frontier experience.

Americans today are still a migratory people, and until very recently California was the chief lodestar. But as we speed down interstate highways alongside the Platte River or jet over the Rocky Mountains in wide-bodied comfort, we have little idea of life on the trail in 1848. For this we must turn to the diaries of the men and women who made the long trek, who gave birth to infants on the wooden beds of wagons and pushed on the next day, and who buried children and parents in unmarked graves to which they would never return.

The view of western migration provided in the following selection, from John D. Unruh's book *The Plains Across,* is rather different from that of most writings on the subject. The author indicates how crowded the trails were during the height of the westward movement, and emphasizes the cooperation of the migrants with one another and with the Plains Indians.

[Between 1840 and 1860] approximately a quarter of a million overlanders had worn the trails to Oregon and California so deeply that in places the ruts are still visible. In that same period over 40,000 Latter-Day Saints traveled portions of those same trails to their Salt Lake Valley refuge, and by 1860 thousands of expectant gold seekers were penetrating the Pike's Peak region. . . .

These masses of westering overlanders do not coincide with the popular media image of widely scattered wagon trains traveling in relative isolation. Indeed, particularly between 1849 and 1853, most overlanders longed for privacy instead of the congested trails, crowded campsites, and overgrazed grasses they were experiencing. So many overlanders, for example, set forth from near St. Joseph on the same day in 1852 that teams traveled twelve abreast. Franklin Langworthy reported in 1850, from near South Pass, "The road, from morning till night, is crowded like Pearl Street or Broadway," noting also that fathers had actually become separated from their sons in the "endless throng" and did not meet again until their arrival in California. Bennett C. Clark's company, in 1849, traveled late into the night near Ash Hollow in a desperate search for a vacant campsite.

Statistically inclined emigrants kept track of trail traffic during noon stops, on rare rest days, early in the mornings, and on particularly dusty days. James B. Persinger reported that their company passed 200 wagons early one 1850 morning, were passed by 100 another noon, and passed at least 500 more another day. Joseph Price wrote to his wife from Pacific Springs the same year that the 160 wagons which passed that point on June 27 was a smaller number than usual. . . .

Not anticipating this trail congestion, emigrants during the gold rush consciously endeavored to travel in companies, formally or informally organized, just as they had in previous years when the trails had not been so crowded. The emigrant goal was always to insure that sufficient manpower would be available for whatever contingencies might arise: bridging or fording a stream, climbing a mountain, rounding up stampeded stock, resisting Indian attack. This vast armada of overlanders swarming together along the trails, especially during the gold rush, often created friction; tempers periodically flared as drivers jockeyed for position on the dusty main trail, and on occasion one traveling company passed another only after an actual race.

Such frustrations, however, were much overshadowed by the omnipresent emigrant interaction, which contributed so significantly to the success of the overland migrations. It is this cooperative quality of the migrations which scholars have so largely overlooked. Two neglected phases of emigrant interchange revolve around travelers who began the westbound journey only to turn back, and over-landers who traveled the trails eastward from the Pacific Coast to the Missouri and Iowa frontiers. For many westbound emigrants, the significant exchanges deriving from interaction with west-to-east trail travelers proved an unexpected bonus.

Although most of the turn-arounds were products of the gold rush years, a few overlanders had reconsidered the wisdom of their proposed venture ever since the overland movement had begun. In 1841, in fact, nearly 10 percent of the de-parting caravan of California- and Oregon-bound overlanders, Jesuit missionaries heading for the Flathead Indian territory, and other tourists and trappers made their way back to the Missouri settlements. . . .

. . . Since many of them had gone at least as far as Fort Kearny, and some to Fort Laramie and even beyond, their knowledge and advice were helpful to those pressing on. Indeed, the oncoming hordes so desired information—even if it was slightly exaggerated—that they pestered all returnees they met, unless there was serious sickness among them. . . .

Through information and mail service (one "goback" forty-niner brought back several letters), the turn-arounds provided their major assistance. But numbers of westbound overlanders who had suffered losses or had discovered outfitting er-rors or omissions were also much aided by this unexpected opportunity to pur-chase draft animals, wagons, tents, provisions, and other needed materials, since turn-arounds were usually willing to part with much of their outfit which they would not now be needing. On the other hand, a few returnees, having lost their draft animals, were forced to rely completely upon the charity of westbound emi-grants in order to return to the frontier settlements. It is difficult to estimate the actual numbers of overlanders who retraced their steps, but in 1849, 1850, and 1852 there were certainly hundreds, and the yearly total probably approached and may even have surpassed 1,000 in 1850 and 1852.

Hasty conversations on the trail or at noon and evening encampments with eastbound overlanders direct from Oregon or California provided the most help-ful and reliable sources of information to westbound emigrants. Such returning travelers were able to provide accurate—and sometimes disheartening—data on how far it really was to the mines, rumors notwithstanding, and whether the Indians evidenced hostile or friendly intentions. They also furnished advice re-garding the various cutoffs, the availability of supplies at forts and trading posts, the presence of ferries at the various river crossings, the prices being charged there, and the location of buffalo herds. On occasion these eastbound parties also served as escorts for turn-arounds. . . .

Because west-to-east travelers were able to answer questions on the two matters of most interest and concern to overland emigrants—conditions on the trail and in California and Oregon—they were plied with questions by oncoming overlan-ders even more persistently than were the turn-arounds. And since eastbound travelers encountered almost the entire westbound migration this could become extremely frustrating, especially in years when 50,000 overlanders were trailing west. One 1850 party simply kept their mules going at a rapid pace, never stopping to entertain the "hundreds" of queries with which they were peppered, although they did shout back answers until they could no longer be heard. . . .

There was cause for eastbound overlanders being circumspect, especially those coming from California with gold dust in their possession. Enoch Conyers, while riding some distance from the main trail in 1852, encountered a solitary eastbound traveler encamped for the night. Upon first questioning, the man claimed to be a discouraged turn-around. When Conyers recognized him as his uncle, however, the solitary traveler admitted to be returning from California with considerable gold in his possession. He explained that he frequently camped far from the main trail and if seen claimed to be a turn-around. He had adopted this strategy because he feared robbers—especially "white Indians"— although he had barely survived a harrowing attack from real Indians shortly after crossing the Sierra Nevada Mountains.

Conyers's uncle had been more fortunate than a number of eastbound overlanders who fell victim to Indians and "highwaymen." . . . A particularly dangerous year for eastbound travelers was 1856, when the bodies of at least eight returning Californians were found along the Humboldt River after apparent robbery-murders. . . .

Although the impact of turn-arounds and eastbound overland travelers upon the overland emigrations was significant, the most important cooperation and interaction obviously prevailed among the much greater number of westbound overlanders. Because attrition, traveling company splits, combinations, and recombinations were so common to the overland emigrating experience, the matter of conveying advice, progress reports, and other newsworthy information to relatives, friends, and former traveling companions was extremely important. The "roadside telegraph" which the overlanders devised was a crude but surprisingly effective means of communication. Anyone wishing to leave a message would write a short note and place it conspicuously alongside the trail so that those following behind would be certain not to pass it by. . . . Even human skulls were used. With surfaces which had been smoothed and whitened by the elements, these skulls and bones were strikingly visible, especially when hung on a stick by the side of the trail. The inscriptions, when not purposely rubbed out, lasted a long time. Lodisa Frizzell in 1852 was still able to read penciled messages written in 1849.

Most overlanders were careful not to disturb these precious sources of information. Messages specifically directed to individual emigrants or particular companies were removed, but most others, after having been studiously read, were not otherwise disturbed. . . .

The roadside messages frequently communicated advice and information reflective of the cooperative concern most overlanders had for each other's safety and progress. The advice was often especially helpful to the many greenhorn travelers of the gold rush period. For example, forty-niner James Wilkins's outfit gratefully followed the recommendation on a trailside notice for avoiding a twenty-mile desert. The notice, according to Wilkins, had been posted "by a philanthropic Kentuckian" who had backtracked specifically to share his discovery of the alternate route for the benefit of those behind. Alonzo Delano found a signboard beyond Fort Laramie which read, "Look at this—look at this! The water here is poison, and we have lost six of our cattle. Do not let your cattle drink on this bottom." At a poisonous waterhole the next year James Evans commented, "Happy is the man who can read!" after observing a myriad of signs warning against tasting the water in phrases such as "He drank of this water and died" and "For God's sake do not taste this water." In addition to cautioning against bad water and grass, overlanders erected signs directing their comrades to fresh-water springs some distance off the road, or admonishing that this was the last available water or the last good grass before a desert stretch was to be crossed. So-called "cutoffs" which saved neither time nor energy were forcefully denounced. Harriet Ward spoke for many grateful overlanders after following a signpost's directions to reach a refreshingly cool spring some distance off the road in 1853: "Oh! what a pleasure to meet with such little mementoes of disinterested benevolence from strangers!"

A great many roadside communications dealt with Indian depredations, warning oncoming overlanders that losses of stock and human life had occurred at a particular location. Such announcements probably served the dual purpose of alerting emigrants to potential dangers as well as reporting the loss of animals, so that if any were subsequently found by other overlanders, the initial owner could claim the animal. Forty-niner John Edwin Banks even saw a notice offering a 200-dollar reward for five stolen horses and the persons who had committed the theft. . . .

. . . In 1849 some overlanders who had gone via Salt Lake changed their minds and traveled the southern trail to California in lieu of the usual Humboldt River route, having been influenced by rumors that Missouri packers had coldbloodedly killed three Indians and burned the grass for 200 miles to impede the progress of overlanders. As a result the trails were reportedly aswarm with revenge-minded Indians and completely unsafe. . . .

Most unplanned route changes, however, stemmed from the favorable accounts about shortcuts and cutoffs which wishful overlanders helped propagate. Emigrant diaries reveal much animated discussion and debate, and occasionally votes, as to whether an unknown cutoff should be attempted. Alonzo Delano, recording the deliberations of his company in 1849 regarding the Lassen Cutoff possibility, noted that emigrants from several traveling companies consulted together and that one man even went out thirty miles on horseback to check the new route. Delano's company, prompted by the urgings of its adventurous young men, took the supposed shortcut. Some of the various cutoff rumors were promulgated by interested parties, but there is ample evidence that many of the stories about how much time and distance cutoffs would save were freely circulated by and among emigrants eager for the trip to end but quite ignorant of any definite facts which would corroborate their roseate assertions. . . .

There were numerous other ways in which westbound overlanders cooperated to lessen the demands of the journey, almost always in a cheerful spirit of cooperation without seeking personal gain. Seasoned plains travelers advised novice overlanders of safe places to ford rivers so that expensive tolls could be avoided. Emigrant wagons bogged down in mudholes were pulled out by passing overlanders. Ropes, chains, boats, and bridge-building equipment were shared among different traveling groups. Overland companies encamping close together occasionally set out a mutual guard during the night. Following a rainstorm or stampede it was sometimes necessary for several traveling companies to cooperate in sorting out cattle which had milled together.

Also, emigrants on occasion volunteered to help strangers search for stock which had been stolen by Indians. This was emigrant cooperation at its best, for such errands of mercy could be dangerous. In 1857 one group of forty-two men from seven or eight different trains spent two fruitless days seeking sixty-one head of cattle stolen from an Arkansas train along the Humboldt River. Upon their return a second company was mustered from some of the trains which had come up in the interim, and this second group finally recovered thirty-six head of cattle and killed one Indian—seventy miles distant from where they had begun their search. Emigrant hunting parties killing more buffalo, deer, or other prairie game than needed often shared surplus meats with fellow overlanders.

A less joyous cooperative task was the burial of deceased overlanders. Passing emigrants were often asked to assist members of other traveling companies in digging graves and constructing coffins and grave markers. Most overlanders also stopped to rebury any deceased overlander whom they discovered, as Heinrich Leinhard's company did along the Humboldt River in 1846, after finding a man whose body had not only been dug up (presumably by wolves) but stripped of clothing and mutilated as well.

One of the most prevalent forms of interaction among westering overlanders was the inadvertent visit paid to another group of emigrants. Most frequently this was for the night, but if often occurred at mealtimes as well. While traveling westward, overlanders persistently rode ahead, lagged behind, or wandered off from their traveling company to hunt, explore, fix a wagon, read, sketch a picture, visit, and sometimes sleep. Often they did not conclude their activity quickly enough to be able to reach their own outfit that same day, and gladly accepted the hospitality and protection their fellow travelers readily extended in such circumstances. Captains and other traveling luminaries were also periodically invited to share a meal with captains of trains they were passing—Edwin Bryant in 1846 and J. Goldsborough Bruff in 1849 were frequent guests at other campfires during the course of their respective overland trips.

There was always considerable visiting among overlanders who had chosen to halt for a day of rest and recuperation and who were encamped in fairly close proximity. When the rest day was on Sunday, as it usually was, emigrants from various companies frequently assembled for a religious service. Gregarious overlanders, of course, needed no excuse to stop, chat, and make new friends. Some occasionally went to great lengths to do so, as with the young 1853 overlander who swam the Platte River to visit a company of emigrants traveling on the other side of that waterway. In addition to the interaction between trains on opposite sides of the Platte, on occasion ladies functioned as nurses among the sick in other trains. And, as proof that the amenities of civilized life were not neglected on the plains, Charlotte Pengra reported in 1853 that she gave her sunbonnet pattern to another lady who had admired it while passing by. . . .

Opportunities for purchasing additional oxen to pull an overloaded wagon, an extra wagon tongue, a new or extra wagon or riding horse regularly presented themselves somewhere along the trail. Numerous trades of cattle, horses, and mules were also recorded in emigrant diaries. Particularly in 1849, when most overlanders took too much along and had to lighten their loads for the sake of their draft animals, fantastic bargains in clothing, revolvers, ammunition, food-stuffs, and almost everything else were available at many encampments. As the trip stretched out, many overlanders chose to sell their cumbersome wagons and most of their supplies in order to pack in to California by mule or horse. Some gold rushers made this change very early in the journey, retaining just as little in the way of provisions and supplies as they calculated would be necessary to complete the trip. This meant that mules and horses came to be increasingly valuable in the buying, selling, and trading among the overlanders, while oxen, wagons, and many other supplies and foodstuffs were sold at ridiculously low prices, if they could be sold at all.

An additional problem loomed toward the end of the journey, when overworked animals gave out or fell victim to Indian theft or arrow. Emigrants thus left with no way to transport their belongings sometimes were able to arrange with more fortunate overlanders to have their baggage carried through to the end of the journey, usually for some monetary or equivalent consideration. A few munificent overlanders asked nothing. These were real acts of compassion, since almost everyone's team was considerably worn down toward the journey's end. Along the Humboldt River in 1850, after traveling with his goods on his back for a day, Hugh Skinner secured accommodations in an Illinois wagon, thanks to a lady whose kindness led Skinner to remark, "I have uniformly found the women on the road more alive to the sufferings of their fellow creatures than the men." The bargain made, the emigrant usually traveled with his benefactor, but on occasion forged ahead on foot or with pack animal, planning to retrieve his goods later in California.

Clothing, blankets, and other personal belongings were important to overlanders, but food was crucial. The most significant assistance overlanders rendered to one another was certainly in sharing and selling provisions. A few gold rushers had even begun the journey with virtually no food supply, frankly planning to "sponge" off their better-prepared colleagues. One such 1849 foot traveler from Maine had reached Fort Kearny by such tactics, and figured that he would continue to find enough "Christians" on the route to supply his needs. . . .

In 1850 food was at a premium, especially on the later portions of the overland route. The rapidly increasing number of packers and other gold rushers running perilously low on rations frantically searched for overlanders well enough supplied to part with some of their provisions. The rapidly diminishing number of overlanders retaining surplus provisions happily watched prices skyrocket. Flour commanded up to $2 per pound; one overlander reported a man going from wagon to wagon unsuccessfully offering $50 for three pounds of flour. Hard bread sold at $1 a pound. One small group of hungry emigrants immediately slaughtered the worn-out ox they had chipped in to purchase for $65 from a passing train. . . .

In such precarious circumstances, desperate overlanders resorted to tactics both clever and violent to induce their fellows to offer up precious provisions. . . . After Oliver Goldsmith had been refused foodstuffs by some southern overlanders, his companion, John Root, who possessed a strong southern accent, managed to get some food from the same group. Root apparently used his accent to good advantage on other occasions.

But ruses seem not to have been as much used as force. Goldsmith and four friends, after being told by one emigrant that they could have all the provisions they wanted, but at the steep price of $2 per pound, "marched up to him and said there were five of us to his one and that we intended to take what we needed at our own price, twenty-five cents a pound, which we did." When 1850 emigrant James Campbell encountered begging overlanders who had eaten nothing but frogs for four days, he prudently began sleeping in his wagon to prevent possible thievery. . . .

Often too, westering overlanders took up collections to provide unfortunate emigrants with the means to replace stock, wagons, or provisions. Thus, forty-niner Bernard Reid came upon a seventeen-year-old girl all alone save for her younger brother, who lay in their wagon sick with cholera. Both the mother and father had already died of the dread disease. The oxen were gone, and so was the faithless company with which the family had been traveling. Reid and others immediately took up a collection so that oxen might be purchased, two passing doctors prescribed medicine for the boy, and a Missouri group volunteered to take care of the orphans for the rest of the trip. Another 1850 gold seeker had been left by the trail after having been accidentally shot by one of his company. A passing physician attended to him, and westbound overlanders contributed money for his continuing care. When overlanders fording Thomas' Fork of the Bear River witnessed the drowning of one of the two horses an old man was relying on to take his family to California, they immediately took up a collection so the father could purchase another horse. And at the Green River ferry, in 1854, westbound emigrants again contributed funds to forward on to California the widow of a man who had just drowned.

Another common act of compassion was the attempt to ease the ordeal of desert crossings with "water wagons" manned and financed by overlanders having just completed the trip. Thirst-crazed overlanders were known to offer astronomical sums for a single drink of water during desert crossings. In 1850 on the desert beyond the Humboldt Sink, $5 was offered for a drink of water, and five gallons of water sold for $50. Henry Bloom reported that on the Hastings Cutoff desperate 1850 overlanders offered $10, $20, and up to $500 for a single drink of water. Fortunately for Bloom and his friends, the water wagon arrived before thirst elicited similar offers from them. This humane venture was especially prominent in 1850, when a wagonload of water was sent back every day by the emigrants who had crossed the preceding day. Not only water for the men but grass for draft animals was included, the effort being financed by contributions from the emigrants encamped at the spring which marked the welcome end of the treacherous long drive. An 1850 physician noted that their group had sent two relief loads back at a cost of $25 per wagon, the funds having been generously subscribed by passing overlanders. The wagon drivers gave the water free of charge to destitute overlanders, but those with money were charged from $1 to $5 per gallon. . . .

An additional legacy of the gold rush contributing considerably to emigrant interchange, albeit in a strange manner, was the trail of debris the greatest "litterbugs" of American history left in the wake of their transit across the West. Some traces had remained of the westward march of the overlanders of the 1840s, but since almost twice as many overlanders trailed westward in 1849 as in the entire previous decade, it was only natural that their residue would be greater. Further, their leavings were compounded by the overloaded wagons with which they had begun. They soon realized that the basic question was what they could do without, since their draft animals could never survive pulling such heavy loads. . . .

Many forty-niners began disposal operations as soon as they launched out onto the prairies. In the long run theirs was the wisest decision, providing they did not throw away too much. So much was abandoned within fifty miles of St. Joseph in 1849 that one emigrant indicated he would never go to California if he could have all that had been sacrificed that early in the journey. Persons went out from the outfitting points to collect the usable debris and brought back wagonloads of bacon, ham, flour, bread, beans, stoves, tools, medicines, extra wagon wheels and axle-trees, clothing, and similar items, which were presumably resold or used by the scavengers. After viewing the perfectly good food and other materials along the trail, one forty-niner wrote: "If I was going to start again, I would get a light wagon for mules, and gather up the rest of my outfit along the road."

While debris accumulated everywhere, much of the abandoned merchandise was concentrated in the Fort Laramie vicinity. Many overloaded forty-niners had endeavored to persevere as far as the fort, where they anticipated profitable sales of their excess supplies. Upon discovering that the traders there needed none of their surplus commodities—which could be picked up along the trail for nothing in any case—the overlanders had no alternative but to begin dumping. Joseph Berrien reached the fort on May 30, well in the forefront of the 1849 migration, and dubbed the area "Camp Sacrifice" because of all that had already been left there. More than 20,000 pounds of bacon alone had been abandoned near the fort before June 1, and the great masses of overloaded emigrants were still to come. Howard Stansbury, en route to an exploration of the Great Salt Lake Valley, enumerated some of the debris he saw in the Deer Creek area: "The road has been literally strewn with articles that have been thrown away. Bar-iron and steel, large blacksmiths' anvils and bellows, crow-bars, drills, augers, gold-washers, chisels, axes, lead, trunks, spades, ploughs, large grind-stones, baking-ovens, cooking-stoves without number, kegs, barrels, harness, clothing, bacon, and beans, were found along the road in pretty much the order in which they have been here enumerated." Virtually everything imaginable was found at least once somewhere along the overland trail: weapons, ammunition, tobacco, an iron safe, a Gothic bookcase, law and medical books—even a diving bell and accompanying apparatus.

If anything expendable remained in the wagons, it rarely lasted beyond the desert crossing to either the Carson or Truckee rivers. Here not only supplies but wagons and draft animals were left behind in ever-increasing numbers. Estimates of the number of abandoned wagons on the forty-mile desert ranged as high as 2,000 in 1850. Overlanders had already been passing and bemoaning the foul-smelling carcasses of dead animals—the victims of overwork and alkali poison-ing—ever since leaving the Upper Platte ferry; what they witnessed on the desert crossings was merely the culmination. Though such tribulations were by no means unique to California gold seekers (Oregon-bound Maria Belshaw counted 190 dead animals along a 321-mile stretch of the Snake River in 1853), the debris, destruction, and stink reached their most astounding proportions on the deserts beyond the Humboldt Sink during the gold rush. . . .

A few gold rushers attempted a count. One 1850 traveler counted 2,381 horses and mules, 433 oxen, and 787 wagons, estimating the value of this and all other property left on the Carson Desert at $100,000. A subsequent tabulation of 4,960 dead horses, 3,750 dead oxen, and 1,061 dead mules led another observer to appraise the value of the abandoned property at $1 million. . . .

"The Dalles at present form a kind of masquerading thoroughfare, where emigrants and Indians meet, it appears, for the purpose of affording mutual aid." Jesuit missionary Pierre-Jean De Smet thus described, in 1846, a scene near the end of the overland route into Oregon's Willamette Valley. He could have written similarly of a multitude of other places along the Oregon-California Trail where overland emigrants and Indians met for purposes of aid and trade. That such beneficial interaction occurred, frequently and with considerable significance, contradicts the widely disseminated myth of incessant warfare between brave overlanders and treacherous Indians. The mass media view is not, of course, completely erroneous: Indians did kill hundreds of overlanders on the trails before the Civil War. The preoccupation with Indian depredations, however, has resulted in radical distortion of the historical record. Moreover, the depredations which did occur can be understood only in the context of the number and nature of Indian-emigrant encounters along the overland trails. . . .

While a relatively small number of overlanders relied upon Indians for route information or trail guidance, many overlanders willingly entrusted their stock, wagons, belongings, and even their families to Indian swimmers and boatmen at dangerous river crossings all along the trail. . . .

. . . [I]t was the Oregon overlanders during the 1840s and the early 1850s who relied most extensively on this form of Indian assistance. In doing so they were presumably following the advice of writers such as J. M. Shively, who had explicitly stated in his 1846 guidebook that "you must hire an Indian to pilot you at the crossings of Snake river, it being dangerous if not perfectly understood." Elizabeth Wood secured an Indian pilot after first attempting to ford the Snake River without one, perceiving, "It is best in fording this river to engage a pilot." Amelia Stewart Knight obviously agreed in 1853, remarking that there were many droves of cattle that could not be gotten across the Snake River without Indian help. Emigrant provisions, personal belongings, and wagons were also often put into Indian canoes to be rowed across raging rivers.

Payment was generally made in articles of clothing or in ammunition. James Longmire discovered on two occasions in 1853 that Indians were by no means devoid of effective bargaining techniques. At the Salmon Falls crossing an Indian, after swimming a few horses over the Snake River, mounted one of the best horses and rode off, while his employers remained helpless on the other side of the river. Later, in crossing horses over the Columbia River, Chinook Indians suddenly halted their exertions in midstream, demanding more money to complete the project. They got it, since any further delay would likely have been disastrous. Usually, however, the bargain, once made, was lived up to by both parties. . . .

Some of the 1843 overlanders who avoided Indian pilots and boats fared disastrously. The Applegate company constructed their own canoes, which they manned themselves with such lack of skill and luck that three in their party drowned and another was crippled for life. Sarah Cummins praised the Indians who helped their party portage around the Cascades in 1845 as "careful and considerate helpers. Not one deserted the ranks." She also stated that not a single dishonest act had been noticed. Mary Jane Long recalled how the Indians taking their party down the Columbia in 1852 had caught fish, built campfires, and brought up spring water while encamped. Once they even went back to a previous encampment to retrieve a gun which her father had inadvertently left behind but had not yet missed. Of course not everyone who took passage in Indian canoes was ecstatic about the experience. David Maynard, for instance, grumped in 1850, "We had a hard time, in consequence of the Indian being so damned lazy." Most emigrants, however, made the trip safely and with considerable respect for the skill of the native boatmen.

Indians aided overlanders in numerous other ways. Always eager to find ways of getting letters back to family and friends in the States, emigrants periodically negotiated with passing natives to transport letters back to the eastern settlements. At least some of these messengers faithfully fulfilled their trust, since many of the letters reached their destination. Forty-niners William Wells, for example, wrote to his wife from along the Kansas River: "This probably is the last chance I shall have to write to you and I do not know that you will even get this one. We have hired an Indian to take our letters to Independence—he may take them and he may not." One 1849 episode revealed both the shrewdness and trustworthiness of some Indian entrepreneurs. Although some of the forty-niners were dubious about the project, Reuben Shaw's company negotiated with three Sioux braves to carry numerous letters back to Council Bluffs. The Indians sagely refused a package deal for all the letters but instead bargained with each individual sender, thereby securing far more clothing, notions, tobacco, and jewelry. Shaw bartered a calico shirt for his letter and wrote, "The Indians got the shirt, and several months later I had the satisfaction of knowing that my wife received the letter.". . .

Even more astonishing to overlanders normally approaching all Indians with considerable suspicion, at least at the beginning of their overland trek, were the occasional acts of kindness and compassion by the Indians. Seeing William Johnston's difficulty in getting his mule-drawn wagons up the steep banks of Wakarusa Creek, a Shawnee Indian brought his pair of oxen to help pull the wagons up. An Indian with an extra horse overtook John Minto, who was walking ahead of his traveling company to Fort Hall, offered him a ride, and even gave Minto a saddle when he had trouble riding bareback. Another Indian brought wood and kindled a fire for John Zeiber's family at the Elkhorn River crossing in 1851 while Zeiber was occupied with fording wagons. . . .

James Evans was involved in a touching encounter on the Humboldt Desert in 1850. Exhausted and struggling on foot toward the Truckee River, Evans met a nearly naked Indian carrying a little tin bucket filled with water for thirsty emigrants—

"When we met he offered me the bucket exclaiming, 'Watty, Watty, Oh! white man—watty!'" Evans declined because he was not in as dire straits as some he had passed, and urged the Indian to minister to them instead. "He went on, and I afterwards learned that he came up to the famishing man and after giving him two or 3 drinks of water brought up an Indian poney, put the white man on him and took him on until he came to Trucky River! Oh! such generosoty! and pray, why do not those Emigrants who are ahead have the same feelings of humanity?" Even the much-despised Digger Indians had their moments: Silas Miller reported a daring 1852 rescue of a drowning emigrant by two Digger braves. The Indians were rewarded for their heroics with suits of clothing and a two-month supply of provisions. . . .

. . . [D]uring the course of their trip virtually every overlander met at least a few Indians anxious to "swap." Most encountered a great many. Though some emigrants did manage to purchase certain items outright from native entrepreneurs, almost all the trading was conducted on the barter principle, since specie had little appeal for most prairie or mountain tribes. Many emigrants quickly learned, much to their surprise, that Indians were not easy marks in the bargaining process. Indeed, the traditional stereotype of the easygoing Indian, victimized in his every dealing with the white man, is simply not accurate. Finley McDiarmid, for example, found the Snake Indians to be "very sharp traders not easily cheated"; Cecelia Adams portrayed the Walla Wallas as "pretty shrewd fellows for money"; William Kelly suggested that the crafty Sioux compared favorably with wily British merchants; and Ansel McCall stated that the Sioux "in every case get the best of the bargain.". . .

Trade and aid were extremely significant aspects of the almost infinite variety of emigrant-Indian encounters. But they have been too often bypassed in the usual concentration upon pitched battles, scalps, and massacres. Initially the westbound emigrant wagons were strange curiosities to the natives in the same way that the overlanders were fascinated by the Indian life-style and customs. Accordingly, interaction, trading, and mutual aid prevailed throughout most of these crucial two decades of overland travel.

An analysis of the type and pattern of emigrant-Indian interaction during the antebellum era does suggest, however, that the overland emigrations quickened and perhaps made inevitable the military conquest of the western Indians. Almost from the very first, the perceptive plains Indians had recognized the threat the overland caravans represented to their way of life. Therefore, one of their first responses was to demand tribute of the passing trains. This tactic was employed at least as early as 1843. An 1845 overlander, speculating on the origin of this Indian tax, believed the practice to have begun with frightened emigrants willing to promise almost anything to travel safely. But it seems clear that tribute demands, which were most widely experienced by overlanders during the gold rush period, were grounded in more than simple repetition of a previous chance success. Emigrants continually reported that the Indians who came to demand tribute explained also why they were requesting the payments. The natives explicitly emphasized that the throngs of overlanders were killing and scaring away buffalo and other wild game, overgrazing prairie grasses, exhausting the small quantity of available timber, and depleting water resources.

FOR FURTHER STUDY

1. Consider the preparations for a journey from Independence, Missouri, to Oregon or California. What would be essential in terms of food, clothing, housing, transportation, medicine, and tools? What mistakes in planning seem to have been the most common?

2. Gold was important in the great migration described by Unruh, but millions of people stayed home in the settled communities of the East, and many went to Oregon and other areas rather than responding to the lure of gold in California. In social and psychological terms, rather than in terms of striking it rich, how do you explain the motivation of the people who left their homes and went west?

3. How do the activities and behavior of the migrants along the trail, and the things they brought with them, indicate an attempt to preserve the life and values they had known in the East?

4. Suppose you were a contemporary Hollywood screenwriter/director with a knowledge of Unruh's work and an interest in doing a different kind of motion picture of the migration. How would it differ from the classic Western saga?

5. For some states entry into the Union depended on special circumstances, such as whether or not slavery would be allowed. But in general, the date of admission indicates that the area had become fairly well populated with a settled society. Explain why California (1850), Oregon (1859), Nevada (1864), and Colorado (1876) were developed to the point of statehood well before the Dakotas, Montana, Washington, Idaho, and Wyoming, which were admitted in 1889–1890.

FOR FURTHER READING

The first historian to call attention to the great significance of the frontier in American history was Frederick Jackson Turner; see especially his book *The Frontier in American History* (1920). In *The Great Plains* (1931), Walter Prescott Webb examined the unique natural environment of the area and how it affected settlers' lives. Two works by Ray A. Billington, *Westward Expansion: A History of the American Frontier*, 3rd ed. (1967) and *The Far Western Frontier, 1830–1860* (1956), are very useful.

The ultimate peril of the westward journey, being trapped in a mountain blizzard, is described in George R. Stewart, *Ordeal by Hunger: The Story of the Donner Party*, rev. ed. (1960). Recently a large number of excellent studies of the westward movement have been published, including John M. Faragher, *Women and Men on the Overland Trail* (1979), Julie R. Jeffrey, *Frontier Women: The Trans-Mississippi West, 1840–1880* (1979), Sandra L. Myres, *Westering Women and the Frontier Experience, 1800–1915* (1982), Glenda Riley, *Frontierswomen: The Iowa Experience* (1981), and Lillian Schissel, *Women's Diaries of the Westward Journey* (1982). There are other special studies, including Duane A. Smith, *Mining America: The Industry and the Environment, 1800–1980* (1987), and David J. Wishart, *The Fur Trade of the American West, 1807–1840* (1979). Two good treatments of the forty-niners are John W. Caughey, *The California Gold Rush* (1975), and Neal Harlow, *California Conquered: War and Peace on the Pacific, 1846–1850* (1982).

Theodore Gentilz, *Invitation to the Dance*, (Details). Daughters of the Republic of Texas Library, Yanaguana Society Collection.

This San Antonio night scene shows horse riders wearing Tejano clothing as they visit a typical thatched-roof house.

EARLY TEXANS—THE COMMON GROUND BETWEEN ANGLOS AND TEJANOS IN REPUBLICAN TEXAS

JESÚS F. DE LA TEJA

$\mathcal{A}$s we discovered in the first reading in this volume people from different traditions who meet in the same territory often borrow from each other as they gradually learn to live together. When nineteenth-century Americans entered Texas in the 1820s and 1830s they saw land that could grow the southern staple, cotton. However, the land was already owned and occupied by Mexicans, Tejanos, who had lived in the area for many years. By 1836, some migrants were convinced that Texas should be free of Mexican rule and that eventual statehood was necessary for the region. Some easterners even thought that conquering the territory and its residents was better for humankind, as a whole.

Despite the conflicts between Americans and Tejanos, much was shared by the groups. As more and more easterners moved into the area they found they had much to learn from the Tejanos who had already adapted to the challenging environment.

This article highlights the exchanges in ranching techniques, food production and cooking, and dress between Anglos and Tejanos. It points out that Anglo-Texans often ended up dressing like Tejanos, eating their foods, enjoying their entertainment, and farming the land much like these residents.

From the *Journal of the Early Republic,* Vol. 18:1, (Spring 1998), pp. 74–98. Copyright © 1998 by the Society for Historians of the Early American Republic. Reprinted by permission.

. . . This essay focusing primarily on Tejanos, points out how the two "early Texases," one largely descended from southern United States colonial and early national experiences, the other from Mexican colonial culture, compared. The evidence demonstrates that despite suspicions, and sometimes overt racism and antipathy, there existed between early Texans and Tejanos much common ground. In what they ate, how they lived, what they enjoyed, and what they suffered, Tejanos and Texans had more in common than they realized. . . .

Corn—*maiz* to the Spanish world—was easy to grow under a variety of conditions; could be consumed before ripening; and was the most important gift of the New World to the Old. It was already being grown in Texas when the first Hispanic settlers arrived in the early eighteenth century to establish permanent residence. For hundreds of years the Caddoan people of East Texas, part of the Mississippian culture group, had raised corn, as had the Jumanos of the trans-Pecos and, perhaps, even the ancestors of the Lipan Apaches. What the Spanish colonial settlers and missionaries introduced was the application of Spanish technologies—plowing, *acequia* irrigation, and new varieties of the staple. Even in the advanced state of decay in which Hispanic agriculture found itself following the hostilities of the 1830s, Thomas W. Bell, a Texas army recruit could recognize that "the country around this place or rather immediately in the valley of the San Antonio river has been in a high state of cultivation. . . . By ditches from the river the whole valley has been irrigated and thus entirely obviate the necessity of rain in the cultivation of the soil."

The importance of corn to both the Anglo-American population and the Tejanos cannot be overstated. Boiled ears of corn and mush kept many a family from starving on both the Anglo-American and Mexican frontiers. . . . For both Mexican and Anglo-American frontier farmers, corn was the first crop in the ground, and its hardiness, versatility, and quick consumability making it much more popular than wheat. An 1840 immigrants' guide to Texas reported that

> at present but little else than corn and rye, and very little of the latter grain, are cultivated in any part of the country. This crop gives bread to the family, fattens their pork, feeds their working horses and oxen, and furnishes corn blades, usually called fodder, which serve here all the purposes of hay in the northern states. Thus this one single article, comprises nearly all the products of field husbandry throughout the republic.

As a matter of fact, from Spanish-colonial times until the last days of the republic wheat remained an imported luxury.

If the Republic-era Tejana used a *metate* and *mano* while the Anglo-American frontierswoman used an Armstrong mill, the result was the same: a coarse meal that could be used in numerous ways. In the absence of American grinding tools, some Anglo women adopted Mexican methods, as Mrs. Dilue Harris reminisced: "Mrs. Roark had a Mexican utensil for grinding corn, called a *metate*. It was a large rock which had a place scooped out of the center that would hold a peck of corn. It had a stone roller. It was hard work to grind corn on it, but the meal made good bread." The *tortilla* may have had its counterpart in cornbread, but the tamale stood alone as the one Mexican item that appears to have won universal approval (other than silver) from Anglo-Americans otherwise quick to disparage everything Hispanic. J. C. Duval, gave an unqualified endorsement: "I have often 'worried them down' . . . without being fatigued, and I can recommend them as an excellent dish." So did Captain W. S. Henry, United States Army, who had the opportunity to try tamales while in Corpus Christi in August 1845. "This afternoon, at Mrs. B.'s, I ate a Mexican preparation called *themales*," he wrote. "It is made of corn-meal, chopped meat, and Cayenne pepper, nicely wrapped in a piece of corn-husk, and boiled. I know of nothing more palatable."

Livestock provided food, clothing, transportation, and entertainment not only for Tejanos, but Indians and Anglos as well. From an early date Texas acquired a reputation as prime ranching country, and Tejanos as natural pastoralists. . . . William Bollaert's description of Tejano *vaqueros* in 1843 could easily be applied to later cowboys: "*Rancheros* . . . [are] a rude uncultivated race of beings, who pass the greater part of their lives in the saddle. . . . Unused to comfort, and regardless alike of ease and danger, they have a hardy, brigand sun-burnt appearance, especially when seen with a slouched hat, leather hunting shirt, leggings and Indian mocassins, armed with a large knife, musket, or rifle, and sometimes pistols." Somewhat later, Frederick Law Olmstead, who was quite condescending in his remarks about Tejanos, described them as "excellent drovers and shepherds." The anonymous informant of *Texas in 1837* asserted that the landscape drew people and livestock together: "Almost all of them have given their attention to the growth of stock and have bestowed no more labor upon agriculture than was necessary to supply their own limited wants." A decade later an old Texas settler put it more bluntly commenting, "The most profitable business which a person can follow in this country is stock-raising; especially if he has but a small force." No wonder that the oft-described "indolent" Tejanos had been raising stock as their principal profit-making business for generations.

Tejanos, moreover, had learned to make as much use of cattle as Comanches did of buffalo. One Anglo-American observer was struck by the variety of uses to which Tejanos subjected rawhide.

> Some say Texas is made of rawhides & Spanish horses. Bless me, they apply rawhides to more uses than we can conceive of. Rawhides constitute the carpets, chairbottoms, cots, beds, shelves, partitions, wagon beds, packs, withers, ropes, saddle-trumpery in part, and numberless other contrivances of the Mexicans. The lariat for noosing wilde horses, or stacking [*sic.*] horses out to grass, is braided rope of rawhide strands.

He might well have added that Tejanos made soap and candles from the tallow and jerky from the dried beef, just as did Anglo-American frontier folk. Yet, Tejanos did draw the line at certain uses, as the French visitor Auguste Frétellièr remarked in 1843: "sweetbreads, calves' flesh and head not being appreciated by the Mexicans, they gave them to us for nothing."

The first commercial cattle drives from Texas took place by the early 1770s. From that time forward, what little export earnings—legal and illegal—Tejanos experienced came from the livestock trade. Cattle drives to Coahuila, while legal, were not as lucrative as drives to Louisiana, where the booming frontier market created a steady demand. Picking up on Tejano tradition, Texan stockmen continued to take their herds into Louisiana, more often than not breaking the same kinds of laws that had been passed in colonial Texas for similar reasons. "Before the Revolution," one contemporary observed, "the Texian found a market for his cattle at New Orleans, where they were driven in large droves, and at the island of Cuba. . . . Cattle are still driven across the Sabine, notwithstanding the great exertions of the authorities to prevent it."

One of the more careful and observant visitors to the western frontier, a German by the name of W. Steinert, distinguished among various classes of horse and mule stock. American and "Spanish" horses were the best and most valuable, costing $100 or more. More common was the "Mexican" horse, "which is very hardy and makes out on ordinary feed," and which could be had for between $10 and $30. Below this was the mustang, to which the author of *Texas in 1840* referred: "the mustangs cannot be used much because they rarely become entirely tame. You can buy them for five to ten dollars, but as a rule they run off if they have not been thoroughly tamed. Catching and taming them is breakneck work, and it is performed mostly by Mexicans." As for mules, the American variety cost between $70 and $100, while Mexican mules went for no more than $60, and could "also be bought very cheaply from the Indians." . . .

Not surprisingly, Tejanos and Texans shared the concept of utility in their fashions. Once again, the frontier environment dictated the choices that people made. That the results could be strikingly dissimilar in outward appearance has obscured the underlying similarity of function. In the absence of an efficient commercial network and a stable and sufficient money supply, people made do with few garments and created their own fashion trends. . . . Homespuns, home-tanned and home-sewn, were the order of the day for most people in the republic era. Furthermore, a considerable number of people went barefoot or made use of home-constructed shoes.

Aside from the "style," there is little to distinguish the Anglo-Texan from the Tejano. As a matter of fact, from the Mexican perspective, Tejanos had already abandoned their cultural heritage in this regard. Two members of General Manuel de Mier y Terán's boundary commission to Texas in 1828 found Tejanos to have come under foreign influence in their customs. Jean Louis Berlandier, the expedition botanist, noted that "in their gatherings, the women prefer to dress in the fashion of Louisiana, and by so doing they participate both in the customs of the neighboring nation and of their own." The commission's artist, Lieutenant José María Sánchez, was even more critical of Nacogdoches Tejanos: "Accustomed to continuous commerce with the North Americans, they have imitated their customs, and so it may truthfully be said that they are Mexican only by birth, for even the Castilian language they speak with considerable ignorance." In 1846, William McClintock also noted that among Béxar women fashion seemed to favor that of the States: "the dress is purely American in style and material, some times rich and costly, but always plain and simple, white being the color most worn by both sexes."

Women's dress got no simpler than when they went about their daily chores. Climate and custom conspired to create situations of which some observers could not fail but take inspirational note. The hot work of preparing tortillas, from the grinding of corn on metates to cooking the flat cakes on the round clay or iron griddles known as *comales,* often made comfort and modesty incompatible. So did doing the wash. Robert Brahan, who arrived in the San Antonio area in the 1850s, was pleasantly confronted by the way Tejanas went about that particular chore. "Our washing days fri. & saturday," he commented, "hundreds of Mexican females (styled Greasers) can be seen in the stream up to their knees scrubbing away with only one light garment on, without sleeves, low on the breast & very short."

Certainly men's apparel was more typically Mexican, at least in the vicinity of San Antonio. As Bollaert's description of ranchero attire makes clear, however, field work demanded a style almost indistinguishable from Anglo-American frontier fashion. Typical evening wear included the short jacket, wide-brimmed hat, and colorful sash. Daily dress, at least for the laboring general population, was simple and functional. "The men mostly at this season dress in white, a crimson silk sash about the waist superseded the use of suspenders," William McClintock noted. . . . When the weather is cool which is the case every few days, they throw a Mexican blanket of rich and varigated colors over the shoulders. These blankets are worth from fifty to seventy five dollars."

Aside from tamales, the Mexican, or Saltillo blanket, seems to have left the most unequivocally positive impression on observers. Lieutenant George Mead of the United States Army, camped at Corpus Christi, noted the quality and colorfulness of the blankets. . . . Steinert complements this imagery, noting that the Mexicans "are excellent horsemen, and their saddles are often highly ornamented. While riding their horses they throw artistically woven blankets around their bodies in a becoming manner."

Whether picket hut or *jacal,* the form and function of housing were similar—simple, labor-saving, inexpensive, easy to abandon and rebuild. In the absence of sawmills, or money with which to purchase dressed lumber, early Tejanos continued to employ the building techniques of their Mesoamerican forebears. The *jacal* may have been crude, but it served its purpose well from the time of the earliest Spanish colonial settlement in the region until the end of the nineteenth century. John Leonard Riddell, passing through San Antonio in September 1839, found the population at work throwing up a new subdivision, most probably what became known as La Villita, and described the *jacal* quite elegantly.

Four-fifths of the houses are thatched with a kind of reed, the cat tail flag . . . it may be, but I think it is some kind of sedge or grass. Some are in progress of erection on the Alamo side of the river, and from them I gathered some idea of the Mexican mode of building. A trench is dug around in a square for about 1 foot deep for the foundation of the walls. Timbers unhewn 4 to 6 inches in diameter, and as high as the house is designed to be, are set in this trench, side by side and on end, and bound together some 5 or 8 feet above the ground with thongs of raw hide. A few poles are attached by rawhide horizontally for supporting the roof, which is thatched with reeds. The inside is plastered with mortar, except over head and under foot. The naked ground serves universally for floor.

This common structure in which the poor lived could be found masquerading behind a clapboard façade in Houston about the same time. . . . The "picket huts" abounded among the Anglo-American settlers of central Texas during the first decades of settlement.

Only when one went up the social ladder to the few prominent families that made up a threadbare elite in every frontier town, could notice be taken of the divergence between Spanish-Mexican and Anglo-American forms. Construction in stone held the same symbolism for Tejanos as dressed-lumber construction held for Anglo Americans. Mary Maverick seems to have had no problem with the "Barrera place," a stone house at the northeast corner of Commerce and Soledad streets, which her husband bought in 1839 and which remained the family residence for a decade. Her description of the place is matter-of-fact and devoid of negative language. "The main house was of stone," she remembered, "and had three rooms . . . [and] a shed in the yard along the east wall of the house towards the north end." Other Anglo families also moved into the better homes surrounding the plazas, for some time sharing the space with the descendants of the people who had built them.

Though some of the Tejanos' architecture performed its function suitably for Anglo immigrants, it nevertheless remained distinct. The exotic nature of this more durable architecture was noted by many a traveler through San Antonio. According to J. C. Duval, "at that time there were but few Americans in the place, and as all the houses were built in the Spanish or Morisco style, it presented a novel appearance to us." A different Old World comparison was made by J. W. Benedict, who also visited Béxar in the late 1830s: "San Antonio de Bexar is a somber looking town," he observed. "The original town is built from hewn stone and from its antiquity presents a very Gothic appearance being built about a century since." . . .

Tejanos had as rich a social life as Texans. . . . Their vices were the same, and their entertainments were similar in form and often in function. Perhaps it was the town-centered living pattern of Tejanos that appeared to Anglo observers to indicate a more desultory and dissolute way of life. Anglo-Americans often became converted to the new ways they discovered among the Tejanos, however, which suggests that Mexican behavior may not have been as strange as some of the writings might indicate.

The daily siesta and regular bathing were features of Tejano life that, according to some writers, symbolized the population's "unconcerned indolence and ease." William Bollaert made quick work of the Tejano's work-day, stressing the portion of leisure over strenuous activities among Béxar's town population. "Early in the morning they go to mass, work a little on the *labores*, dine, sleep the *siesta*, and in the evening amuse themselves with tinkling the guitar to their *dulcinea*, gaming, or dancing," he scorned. J. W. Benedict did not even give Tejanos the credit of working in the morning: "People here are very Indolent[,] scarcely any person stirring in fore part of the day."

In the Tejano's way of life, however, "loafing" seemed to some to be a good adaptation to the environment. W. Steinert, the meticulous German observer, had the following advice for would-be settlers: "you should never ride horseback during the noon hours; from eleven to three o'clock you should look for a shady place." Mary Maverick's memoirs make equally clear that the Tejanos' behavior was rational. "During this summer [1841], the American ladies led a lazy life of ease," she remembered. "We fell into the fashion of the climate, dined at twelve, then followed a siesta, until three, when we took a cup of coffee and a bath." And some Anglo observers seem to have quickly accepted this particular daily ritual. "From early evening until the soft hour of twilight the inhabitants flock to the river to bathe," William Bollaert noted; "and then the bronze-like forms of southern nymphs may be seen joyfully gamboling in the limpid stream, with their arch looks and their dark hair floating over their shoulders."

After the bath, dances and gambling were the norm. Superficially, these events proved for Anglos the indolence of the Tejano population. Immediately following his description of the lazy characteristics of Tejanos, for example, the unnamed traveler who visited San Antonio in 1837 commented, "The evening is spent by a large portion of the population at the fandango, a kind of Spanish waltz. There are seldom less than three or four of this description of dances during the night in different portions of the city." Fretéllièr has left us one of the better descriptions of such an occasion:

> The sound of the violin drew us to the spot where the *fête* was in full swing. It was in a rather large room of an adobe house, earthen floored, lighted by six-tallow candles placed at equal distances from each other. At the back a great chimney in which a fire of dry wood served to reheat the *café*, the *tamales* and *enchiladas*: opposite, some planks resting on frames and covered with a cloth, formed a table on which cups and saucers were set out. . . . At the upper end of the room, seated on a chair which had been placed on an empty box, was the musician, which was a violin. . . . The airs, for the most part Mexican, were new to me. The women were seated on benches placed on each side of the room. . . . The dance which I liked best was called the quadrille. It is a waltz in four-time with a step crossed on [e]very slow measure. . . . When the quadrille is finished, the cavalier accompanies his partner to the buffet, where they are served a cup of coffee and cakes. Then he conducts the young lady to her mother or to her chaperon to whom the girl delivers the cakes that she has taken care to reap at the buffet. The mother puts them in her handkerchief, and if the girl is pretty and has not missed a quadrille, the mama carries away an assortment of cakes to last the family more than a week.

Fandangos were typically associated with gambling, a pastime that seems to have captivated the attention of all manner of people. William Kennedy described games of chance as "one of the prominent vices of the South." He went on to add that "among all ranks and classes in Mexico, the mania for gambling ruinously prevails." A decade later William McClintock made similar observations. Gamblers had by then descended on San Antonio in order to profit off of the United States Army personnel stationed there, and "day and night, with unremitting zeal and application they ply their infamous trade." Apparently, the Mexican population was also consumed in this gaming frenzy. So much so, McClintock added, that "yesterday saw, (and the like may be seen on any Sabbath) many Mexicans leave chapel even before mass was concluded, and repair to the gaming table; where they spent the remainder of the day, and perhaps the whole night." To this sin may be added the sacrilege observed sometime earlier by another traveler. "So strong is this passion," this outsider commented, "that even the priests sometimes forget their sacred office and are seen dealing monte, the favorite game of the Mexicans."

Other forms of entertainment, some familiar to Anglo-Americans, were also evident among the Tejanos. In these activities, at least some Anglos perceived a kind of cultural resistance on the Tejanos' part. William Bollaert asserted that "although San Antonio is governed by Texan laws, Mexican customs prevail; rope dancing, tumbling, and plays on Sunday." He described one performance of "maromeros" he witnessed:

> The company consisted of a comical Payaso, or clown, three young men and one female. The performance was *al fresco* in the court yard of a house in a public square. At the foot of the tight rope was made two large fires, this being the only illumination for actors and audience. The rope dancing over, tumbling commenced, this being finished, upon a rude stage, a comedy and two farces followed, the three pieces occupying about twenty minutes. I cannot speak favourably of the polite composition of the dramas represented; it was indeed very *low comedy.*

In the mid-1850s Anglo-American and Mexican cultures were still coexisting. Frederick Law Olmstead noted critically that a not very good theater company provided tragedies to the local American population, while Tejanos enjoyed an amusement of a different order. "There is a permanent company of Mexican mountebanks," Olmstead observed, "who give performances of agility and buffoonery two or three times a week, parading, before night, in their spangled tights with drum and trombone through the principal streets."

Horse racing was one activity that Anglos, Indians, and Tejanos shared in common. Although Mexican frontier horse racing differed in form from the Anglo-American pastime, it served similar functions. Races meant opportunities for social interactions, for showing off of personal skills and mastery of good horse flesh, and for gambling. J. C. Duval's description of a meet in San Antonio around 1840 may in part be a fanciful old-age reminiscence, but it is an example of the ameliorative powers of such events.

> It was indeed a strange and novel scene that presented itself to our view. Drawn up in line on one side of the arena, and sitting like statues upon their horses, were the Comanche warriors, decked out in their savage finery of paints, feathers and beads, and looking with Indian stoicism upon all that was going on around them. Opposite to them, drawn up in single file also, were their old enemies upon many a bloody field, the Texas Rangers, and a few Mexican rancheros, dressed in their steeple crown, broad brim sombreros, showy scarfs and "slashed" trowsers, holding gracefully in check, the fiery mustangs on which they were mounted.

The competition itself consisted of various skill events, including picking up objects on the ground, target practice while riding at a full gallop, and breaking in wild horses. In other words, the spectators were witnessing a kind of proto-rodeo, complete with exotic costumes, Indians, vaqueros, trick riders, and bronco busters.

Secular and religious events of various kinds are used by people, consciously and subconsciously, to celebrate their common bonds. The calendar of holidays in early Texas was . . . full. . . . The anniversaries of the battle of San Jacinto, the Texas declaration of independence, the Fourth of July, and Christmas as those holidays generally celebrated. . . . Yet, in the 1840s Mexican Texans continued to celebrate feasts, some old and some recent, analogous to Anglo-American holidays.

In the early 1840s Tejanos still commemorated Mexican independence on September 16, according to Mary Maverick. As early as the 1820s, the celebration in San Antonio included processions, speeches, Catholic Mass, and dancing—a ball for the town's prominent families and dances for the general population. At La Bahía, the event's symbolism was so obvious that it did not escape comment by Mrs. Teal.

> It was Independence Day of the Indians of Mexico and was being celebrated on the 16th of September, 1832. Inside a gaily decorated carriage sat a little Indian girl, dressed in all the splendor of Indian royalty; long lines of white ribbons were fastened to the carriage and held by twelve elegantly dressed Spanish ladies who walked on either side, while the carriage was pushed forward by officers of high rank, and soldiers marched in front.

Tejanos also continued to commemorate the feast of Our Lady of Guadalupe, a holiday that since colonial days had marked the beginning of the Christmas season. Mary Maverick's description of the event in the early 1840s suggests that Tejano society continued to demonstrate internal cohesion, despite the Anglicizing forces at work. After a "grand" procession through the streets on December 12, "the more prominent families taking the Patroness along with them adjourned to Mr. José Flores' house on the west side of Military Plaza, where they danced most of the night. . . . It was all quite a novel and interesting scene to me." As a matter of fact, one of the problems encountered by the new European clergy, who took over the church in 1840, probably resulted from the continued devotion to Guadalupe. According to William Bollaert, "The Sacristan or vestry clerk was polite and communicative; he told me they were in a 'difficulty,' not knowing exactly to whom the church was dedicated, San Fernando, or Our Lady of Guadalupe, or San Antonio." There is other evidence that San Fernando church remained Mexican in practice to the end of the republic. For instance, William McClintock commented that "there has been a few pews erected in the chapel, I suppose for the convenience and comfort of American citizens. But the Mexicans seat themselves on the floor. . . ."

The public and communal character of Catholicism was certainly lost on most writers, even those who avoided calling the Tejanos' faith superstition. J. C. Duval, . . . claimed that it would have been "very easy" for him to have "passed" for Catholic, as "Catholicism (at least among the lower class of Mexicans) consists mainly in knowing how to make the sign of the cross, together with unbound reverence first, for the Virgin Mary, and secondly for the saints generally—and the priests." The somewhat harsher terms of a 1837 informant nonetheless convey the same sense of public religiosity: "every Mexican professes to be a Catholic and carries about his person the crucifix, the rosary, and other symbols of the mother church. But religion with him, if one is permitted to judge of the feelings of the heart by outward signs, is more a habit than a principle or feeling."

Minor religious holidays, such as St. John's and St. James's feasts, often proved perplexing to observers. Steinert could do little but describe in bewilderment one such celebration. "Yesterday [August 1, 1849] the local Mexicans celebrated Saint Peter's day, and none of them worked," he puzzled. "The ladies wore white dresses. In the afternoon the young people of both sexes dashed through the streets on horseback and yelled. Mud splashed up to their ears, and the muddier they became the better. I was not able to find out what sense there was to all these doings."

Not all reactions to Tejano Catholicism were negative. John Brown, on moving his family to San Antonio in the early 1830s, had his children baptized. His son reminisced that "as a child I accepted the faith most cheerfully," until his Presbyterian grandmother "took me in hand and taught me to love the scriptures." The ceremonial and celebratory character actually became an attraction for Anglo-Americans. Nacogdoches businessman Adolphus Sterne, on business in Austin at the end of 1841, commented in his diary, "all hands gone to San Antonio to Spend Christmas." And for Irish immigrants, the Tejano variant on their own faith seemed not at all strange, as Mrs. Teal's reminiscence of a wedding at La Bahía shows. "After the ceremony the Mexicans fired a salute of ten guns," she recalled. "The marriage services were concluded by a Mexican priest, before daylight, at the church in La Bahia."

Everyday life in Republic-era Texas was rough and violent. For Tejanos, it was marked by uncertainty about the future and a great deal of disconnectedness from the past. The rapid improvement of the country largely bypassed them. Still, evidence exists that Mexican Texans did not necessarily view their position in society as inferior; nor did antagonism color all relations with Anglo Texans. Among the many negative depictions of Tejanos as a group, sympathetic comments appear. Mrs. Teal reminisced that in the Refugio County area southeast of San Antonio, the settlers, "surrounded by Mexicans and Indians, . . . learned to fear neither, as they were never harmed during all the long years they lived among them." Auguste Fretéllièr, a Frenchman and friend of the artist Gentilz, was very positive about getting to know the Tejano population of San Antonio. He noted approvingly, "My mentor spoke Spanish very well, so I made rapid progress and in a little while I understood much better the Mexican character which pleased me infinitely—they were very polite, always gay and very obliging."

At the same time, Texans, in regarding Tejanos as "Mexicans," that is foreigners, were in the process of dissolving that uneasy partnership that had been created during the Mexican era. Promises that the laws would be published in Spanish went unfulfilled. Manipulation of the legal system led to land loss. Association with the enemy—Mexico and Indians—licensed indiscriminate violence against them. Identification with Catholicism made them the enemies of progress and enlightened thinking.

The history of Texan-Tejano relations in the second half of the nineteenth century is, therefore, one of increasing intolerance and segregation. Even as they accepted words into their vocabulary, livestock practices and equipment into their economy, legal principles into their system of law, and a number of dishes into their cuisines, Anglo-Texans increasingly excluded the Tejanos themselves. Even so, . . . Tejanos managed to retain much of the culture they inherited from "early Texas," and continued to participate in Texas society, whether or not that participation was fully recognized and appreciated.

 ## FOR FURTHER STUDY

1. How did corn growing and the products prepared from corn demonstrate what Anglos learned from the Tejanos?

2. Describe how Spanish ways of caring for cattle and processing them was important to early Texas.

3. What shows that Tejanos borrowed from their contact with Anglos—especially those in Louisana?

4. How did both Anglos and Tejanos adapt to the Texas climate?

5. Leisure activities also reflected differences and adaptations. Describe two including the early rodeo.

6. How did Tejano religious practice continue and what did Anglos think of it?

FOR FURTHER READING

For an earlier study see Arnoldo de Leon, *They Called Them Greasers: Anglo Attitudes Toward Mexicans in Texas, 1821–1900* (1983) and for a more detailed history of Tejanos in one area of Texas see Timothy M. Motovina, *Tejano Religion and Ethnicity: San Antonio, 1821–1860* (1995) and Arnoldo de Leon, *The Tejano Community, 1836–1900* (1982). For other similar histories of the treatment of Hispanic peoples see Leonard Pitt, *The Decline of the Californios: A Social History of the Spanish-Speaking Californians, 1846–1890* (1966). For a Mexican perspective see Gene Brack, *Mexico Views Manifest Destiny, 1821–1846* (1975). See also David J. Weber, *The Mexican Frontier, 1821–1846: The American Southwest under Mexico* (1982). More general treatments include Robert J. Rosenbaum, *Mexican Resistance in the Southwest: "The Sacred Right of Self-Preservation"* (1981), M. S. Meir and Feliciano Rivera, *The Chicanos: A History of Mexican Americans* (1972), and Albert Camarillo, *Chicanos in a Changing Society: From Mexican Pueblos to American Barrios in Santa Barbara and Southern California, 1848–1930* (1979). For the diary of an easterner see William F. Gray, *From Virginia to Texas, 1835* (1985). For one of the famous characters in this period see Mark Derr, *The Frontiersman, The Real Life and Many Legends of Davy Crockett* (1993). For the entire frontier see Gregory H. Nobles, *American Frontiers: Cultural Encounters and Continental Conquest* (1997).

(left) Library of Congress; (right) The Valentine Museum, Cook Collection, Richmond, VA.

These young soldiers from the Union and Confederate armies were like those who explained why they were fighting in letters they wrote home to friends and relatives.

WHY SOLDIERS WENT TO WAR

JAMES M. MCPHERSON

*M*uch of what we learn about the Civil War concentrates on the causes of the conflict or on the heroic actions on its battlefields. The background of the war is full of the images of novelist Harriet Beecher Stowe's *Uncle Tom's Cabin,* the protests and political actions of abolitionists, and the Lincoln-Douglass debates. After the firing on Fort Sumter in 1861 we concentrate on the war itself, its battles and personalities. We seem to think that the reasons that caused the war to begin persisted throughout its campaigns. What we are missing is an entire range of other decisions made by individual soldiers who had to chose to join the war and remain in it. The words of the leaders, especially President Abraham Lincoln at Gettysburg and in the Emancipation Proclamation, do not explain why men came and stayed. Policy makers like Lincoln often chose their words carefully, and their guarded comments seldom expose their own personal beliefs. They certainly cannot explain the actions of those who actually fought. Fortunately, soldiers who fought on both sides did reveal their personal beliefs in letters sent home to family and friends. Analyzing participants' comments about the war offers new insights about it.

It may seem strange to think that this is a new approach but by the 1890s most Americans wanted to heal the wounds left by the war. So they ignored the importance of slavery as a cause and concluded that the war was simply an heroic fight between brothers. To correct this view, James McPherson read hundreds of letters from soldiers on both sides to see what they said about why they were fighting. He also traced their views as the war progressed to see if events changed their thoughts. This essay lets the reader experience the words of soldiers on both sides—many by writers who did not live to see the war end. They allow us to understand the war from the inside—from its participants—not from those who planned the battles but from those who fought them. Sometimes the soldiers write to convince themselves they made the right choice when they joined the fight. Sometimes they write to bolster the spirits of those worrying about them at home. When they talk about why they are risking their lives, however, they reveal the heart of the conflict.

Make sure you can trace how the views of both sides changed as the war went on. Notice how they responded to the fortunes of their side in the war. Be sure to look for the importance of the Emancipation Proclamation to the soldiers of both sides.

In his Second Inaugural Address, on March 4, 1865, Abraham Lincoln stated a proposition to which most historians today as well as most Americans of Lincoln's time would assent: slavery before the war had been a "powerful interest. All knew that this interest was, somehow, the cause of the war. To strengthen, perpetuate, and extend this interest was the object for which the insurgents would rend the Union, even by war."

On this issue at least, the president and vice-president of the Confederacy concurred with Lincoln. In 1861 Jefferson Davis justified secession as an act of self-defense against the Black Republicans, whose purpose to exclude slavery from the territories would make "property in slaves so insecure as to be comparatively worthless . . . thereby annihilating in effect property worth thousands of millions of dollars." And in his famous "cornerstone" speech of March 21, 1861, Alexander Stephens maintained that the Republican threat to slavery was "the immediate cause of the late rupture and the present revolution" of Confederate independence. The old confederation known as the United States, Stephens continued, had been founded on the false idea that all men are created equal. The new Confederacy, by contrast, "is founded upon exactly the opposite idea; its foundations are laid, its cornerstone rests, upon the great truth that the negro is not equal to the white man; that slavery, subordination to the superior race, is his natural and normal condition. This, our new government, is the first, in the history of the world, based on this great physical, philosophical, and moral truth."

Some Confederate soldiers were equally plainspoken in their avowals of slavery as the cause for which they fought. On the eve of secession, a young lawyer in Shreveport looked forward to "a great cotton slave Republic—with a future the most auspicious that ever waited on earthly government." He lived to see the rise but not the fall of this republic, for he was killed at Gettysburg. A lieutenant in the 28th Mississippi told his wife in 1863 that "this country without slave labor would be completely worthless. . . . If the negroes are freed the country . . . is not worth fighting for. . . . We can only live & exist by that species of labor: and hence I am willing to continue to fight to the last." A captain in the 8th Alabama likewise vowed "to fight forever, rather than submit to freeing negroes among us. . . . [We

---

From *What They Fought For 1861–1865,* by James M. McPherson. Copyright © 1994 by Louisiana State University Press. Reprinted by permission of Louisiana State University Press.

are fighting for] rights and property bequeathed to us by our ancestors." And a Georgia officer, owner of forty slaves, reassured his wife, who in 1863 expressed doubts about the future of slavery, that if the Confederacy won the war "it is established for centuries."

Several Confederate soldiers welcomed Lincoln's Emancipation Proclamation for bringing the real issue into the open. The "Proclamation is worth three hundred thousand soldiers to our Government at least," wrote a Kentucky cavalry sergeant who rode with John Hunt Morgan. "It shows exactly what this war was brought about for and the intention of its damnable authors." And a Virginia captain, a small slaveholder in the Shenandoah Valley, believed that "after Lincoln's proclamation any man that would not fight to the last ought to be hung as high as Haman."

Confederate prospects for victory appeared brightest during the months after the Emancipation Proclamation, partly because this measure divided the northern people and intensified a morale crisis in Union armies. Slave prices in the South rose even faster than the rate of inflation during that springtime of Confederate confidence. A number of soldiers wrote home advising relatives to invest in slaves. The famous "boy colonel" of the Confederacy, the planter's son Henry Burgwyn, who became colonel of the 26th North Carolina at the age of twenty-one, urged his father in February, 1863, to put every cent he had into slaves. "I would buy boys & girls from 15 to 20 years old & take care to have a majority of girls," he wrote. "The increase in number of your negroes by this means would repay the difference in the amount of available labor. . . . I would not be surprised to see negroes in 6 mos. after peace worth from 2 to 3000 dollars." Gettysburg cut short his life before he could witness the collapse of his dreams.

But Gettysburg did not discourage Colonel E. Porter Alexander, Longstreet's chief of artillery, who won fame in that battle for directing the barrage that preceded Pickett's charge. Three weeks after the battle, Porter advised his wife to buy a wet nurse for their twins, for "Carline & her baby wd. be a fine *speculation* at $2000." Even as late as January, 1865, an officer from low-country South Carolina wrote to his fiancée that "now is the time for Uncle to buy some negro women and children on the principle that if we don't succeed the money won't be worth anything and if we do slaves will be worth a 1000 times more than now."

But such candid discussions of slavery were the exception rather than the rule. Even in private letters, Confederate soldiers professed more often to fight *for* liberty and *against* slavery—that is, against their own enslavement to the North. "Sooner than submit to Northern Slavery, I prefer death," wrote a South Carolina captain to his wife in 1862, a phrase repeated almost verbatim by many soldiers. They filled their letters and diaries with references to "the ruthless invader who is seeking to reduce us to abject slavery." "The Deep still quiet peace of the grave is more desirable than Vassalage or Slavery." We must "die as free men or live as slaves"; better far "to die rather than be slaves." Such remarks are rescued from bombast by knowledge that all four men who wrote them—two lieutenants, a sergeant, and a private—were killed in action.

Those soldiers were using the word *slavery* in the same sense that Americans in 1776 had used it to describe their subordination to Britain. Confederates claimed to fight for the same liberty their forefathers had won in 1783. . . .

. . . Many Americans in Thomas Jefferson's time felt acutely the paradox of fighting for liberty while holding other people in slavery. There was no shortage of Yankees in 1861 to point out the same paradox in Confederate professions. "The *perfect* liberty they sigh for," said Abraham Lincoln, is "the liberty of making slaves of other people." But Confederate soldiers, unlike many of their forebears of 1776, seemed unconscious of the paradox. In the countless references to liberty, freedom, justice, equal rights, and the like in their letters and diaries, I have found but one reference to any sense of inconsistency between the ideas of fighting for liberty and for slavery. A low-country South Carolina planter's son in Hampton's Legion considered all this talk about liberty and the rights of man "simple non-sense; I for one am fighting for the maintenance of no such absurdity. . . . Every reflecting child will glance at the darkey who waits on him & laugh at the idea of such an 'abstract right.'"

Absurdity or not, most Confederate soldiers believed that they were fighting for liberty *and* slavery, one and inseparable. A young physician from Louisville who joined the 4th Kentucky Confederate Infantry wrote that "We are fighting for our liberty, against tyrants of the North . . . who are determined to destroy slavery." . . . A planter's son who with two brothers fought in the 16th Mississippi wrote home in 1863 that he had been offered $3,500 for his body servant but was holding out for $4,000. When one of his brothers was killed at Cold Harbor, the soldier consoled their mother that "he died that we might live free men." . . .

During the antebellum period many southerners had avoided using the words *slaves* and *slavery,* preferring instead *servants* and *southern institutions.* Some Confederate soldiers kept up this practice even in private letters, referring to "our own social institutions," "the integrity of all our institutions," "the institutions of the whole South" as the cause for which they fought. In 1863 a young North Carolina officer stopped for a meal in the home of a Pennsylvania farmer during the Gettysburg campaign. He described the scene to his mother: "They live in real Yankee style wife & daughters & a help doing all the work. It makes me more than ever devoted to our own Southern institutions." A Georgia lieutenant in Longstreet's corps was a little more explicit. "Pennsylvania is the greatest country I ever saw in my life," he wrote his wife. "Molie if this state was a slave state and I was able to buy land here after the war you might count on living in Pennsylvania."

Most of the soldiers quoted so far came from slaveholding families. They tended to emphasize the right of property in slaves as the basis of the liberty for which they fought. This motive, not surprisingly, was much less in evidence among nonslaving soldiers. But some of them emphasized a form of property they did own, one that was central to the liberty for which they fought. That property was their white skins, which put them on a plane of civil equality with slaveholders and far above those who did not possess that property. Herrenvolk democracy— the equality of all who belonged to the master race—was a powerful motivator for many Confederate soldiers.

Even though he was tired of the war, wrote a Louisiana solider in 1862, "I never want to see the day when a negro is put on an equality with a white person. There is too many free niggers . . . now to suit me, let alone having four millions." A yeoman farmer from North Carolina facing the Yankees in Virginia vowed to "make them know that a white man is better than a nigger." . . . Many northern soldiers shared the bewilderment of a Wisconsin private who wrote home describing a conversation with Confederate prisoners captured in the Atlanta campaign: "Some of the boys asked them what they were fighting for, and they answered, 'You Yanks want us to marry our daughters to the niggers.'"

Such sentiments were not confined to nonslaveholders. Many slaveholding soldiers also fought for white supremacy as well as for the rights of property. An Arkansas captain was enraged by the idea that if the Yankees won, his "sister, wife, and mother are to be given up to the embraces of their present 'dusky male servitors.'" After reading Lincoln's Proclamation of Amnesty and Reconstruction in December, 1863, which stipulated southern acceptance of emancipation as a condition of peace, another Arkansas soldier, a planter, wrote his wife that Lincoln not only wanted to free the salves but also "declares them entitled to all the rights and privileges as American citizens. So imagine your sweet little girls in the school room with a black wooly headed negro and have to treat them as their equal." Likewise, a Georgia lieutenant wrote to his wife from the trenches on the Chattahoochee that if Atlanta and Richmond fell, "we are irrevocably lost and not only will the negroes be free but . . . we will all be on a common level. . . . The negro who now waits on you will then be as free as you are & as insolent as she is ignorant."

It would be a mistake, however, to assume that Confederate soldiers were constantly preoccupied with this matter. In fact, only 20 percent of my sample of 374 southern soldiers explicitly voiced these proslavery convictions in their letters and diaries. Not surprisingly, the proportion of soldiers from slaveholding families expressing such a purpose was double that from nonslaveholding families—30 percent compared with 14 percent. Ironically, the proportion of Union soldiers who wrote about the slavery question was much greater, as we shall see. There is a ready explanation for this evident paradox. Emancipation was a salient issue for Union soldiers because it was controversial. Slavery was not salient for Confederate soldiers during most of the war because it was not controversial. They took slavery for granted as part of the southern way of life for which they fought, and did not feel compelled to discuss it. Although only 20 percent of the soldiers avowed explicit proslavery purposes in their letters and diaries, *none at all* dissented from that view. . . .

A year before Lee surrendered at Appomattox, a southern private noted in his diary that Confederate victory was certain because "we are fighting for our property and homes; they, for the flimsy and abstract idea that a negro is equal to an Anglo American." He was wrong. Few Union soldiers professed to fight for racial equality. And while the abolition of slavery was one of the two great results of the Civil War—the other being preservation of one nation indivisible—not many Union soldiers claimed to fight *primarily* for that purpose.

Four decades ago Bell Wiley wrote that scarcely one in ten Union soldiers "had any real interest in emancipation per se." If by "per se" Wiley meant "in and of itself alone," one in ten may even be an exaggeration. Rare indeed were two soldiers, one from Wisconsin and the other from Maine, whose letters home contained such sentiments as: "I have no heart in this war if the slaves cannot go free. . . . [Our cause is] nobler even than the Revolution for they fought for their own freedom, while we fight for that of another race. . . . If the doom of slavery is not sealed by the war I shall curse the day I entered the Army or lifted a finger in the preservation of the Union."

But if "emancipation per se" meant a perception that the abolition of slavery was inseparably linked to the goal of preserving the Union, then almost three in ten Union soldiers took this position during the first year and a half of the war, and many more were eventually converted to it. In November, 1861, a Massachusetts officer and Harvard graduate declared that "slavery has brought death into our own households already in its wicked revolt against the government. . . . There is but one way, and that is emancipation; either that or we must succumb and divide." A stonemason who served as a private in another Massachusetts regiment considered "the object of our government as one worth dying to attain—the maintenance of our free institutions which must of *necessity* result in the freedom of every human being over whom the stars and stripes wave." Or as a twenty-year-old farm boy in the 1st Minnesota Infantry put it more succinctly in December, 1861: "The war will never end until we end slavery."

But this was far from a universal opinion among Union soldiers. At times during the first two years of the war, for every soldier who held this opinion another expressed the opposite conviction: that emancipation was an unconstitutional and illegitimate war aim. Whereas a tacit consensus united Confederate soldiers in support of "southern institutions," including slavery, a bitter and explicit disagreement about emancipation divided northern soldiers. For six months during the winter and spring of 1862–1863, this question seriously sapped Union army morale. But unlike Confederate opinion on slavery, which remained relatively constant until the final months of the war, Union opinion was in a state of flux. It moved by fits and starts toward an eventual majority in favor of abolishing slavery as the only way to win the war and preserve the Union.

During the war's first year, the slavery issue seldom came up in the letters of most northern soldiers, for at this time the official war aim was only restoration of the Union. Nevertheless, during that year some soldiers predicted that the war must also become a fight to abolish slavery. A young schoolteacher who enlisted in the 5th Wisconsin declared in August, 1861, that "I have been talking all my life for the cause of liberty but now the time is nigh at hand when I shall have a chance to aid by deed this cause." A farmer's son from Connecticut dropped out of Yale after his sophomore year in 1861 and enlisted in a cavalry regiment, as he explained to his mother, to fight "for Liberty, for the slave and the white man alike. . . . I have turned out to be a right out and out Abolitionist. The guaranties of the Constitution to Slavery, I claim, have been, one and all forfeited by the rebel slave owners." In July, 1861, a Union naval officer asserted that there would never "be peace between the two sections until slavery is so completely scotched [that] . . . we can see plainly in the future free labour to the gulph. . . . I think myself the Southerners are fighting against fate or human progress." What is remarkable about this last quotation is that it came not from a Yankee fanatic but from Percival Drayton, a native of South Carolina and scion of a prominent planter family, whose brother Thomas Drayton became a Confederate general.

Experience in the South reinforced the convictions of most antislavery soldiers. After talking with a slave woman in Virginia who described the brutal whipping of her husband in a matter-of-fact way, a private in the crack 83d Pennsylvania wrote in January, 1862: "I thought I hated slavery as much as possible before I came here, but here, where I can see some of its workings, I am more than ever convinced of the cruelty and inhumanity of the system." More typical than such humanitarian concerns, however, was a contempt for southern ignorance and backwardness, which many Yankee soldiers attributed to slavery. An Ohio farmer's son who marched through Tennessee remarked on "how far behind the North they are in improvements of every kind. . . . The institution of slavery is as much a curse to the whites as the blacks and kills industry and improvements of every kind. Slavery has deadened all enterprise and prosperity. School houses are a rare sight." . . .

By the summer of 1862, antislavery principle and pragmatism fused into a growing commitment to emancipation as both a means and an end of Union victory. This development represented a significant hardening of northern attitudes toward "traitors," whose rights of property—especially property in slaves—were entitled to little respect. "We have been . . . playing with *Traitors* long enough" was a typical phrase in soldiers' letters. . . .

Officials in Washington came to the same conclusion. In July, 1862, Congress passed the second confiscation act and Lincoln made his momentous decision to issue an emancipation proclamation. It would not become public for two months, but meanwhile the work of practical emancipation went on. "That bill to confiscate the rebel property is just what we want," wrote a Rhode Island sergeant. "If a rebels property gits eney favers from eney of our Soldiers you can call me a poore judge." The colonel of the 5th Minnesota wrote from northern Alabama in September, 1862, that "I am doing quite a business in the confiscation of slave property. . . . It certainly makes the rebels wince to see their 'niggers' taken off which is a source of private satisfaction to me. . . . Crippling the institution of slavery is . . . striking a blow at the heart of the rebellion."

But a good many Union soldiers disagreed. A backlash of antiemancipation sentiment began to surface in the letters of a number of them in 1862. This sentiment brewed up from a mixture of racism, conservatism, and partisan politics. The experiences and observations in the South that made some soldiers more antislavery made others more antiblack. "No one who has ever seen the nigger in all his glory on the southern plantations will ever vote for emancipation," wrote an Indiana private. "If emancipation is to be the policy of this war . . . I do not care how quick the country goes to pot." . . . An artillery major from New York, a Democrat like so many officers in the Army of the Potomac under McClellan, wrote that if Lincoln caved in to "these 'black Republicans'" and made it "an abolition war[,] . . . I for one shall be sorry that I ever lent a hand to it. . . . This war [must be] for the preservation of the Union, the putting down of armed rebellion, and for that purpose only."

This major spoke for a substantial number of Union soldiers. After all, at least two-fifths of them were Democrats and another tenth came from border states. Their resistance to any notion of turning the war for Union into a war against slavery was one reason for Lincoln's hesitancy to do just that. The cause of Union united northern soldiers; the cause of emancipation divided them. Letters and diaries mention vigorous campfire arguments about slavery. A Massachusetts sergeant made the following entry in his diary for February 4, 1863: "Had a jaw on slavery in the evening, & Jim did n't agree with the rest of us, & so he got mad." . . . At about the same time an Indiana corporal wrote in his diary: "At night got into an argument, with a man that believed Slavery is right.—Had a warm time." . . .

It was no accident that these heated discussions took place during the winter of 1862–1863. The Emancipation Proclamation provoked a new level of consciousness about the relationship of slavery to the war. Soldiers who had advocated an antislavery war from the beginning naturally welcomed the proclamation. . . . A Minnesota corporal wrote approvingly to his wife: "Abraham 'has gone and done it' at last. Yesterday will be a day hallowed in the hearts of millions of the people of these United States, & also by the friends of liberty and humanity the *world* over." . . . Several soldiers rang changes on the theme expressed by a New York private: "Thank God . . . the contest is now between Slavery & freedom, & every honest man knows what he is fighting for."

These were the idealists. The pragmatists weighed in with equally forceful, if less elegant, expressions. "I am no abolitionist," wrote an enlisted man in the 55th Ohio, "in fact despise the word," but "as long as slavery exists . . . there will be no permanent peace for America. . . . Hence I am in favor of killing slavery." An Indiana sergeant told his wife that while he had no use for free blacks, he approved the Emancipation Proclamation "if it will only bring the war to an end any sooner I am like the fellow that got his house burned by the guerrillas he was in for emancipation subjugation extermination and hell and damnation. We are in war and anything to beat the South." As for those who howl that we are now "fighting for the nigger," rather than for Union, wrote a forty-year-old Ohio private to his wife, "if they are such fools as not to be able to see the difference between the means employed, and the end in view, let them remain blind."

But plenty of soldiers believed that the proclamation *had* changed the purpose of the war. They professed to feel betrayed. They were willing to risk their lives for Union, they said, but not for black freedom. The proclamation intensified a morale crisis in Union armies during the winter of 1862–1863, especially in the Army of the Potomac. The removal of McClellan from command, the disaster at Fredericksburg, and the fiasco of the Mud March had caused morale in that army to plunge to an all-time low. Things were little better in Grant's army on the Mississippi, where the first attempts against Vicksburg had come to grief.

Desertion rates in both armies rose alarmingly. Many soldiers blamed the Emancipation Proclamation. The "men are much dissatisfied" with it, reported a New York captain, "and say that it has turned into a 'nigger war' and all are anxious to return to their homes for it was to preserve the Union that they volunteered." Enlisted men confirmed this observation with a blizzard of bitter comments in letters home. "I am the Boy that Can fight for my Country," wrote an Illinois private, "but not for the Negros." . . . At the end of 1862 [an] . . . Illinois soldier with a wife and children reflected on the "cost of freeing the Black Devils. No less than 300,000 of our own free white citizens have already been sacrificed to free the small mite that have got their freedom. . . . I consider the life & Happiness of my family of more value than any Nigger."

How widespread were such attitudes? How dangerous were they to the morale and cohesion of Union armies? The answers are difficult to quantify precisely. For a time during the winter of 1862–1863, antiemancipation expressions seemed to outnumber those on the other side. And morale certainly declined—although defeatism and lack of faith in Union leaders may have had more to do with this than the Emancipation Proclamation. In any case, the decline of morale proved short-lived, for the Union armies did not fall apart and soon won some of their most decisive victories of the war. And of the soldiers in my sample who expressed a clear opinion about emancipation as a war aim at any time through the spring of 1863, two and one-half times as many favored it as opposed it: 36 percent to 14 percent. If we apportion those who did not comment on the subject evenly between the two sides, the picture would conform with the results of a poll in March, 1863, in the 15th Iowa, a fairly typical regiment. Half of the men endorsed the Emancipation Proclamation, a quarter opposed it, and the other quarter did not register an opinion. . . .

. . . The evidence indicates that proemancipation convictions did predominate among the leaders and fighting soldiers of the Union army. And that prevalence increased after the low point of early 1863 as a good many antiemancipation soldiers changed their minds. Two factors played a part in their conversion. The first was a dangerous rise of copperheadism on the home front during the first half of 1863. Peace Democrats zeroed in on the Emancipation Proclamation in their denunciations of Lincoln's unconstitutional war and their demands for a negotiated peace. This produced an anticopperhead backlash among Union soldiers, including many Democrats, that catapulted some of them clear into the Lincoln camp on emancipation. . . .

As colonel of the 67th Ohio, Marcus Spiegel was the highest-ranking officer of the Jewish faith in the Civil War. As a Democrat he denounced the Emancipation Proclamation, writing to his wife in January, 1863: "I am sick of the war. . . . I do not fight or want to fight for Lincoln's Negro proclamation one day longer." But when his men began to say the same thing, repeating what they had heard from home or read in Democratic newspapers, Spiegel grew alarmed. "Stand by the government right or wrong," he told his regiment. By April, 1863, he had repudiated the Democratic party; by January, 1864, a few months before he was killed in the Red River campaign, he wrote his wife from Plaquemines Parish, Louisiana, that "since I [came] here I have learned and seen more of what the horrors of Slavery was than I ever knew before. . . . I am [in] favor of doing away with the . . . accursed institution. . . . I am [now] a strong abolitionist."

The second factor that converted many soldiers to support of emancipation was a growing conviction that it really did hurt the enemy and help their own side. In this respect the contribution of black soldiers—whose enlistment was a corollary of the emancipation policy—did much to change the minds of previously hostile white soldiers. A junior officer in the 86th Indiana reported in March, 1863, that men who two months earlier had damned the "*abolition war*" and threatened to desert now favored both emancipation and black soldiers. "We use all other kinds of rebel property," he wrote, "and they see no reason why we should not use negroes. Every negro we get strengthens us and weakens the rebels. The soldiers now say if there can be negroes enough raised to conquer the rebels let them do it." . . .

Not all antiabolitionist soldiers experienced such a conversion. An Indiana private decided against reenlisting for another three-year hitch because the war had become a crusade "to Free the Nigars . . . and I do not propose to fight any more in such a cause." A private in the 6th Kentucky complained in the spring of 1864 that "this is nothing but an abolition war. . . . I am a strait out Union and Constitution man I am not for freeing the negroes." His brother in the same regiment agreed and added a wish that "old abe lincoln . . . had to sleep with a negro every night as long as he lives and kiss ones ass twice a day."

But this was a distinctly minority view among Union soldiers by 1864. When Lincoln ran for reelection that year on a platform pledging a constitutional amendment to abolish slavery, he received nearly 80 percent of the soldier vote—a pretty fair indication of army sentiment on slavery by that time. . . . A Michigan sergeant in his forties, also a farmer, wrote his wife from Georgia in the spring of 1864 that "the more I learn of the cursed institution of Slavery, the more I feel willing to endure, for its final destruction. . . . After this war is over, this whole country will undergo a change for the better . . . abolishing slavery will dignify labor; that fact of itself will revolutionize everything." He never experienced disappointment with this vision of the future; an enemy sharpshooter ended his life near Atlanta in August, 1864.

Had the Michigan sergeant lived to witness the North's retreat from Reconstruction in the 1870s and the South's disfranchisement and formalized segregation of blacks in the 1890s, he might have wondered whether the abolition of slavery had revolutionized everything after all. By the 1890s the road to reunion between men who wore the blue and gray had paved over the issues of slavery and equal rights for freed slaves. Middle-aged veterans in the Grand Army of the Republic and the United Confederate Veterans held joint encampments at which they reminisced about the glorious deeds of their youth. Many of them reached a tacit consensus, which some voiced openly: Confederate soldiers had not fought for slavery; Union soldiers had not fought for its abolition. It had been a tragic war of brothers whose issues were best forgotten in the interests of family reconciliation. In the popular romanticization of the Civil War, the issue of slavery became almost as invisible as black Union veterans at a reunion encampment. Somehow the Civil War became a heroic contest, a sort of grand, if deadly, football game without ideological cause or purpose.

Some veterans, however, dissented from the tendency to blur the issues of the war, especially slavery. Their most eloquent spokesman was Oliver Wendell Holmes, Jr. Twenty years after he had described the Union cause as "the Christian crusade of the 19th century," Holmes declared in a Memorial Day address to other veterans in 1884 that "in our youth our hearts were touched with fire. It was given to us to learn at the outset that life is a profound and passionate thing." Like Holmes, many Civil War soldiers felt a profound and passionate commitment to the idelogical purposes for which they fought. If some of them later forgot this, there is no better way to recover what motivated them from 1861 to 1865 than to read their letters and diaries written in the immediacy of experience. Only then can we truly understand what they fought for.

 ## FOR FURTHER STUDY

1. What effect did the Emancipation Proclamation have on both Confederate and Union soldiers?

2. Why did some Southerners say they were fighting against slavery?

3. Did Southern soldiers whose families owned slaves think they were fighting to preserve slavery?

4. Early in the war most Union soldiers did not think they were fighting for abolition. What were they fighting for? After 1862 how and why did antislavery and pragmatism join to support emancipation?

5. How does the nature of the sample used by the author influence the essay and its results—are there groups of soldiers we do not hear from because they seldom write? If we know that the mails were disrupted, does this influence the author's findings? How?

FOR FURTHER READING

There are more books and articles on the American Civil War than on any other aspect of American History. Many aspects of army life are treated in Bell I. Wiley, *The Life of Johnny Reb* (1943) and *The Life of Billy Yank* (1952). Newer works on soldier life include Michael Barton, *Goodmen: The Character of Civil War Soldiers* (1981), Gerald E. Linderman, *Embattled Courage: The Experience of Combat in the American Civil War* (1989), Reid Mitchell, *Civil War Soldiers: Their Expectations and Their Experiences* (1989), and Glenn M. Lindend and Thomas J. Pressly, *Voices From the House Divided* (1995). For women see Elizabeth D. Leonard, *Yankee Women: Gender Battles in the Civil War* (1994), Catherine Clinton, *Tara Revisited: Women, War, and the Plantation Legend* (1995), and Jacqueline Jones, *Labor of Love, Labor of Sorrow* (1985). For African Americans see Clarence L. Mohr, *On the Threshold of Freedom* (1986), Ira Berlin et al., eds., *Freedom: A Documentary History of Emancipation, 1861–1867* Series II, *The Black Military Experience* (1982).

For an overview of the whole war see Peter J. Parrish, *The American Civil War* (1985), and Philip S. Paludan, *"A People's Contest": The Union and the Civil War, 1861–1865* (1989). James M. McPherson, *Battle Cry of Freedom: The Civil War Era* (1988) and Charles Royster, *The Destructive War* (1991) are good, one-volume studies. For a look at the result of the war see Gabor S. Boritt, ed., *Why the Confederacy Lost* (1992). Excellent, single-volume biographies include David Donald, *Lincoln* (1995), Alan T. Nolan, *Lee Considered* (1991), and William C. Davis, *Jefferson Davis* (1991).

CHAPTER 21

Edward Lamson Henry, *Old Westover Mansion*, (detail), 1869. Corcoran Gallery of Art, Gift of the American Art Association, (00.11)

Union troops occupy a southern plantation near the end of the Civil War.

WHEN THE YANKEES CAME: THE REALITIES OF LIVING IN THE OCCUPIED SOUTH

STEPHEN V. ASH

*V*ery seldom have people who live in the United States been subjected to military occupation by hostile armies. During the Revolutionary War the British occupied New York City, but they rarely occupied the interior where ordinary citizens lived. When the British armies passed through various rebellious colonies some residents joined their armies, especially in the South where slaves made their way to British forces to be free. The only other large-scale occupation was during the Civil War when Northern armies controlled parts of the South. Of course, there were interior portions of the Confederacy which remained out of reach, but where the Union army controlled Southern territory they established garrisoned towns which protected their occupants from the Confederate armies or from local insurrections. Some southern residents sympathized with the Union cause and fled to the safety of these Union areas. Others felt liberated by the decline of the aristocracy and lashed out at those who had treated them poorly. African Americans, too, had new-found freedom and some rebelled and joined Union forces while others remained loyal to their former masters. Women in occupied territory were fearful that they would be attacked while their men were at war—both by occupation troops or by others. In the shadows there were many loyal to the Confederacy who wanted to strike blows against the North. Others took advantage of the lawlessness to take what they could from abandoned houses, sparsely occupied towns, and vulnerable residents.

The liberation of the slaves of the South has been called the jubilee, but according to Stephen Ash in the following selection, there was "the other jubilee" when the Northern presence changed the embedded social system in the South. As you read be aware that when Ash uses the term *yeoman* he means a farmer or small landowner who has more than poorer whites but could easily be overwhelmed by the occupying troops and lose crops and animals. Also, at several points when Ash refers to oaths he means loyalty oaths which required Southerners to say they were loyal to the Union, not the Confederacy, before they could be given shelter in garrisoned towns or other forms of help.

In September 1862 planter John Pool and a number of other prominent citizens of Bertie County, North Carolina, met in Windsor, the county seat, to discuss matters of common concern. Bertie County was on the Confederate frontier, within reach of the Federal forces at Plymouth. There were no Confederate troops in the area, the Yankees had raided the county several times, Union gunboats had been seen on the nearby Roanoke and Chowan Rivers, and some slaves had escaped to the Federal lines. Pool and the others mulled over these troubling facts and came to some conclusions. Three days later Pool sent a report of the meeting to Governor Zebulon Vance.

"Several months spent in this state of constant danger and anxiety has enabled the thinking men of this county to see what [is] necessary to be done more clearly, perhaps, than can be seen by those at a distance," Pool told the governor. The proximity of the Federal post and the county's vulnerability to raids, he said, posed great dangers. The threat of further slave losses would inevitably force masters to remove themselves and their remaining slaves to the interior. "If the slaveholders, being men of means, flee upon the approach of danger and leave the poorer classes . . . exposed not only to the enemy but to the gangs of runaway slaves, it will produce a state of things and of feeling much to be dreaded. Is it not the duty of the influential slave-holder to remain and to exert himself to preserve social order and to prevent an entire disruption of society?" The only solution, Pool insisted, was to station a military force in the county strong enough to deter slave desertions and fend off Federal raids.

There was still another danger, however. Slaves were not the only ones running off to the Union army. "[T]he attempted execution of [the military conscription] law has driven many [men] of not very reliable character to the enemy at Plymouth," Pool pointed out, "and many more of little better character are in readiness to repair to Plymouth or to the gunboats if its further execution is attempted." There were not enough dependable men left in the community "for efficient police duty." Unless the county was exempted from conscription, the disaffected poor whites, taking advantage of the proximity of the enemy, would become wholly ungovernable. "The substantial men of the county," Pool concluded, "dread to see the others made their enemy."

Such fears plagued people of substance throughout the occupied South, for the coming of the Yankees generated shock waves that threatened to unsettle class relations as thoroughly as they unsettled political and racial relations. Aristocrats and plain folk—like secessionists and Unionists, masters and slaves—found themselves in a radically altered environment with new relations of power, new perils, and new possibilities. . . .

. . . Having found in the South the backward, undemocratic society that their preconceptions had prepared them to find, and having concluded that the continued existence of such a society on American soil would perpetually threaten the Union, the invaders were determined to transform the South, to remake it in the North's image. "The more we learn of the despicable social condition of the South," wrote a Union soldier in North Carolina in 1863, "the stronger appears the need of the purification which, in the Providence of God, comes of the fire and the sword."

Ridding the South of the blight of slavery was the first step toward purification, but several other tasks remained. One was to suffuse the South with Northern ideals and practices. "We have not only to conquer the South," declared the Indiana reformer Lyman Abbott in 1864, "—we have also to convert it. We have not only to occupy it by bayonets and bullets,—but also by ideas and institutions." . . . Northerners acknowledged that the task would be formidable. "It will be no easy matter to awaken aspirations in the minds of [the Southern masses]," wrote a Boston newspaper correspondent in Tennessee in 1862. "They have been so long inert, so long taught to believe that labor is degrading, that rapid progress of Southern society cannot be expected immediately, unless emigration infuses a new vitality into the community."

Indeed, the idea of colonizing the South with industrious Yankees appealed to many Northerners. "The very soil," one soldier remarked, "seems to pray for an infusion of Northern blood and Yankee ingenuity." Immigrants from north of the Mason-Dixon line would spread the gospel of hard work and free labor that had made their country great. New England abolitionist Eli Thayer, who had joined a similar crusade in Kansas in the 1850s, proposed in 1862 to lead a force of several thousand armed Northern settlers into Florida, where they would establish free labor farms, "crowd out slavery," and begin the "economic reconstruction" of the South. Thayer's plan came to naught, but many of the men who traveled south individually to lease abandoned plantations had more in mind than just a fast dollar: they saw themselves as pioneers bringing civilization—in the form of free labor and up-to-date methods of husbandry—to the wilderness. Other Northerners called for similar efforts to invigorate Southern commerce and industry.

The South needed more than just free labor and Yankee enterprise, however. It also needed what one Northerner termed "*moral reconstruction* . . . some radical change in the thoughts, convictions, sentiments and characteristics of the people . . . a change which shall make them, at heart, a better race, and thus fit them to appreciate free institutions and a higher civilization." . . . Northern books must be placed in the hands of the Southern people, Northern-born editors must set the South's newspaper presses humming and proclaim the good news of progress, Northern men of God must carry the true gospel of Christ throughout Dixie.

Northerners heeded these calls. In New Orleans, Memphis, New Bern, and many other places, Northern editors (some of them army officers) established newspapers or, with the cooperation of military authorities, took control of existing secessionist papers. Yankee ministers, missionaries . . . also flocked to the garrisoned towns. In a number of cases obliging commandants deposed Rebel preachers and turned their church buildings over to the newcomers. In New Orleans a group of army chaplains formed the Union Ministerial Association, dedicated to the moral cleansing of that sin-ridden city, and persuaded the military commander to close the saloons, billiard parlors, theaters, and racetracks on Sundays.

Whereas some Northerners were content to let moral suasion by itself transform the heathen South, others argued for a direct assault on the structure of Southern society. The campaign against slavery was one part of that assault, but only one. The North must also march against the Southern aristocracy, that relic of the feudal past, a class that supposedly monopolized wealth and power, tyrannized slaves and poor whites alike, and had broken up the Union for its own nefarious purposes.

Nothing that Northerners saw in the occupied South caused them to modify their long-standing beliefs about the aristocracy. One Northerner in Nashville observed that until the Union army arrived, "the leading families had had things all their own way." Northerners also noted the fervent secessionism and bitter hostility of nearly every aristocrat they met. A soldier in Virginia offered this maxim: "Find a well-dressed lady, and you find one whose hatred [of Yankees] will end only with death."

Aristocratic hegemony must be destroyed, many Northerners agreed. One of Sherman's officers denounced the "selfishness of the so-called 'chivalry,' whose energy and audacity have been [the rebellion's] motive power. . . . [N]othing can secure the safety of the nation short of blotting out their influence, and if necessary their existence, as a class. . . . [They have] from the first lorded it over the South, and would put their foot upon all our necks if they could." An officer in Tennessee put it more succinctly: "the bad rich men," he said, "must feel our power."

While Congress debated the propriety of a systematic program to depose the Southern aristocracy, occupation officials and commanders in the field took matters into their own hands. Many singled out aristocrats for punishment or coercion. In Tennessee, military governor Johnson (who, though a Southerner himself, shared the Northerners' desire to humble the South's elites) arrested a number of the state's most prominent planters, jurists, and politicians and jailed them, in some cases for months, until they took the oath. In Louisiana, General Nathaniel P. Banks ordered "that the leading families who have been strongly identified with secession" must take the oath or go to Rebel territory. A Union general in Tennessee urged that all aristocrats be expelled from the occupied regions, even those who took the oath and posted bond for good behavior: "If they are sent away," he reasoned, "their presence and their influence are gone." Many commanders also targeted the property of aristocrats for seizure or destruction. . . .

With the closed South opened up, slavery eradicated, and the aristocracy brought low, one mission remained: to elevate the degraded white masses. Faced with overwhelming evidence that secessionism and resistance cut across class lines, Northerners had abandoned their original assumption that the Southern plain folk had been tricked or bullied into supporting the rebellion, and they no longer expected the plain folk as a whole to rally spontaneously around the Stars and Stripes as the Unionists and blacks did. But they continued to believe that the mass of Southern whites was a benighted, destitute class ground under the heel of the aristocracy.

Rare was the Yankee who recorded his observations of Southern society during the war without mentioning the degradation of the poor whites. (Most Northerners continued to lump all nonelite Southerners into an undifferentiated mass, which they labeled poor whites.) A Union officer in Falmouth, Virginia, wrote that there were only two families of quality in the town: "As for the rest of the inhabitants, they are what is called poor whites, and are very poor indeed, both mentally and physically." . . . Having spent some time among the people of southeastern Virginia, Lieutenant Colonel Alvin Voris concluded: "Poor white folks, mules, niggers, horned cattle and worn out horses occupy the same glorious level. . . . Southern Society does very well for the aristocracy but for nobody else."

The plight of the poor whites touched the hearts of many Northerners. . . . Northerners . . . were struck by the similarities between the poor whites and the freed slaves and decided that the whites were as worthy of benevolence as the blacks. "Shall we not succor them," asked the Reverend Joseph P. Thompson, of New York, who addressed a meeting of philanthropists in Washington early in 1865. "Shall we not relieve their miseries, and trust that God will soften their hearts . . . ?"

Education was the key, many Northerners believed. Teaching the poor whites to read and write and think would not only elevate them morally and socially, it would also free their minds from the baneful influence of the aristocracy and thus help ensure the future safety of the Union. "[I]f the masses of the people in the south had been properly educated," wrote a Union soldier in Arkansas, "this rebellion would never have arisen[.] [I]t is on account of the ignorance of the people that ambitious demagogues have been able to work on the superstitious credulity of the masses for the advancement of their own ambitious schemes." Idealistic Northerners, many of them women, packed their bags and headed south to uplift the poor whites with the aid of the three Rs. "The whole North must become one mighty nation of teachers," a New Hampshire woman declared, "*then—DisUnion*—can never exist." If the older generation of poor whites was corrupted beyond redemption, the younger generation might still be reached. "Yes," announced the Reverend Mr. Thompson, "I will take this poor, naked, starving boy, no matter who his father was or where he is, I will take him by the hand; . . . I will teach him to read; . . . I will teach him that he has a country. . . . And I will sow that land of rebellion thick with these regenerated children." . . .

If there was a strain of elitist contempt among Northerners in the occupied South, there was also a strain of real radicalism. Some Yankees were determined to incite the poor whites against the aristocracy. Although for some this was simply a social means to a political end—an attempt to win the poor whites to the Union cause by convincing them that the Confederacy was ruled by a despotic planter oligarchy—for others the ultimate goal was nothing less than social revolution. The first issue of the *New Era,* a newspaper published under Federal aegis in Fort Smith, Arkansas, denounced the Southern aristocracy as "that abominable set of men who . . . [have sought] the total enslavement and the subversion of the rights of the great mass of the laboring white population" and looked forward to the day of deliverance. . . .

And so the Yankees embarked on their righteous social crusade in the South. It remained to be seen how Southerners themselves would respond to the Northern agenda, and to the other dangers and opportunities that surfaced in the roiling wake of the Union army.

It was not Yankee manifestos, but hunger and hardship, that first tested the commitment of the plain folk to the old order in the occupied South. Before the war, Southern yeomen as a class had rarely known want. Their economic independence and comfortable, if not luxurious, existence were in fact key props of class unity and social order in the antebellum South. Poor whites, propertyless and unskilled, had enjoyed far less comfort and no independence, but they could always rely on paternalistic aristocrats, generous neighbors, or local government to relieve their suffering, as could any yeoman family that happened to fall on hard times.

All this began to change with the coming of the Northern invaders. Yeomen saw their crops seized, their herds decimated, their shops ransacked, their boats burned. Poor whites were thrown out of work as agriculture, industry, and trade declined. (Aristocrats suffered too, of course, but they generally had greater reserves of provisions or valuables to fall back on than the plain folk had.) The poor, in particular, were often left wholly destitute. In June 1863 a Pennsylvania soldier in northern Virginia spoke with a young woman, an overseer's wife, who "gave me such a story of struggles to keep alive, to get enough to keep from starving, as made all the hard times I have ever seen seem like a life of luxury. I did pity her. On such as she, the poor whites of the South, the burden of this war is heaviest."

In no-man's-land at least, the traditional sources of relief dried up. Aristocrats and other neighbors, hard pressed themselves, could offer little to the sufferers, and the country churches were disrupted and county governments defunct. In the garrisoned towns, municipal governments were in many cases revived, but they were generally in no financial condition to offer relief. In both no-man's-land and the garrisoned towns, therefore, the needy did what they had to do: they appealed to the occupiers for help and thereby, tacitly at least, acknowledged the bankruptcy of the old order.

On the Confederate frontier economic disruption was less severe, local government and communal institutions survived, and formal and informal measures of relief generally continued. But there was still enormous privation, and the plain folk endured more than their share. Another challenge to class unity arose on the frontier in the form of discriminatory Confederate and state legislation, particularly laws exempting large slaveholders from the draft or militia duty. "[T]he Law now makes the rich man superior to the poor," a northern Mississippian complained in 1862, "forcing the poor [to] the [battle]fields, . . . showing to the world that the rich is to[o] good to become food for bullets." Even after such laws were repealed, the fact remained that yeoman and poor white families suffered economically from the conscription or enlistment of husbands and sons far more than did aristocratic families, whose resources of wealth and black labor sustained them.

Everywhere in the occupied South, hardship and want uprooted many of the plain folk. Thousands of men and women—most of them poor whites but some of them yeomen stripped of their livelihood—restlessly roamed the countryside. "Yesterday a man & his wife stopped here & asked for something to eat," wrote Mary Fielding of northern Alabama in the summer of 1862. "They complained bitterly of the hard times; said they were from Giles County [Tennessee] & had *tramped* over three or four counties in search of work but could find none." . . . Other transients followed the Union armies, scavenging in abandoned campsites for scraps of food and clothing.

Increasingly, the displaced plain folk migrated (like the freed blacks) to the garrisoned towns. As the war went on the towns filled with these people, who were, in a sense, refugees-in-reverse, having taken the opposite path from those Southerners who fled to Rebel territory when the Yankees came. By early 1865 an estimated eighty thousand white refugees had come into the Federal lines. Some were Unionists escaping Rebel persecution, others were deserters from the Confederate army; but mostly they were indigent poor whites, dispossessed yeomen, or people of either class who were fed up with the onerous and inequitable demands of the Confederate government. By going to the army posts, these men and women were not proclaiming their conversion to the cause of the Union; they were simply seeking a haven from affliction. William King met one such refugee in Marietta, a man who had been living comfortably on his small farm thirteen miles from town until a gang of Yankee stragglers cleaned him out, forcing him to look for work in the town. . . . Another man traveled to Pensacola from the countryside "for protection"; the Rebel authorities, he said, had "threatened me for keeping my boys from the war." In late 1864, at another post, a Georgia man sought refuge: he had been a railroad engineer, "but since Sherman has destroyed nearly all the railroads in the interior, I thought they might want me to take a musket, so I concluded to leave them."

The Federal policy was generally to accept all such refugees, especially those fleeing Rebel conscription, as long as they were willing to take the oath. At many posts they were housed in special camps or shelters, often at the expense of rich secessionists levied on by the occupation authorities. Even with government support, many refugee camps became scenes of squalid misery, and so Northern humanitarian agencies stepped in to help—notably the American Union

Commission, headed by the Reverend Joseph P. Thompson, which provided food, clothing, blankets, and medicine. The refugees were also objects of earnest attention from the Northern teachers and missionaries who came south to uplift the masses. . . . When the burden of supporting them became too great, the government sent them to Northern cities where they could find employment. . . .

. . . A good many of the plain folk—especially poor whites—both inside and outside the garrisoned towns began seizing opportunities denied them under the old regime. From their perspective, military occupation was in some ways a liberating experience, for it undermined traditional forms of authority and control and knocked aside many of the formal and informal barriers that the South's stratified society put in the way of ambitious plebeians. For these men and women, as for the slaves, Union invasion heralded the "year of jubilee." In Louisiana, poor whites took advantage of the waning power of the planters by trading with blacks on the plantations, a practice strictly prohibited in the old days. An Alabama man living at the post of Huntsville developed a lucrative trade in army horses—most of them stolen or purchased illegally from Union soldiers—and was heard to remark that "now was the time to make a fortune, if he did not do it now before the war was over he never could."

Above all, many of the poor sought to stake a claim to land. So many homesteads had been abandoned in the occupied South that it seemed almost a new frontier, with good land for the taking. In Pointe Coupee Parish, Louisiana, landless whites settled on rich, parish-owned land along the levee that formerly had been leased to planters. On Amelia Island, Florida, the provost marshal noted that a number of farms belonging to men in the Confederate army "have been farmed by white persons who have taken possession of the place." From Bolivar County, Mississippi, came a report that "refugees from the hills are flocking in & settling all the vacant places." . . .

Opportunism unleashed by the breakdown of traditional authority, restlessness provoked by hunger and resentment, radicalism propounded by the Yankees—these ingredients made up a volatile brew. But if it seemed that the occupied South might be primed for an explosion of popular insurgency, there were at the same time factors at work that continued to bind the plain folk to the old elite.

For one thing, the great majority of poor whites and yeomen in the occupied South—even those who accepted food and shelter from the occupiers—continued to view the Yankees as invaders and to join with the aristocracy in opposing the Northern "violation" and "pollution" of their land. Many of them rode side by side with aristocrats in the guerrilla gangs (which carried out attacks not only against Union soldiers but also against the Northern plantation lessees who colonized the South). They proved utterly impervious to Northern attempts to "regenerate" them and turn them into "proper" middle-class citizens on the Yankee model.

Race, too, remained a powerful cohesive force. Whites of all classes stood shoulder to shoulder against the attempts of blacks to gain liberty. . . . Northerners were frequently amazed at the extent to which racism encouraged the Southern plain folk to identify with the slaveowning elite. One recorded a conversation he had in Mississippi with a woman who had never owned a slave "or ever expected to do so": "We-uns didn't want to fight, no-how," she told him when he broached the subject of secession. "You-uns went and made the war so as to steal our niggers."

If race and culture continued to unite plain folk and aristocrats in the occupied South, there were signs that politics and property might yet drive them apart. As the occupation continued, a small but vocal number of citizens began to echo the Northerners' call for social revolution. Almost to a man, they were Unionists—some of them no doubt being among the minority of plain folk who had always resented aristocratic domination, others perhaps converted to radicalism by their brutal treatment at the hands of the Rebels.

Whatever the source of their discontent, those who could do so in safety began to speak out publicly for the overthrow of the old order. On Virginia's eastern shore, citizen J. G. Potts published an appeal to "Mechanics, Tenants, and Laborers," denouncing the "overbearing small-potatoe aristocracy who have governed you most despotically" and urging his readers "to commence with the fifth task of Hercules, and sweep . . . [the aristocracy] out root, stump and branch. Now is the time to trample under foot this petty despotism." An editorial in the *Nashville Daily Times and True Union,* a Unionist newspaper, asserted: "The rapacious slaveocracy have seized all the valuable lands and driven the non-slaveholders from nearly all the soil which is worth possessing. . . . Slavery must be destroyed immediately, . . . in order to produce a division of overgrown farms among the farmers of small means." A letter to the editor in the same newspaper reminded readers of how things were before the Yankees came, when "slaveholders possessed and exercised all social powers. A non-slaveholder was nothing but a poor white man, and his wife and daughters were nothing but poor white trash. . . . Oppressed and cruelly wronged fellow-sufferers, shall we longer remain the base slaves of these cold-hearted aristocratic few?" . . .

In some of the garrisoned towns native and Northern radicals joined hands and tried to create a class-based political movement. In Memphis, the *Union Appeal* published a notice of a political rally intended as a protest not only against the secessionists' "unholy rebellion" but also against Southern aristocrats, who "looked upon all labor as disgraceful, and white laborer as *less* than a negro. . . . Come out, working men, mechanic and laborer; enter your protest against tyranny." In the garrisoned towns of eastern North Carolina, radicals founded Free Labor Associations and enrolled Unionist poor whites and yeomen. . . . The leader of the associations, Charles Henry Foster, a New England native who had moved to North Carolina before the war, announced that he "was pledged, and his oath registered in Heaven, to the extirpation of the accursed negro-driving aristocracy."

The appeal of these populist campaigns was limited. Even among Unionists, the committed radicals and their fellow travelers were a small minority, and most poor whites and yeomen had no wish to be associated with Unionism in any form, whether radical or conservative. But if revolutionary speeches and editorials failed to spark a class-conscious political movement among the plain folk, there was nevertheless growing popular hostility toward aristocrats. Though most humble folk in the occupied South continued to identify the Union army as the principal author of their woes, many came to believe that the aristocracy deserved at least part of the blame. A poor white farm laborer in middle Tennessee complained to Andrew Johnson that "there is a Plenty of [rich] men that helpt get up the rebellion & Promised [poor] men that if they would go into the servis there wives & Children should hav a plenty [to eat] that is [now] a Litting them seffer." A man in Memphis who had deserted from the Confederate army and sought sanctuary in the Union lines explained: "I got tired of fighting for a lot of old Rich Planters. . . . Here I was fighting to save their negroes and property and them remaining at home, living in all the luxuries of li[f]e."

Some of the more resentful plain folk got even with their aristocratic neighbors by informing on them. Planter Colin Clarke in Virginia complained that a number of poor whites in his community had deserted from the Rebel army and returned home and were now "in league with the enemy. . . . They have already carried in lists of the names of gentlemen [who are] rabid secessionists." . . .

Moreover, there were hints that the suffering and the opportunism of the plain folk, especially the poor whites, might ultimately pose a direct threat to people of property. A man living in the northern Virginia countryside reported that the poor were close to starvation while "there are some about here that could spare bread stuff but they wont [except] at high prices"; one citizen he knew had been heard to say that "the suffering females had better raise [up] & take corn by force." An anxious property owner in an area of no-man's-land on the North Carolina coast prayed that the Confederate government would reassert its authority there. . . . A number of poor whites, he said, had been stealing fence rails and threatening to seize farms from their owners: "some of those fellows have already said they will cultivate any mans land they please."

Thus it seemed that resentment and hunger and ambition might do what the appeals of radical Yankees and Unionists could not: set the classes at odds and usher in a new order. But questions remained: how would the defenders of the old order answer these challenges? Would they prove impotent, or did they still command the power to preserve the world as it was?

People of property in the South, especially aristocrats, had always distrusted the poor. . . . "You know the lower classes of [eastern North Carolina] have always been very degraded," remarked one plantation lady in 1863. "They could always be bought." A Confederate general in southern Louisiana spoke for many of that region's elite when he described the poor whites there as a "miserable, mixed breed, commonly called Dagos or Acadians, in whom there is not the slightest dependence to be placed." Indeed, many Southern property owners, especially members of the upper class, pictured the world in the starkest terms, as an arena of unending conflict between haves and have-nots. . . .

Aristocrats had successfully restrained the mob in the antebellum years, and when they perceived dangers to the social order in the wake of Lincoln's election, they had headed off trouble by leading the South out of the Union. But invasion and occupation resurrected those dangers, spawned new ones, and confronted the South's ruling class with its greatest crisis.

Standing on the wide verandas of their homes, aristocrats in the occupied South looked about and were deeply troubled by what they saw. For one thing, continuing privation threatened to drive the plain folk to desperation. (Privation was not unique to the occupied South, of course—it was epidemic in the Confederate interior, too—but it was enormously aggravated in the occupied regions by devastation and economic disruption.) The sympathy that aristocrats expressed for the sufferers was often tinged with nervousness. "The poor people will be in a sad plight here," wrote a North Carolina planter whose neighborhood had just been raided by Federal troops, "& I would not be surprised if there should be a good deal of roguery going on."

Another development that worried aristocrats was the breakdown of authority in no-man's-land, which threatened to untether the villainous impulses of poor whites. A resident of tidewater Virginia denounced certain "men of the low class" who had deserted from the Confederate army and now infested his neighborhood: "Some of them," he averred, ". . . expect to live by stealing." Planters in Jefferson Parish, Louisiana, complained that "there are many white Persons and Negros running about in this Parrish . . . without any ostensible means of a livelyhood and we are daily Robbed of our goods and chattles." Moreover, the numbers of the "dangerous" sort were swelling: every dispossessed yeoman was an addition to the ranks of the propertyless. . . .

Worse yet, it appeared that the Yankees were determined to do exactly what people of substance had long feared they would do: stir up the poor whites, who—dimwitted and devoid of character as they were—would be easily swayed. A North Carolina plantation lady believed that some of the rabble had been enticed into joining the Union army with offers of a share in the spoils of war. She described them as "poor ignorant wretches who cannot resist a fine uniform and the[ir] choice of the horses in the country & liberty to help themselves without check to their rich neighbors belongings."

As lower-class unruliness waxed in the occupied regions, the elite's ability to suppress it waned. Aristocrats had long dominated the South through the exercise of political and economic power and moral authority. But with the coming of the Yankees that power and authority were compromised, especially in the garrisoned towns and no-man's-land.

For one thing, many aristocrats fled the occupied regions when the Federals first appeared or were later banished by them. Furthermore, in garrisoned towns the occupation authorities displaced the political institutions through which aristocrats had wielded power or, if they allowed those institutions to continue, usually deposed aristocratic officeholders, while in no-man's-land political institutions for the most part simply ceased to function. From a political standpoint, the coming of the Union army produced, as one Northerner wrote, "a convulsion, an upheaval," a virtual "earthquake, overturning aristocratic pride, privilege, and power."

The economic emasculation of aristocrats was less abrupt and less complete than their political dethronement, but it was nevertheless telling. Nearly all aristocrats in the occupied regions suffered severe financial losses—not only from military seizures and destruction and the disruption of agriculture and trade, which touched all classes, but also from the loss of slaves and the devaluation of Confederate currency and bonds, which hurt aristocrats especially. "Gloom & despondency [are] on the countenance of all property holders," Tennessee planter John H. Bills reported in the summer of 1862. "Desolation of crops, loss of stock, insurbordination of negroes, runaways & etc. exceed description. No one knows [if] he is worth a cent today." Some were wiped out financially. After repeated Federal raids on his two plantations, a Virginia aristocrat declared that he had "lost nearly every thing I had save my land" and now found himself "poor and needy with a large family dependant on me. . . . I am ruined and undone."

The decline of aristocratic fortunes had significant social consequences. Obviously, the ability of elites to control events through sheer economic might was curtailed. So too was their ability to offer paternal largess to their plebeian neighbors, a custom that, in the past, had worked to forestall popular unrest and to bolster the moral authority of the aristocracy. A Mississippi man whose much-ravaged community was a scene of "great distress among the people" told of a neighboring planter whose "corn-crib, which he has thrown open to the poor with a generous hand, has relieved many suffering families, [but] now that he has given away all that he can possibly spare, I do not know what arrangements the people can make to get their daily bread." The moral authority of aristocrats was weakened, too, when they appealed to the occupiers for relief, as some were eventually forced to do. A Union general on the North Carolina coast reported that he was provisioning not only the poor citizens but also some "who have but lately been in affluent circumstances, but who now have nothing but Confederate notes, city shin-plasters, worthless notes of hand, unproductive real estate, and negroes who refuse to acknowledge any debt of servitude."

The sight of . . . [aristocrats] lining up for Yankee handouts alongside the wretched rabble was no doubt shocking to many people in the occupied South. So, too, was the sight of elite ladies and gentlemen wielding brooms, hoes, washtubs, and milk pails. The loss of their slaves compelled a great many aristocrats to take on unaccustomed duties. "Some planters have not even one servant left," a Louisiana man wrote in 1863. "[W]ives and daughters have to take the pot and tub, the men, where there are any, take to the field with the plough and hoe." Most found such chores not only laborious, but deeply humiliating. "I cannot see how we are to get through the winter," sighed a Tennessee lady who had lost all but one house servant, "for I do *hate* to work. . . . We are all tired *to death* by seven oclock." . . .

Drudgery and beggary were not the only humiliations some aristocrats had to endure. Every day of occupation brought mortifying reminders that their power had been usurped by outsiders and that they could no longer exercise the command they had been born and bred for. Many a proud aristocrat was humbled at the hands of vengeful Yankees or assertive blacks. On the last day of 1862, planter Edward Carter Turner summed up the year's events as the northern Virginia aristocracy had experienced them: "Any lying negro who felt disposed to do so could involve in the most serious difficulties the first men in the land. . . . [E]xcellent & worthy citizens were stripped of property & otherwise shamefully treated [by Federal authorities] upon the testimony of some unprincipled slave." In Tennessee, George A. Washington, one of the South's wealthiest planters, was set upon by a band of Union soldiers at his home and, according to his wife: "For two mortal hours, threats, curses, jeers and taunts . . . were heaped upon him and . . . pistols were snapped in his face and shaken over his head, my prayers and tears were made a scoff and jest, a band of indians could not have taken more devilish delight in tormenting a prisoner." The ultimate humiliation befell William Clopton, described scornfully by the Union officer who arrested him as a "high minded Virginia Gentleman." Clopton was known "as the most cruel Slave Master in this region," the officer reported, and after his arrest a number of his runaway slaves came forward and testified to his brutality. Though Clopton "put on the character of Snivelling Saint" while in custody, the officer decided to administer "Poetical justice." Stripping off Clopton's shirt, he handed a whip to the blacks and watched with satisfaction as four of them "took turns in settling some old scores on their masters back."

Deprived of power, position, and property, many aristocrats, like Clopton, bowed meekly in the presence of the conquerors. "[T]hese people are cowed by the force of the Gov't," declared the Union officer in charge of recruiting black soldiers in Tennessee. "Slaveholders of all classes—[including] . . . the most aristocratic man and the most aristocratic lady—come . . . to talk with me about their slaves, and are the most polite people I ever saw." Some who had been singled out by Federal authorities because of their prominence longed for anonymity. "It is a happy thing these days to be obscure," sighed Elizabeth Harding, of Tennessee, whose husband was under arrest and whose elegant plantation near Nashville was being pillaged almost daily, "and a man's safety now depends on his insignificance; how I envy such quiet and seclusion, as is to be found in the hills and hollows."

The abasement of the aristocracy aggravated the unrest among the plain folk. Old habits of deference to the elite seemed, to some, absurdly out of place in this new world. Why submit to the moral authority of a man who could barely feed his own family, who could not control his slaves, who worked in the fields like a common laborer, who prostrated himself at the feet of the Yankee occupiers?

With their influence withering and disorder spreading, some aristocrats swallowed their pride and called on the occupiers for help. The planters of Jefferson Parish, Louisiana, for example, acknowledging that they had "no available means of suppressing" the outbreak of lower-class thievery in their community, pleaded with the parish provost marshal to form a police patrol. Such appeals were of little avail, however (except in the garrisoned towns). Restlessness and resentment among the lower orders seemed only to grow, fueling in turn the fears of the threatened elite. In 1864 a Mississippi aristocrat described the situation in Yazoo and other counties near the Union lines, which were being inundated by a "filthy, base, disloyal, deserting, stealing, murdering population" that had fled the Confederate interior. "They ought to be hung," he declared. "They pretend to go there to get corn to live on, but their real object is to avoid our army, steal, plunder, and be with the Yankees. I . . . know them to be a base, vile & worthless set who never made a good or honest living. . . . They are all as rotten as Hell." A few weeks later he warned that "this tide is still rolling on, swelling and enlarging." Many of this rabble, he said, have "seized upon [abandoned] places & supplies at will and are exhorting all behind to follow, alledging that they can thus keep out of the army, have plenty to trade with the yankees and ultimately the yankees will reward them with the places they have thus located upon."

Was there even worse in store? Some aristocrats suspected so. As early as February 1862, planter Charles Pettigrew, of Washington County, North Carolina, began carrying a gun. "The low whites are not to be trusted at all," he thought. "They would betray or murder any gentleman." As the months went by, more people of substance in Washington County and across the occupied South watched nervously for signs of insurrection.

The worst nightmares of the aristocracy did not come to pass. The masses did not rise in murderous fury; no tumbrels or guillotines appeared. But if aristocrats' lives were spared, their property was not. Before the war was over, many sections of the occupied South witnessed open assaults on property by the propertyless. Hunger, resentment, and opportunism were the impulses behind these assaults, but it was the disruption of traditional authority that unleashed those impulses.

Open attacks on property were least common in the garrisoned towns, because the Federals—however much they desired to revolutionize Southern society— could not tolerate disorder in their strategic enclaves. No sooner did they capture a town, in fact, than they cracked down on the unruly poor. For example, when Union troops entered Savannah and found (as they had found in other cities abandoned by the Rebel army) "a lawless mob of low whites and negroes pillaging and setting fire to property," their first order of business was to disperse it. Thereafter, in Savannah and other garrisoned towns, the occupation authorities rigorously policed the underclass and responded promptly when trouble broke out.

Even so, people of property in the towns saw ample evidence that the propertyless would eagerly redistribute wealth if they had the chance. A woman who lived in Rome, Georgia, while it was garrisoned in 1864 listed her family's personal property that was "stolen and taken off, some by the Yankees and a great deal by the poor people and negroes, who are almost as bad as Yankees about stealing. . . . [T]he white women would come in Mother's yard in the broad daytime and steal peaches and apples, and she did not dare say anything to them for fear that they would tell the Yankees some great story on her." In another Georgia town poor whites brazenly hauled away furniture and other belongings from houses abandoned by families who had fled the Northern invasion. In some of the towns that the occupiers were forced to evacuate, plundering broke out as soon as the garrison troops marched away.

On the Confederate frontier the propertied classes could, and did, appeal to Confederate and local authorities to rein in the restive underclass. But the authorities were sometimes powerless to act. For one thing, in some sections of the frontier that lay relatively close to Union lines poor whites sought refuge with the invaders and then used the Federal posts as bases for larcenous raids into the frontier. This was the predicament that John Pool and his aristocratic friends eventually faced in Bertie County, North Carolina. "[D]isorderly white persons have left here & congregated at [the post of] Plymouth," Pool wrote in July 1863. From there, he said, they found it easy to return to the county by river and "commit depredations." He cited one instance in which "pirate bands from Plymouth" robbed a plantation of fifteen thousand dollars' worth of property. A Florida citizen reported in 1864 that a number of poor white families in his community had gone to the Union lines and many others were preparing to go, spurred by a rumor that the Federals were offering provisions, free homesteads, and cash rewards for cattle and slaves driven in from the frontier. . . .

Even some of the poor who remained on the frontier dared to strike against the propertied, emboldened by the proximity of the Union army. In Cherokee County, Alabama, Sarah Espy reported that as one of her neighbors was threshing wheat, a group of poor white women "came and impressed 70 bush[els] of it. This looks like a bold thing, but we shall hear of more no doubt." John Pool noted that several gangs of draft dodgers were lurking about Bertie County and committing robberies; one party had visited the home of a widow and confined her in her house while they broke into her food stores. "No military force can reach them," Pool explained, "because as soon as they become [alarmed] they will go over to the enemy, either by crossing the Chowan or by signalling some passing gunboat in the Roanoke."

When Union troops passed through on one of their occasional forays into the frontier regions, some poor whites abandoned all restraint. A Louisiana planter returned home after a raid had disrupted his community and "found that my . . . place had been broken up & robed by the disserters—rogues who have long infested the neighborhood—and every thing taken off the place which could be moved." Workers at a gristmill in North Carolina took advantage of a raid to pillage their employer's supplies, stealing bacon and other goods that they concealed when the employer later came looking for them. . . .

It was in no-man's-land, where anarchy reigned, that the restless poor were least inhibited. The countryside surrounding Plymouth, for example, witnessed repeated assaults on property by propertyless whites, some of whom were enrolled as Unionist home guards or Federal soldiers. "[S]hortly after you left," a correspondent informed Josiah Collins, who had left his large Washington County plantation in charge of an overseer, "the Union men . . . united and bid defyance to ownership of property . . . and went plundering and destroying with impunity in every direction." The estates of Collins and other planters, and even the farms of some of the more prosperous yeomen, were stripped of crops, livestock, equipment, fencing, and furniture. Another friend told Collins of depredations by the Union army but added that families in the neighborhood were guilty, too: "many of the country people have supplied themselves with corn from your plantation & several of [your stolen] horses have not gone far from home." In many cases personal property that was not carried away was maliciously wrecked. A number of poor whites in the Plymouth region squatted defiantly on planters' land and claimed it for themselves—sometimes provoking violent confrontations with blacks who had the same idea.

One of the most dramatic poor white uprisings in no-man's-land took place in the eastern highlands of middle Tennessee, at a place known as Beersheba Springs. Aristocratic families had been vacationing there since the 1850s, staying at the large resort hotel or in private cottages and enjoying the restorative waters. In the summer of 1863 a number of aristocrats, including Virginia French, gathered at Beersheba believing that the area was safe. They were unaware that the local poor whites, whom they condescendingly dubbed the "mountain people," had grown mutinous.

French's diary vividly records the events of that summer. Beginning in June there were reports of lawless bands in the neighborhood (French suspected that they might be renegade Yankees or Confederate deserters), and three times in July robber gangs struck at the resort. On the third occasion French noted her suspicion that "the mountain people assisted too." The next day all doubts disappeared. "Scenes enacted here today beggar description," French wrote:

> Early in the morning the sack of the place began. . . . [T]he mountain people came in crowds and with vehickles of all sorts and carried off everything they could from both hotel and cottages. . . . Gaunt, ill-looking men and slatternly, rough barefooted women stalking and racing to and fro, eager as famished wolves for prey, hauling out furniture—tearing up matting and carpets. . . . A band would rush up and take possession of a cottage—place a guard, drive off every one else, stating that this was theirs.

French saw one woman enter a cottage and carry away Latin, French, and theology books: "The woman, who did not know a letter to save her life, said 'she had some children who were just beginin' to read and she wanted the books for them—she wanted to encourage em!'" At another cottage a group of mountain people "held an orgie the whole night, singing, shouting, and it is believed dancing." " '[T]he masses' had it all their own way on this memorable day," French concluded, "—the aristocrats went down for the nonce." The next day the mountain people returned for more plunder, and they made sporadic raids throughout the summer.

As sensational as such episodes were, the conflict that they evidenced was singularly muted. Of all the struggles that convulsed the occupied South—including those of Rebels versus Yankees, secessionists versus Unionists, and whites versus blacks—the struggle of the propertied versus the propertyless was the most restrained. Dead bodies of insurgent poor whites did not litter the countryside as the bodies of insurgent blacks and Unionists and invading Yankees did.

The reason is probably this: despite their oft-expressed fears, aristocrats came to understand that the unruly plain folk did not fundamentally threaten the social order. The poor and dispossessed overwhelmingly rejected real radicalism and violence against persons. Their vision of the year of jubilee did not embrace revolution; they demanded merely a less inequitable share of sustenance, property, and opportunity than was their customary lot. And only a minority of the underclass made even those limited demands; most just endured their fate in silence and tried to get along the best they could with the little they had.

Perhaps things would have turned out differently if the war had continued beyond the spring of 1865. The further agitation of the plain folk, and the further degradation of the aristocracy, might well have snapped the weakened but still intact bonds of deference and paternalism that united the white South. If so, then Appomattox signaled not the extinction, but indeed the salvation, of the old order.

FOR FURTHER STUDY

1. What important changes did some Northerners think were necessary for the South to be truly reformed? Why? In what ways were some of the initiatives revolutionary? Do you think these ideas reflected Northern feelings of cultural superiority?

2. What was the state of poor whites in the occupied areas? Who could they go to for relief?

3. How did resentment, hunger, and ambition make some Southerners challenge the aristocracy? How did they get back at them?

4. What did the aristocrats think of poorer residents? What power and control did they lose? What were they forced to do to get by? How were some, especially Clopton, treated for their former deeds?

5. How was the property of aristocrats treated in the garrisoned towns? On the frontier? In the no-man's-land? At Beersheba Springs?

6. What limited the actions of the unruly plain folk?

FOR FURTHER READING

For general materials on the Civil War see For Further Reading for 20. For the political side see Ralph H. Wooster, *Politicians, Planters, and Plain Folk: Courthouse and Statehouse in the Upper South, 1850–1860,* (1975). For Northerners in the South see Lawrence Powell, *New Masters: Northern Planters during the Civil War and Reconstruction,* (1980) and Richard N. Current, *Northernizing the South,* (1983). For one community see Wayne K. Durrill, *War of another Kind: A Southern Community in the Great Rebellion,* (1990). Randall C. Jimerson, *The Private Civil War: Popular Thought during the Sectional Conflict,* (1988). For a city see Gerald M. Capers, *Occupied City, New Orleans under the Federals, 1862–1865,* (1965).

CHAPTER 22

Culver Pictures, Inc.

Cartoonist Thomas Nast's comment on the racial violence that swept the South during Reconstruction.

Political Violence During Reconstruction

Samuel C. Hyde, Jr.

$\mathcal{W}$hen the Civil War came to an end after four long and bloody years, the United States faced the daunting problems of repairing the various damages the war had brought and creating a new foundation for the nation's future. Many of the problems centered in the defeated South. Not only had the war brought widepread physical and economic devastation to the section, but it was also necessary to fashion a new political system to replace the Confederacy, to decide how and when to readmit the Southern states to full political partnership in the Union, and, perhaps most daunting of all, to devise ways of incorporating four million ex-slaves into the economic, social, and political structure of the South on a basis other than slavery.

Shortly after the war ended, many in the North concluded that, despite their defeat, those in control in the South were determined to keep things as they had been before the war. That included keeping African Americans in a status as close to slavery as they could devise. Accordingly, under the political leadership of the Radical Republicans in Congress, the federal government created the Freedmen's Bureau to provide various kinds of aid for ex-slaves, oversaw Southern state governments, imposed qualifications for voting and other forms of political activity that temporarily excluded many prominent ex-Confederates, created stringent conditions for readmitting the Southern states to the Union, and in the meantime treated the South as conquered territory with federal troops acting as what amounted to an occupying army. All this was in the hope of creating a new political situation in the South and making secure the new rights of ex-slaves to full citizenship that supposedly became law with the adoption of the Thirteenth, Fourteenth, and Fifteenth Amendments to the Constitution.

In the end, however, the effort to impose a new social and political order on the South failed. The following selection offers some insights about the reasons for this failure. It deals with a small part of the South, the so-called Florida parishes (counties) in the "piney woods" section of southeastern Louisiana, but similar events occurred throughout the South and ultimately they meant that Reconstruction would not result in the political and social transformation of the South that some Northerners hoped to accomplish.

The catastrophe that secession and the war represented for all white social classes in eastern Louisiana . . . encouraged the plain folk to reassess their fealty to the planters. Linus Parker declared that his reflection on the events leading to secession and its results had led him to "wonder at the hollowness of the whole affair." In a chilling reference to the piney-woods tradition of political powerlessness, the Greensburg *Weekly Star and Journal* urged its readers to action by declaring. "You will have a government made for you if you do not make it for yourself." The *St. Helena Echo* reminded the people that the man who works the land has always been oppressed by "class legislation" initiated by the "lordly planters." Calls for the revival of the independent, self-sufficient life-style that characterized the region in less complicated times proved a popular theme of the piney-woods press during the immediate postwar period. The Greensburg *Journal* exhorted a revival of Jeffersonian principles to liberate the people from the manipulation that led to war, ruin, and subsequent exploitation by Yankees, proclaiming, "Home manufacturing is the true road to independence." Likewise, the Amite City *Democrat* reminded its readers of the near utopian existence inherent in the independent and self-sufficient piney-woods way of life. Many newspapers equated the prevailing deprivation with the people's abandonment of self-sufficiency for the unpredictable and dependent circumstances of the market economy. The *East Feliciana Patriot* urged farmers to plant corn, not cotton: "We never did right in so tilling our soil as to enrich others at our expense and we can never reach that level of independence as long as we allow that great mine of wealth, our soil [to] lie dormant. The surest way of relieving ourselves of debt and becoming independent is to raise everything our soil and climate can afford for human consumption."

The resurgent republican ideal demanded that piney-woods farmers free themselves from all agents of exploitation. This included their northern conquerors as well as their planter overlords, who, many plain folk appeared increasingly willing to believe, had manipulated them. Osyka resident J. W. Courtney argued that the poor had fought and suffered through the war merely to support the life-style of the rich. Proclaiming his refusal to submit further to planter selfishness, Courtney

Reprinted by permission of Louisiana State University Press from *Pistols and Politics: The Dilemma of Democracy in Louisiana's Florida Parishes, 1810–1899,* by Samuel C. Hyde, Jr. Copyright © 1988 by Louisiana State University Press.

declared, "I am determined in my mind not to serve them [planters] any longer they have allways [*sic*] made laws to oppress the poor." Cotton increasingly came to be seen as the tool for exploiting the less privileged. Deliverance from the shackles of King Cotton became synonymous with independence in the piney-woods press. The *St. Helena Echo* declared, "Wealth and prosperity will come only through independence and independence will come only through agricultural diversity." Other country newspapers, such as the *East Feliciana Patriot* and the Magnolia *Gazette,* urged farmers to plant food crops in order to break the cycle of dependence and limit the wealth of rich manufacturers.

Calls for economic independence, coupled with the results of the immediate postwar elections and the commanding presence of the federal military, created conditions favorable to political realignment in eastern Louisiana. As they had in the 1850s, however, the planters would again delay the arrival of realistic democracy in the piney woods by identifying and promoting fear of another common enemy of southern whites. Planter preeminence, though now subject to an alliance with the increasingly powerful merchant-professional class, who also demanded racial unity and home rule, resurfaced in the face of a determined common enemy. Henry Clay Warmoth, a Republican organizer and successor to Governor Wells, correctly surmised that the old elite intentionally fostered hatred in order to maintain its power. According to Warmoth, Louisiana's problem lay "in the contumacy of the old ruling aristocracy, who believe that they were born to govern, without question, not only their slaves but the masses of the white people." By capitalizing on reinforced racial fears and lingering hatred for the Yankees, the elite again presented itself as the protector of the common man. Carpetbaggers, northerners who supposedly carried all their belongings in a satchel made of carpet material as they came south to exploit the defeated region, and local people who supported the efforts of the Republican party, known derisively as scalawags, provided excellent scapegoats. The old elite aggressively promoted contempt for the Republicans and their supporters. One Democratic party circular declared, "Most ill disposed negroes are not half so much deserving our aversion and non-intercourse with them as the debased whites who encourage and aid them, and who become through their votes the office holding oppressors of the people. Whatever of resentment you have should be felt toward the latter and not the colored men." Such statements, typical in the immediate postwar period, implied that the Republicans, not the freedmen, constituted the real enemy. . . . Although significant evidence demonstrates that the piney-woods aversion for rule of the elite had resurfaced, racial fears and the new common enemy would again delay the ramifications of this resentment. . . .

The prevailing perception that many among the prewar elite had been disenfranchised provided the old aristocracy with a powerful propaganda tool. Denying landholding freemen suffrage comprised a fundamental violation of the piney-woods tradition of republicanism. The old elite presented themselves as victims of tyrannical outsiders who sought not to create equality between the races but indeed to make blacks dominant in order to serve their own special ends. The transition in popular perceptions regarding the planter elite would prove decisive in determining the outcome of Radical Reconstruction in Louisiana. Racial solidarity and hostility to outsiders again secured the old elite against the potential for social upheaval. Latent antagonism between white social classes would remain dormant until the common enemy was subdued. . . .

For blacks and white Republicans the advent of Radical Reconstruction represented an unprecedented opportunity. With the future in their own hands, few would willingly relinquish their newfound power, and many would fight to retain it. Most regarded the limitations of some of their number as a product of decades of misrule and brutal oppression. Most local whites, though, viewed the changing circumstances not merely as a loss of control over their own destinies but as an affront to the very idea of order and government. And in eastern Louisiana, as in other areas of the South, the last months of the war had demonstrated an effective means of dealing with a perceived oppressor. With such a vast chasm between the opponents and such bitter lessons learned, the struggle was certain to be painful.

Violence characterized the Florida parishes from the very outset of Reconstruction. Freedmen's Bureau agents, Federal soldiers, and blacks all suffered frequent attacks. The day after the second attempt on his life, Lieutenant Edward Ehrlich reported, "Outrages are committed daily at Amite City." During the summer and fall of 1865, at least sixteen shootings and stabbings occurred in the eastern Florida parishes. Dozens of incidents of assault, battery, and intimidation also were reported. In the few cases local law enforcement sought to prosecute, it failed miserably, often in comical fashion. A jury acquitted George Story of shooting a black woman based on his assertion that he was actually shooting at another man down the street from the victim. The jury apparently not only lacked sympathy for the victim but also considered Story's intentions justifiable.

Federal authorities also proved incapable of dealing with the scope of the violence. Insufficient manpower and a sluggish bureaucracy ensured that before enough evidence could be gathered in one case, several more startling incidents had occurred. Civil authorities refused to share information from ongoing criminal investigations with federal troops and only reluctantly responded to federal demands. The vast majority of local whites refused to cooperate with federal authorities in any way. When summoned to appear before the local Freedmen's Bureau agent, Amite City resident Mark Day responded simply, "To hell with the Yankee."

Although blacks suffered greatly from acts of violence, many proved willing to defend themselves, and others resorted to violence to obtain their own ends. Many blacks who spoke in support of the Democrats became victims of black-on-black terror. Only moments after Stephen Durden, a black resident of Livingston Parish, completed a speech supporting the Democrats, a group of freedmen shot and killed him on a public highway. Such incidents increased in the wake of the September, 1867, election. After touring Washington Parish, Freedmen's Bureau agent W. H. Haugen observed that many blacks refused to work, instead resorting to theft, and were "a perfect terror to the country." Armed freedmen also seized several plantations in East Feliciana and St. Helena parishes, threatening to kill anyone who interfered with their operations. Under the heading "An Ugly Sight," the Amite City *Democrat* described the passion of a particular black woman for carrying "a tremendous navy six shooter" with her about the streets of Amite City in search of a "white man who gave her a drubbing." The article concluded, "We hope some of her colored friends will prevail upon her to leave the ugly weapon at home and use the law to protect her." White Republican officials were often accused of instigating these acts of violence. Governor Wells faced accusations that he provided immunity to those who murdered his political enemies.

The level of violence increased dramatically with the emergence of several paramilitary organizations. Prior to this development, despite the presence of numerous thinly disguised "rifle clubs" and other politically inclined groups, most violent incidents had been random acts between individuals. In the wake of the July, 1866, New Orleans race riot, which amounted to no less than a slaughter of blacks by armed whites, however, the necessity of black defensive preparations was manifest. During the spring and summer of 1867, Republican organizers from New Orleans worked aggressively to establish politically inclined self-defense organizations known as Loyal League Clubs among the blacks in eastern Louisiana. Increasing acts of violence against the freedmen, such as the seemingly daily incidents at Amite City, and inequitable labor practices encouraged a newfound militancy and willingness to defend themselves. Throughout the summer of 1867, local Freedmen's Bureau agents and federal officers reported growing political agitation among the freedmen. White residents became increasingly tense with the discovery of each new "incendiary" tract issued by the New Orleans Radical Club, headed by Warmoth and others. Warmoth created near panic in February, 1868, when he proclaimed before a black audience in New Orleans that exConfederates were "traitors and treason under the Constitution is punishable by death." Union army veteran A. J. Sypher confessed that his formation of a black militia in Rapides Parish "greatly exasperated the majority of the white people in the parish." By August, 1867, Freedmen's Bureau agent James Hough reported that blacks increasingly left work to attend political meetings "where incompetent negroes [created] insubordinate feelings." Hough further noted that armed groups of blacks regularly established picket posts along the public roads and that "travellers passing by [were] halted and subjected to annoyance." Suspicions of impending trouble became a reality in the volatile circumstances surrounding the September, 1867, election.

One of the most militant black paramilitary organizations emerged in western St. Helena Parish. This Loyal League Club embodied the recognition among many blacks that realistic protection from increasing racial attacks rested with themselves. Led by a mulatto farmer named Thomas Turner, the group created consternation by publicly parading with arms and threatening local whites. Hough described Turner as "very troublesome and the terror of all whites in his neighborhood." In the summer of 1867, Turner announced that he had received authority from the commanding officer of the local federal garrison "to hang all the whites." On the roads in lower St. Helena he posted pickets who loudly proclaimed their intentions. On the eve of the September 27, 1867, election, Turner mobilized his forces. Rather than marching on Greensburg as local residents expected, Turner instead headed for Amite City. During the afternoon of September 27, he arrived outside the town at the head of an armed band, which estimates placed at anywhere from 50 to 250. Major James Offley, commanding the federal garrison, informed the militiamen that they would not be permitted to enter the town as an armed body. To the horror of local whites, Offley allowed the blacks to conceal their weapons and march into town en masse. Turner's men voted with out incident, then camped on the outskirts of town for several days as a demonstration of their resolve.

In permitting Turner's militia to enter Amite City as an organized body and to camp on the outskirts of town, Offley outraged local whites, most of whom proved unwilling or unable to make the connection between black assertiveness and the daily incidents of racial violence perpetuated against the freedmen. Turner had boasted that he was authorized to hang any whites who interfered with his group, and many residents considered the federal commander's actions irrational. Many also remained incensed that Yankee planters had provided arms to some of their black laborers. The Amite City *Times* and other local newspapers angrily contrasted General Sheridan's orders to break up meetings supporting hospitals and monuments for Confederate veterans with his tolerance of secret meetings by armed blacks. The *Times,* though continuing to profess confidence in Major Offley's intentions, declared its own intentions: "The whites can not and will not sit idle and see their families butchered by barbarians. Self defense is God's gift—a deduction from the gift of existence itself."

Limited evidence does indicate that secret white paramilitary organizations functioned in Louisiana prior to the winter of 1867 or the spring of 1868. In a November, 1865, address to the state legislature, Governor Wells announced, "Secret political associations, the members of which are bound to each other by strange oaths, and recognize each other by signs and passwords, are being revived in this city [New Orleans] with affiliations in the parishes throughout the state." Wells failed to speculate on the motives of these secret organizations, nor did he provide any evidence to support his allegations. If the evidence is sparse concerning white paramilitary organizations statewide, even less exists to indicate their presence in the Florida parishes prior to the first months of 1868. It should be noted that white-on-black violence remained so universal and difficult to prosecute that prior to 1868 there was no need for organized white terrorist groups. Substantial evidence indicates that the explosive conditions surrounding the elections in the fall of 1867 and the spring of 1868 promoted the rapid growth of white secret societies across Louisiana. Although many supporters of these groups insisted that they emerged as a response to black assertiveness, they clearly functioned less for self-defense and more as mechanisms for the maintenance of white supremacy. The Knights of the White Camellia and the Ku Klux Klan emerged as the principal groups to fulfill this mission.

Historians have frequently misunderstood the relationship between these two white supremacy organizations. Despite the recurrent misconceptions, both groups functioned separately, with different methods, if not different purposes. In the winter of 1867 and 1868, the first reports of a Ku Klux Klan in Louisiana began to circulate. Organized in Tennessee in 1866, the Klan initially functioned as a social club for Confederate veterans. By early 1867 Klan members had recognized that their secrecy enabled them to function effectively as regulators as well. Ample evidence suggests that by the spring of 1868 several Klan dens existed in the Florida parishes as well as in upstate Louisiana and southwestern Mississippi. The Klan combined an unqualified commitment to white supremacy with a murderous contempt for aspiring blacks and white Republicans. Terror served as the weapon of choice for Klansmen. Murder, arson, and intimidation all played an integral role in the Klan's nightly adventures. Their violent activities demanded absolute secrecy; few ever admitted membership. Klansmen in eastern Louisiana conformed to the stereotype of white-hooded and shrouded specters who traveled late at night and terrorized with impunity.

The Ku Klux Klan's obsessive secrecy has caused some historians to question its existence in Louisiana during Reconstruction or to assume that it functioned as the more popularly recognized Knights of the White Camellia. In contrast to the Klan, though, the White Camellia originated in Louisiana with slightly different intentions. Whereas the former combined fealty to white superiority with a determination to terrorize its enemies into submission, the latter incorporated a similar commitment to white supremacy into a political and economic agenda. Although equally brutal in their condemnation of assertive blacks and white Republicans, the Knights of the White Camellia who operated in the Florida parishes seldom engaged in terror. Instead, they typically incorporated menacing persuasion with economic intimidation to achieve political ends. The combination of the terror of the Klan and the economic strangulation of the Knights proved a powerfully persuasive arrangement.

Members of the White Camellia openly admitted their affiliation, though the very same men denied any knowledge of the Klan. Local residents apparently felt justified in their determination to preserve the superiority of the white race but proved reticent in discussing an organization that encouraged murder. When congressional investigators in the spring of 1869 repeatedly insisted that the Knights of the White Camellia constituted nothing more than a pseudonym for the Ku Klux Klan, prominent Tangipahoa merchant Charles Kennon exploded: "I know that it is not the Ku Klux. I have never heard it called so." Some residents belonged to both, but the different oaths they took for these groups indicate their contrasting emphases. In swearing loyalty to the White Camellia, one committed himself to "defending the social and political superiority of the white race and in all places to observe a marked distinction between the white and African races." Furthermore, initiates pledged to "vote for none but white men for any position of honor, profit or trust, and to protect and defend persons of the white race against the encroachments and aggressions of an inferior race." Although it contained an extreme commitment to racial superiority and required an apparent willingness to defend that principle, the oath did not include an overt call to violence. A Klansman pledged to "reject and oppose the principles of the radical party in all its forms, and forever maintain that intelligent white men shall govern this country." After swearing to protect "females, widows and their households," the Klansman further pledged his life: "[I will] obey all instructions given me by my chief, and should I ever divulge or cause to be divulged any secrets, signs or passwords of the Invisible Empire, I must meet with the fearful and just penalty of the traitor, which is death, death, death, at the hands of my brethren." Although abundant evidence demonstrates the violent activities of the Klan, no available evidence indicates that the Knights of the White Camellia participated in violent activities in the Florida parishes.

During the course of Reconstruction, Florida-parish blacks endured constant physical assaults, continual efforts to retain them as virtual slaves, sustained discrimination in all areas, and universal denial of long-overdue civil rights. Without the backing of guns, their desire to enjoy the fruits of liberation from bondage would have ensured their destruction in eastern Louisiana. Yet their organized efforts to protect themselves did result in extreme racial sensitivity on the part of whites long accustomed to black passivity and subordination. By fanning the flames of this racial hysteria, the old elite recovered much of their influence. The near universal support among whites attained by the postwar leadership enabled these men aggressively to pursue their primary purpose, recovery of political control. As in the antebellum period, though, not all whites shared the same priorities. If most whites feared black empowerment and demanded government led by native conservatives, the divergence in priorities exemplified by the nebulous distinctions between the White Camellia and the Klan symbolized a contrast between the white groups that was central to the chaotic conditions of the late nineteenth century. The two organizations shared many of the same ideals and members, but in eastern Louisiana political control proved primary to the White Camellia, whereas Klansmen typically regarded racial dominance as preeminent. The differences in the priorities and methods of these two groups contributed to a growing schism between piney-woods whites in the late nineteenth century from which emerged violently competitive factions.

The distinctions between the two organizations sharpen when their day-to-day operations are examined. The membership of the White Camellia represented the best elements of white society. Most of their leaders in eastern Louisiana, including Tom and John Ellis, John Pipes, and J. B. McClendon, represented the emerging business and professional class, which provided leadership in the immediate postwar period. Others, such as former state senator and Washington Parish patriarch Hardy Richardson, exemplified the old elite's commitment to the movement. The Klan's obsessive secrecy makes identifying members difficult, but the few in eastern Louisiana whose membership is certain differed from the Knights: they were younger, less affluent, and largely detached from sources of power. Tom Ellis referred to the Klansmen simply as "drinking characters." Other possible Klansmen, such as Robert Babington, a Franklinton businessman and postmaster, represented those associated with both organizations.

In the weeks preceding the November, 1868, election, both white societies initiated offensives that exemplified their respective practices. Having failed in the spring of 1868 to achieve victory through legal means, the Democrats determined to triumph through extralegal activities. The *Daily Picayune* declared in the immediate aftermath of the April election, "The next time an election takes place we will be prepared, and their [Republicans'] intimidation game will not be a very safe one." The most hotly disputed contest in addition to the presidential election and a few local races involved the selection of a congressman from eastern Louisiana. That race pitted an aging Louis St. Martin against a carpetbagger general J. H. Sypher, in a bitter contest characterized by massive fraud and violence.

The white conservative campaign incorporated economic intimidation, psychological terror, and murder. One technique involved a systematic economic lockout of blacks who voted Republican. Acting at the behest of the Knights of the White Camellia, local Democratic executive committees issued protection papers to freedmen who voted Democratic. The papers identified the individual as a Democratic voter who was therefore entitled to retain his employment and to receive valuable services provided by Democrats such as corn grinding and credit extension. Local newspapers and power brokers promoted this effort relentlessly in the weeks preceding the November election. According to congressional testimony, the owners of the Magee Mill and Lumber Company in Washington Parish distributed flyers informing the freedmen that the mill would no longer grind their corn or cut their timber if they failed to vote Democratic. Isham McGee, a black resident of Washington Parish, confirmed that many freedmen voted Democratic simply to avoid losing their jobs or essential services. The Democrats circulated a petition among whites getting them to pledge that they would not buy from or sell to blacks who failed to vote Democratic. Those who refused to sign came under immediate suspicion. In the Florida parishes as in other regions of the South, voting Republican carried a stiff price.

Another part of the Democratic strategy involved the use of terror. This aspect of the multifaceted campaign of intimidation fell to the Ku Klux Klan. To fulfill their part of the scheme, the Klan employed tactics designed to eliminate black leadership and inspire fear in their Republican opponents. During the interim between the April and November elections, the Klan sought to "turn over" Republican activists. Johnson E. Yerks, a leading St. Helena Parish Republican, informed a congressional investigating team that several prominent blacks presented letters urging them to "turn over" or face death. Yerks himself received a menacing letter signed only "KKK." Headed "Crow Hall Midnight," the letter warned that Yerks was suspected of Radical principles and should beware the hour of midnight. Other prominent Republicans received similar letters. H. H. Bankston testified that the Klan placed cards with mystic warnings on his door and those of other known Republicans. As the election neared, the Klan began making nightly raids in full costume. Black Washington Parish residents Isham Buckhalter and Isham McGee received midnight visits from large groups of Klansmen. Both declared that the Klansmen "dressed in sheets from the top of their heads to their horses' heels" and "wore false faces." The nightriders warned the blacks to vote Democratic or die. Buckhalter testified that blacks knew the Klan members were men and not ghosts but added that most believed they would be killed if they voted Republican.

Republican activists had good reason to fear the Klan. In the two weeks preceding the November election, armed Klansmen in groups fifty to one hundred strong made nightly rides through the streets of Greensburg and Franklinton, creating fear and consternation among friend and foe alike. Other groups of Klansmen made discreet yet menacing midnight rides near the homes of Republican organizers. Even more disturbing, Klansmen unexpectedly dynamited trees late in the evening near Republican homes, greatly heightening the anxiety of the inhabitants. William H. Wilder and H. H. Bankston both declared that the "tree burstings" created extreme fear among local Republicans, black and white. Wilder described panicked families huddled in their homes, waiting to be attacked and afraid to venture out for sustenance, much less to vote. Word circulated later that the tree burstings served as a signal to Klansmen that the election should proceed without violent interruption, indicating that the Klan recognized their campaign of terror had been successful. With little physical harm, the Klan's nocturnal activities effectively neutralized a significant portion of the Republican electorate.

Some black leaders, however, refused to "turn over," so in the days immediately preceding the election, the Klan, seemingly exasperated by their intransigence, systematically eliminated the black and significantly weakened the white Republican leadership. Congressional candidate J. H. Sypher emerged as the principal candidate for elimination. Sypher, widely regarded as ruthless and opportunistic, along with his brother had engineered the appointment to local office of numerous Republicans in eastern Louisiana. His frequent speeches to largely black audiences encouraging self-defense and support for the Republican party enraged many whites in the Florida parishes.

Ten days before the November election, armed groups of whites broke up Republican meetings at Greensburg and Tangipahoa, where Sypher had planned to speak. Rumors circulated that prominent Republicans, including Sypher and John Kemp, president of the local black Republican club, would be killed that night. Learning of the rumors, Sypher wisely cut short his visit to Greensburg and canceled his appearance at Tangipahoa. Kemp received a final warning, which he answered with a telegram to Governor Warmoth requesting troops. Unfortunately for Kemp, his message fell into the hands of Klansmen, who intercepted the youth attempting to send it in a nearby village. Late that evening a body of Klansmen crossed the state line below Osyka, Mississippi, heading south. The Klan routinely employed neighboring dens in extreme cases in order to hamper identification. The nightriders entered the village of Tangipahoa and inquired at the hotels for Sypher. Learning of the absence of their prize, they proceeded to Kemp's home outside of town and murdered him. Six days later, Jim Beekham, leader of a black militia forming in western Washington Parish, met a similar fate. Black Republican organizers Squire Roberts and Mumford McCoy barely escaped with their lives. The Republican mayor of Amite City placed Roberts under arrest for disturbing the peace on election day and probably saved his life. McCoy, a Greensburg blacksmith and legislative candidate, received a postelection visit from a group of white men who denounced his activism. The visitors warned McCoy that if any whites should be harmed, he would be held personally responsible and that as retribution the Klan would cut off his head. McCoy understandably fled the parish the same day. Many other less prominent freedmen suffered similar abuses, including Bill Wheeler, whose eyes were gouged out at Greensburg, and Daniel Lee and Marshall Thompson, both bushwhacked near Amite.

In addition to Sypher, the Klan also targeted other prominent white Republicans. James B. Wands, a former Union naval officer from New York, aroused the ire of Democrats by securing from Warmoth appointments as local tax collector and state representative. If the onerous burden of Reconstruction taxation did not in itself condemn Wands, his aggressive support of the Republican cause did. In the days preceding the November election, Wands distributed Republican ballots in Livingston, St. Helena, and Washington Parishes. Warned of a plot to kill him, Wands fled Franklinton the evening before the election and camped in the woods as Klansmen searched the area. David Hennessy, a member of Warmoth's newly created Metropolitan Police Force and a registrar of voters in Washington Parish, was not so lucky. The day before the election, the third attempt to kill Hennessy proved successful. Mass torchlight counterdemonstrations by Republicans and Democrats in Clinton and Jackson avoided bloodshed only because both sides recognized the horrific casualties that could result. Describing a provocative Democratic procession near Olive Branch in East Feliciana Parish that stumbled into a similar Republican procession, Willie Dixon declared, "We came very near having a bloody battle with them." A timely absence from the region was all that saved Republican congressman J. P. Newsham of West Feliciana from death at the hands of an outraged mob. Numerous bloody encounters between individuals contributed to an incredibly high level of tension by election day in the Felicianas and East Baton Rouge. In the wake of massive election-day violence and fraud, Freedmen's Bureau agent J. W. Coleman reported from Baton Rouge that "the Bureau appears to be the only protection the freedmen have."

The pressure applied to black voters came from friend and foe alike. To counter Democratic threats and intimidation, white Republicans warned that blacks who failed to vote, and vote Republican at that, would not receive their share of land and mules. Republicans routinely promised the freedmen that once they were in power, their supporters would be appropriately compensated. Moreover, the federal garrisons increasingly demonstrated an unwillingness to intervene on behalf of black Republicans. Prominent Republican William Wilder declared, "The soldiers are worse on the negroes than anybody else." Thus, blacks had the option of risking their lives by voting Republican or of forfeiting their only realistic hope for economic advancement by voting Democratic. Unfortunately for the freedmen, this unenviable predicament would only get worse.

The 1868 Democratic campaign of terror proved remarkably successful. By employing the lessons in brutality learned from the war, the Democrats effectively neutralized much of their opposition. Political violence claimed the lives of at least 204 black and white Republicans statewide. Rowdy, armed Democrats congregated about most precincts, intimidating all who sought to vote Republican. Colorized ballots made a voter's preference easily identifiable, thus expediting coercive efforts. Only precincts guarded by federal troops recorded any Republican votes. White and black Republicans voted Democratic at most polling stations in St. Helena and Washington Parishes or faced the consequences of failing to vote. Their votes contributed to huge Democratic majorities in both parishes. On the other side, the extent of their defeat alarmed both state and national Republican leadership. Barely 40 percent of the region's Republicans cast ballots for their party's ticket. Except in West Feliciana, where the Republicans scored a substantial victory, every parish in eastern Louisiana returned a Democratic majority. The margin of victory ranged from slightly more than one hundred votes in East Baton Rouge to a 100 percent Democratic vote in Washington.

The Republican's two-to-one majority among registered voters in the plantation parishes easily offset a similar Democratic majority in the piney woods. Despite the regional preponderance of Republicans, what the Democrats had failed to accomplish through persuasion in April, 1868, they achieved splendidly only seven months later. The key to success remained the unqualified application of violence. Moreover, Democratic efforts contributed to an emerging societal phenomenon. The secret societies, and nightriding in particular, promoted an important camaraderie among country whites. With a dearth of opportunity for fraternizing in rural areas, Republican bashing became an important outlet and social activity. Ominously, violence was at its core. With startling alacrity, violence progressed from a common element in the piney woods of Louisiana and southwestern Mississippi to an integral aspect of every resident's very existence. Long acceptable in affairs of honor, unrestrained brutality emerged as the principal means of societal regulation and governance. Significantly, violence became an aspect of behavior not merely accepted but expected. The events of the 1860s clearly demonstrated that the old adage "violence does not solve anything" was nonsense. . . .

Despite the fact that their leadership had plunged the region into war and catastrophe, during Reconstruction the old elite again emerged dominant. By promoting racial fears and encouraging popular contempt for the Republican government, antebellum power brokers identified another enemy common to the white population, Republicans and assertive blacks, who provided a focus to rally the commoners behind the elite. Again the aspirations of the plain folk would be subsumed by the necessity for unity behind the natural leadership of the planters. But the contest for political dominance between the old elite and the Republicans produced some important lessons that would have an impact on regional development. Planter attacks on Republican leadership seemed to confirm the intrinsic corruption of government, and their calls for the violent overthrow of the Republicans reinforced an inclination toward extralegal means in eastern Louisiana. . . .

FOR FURTHER STUDY

1. Who were the so-called "carpetbaggers"? "Scalawags"? What was the attitude of most white Southerners toward the people to whom they applied these terms?

2. According to the author, at the end of the war there was some indication that lower class Louisianans were inclined to challenge the continued leadership of the planter elite. Why do you suppose they wanted to do this? Why did the challenge prove unsuccessful?

3. Many of the actions the author describes were clearly illegal, but few of those who committed these acts were even prosecuted, let alone convicted. How do you explain this? Why were the perpetrators usually able to get away with what they did?

4. What were the main similarities and differences between the Ku Klux Klan and the Knights of the White Camelia in regard to such things as goals, membership, and tactics?

5. One of the implications of the selection is that the recent experience of war made violence a more thinkable and usual way of dealing with problems than it had been. Bear this in mind when you consider the other wars in which the United States has been involved. Did they result in an increase in the amount of internal violence?

FOR FURTHER READING

Two general histories of Reconstruction are Kenneth Stampp, *Era of Reconstruction, 1865–1877* (1965) and Eric Foner, *Reconstruction: America's Unfinished Revolution, 1863–1877* (1988). The subject of political violence is dealt with in George Rabel, *But There Was No Peace: The Role of Violence in the Politics of Reconstruction* (1984). Ted Tunnell, *Crucible of Reconstruction: War, Radicalism, and Race in Louisiana, 1862–1877* (1974) offers another perspective on and a more detailed treatment of events in the state this selection deals with. On race relations see Vernon C. Wharton, *The Negro in Mississippi* (1965), Herman Belz, *Emancipation and Equal Rights* (1978), and Howard Rabinowitz, *Race Relations in the Urban South* (1978). Allen W. Trelease provides a general history of the Ku Klux Klan in *White Terror: The Ku Klux Klan Conspiracy and Southern Reconstruction* (1971). The people who came to the South from the North in the days after the Civil War are the subject of Richard N. Current, *Those Terrible Carpetbaggers: A Reinterpretation* (1988).